Athanor
Semiotica, Filosofia, Arte, Letteratura

Serie annuale del Dipartimento di Pratiche Linguistiche e Analisi di Testi
Sezione di Filosofia e Scienze del Linguaggio
Diretta da Augusto Ponzio

anno XV, nuova serie, n. 8, 2004

Alle spese di pubblicazione di questo fascicolo ha partecipato con un contributo
l'Università di Bari

Dipartimento di Pratiche Linguistiche e Analisi dei Testi
Sezione di Filosofia e Scienze del Linguaggio
Facoltà di Lingue e Letterature Straniere
Via Garruba 6, 70122 Bari
Tel. e fax 0805717460

Meltemi editore
via Merulana 38, 00185 Roma
tel. 064741063 - fax 064741407
www.meltemieditore.it
info@meltemieditore.it

THE GIFT, IL DONO
A feminist analysis

a cura di Genevieve Vaughan

Presentazione

Questa raccolta di articoli è il prodotto di un network internazionale di donne che abbracciano, in un modo o nell'altro, l'idea della logica del dono come base di un mutamento di paradigma per il cambiamento sociale. Molte delle donne si sono conosciute, in un primo momento, al convegno tenutosi all'università femminista di Loten in Norvegia nel 2001. Al convegno, organizzato dalla norvegese Berit As e dall'italiana Paola Melchiori, sono state invitate donne dal sud e dal nord per condividere le loro esperienze e le loro idee di cambiamento. Molte di loro erano interessate all'idea dell'economia del dono e diventarono il fulcro di un network che da allora si è incontrato e ha tenuto seminari in diversi luoghi del mondo, e in diverse occasioni, comprese quelle dei Forum Sociali Mondiali in Brasile e in India.

La pratica del dono esiste in molti luoghi ma viene resa invisibile dal capitalismo patriarcale. Essa si esprime nelle strutture economiche delle culture indigene. All'interno del capitalismo, essa è visibile in alcuni fenomeni di vasta scala quali il lavoro domestico gratuito delle donne e le rimesse inviate dagli immigrati alle loro famiglie nei paesi di origine. È possibile anche, ed in alcuni di questi articoli se ne fa l'ipotesi, che la pratica del dono sia la base della comunicazione. Lo scambio, cioè dare per rice-

Presentation

This collection of articles is the product of an international network of women who embrace in one way or another the idea of the logic of gift giving as the basis of a paradigm shift for social change. Many of the women first met each other at a meeting at the Feminist University in Loten, Norway in 2001. The meeting, which was organized by Norweigen Berit As and Italian Paola Melchiori, brought together women from South and North to share their experiences and ideas for change. Many of the women there were interested in the idea of the gift economy and became the core of a network which has since met and given presentations in numerous places around the world, including workshops at the World Social Forums in Brazil and India.

Gift giving exists in many places but is made invisible by Patriarchal Capitalism. It has structured viable economies in indigenous cultures. Inside Capitalism it can be seen in such large-scale phenomena as women's free housework, and the remittances sent by immigrants to their families in their home countries. A case can be made that gift giving is the basis of communication. Exchange, giving in order to receive a quantitative equivalent, is its determined opposite.

The logic of gift giving forms the basis of a paradigm that is radically different from the

vere un'equivalente quantitativo, ne è l'esatto opposto.

La logica del donare forma la base di un paradigma che è radicalmente diverso dalla visione del mondo basata sulla logica dello scambio. Il vecchio/nuovo paradigma, sebbene non sia riconosciuto, è già ampiamente diffuso e potrebbe essere la base di un'organizzazione sociale migliore.

È appropriata a questa raccolta di articoli, che è espressione del movimento internazionale delle donne, la pubblicazione come volume della rivista *Athanor* in inglese in Italia, con l'aiuto di Augusto Ponzio e Susan Petrilli dell'Università di Bari. Le autrici porgono i loro sentiti ringraziamenti per il dono di ospitalità che le ha accolte in queste pagine. Gli articoli presenti in questa edizione di *Athanor* e il fatto stesso della loro pubblicazione sono esempi della pratica del dono, collettiva e collaborativa, di cui c'è bisogno per creare un mondo migliore.

worldview based on the logic of exchange. The new/old paradigm, though unrecognized, is already widespread and could be the basis of a better way of organizing society.

It is fitting that this collection of articles, which is an expression of the international women's movement, is published as a volume of *Athanor* in English in Italy, with the help of Augusto Ponzio and Susan Petrilli of the University of Bari. The authors extend their heartfelt thanks for the gift of hospitality that has welcomed them to these pages. The articles in this issue of *Athanor* and the very fact of its publication are examples of the collective and collaborative gift giving that are needed to make a better world.

Oggi nel mondo coesistono due paradigmi economici di base, logicamente contraddittori ma anche complementari. Uno è visibile, l'altro invisibile; uno fortemente apprezzato, l'altro sottovalutato. L'uno è collegato con gli uomini, l'altro con le donne. Quello che dobbiamo fare è dare valore a quello collegato con noi donne per causare uno spostamento fondamentale dei valori con cui gestiamo le nostre vite e le nostre politiche.

Il mio primo approccio all'idea del dono, come principio economico di base e come principio di vita, è stato quando lavoravo sul linguaggio e la comunicazione. Più tardi, come femminista, ho capito che il mio lavoro domestico gratuito e il mio lavoro di madre nel crescere i figli era in effetti un dono, e che le donne di tutto il mondo lo praticano.

L'attuale sistema economico, che dicono sia naturale e troppo diffuso per poter essere cambiato, si basa su una semplice operazione a cui gli individui partecipano a più livelli e in momenti diversi. Questa operazione è lo scambio, che si può descrivere come un dare per ricevere. La motivazione che sta alla base dello scambio è egocentrica, poiché ciò che è dato ritorna sotto altra forma al donatore per soddisfare i propri bisogni: soddisfare i bisogni altrui è un mezzo per soddisfare il proprio bisogno. Lo scambio impone l'identificazione delle cose scambiate, come pure la loro misurazione e la dichiarazione della loro equivalenza in modo da soddisfare il criterio che nessuno di coloro che scambiano dia di più di ciò che riceve. Quindi lo scambio richiede più visibilità; attrae l'attenzione, sebbene sia praticato tanto spesso che la sua visibilità è diventata un luogo comune. Il denaro entra nello scambio prendendo il posto dei prodotti e ne riflette la loro valutazione quantitativa.

Quella che sembrerebbe una semplice interazione umana, lo scambio, dato che viene operata così spesso, diventa una sorta di archetipo o di calamita per altre interazioni umane, rendendo se stesso – e qualsiasi cosa gli assomigli – apparentemente normale, mentre tutto il resto è follia. Per esempio, si parla di scambio d'amore, di conversazioni, sguardi, favori, idee.

Ma c'è anche un certo tipo di somiglianza tra lo scambio e la definizione linguistica: la definizione opera una mediazione stabilendo se un concetto appartenga o meno ad una determinata categoria, così come, mediante la monetizzazione di una determinata attività, se ne definisce l'appartenenza o meno alla categoria del lavoro. La stessa visibilità del-

* Offro la traduzione di questo articolo, pubblicato in inglese in *Ms.Magazine* nel 1990, come breve introduzione per i lettori italiani.

lo scambio è auto-confermativa, mentre altri tipi di interazione sono rese invisibili o inferiori per contrasto o per descrizione negativa. Ciò che è invisibile sembra essere senza valore, mentre ciò che è visibile viene identificato con lo scambio che si riferisce ad un certo tipo di valore quantitativo. Inoltre, dato che viene asserita un'equivalenza tra ciò che diamo e ciò che riceviamo, sembra che chiunque possieda di più abbia prodotto altrettanto o dato altrettanto e valga, quindi, in qualche modo, di più di quelli che possiedono meno. Lo scambio mette al primo posto l'ego e gli permette di crescere e svilupparsi in modi che enfatizzano modelli di comportamento competitivo ("prima io") e gerarchico. Questo ego non fa intrinsecamente parte dell'essere umano ma è un prodotto sociale derivante dal tipo di interazioni umane con cui è collegato.

Il paradigma alternativo, che è nascosto – o quantomeno mal identificato – è quello del prendersi cura dell'altro (*nurturing*) ed è orientato verso l'altro (*other-oriented*). Esso continua ad esistere perché si basa sulla natura degli infanti, che sono dipendenti ed incapaci di ripagare il donatore. Se i loro bisogni non fossero soddisfatti unilateralmente, essi soffrirebbero e morirebbero. La società ha attribuito il ruolo di curatrici a noi donne poiché diamo loro la vita e abbiamo il latte per nutrirli.

Poiché una grande percentuale di donne si prende cura dei bambini, esse sono portate ad avere un'esperienza che va al di là dello scambio. Ciò richiede un orientamento verso l'interesse per l'altro. I premi e le punizioni coinvolti in questa relazione hanno a che fare con il benessere dell'altro. La nostra soddisfazione ci viene dalla sua crescita e felicità e non solo dalla nostra. Nel migliore dei casi, ciò non comporta nemmeno il nostro impoverimento o sfruttamento. Dove c'è abbastanza, noi possiamo nutrire gli altri abbondantemente. Il problema è che di solito siamo in presenza di scarsità di risorse, la quale viene creata artificialmente dal sistema per poter mantenere il controllo, così che l'orientamento verso l'altro diventa difficile e ci esaurisce. Di fatto lo scambio impone uno stato di scarsità, perché, se i bisogni fossero abbondantemente soddisfatti, nessuno sarebbe costretto a rinunciare a qualcosa per poter ricevere ciò di cui ha bisogno.

Si dice che attualmente la terra produca abbastanza risorse per nutrire tutti abbondantemente. Tuttavia ciò non può essere fatto sulla base del paradigma dello scambio. Ma è vero che neanche il paradigma dello scambio e l'egocentrismo che esso sostiene potrebbero continuare in una situazione di abbondanza e libero dono. Ecco perché è stata creata la scarsità a livello mondiale con le spese per gli armamenti ed altro spreco di risorse: 17 miliardi di dollari darebbero da mangiare all'intera popolazione della Terra per un anno, mentre nel mondo sprechiamo questa somma ogni settimana per spese militari, creando così la scarsità necessaria perché possa sopravvivere e convalidarsi il paradigma dello scambio.

Ma se noi identifichiamo il paradigma del dono con il modo di essere della donna, vediamo che esso è già diffuso, poiché le donne costituiscono la maggioranza della popolazione. Anche molti uomini in qualche misura praticano il paradigma del dono. Nelle economie non capitalistiche, come le economie indigene, si trovano spesso importanti pratiche di dono e varie ed importanti leadership femminili.

Per esempio, io credo che molti dei conflitti tra donne e uomini in cui sembra trattarsi di differenze personali, in realtà riguardino differenze del paradigma che usiamo come base del nostro comportamento. Le donne criticano l'egocentrismo degli uomini e gli uomini dicono alle donne che non hanno il senso della realtà e che sono troppo generose. Ognuno cerca di convincere l'altro a seguire i propri valori. Di recente molte donne hanno cominciato a seguire il paradigma dello scambio, cosa che ha il vantaggio immediato di liberarle dalla bieca servitù economica – ed anche il vantaggio psicologico che è dato dalla monetizzazione che definisce la loro come un'attività di valore. Ma la servitù stessa è causata dal paradigma dello scambio.

Quando le persone passano da un paradigma all'altro, resta probabilmente un residuo del paradigma precedente, sicché le donne che intraprendono lo scambio spesso continuano a prendersi cura dell'altro, mentre gli uomini che cominciano a praticare il dono restano maggiormente egocentrici. Ciò è ritrovabile nel caso delle religioni, nelle quali è l'uomo a legiferare sull'orientamento verso l'altro, spesso seguendo il paradigma dello scambio, ed escludendo e squalificando le donne. Infatti, essi fanno apparire l'altruismo così santo da diventare impraticabile per i più (mentre ignorano che esso è spesso la norma per le donne). Un caso analogo è la sindrome della madonna-puttana, in cui la donna è sopravvalutata o sottovalutata, adorata o disprezzata. L'altruismo viene fatto risultare fuori dalla nostra portata, e spesso sembra comportare un sacrificio di sé (per via della scarsità prodotta dall'economia dello scambio), oppure viene visto come uno spreco; le religioni patriarcali predicano la carità in cambio della salvezza dell'anima.

Il dono che viene dall'egocentrismo dello scambio non funziona, come si può vedere al livello degli aiuti tra nazioni. Ci sono obblighi imposti dalle nazioni donatrici che depauperizzano le nazioni riceventi. Un altro aspetto del conflitto tra paradigmi è che il lavoro domestico o altro lavoro non-monetizzato di donne viene visto come inferiore o come non-lavoro; valorizzarlo sovverte il paradigma dello scambio. Forse il lavoro delle donne viene pagato di meno per mantenerle in uno stato di dono depauperato. Ciò che occorre fare non è pagare di più il lavoro alle donne, ma cambiare totalmente i valori, con la conseguente squalificazione della monetizzazione e dello scambio.

Ma in che modo un paradigma non-competitivo e di cura può competere con un paradigma competitivo? Esso è sempre svantaggiato perché la competizione non è un suo valore, né la sua motivazione. Tuttavia è difficile *non* competere senza perdere, convalidando così l'istanza dell'altro. Un altro grande problema consiste nel fatto che se la pratica di soddisfare un bisogno è gratuita, non si dovrebbe ricorrere ad un suo riconoscimento. Ma proprio non richiedendone il riconoscimento, le donne continuano esse stesse ad ignorare il carattere paradigmatico delle loro azioni e dei loro valori.

È chiaro che il paradigma egocentrico è pernicioso. Il suo risultato è il potere dei pochi ed il depauperamento, lo sfruttamento, la morte e l'invisibilità dei più. Dato che l'ego è un prodotto sociale, in qualche modo artificiale, esso deve essere continuamente ricreato e confermato. Ciò può essere fatto anche attraverso la violenza contro l'altro, inclusa la violenza sessuale. Chiunque sia nella posizione di altro viene ignorato, negato, escluso e degradato per confermare la superiorità e l'identità degli ego dominanti. Vorrei evitare qualsiasi discorso morale su questo punto (infatti, io vedo il senso di colpa come scambio interiorizzato da parte di chi si prepara a ripagare per l'errore commesso) e considerare semplicemente i problemi come conseguenze logiche e psicologiche dei paradigmi. La vendetta e la giustizia impongono una resa dei conti. Ma noi abbiamo bisogno di bontà e cura nei confronti dell'altro. Quando troviamo che l'ottantacinque per cento dei carcerati sono stati vittime di abusi subiti dai bambini, dobbiamo capire che la vera questione non è la giustizia. Come la carità, anche la giustizia rende umano lo scambio quanto basta per non farlo cambiare. Abbiamo bisogno di un mondo basato sul dare e sul perdonare, non sulla retribuzione.

A questo punto sembra importante creare strutture di transizione nelle quali la pratica del dare possa essere valorizzata. Strategie come, ad esempio, il commercio per una giusta causa (*cause-related marketing*) nel quale i profitti vengono devoluti a progetti per il cambiamento sociale per soddisfare bisogni, impiegano lo scambio per donare. Anche il movimento dei donatori per il cambiamento sociale valorizza il donare, specialmente quando esso proviene da un modello di abbondanza piuttosto che da un modello di scarsità. Ma anche tutte le persone dei movimenti per la pace, il femminismo, la cura e la terapia, che dedicano il loro tempo e le loro energie a soddisfare bisogni umani e sociali valorizzano il dono. Stiamo facendo ciò che è giusto ma non sappiamo perché. Talvolta screditiamo l'orientamento verso l'altro mentre lo stiamo praticando, perché il modello dello scambio è assai radicato e forte. Abbiamo bisogno di dare i nostri soldi, il nostro tempo e le nostre attenzioni al cambiamento di valori e ad alternative economiche, nuove o tradizionali, che non dipendano dallo scambio e dal mercato. Le donne devono capire che i loro valori e le loro energie sono importanti anche al di fuori della famiglia e non solo al suo interno. I problemi sociali sono essi stessi bisogni che noi dobbiamo soddisfare. Il nostro orientamento verso l'altro deve diventare la norma.

Allora il sogno antico che i potenti depongano le armi e i ricchi rinuncino ai loro beni potrebbe avverarsi, sotto la guida delle donne del mondo. Per esempio, possiamo muoverci all'interno del "primo mondo" nel senso del perdonare il debito del "terzo mondo". Richiamo la vostra attenzione sulla parola *per-donare*.

Traduzione di Amelia Rossi-Landi

GENEVIEVE VAUGHAN   *A BRIEF INTRODUCTION: THE GIFT ECONOMY**

Two basic economic paradigms coexist in the world today. They are logically contradictory, but also complementary. One is visible, the other invisible; one highly valued, the other undervalued. One is connected with men; the other with women. What we need to do is validate the one connected with women, causing a basic shift in the values by which we direct our lives and policies.

I first approached the idea of giving as a basic economic and life principle when I was doing work on language and communication. Later, as a feminist, I realized that in my free homemaking and child-rearing work, I was doing gift labor – as were women worldwide.

The present economic system, which is made to seem natural and too widespread to change, is based upon a simple operation in which individuals participate at many different levels and at many different times. This operation is exchange, which can be described as giving in order to receive. The motivation is self-oriented since what is given returns under a different form to the giver to satisfy her or his need. The satisfaction of the need of the other person is a means to the satisfaction of one's own need. Exchange requires identification of the things exchanged, as well as their measurement and an assertion of their equivalence to the satisfaction of the exchangers that neither is giving more than she or he is receiving. It therefore requires visibility, attracting attention even though it is done so often that the visibility is commonplace. Money enters the exchange, taking the place of products reflecting their quantitative evaluation.

This seemingly simple human interaction of exchange, since it is done so often, becomes a sort of archetype or magnet for other human interactions, making itself – and whatever looks like it – seem normal, while anything else is crazy. For example, we talk about exchanges of love, conversations, glances, favors, ideas.

There is also a different type of similarity of exchange to linguistic definition. The definition mediates whether or not a concept belongs to a certain category, just as monetization of activity mediates its belonging to the category of work or not. The very visibility of exchange is self-confirming, while other kinds of interchange are rendered invisible or inferior by contrast or negative description. What is invisible seems to be valueless, while what is visible is identified with exchange, which is concerned with a certain kind of quantitative

11   * I offer this article, published in *Ms.Magazine* in 1990, as a brief introduction to the idea of the gift as I see it.

value. Besides, since there is an equivalence asserted between what we give and what we receive, it seems that whoever has a lot has produced a lot or given a lot, and is, therefore, somehow more than whoever has less. Exchange puts the ego first and allows it to grow and develop in ways that emphasize me-first competitive and hierarchical behavior patterns. This ego is not an intrinsic part of the human being, but is a social product coming from the kinds of human interaction it is involved in.

The alternative paradigm, which is hidden – or at least misidentified – is nurturing and generally other-oriented. It continues to exist because it has a basis in the nature of infants; they are dependent and incapable of giving back to the giver. If their needs are not satisfied unilaterally by the giver, they will suffer and die. Society has allocated the caretaking role to women since we bear the children and have the milk to nourish them.

Since a large percentage of women nurture babies, we are directed toward having an experience outside exchange. This requires orientation toward interest in the other. The rewards and punishments involved have to do with the well-being of the other. Our satisfaction comes from her or his growth or happiness, not just from our own. In the best case, this does not require the impoverishment or depletion of ourselves either. Where there is enough, we can abundantly nurture others. The problem is that scarcity is usually the case, artificially created in order to maintain control, so that other-orientation becomes difficult and self-depleting. In fact, exchange requires scarcity because, if needs are abundantly satisfied, no one is constrained to give up anything in order to receive what they need.

It is said that the earth produces enough at the present time to feed everyone abundantly. However, this cannot be done on the basis of the exchange paradigm. Nor can the exchange paradigm or the kind of dominant ego it fosters continue in a situation of abundance and free giving. That is why scarcity has been created on a worldwide scale by armaments spending and other wastes of resources: $17 billion would feed everyone on earth for a year and we spend it worldwide every week on the military, thus creating the scarcity necessary for the exchange paradigm to survive and continue to validate itself.

If we identify the gift paradigm with women's way, we see that it is already widespread, since women are the majority of the population. Many men practice it to some extent also. Non capitalistic economies, such as native economies, often have major gift-giving practices and various important kinds of women's leadership.

I believe, for example, that many of the conflicts between women and men that seem like personal differences are really differences in the paradigm we are using as the basis for our behavior. Women criticize men's big egos and men criticize women as being unrealistic, soft-touch, bleeding hearts. Each tries to convince the other to follow his or her values. Recently, many women have begun to follow the exchange paradigm, which has the immediate advantage of liberating them from grim economic servitude – and the psychological advantage that monetization defines their activity as valuable. But the servitude itself is caused by the exchange paradigm.

As people change from one paradigm to the other, there is probably some holdover of the previous paradigm, so that women who take on exchange often remain nurturing while men who take on giving remain more ego-oriented. I see this in the case of religions, in which men legislate other-orientation, often according to exchange, excluding and disqualifying women. Indeed, they make altruism seem so saintly that it is impractical for the many (while ignoring that it is often the norm for women). This is like the madonna-whore syndrome, where the woman is either over- or undervalued, worshiped or despised. Altruism is made to seem above our reach, often with a self-sacrificing side (because of the scarcity produced by the exchange economy), or it is seen as wasteful, spendthrift; charity is given by patriarchal religions in exchange for the soul.

The gift giving done by the big exchange-ego does not work, as we have seen on the scale of aid between nations. There are strings attached by the donor country, which pauperize the recipients. Another aspect of the conflict of paradigms is that housework or other un-monetized women's labor is seen as inferior, or non-work: valuing it is subversive to the exchange paradigm. Perhaps women's labor is paid less than men's to maintain it in a disempowered gift stance. What we need to do is not to pay women's labor more, but to change the values altogether, eventually disqualifying monetization and exchange.

How can a noncompetitive, nurturing paradigm compete with a competitive one? It is always at a disadvantage because competition is not its motivation or its value. Yet it is difficult to *not* compete without losing, thereby validating the other's stance. Another major problem is that if satisfying a need is free, one should not require recognition for it. But by not requiring recognition, women have themselves remained unconscious of the paradigm character of their actions and values.

Yet clearly the ego-oriented paradigm is pernicious. It results in the empowerment of the few and the disempowerment, depletion, death, and invisibility of the many. Since the ego is a social product, artificial in some ways, it needs to be continually re-created and confirmed. This can also be done by violence against the other, including sexual violence. Anyone in the position of the other is ignored, denied, excluded, degraded to confirm the superiority and identity of the dominant egos. I would like to avoid any moral discourse on this point (in fact, I see guilt as internalized exchange, preparing to pay back for the wrong one has done) and simply see the problems as logical and psychological consequences of the paradigms. Vengeance and justice require a balance of accounts. But we need kindness and nurturing. When we find that 85 percent of people in prison have been abused as children, we must realize justice is not the issue. Like charity, justice humanizes the exchange just enough to keep it from changing. We need a world based on giving and for giving, not retribution.

At this point, it seems that it is important to create transitional structures by which giving can be validated. Such strategies as cause-related marketing, where profits are given to social change projects to satisfy needs, use exchange for giving. The social change funding movement also empowers giving, especially when it comes from an abundance rather than a scarcity model. But so do all the people in the peace, feminist, healing, and therapy movements who devote their time and energy to satisfying human and social needs. We are doing the right thing, but we don't know why. Sometimes, we even disparage other-orientation while we are practicing it, because the exchange model is so pervasive and strong. We need to give our money, time, and attention to the change in values, and both new and traditional economic alternatives not dependent on exchange and the market.

13

Women need to realize that our values and energies are important outside the family as well as inside. Social problems are themselves needs that we must satisfy. Our other-orientation must become the norm.

Then the ancient dream that the powerful will lay down their arms and the rich their goods might come true, led by women of the world. We can, for example, move within the "first world" to forgive the "third world" debt. I call your attention to the word *for-give*.

GENEVIEVE VAUGHAN

GIFT GIVING AND EXCHANGE:
GENDERS ARE ECONOMIC IDENTITIES,
AND ECONOMIES ARE BASED ON GENDER

The circumstances of my life brought me to begin thinking about communication as based on gift giving as early as the 1970's. In 1963 as a young woman I married the Italian philosopher, Ferruccio Rossi-Landi and moved to Italy from Texas (USA). The following year he was invited by a group of his colleagues to write about language as seen through the lens of Marx's analysis of the commodity and money in *Capital*. He developed a theory along those lines, which can be seen, in his books, *Il linguaggio come lavoro e come mercato* (*Language as labor and trade*) (1968) and *Linguistics and Economics* (1974). I was completely fascinated by this project and spent a lot of time throughout those years trying to fit the pieces of the complex puzzle together. For me it was as if language and exchange (trade, the market) were in some ways really the same thing – but some of the pieces just didn't fit. There was a sense of sharing and cooperation, a kind of life-enhancing creativity in language that was just absent from most commercial relations as I understood them. During those years I gave birth to our three daughters and was taking care of them. Because I had been concentrating on the comparison between language and exchange I could not avoid noticing that they were learning to talk long before they learned about exchange for money and before they were doing anything that might be called work. Maybe, I thought, it is language that comes first in society and exchange derives from language. It seemed improbable that exchange could have made the same kind of fundamental contribution to our becoming and being human that language did. I knew that the indigenous peoples of the Americas had not had money or markets as such before the European conquest, yet they certainly spoke. Meanwhile I tried not to manipulate my children, or anybody else because that was antithetical to the way I thought human relations should be. The kind of – if you do this, I will do what you want – exchange, seemed to me to be a negative way to behave.

At any rate at the time I would not have thought of looking at communication as gift giving if I had not been trying to distinguish communication from exchange and to find a way to salvage language from the relations of capital and the market and even from work, considered as the production and use of tools. The theory my husband was developing, while fascinating, did not convince me. There was something else. An image came to me. The construction of Marx's analysis as well as of my husband's theory had a false floor. Underneath it was another layer where there was a hidden treasure, or perhaps better, a spring that was welling up, the spring of what I later began to call "the gift economy".

I spent two years in the U.S. in the early 70's with my children, and used the free time I had there, to write and think about language and communication. From the work I did then I published two essays in semiotics journals. The first was "Communication and exchange"(1980) where I developed the idea of communicative need, and described words as the verbal elements people use for communicative need-satisfaction. Money then appeared to be a kind of materialized word, used to satisfy the peculiar communicative need that arises from the mutually exclusive relations of private property. The second essay was "Saussure and Vygotsky via Marx" (1981). I had read L. S. Vygotsky (1962 [1934]) and linked his idea of abstract concept formation with Marx's idea of money as the general equivalent. In Vygotsky's experiment any item of a set could be taken as the exemplar for the concept, but it had to be held constant or the concept did not develop as such. If the exemplar varied, the abstraction would be incomplete and the relevant common qualities would not be separated from the irrelevant qualities. I realized that the general equivalent, money could be understood as the exemplar for the abstraction of the concept of value in the market. Money measures the "common quality" of exchange value[1] in commodities and leaves aside as irrelevant whatever does not have that quality. Whatever is not commodified does not have that quality and thus appears to be irrelevant to the market, outside its "concept".

Although I had read Malinowsky (1922) and Mauss (1990 [1925]) as a student many years earlier, I did not immediately see the continuity between gift giving and communication, perhaps because the term used to describe the process in indigenous cultures was gift "*exchange*" and I had made the distinction between exchange and unilateral need satisfaction. However I remember that by 1978 I had made the connection between communication and the gift giving of indigenous peoples. I also realized at the time that market bias was so strong that everyone, including anthropologists, used the term "exchange" without questioning it[2]. There could be a different perspective though, I thought. If communication was based on gift giving, maybe societies that did not have markets, used gift giving for communication. Then maybe exchange and markets could be seen as altered gift giving, altered communication.

In that year also I encountered another important idea, which redirected my thinking. After my divorce from Rossi-Landi, I began going to a feminist consciousness raising group. There I found out that women's free work in the home is an enormous unrecognized contribution that women are giving, both to their families and to the economy as a whole[3]. Part of that work of course is childcare, the free services that mothers give to children on a daily basis. Satisfying another's communicative need was that kind of thing, I realized, a unilateral gift that, even without an immediate counterpart, establishes a human relation. Even in dialogue, what is happening is not exchange but turntaking in giving unilateral gifts. I speak and you understand what I say, whether or not you reply.

Ferruccio had talked about a kind of inevitability of understanding the verbal products that come ungarbled to one's healthy ears and brain, if one knows the language. It seemed clear to me that if it is inevitable that others understand our words, our giving our words to others and their receiving them will not be contingent upon a reply. If there is a reply, it is couched in the same unilateral gift logic as the previous speaker's words. Even questions, which are asked in order to receive a reply, are verbal products that are given and received

16

as such, unconditionally. That is, they are understood anyway even if no reply is actually given. In the market instead, one does not give up one's product except in exchange for money. Both seller and buyer necessarily participate in the *do ut des* self-reflecting and contingent logic of exchange.

As the years have passed since the 60's when I first began thinking about all of this, it has become more important than ever to distinguish communication from exchange, and to refuse to see the logic of exchange as the basic human logic. In fact I think that as a society we have believed acritically in the fundamental value of the logic of exchange and we have consequently embraced and nurtured an economic system that is extending itself parasitically over the planet, feeding on the unilateral gifts of all. These are unilateral gifts of tradition, of culture, of nature, of care and of love as well as the forced or leveraged unilateral gifts imposed by exploitation, the gifts of cheap or free labor. If we look at exchange as the basic human logic, those who do it best will seem to be the most "human". Conversely, those who do not do it well, or do not succeed in the market, will seem to be "defective", less human[4] and therefore more exploitable. In Capitalism the values of Patriarchy – competition, hierarchy, domination – have been united with the values of the market. In order to understand this merger and justify some startling similarities in what are usually considered widely different areas, we need to look beyond both Capitalism and Patriarchy to underlying patterns.

I used my understanding of the similarity between Vygotsky's concept formation process and Marx's general equivalent to develop a theory of Patriarchal Capitalism[5] in which neither male dominance nor the market economy is primary. Rather both are caused by epistemological distortions and incarnations of our concept forming processes, which are due to the social imposition of binary gender categories. For this reason the values of Capitalism are similar to those of Patriarchy. In Patriarchy, males vie to dominate, that is, to achieve the general equivalent or exemplar position, which has become not just an element in the distribution of goods on the market or a way of organizing perceptions, but a position of "power over" others. In Capitalism, those who have the most, who have succeeded in dominating economically, are the exemplars of the concept "man" extended to "human". This race to the top position can be seen at other levels as well. For example it can be seen in the way that nations vie with each other for supremacy, to become the "exemplar" nation, which dominates economically and militarily. Each area of life, the military, business, religion, even academia, seems to incarnate the concept form as a life agenda rather than merely as a mental process of abstraction. In each area the "exemplar" position is invested with special power or value, and is not seen as just any item that is being used as a point of reference for sorting members of categories. In fact a flow of gifts towards the item in the "top" position is created and justified by the attribution of this special value.

This view of the "top" as the exemplar position allows us to see Patriarchy and exchange as embedded not in our brains or chemistry but in our minds and in society, not in something inevitable but in something we can radically change. It allows us to see the problem as our socialization of boys into the male gender in binary opposition to something else: a gift giving process, which is the *human* way[6]. This socialization varies culturally but the problem has arisen particularly intensely with the Euro-American construction of gender, and its externalization in the economic system of Capitalism. The relation of money, as the exemplar of value, to commodities in the market, is an incarnation of the equivalent position in the concept forming process. This logical structure can extend to all cultures because it is as familiar to them as the way they think. Patriarchy, which puts the father or male leader in the position of exemplar of the human, can infect previously non patriarchal cultures in a similar way[7].

The exchange paradigm

Patriarchal Capitalism justifies itself by a worldview I call the "exchange paradigm", which frames everything in terms of the exchange logic, from the marriage market to military "exchanges", from justice as payment for crimes, to the equations of a self reflecting consciousness. This paradigm arises from and promotes an area of activity, the market, where gift giving is absent or concealed and where Patriarchal males find a non-giving field of endeavor in which to practice their quest for dominance. The seemingly neuter and therefore neutral "objective" exchange approach conceals and denies the importance of unilateral gift giving at every turn, while at the same time making it possible for many hidden gifts to be given to the system. These are for example, the gifts of women's free labor in the home. They are also the gifts contained in the surplus labor of workers, which creates surplus value: that part of the labor that is not covered by the salary and is therefore a free gift to the Capitalist (though constrained and leveraged) from the worker. The gifts given to the system include all the free gifts of nature and culture. These are not viewed within the exchange paradigm as gifts but rather are seen as "deserved" by the investor who extracts, privatizes, exploits and pollutes. The sum of the gifts given to those at the "top" is concealed by renaming it "profit" and it is what motivates the whole system.

Although Capitalism is now being extensively criticized by the anti globalization movement, a clear and radical alternative has not yet been collectively embraced because the logic of exchange itself has not been identified as problematic. Moreover, the logic of the unilateral gift continues to be unrecognized, discredited, and even sometimes despised. The women's movement, while decidedly anti Patriarchal, is not in many of its aspects anti Capitalistic. In fact the links between Capitalism and Patriarchy have not been clearly delineated. Instead it appears that only by being absorbed into the work force as persons with economic agency in the system, have women been able to free themselves from domestic slavery [8], disempowerment and "dependency". As happens in any situation in which the market takes over a previously free area of the world, causing at least short term improvements for some of the inhabitants, some women who have been effectively absorbed by Capitalism have had an improvement in the level of their lives. They have had an increase in personal freedom but have also become dependent on a market situation that is beyond their control. This state of transition, like the transition from pre Capitalist to Capitalist cultures, gives women a chance to participate in and become conscious of both paradigms[9]. The recognition of a shared gift perspective could link the women's movement cross-culturally internally. It could also link it externally with movements of indigenous, colonized and ex-

18

ploited people of both genders who continue to participate consciously or unconsciously in the gift paradigm. This is possible if we can leave aside the biological differences between male and female as the determinants of gender and base solidarity on processes and values coming from economic gender identities.

By recognizing "female" and "male" as economic identities, having to do with the modes of distribution – of gift giving or exchange – we can also look at some cultures as economically 'female' and others as economically "male". The two economic "structures", gift giving and exchange, give rise to characteristic and distinguishable ideological "superstructures", which are the value systems and world views that I am calling the gift and the exchange paradigms. That is, the cultures issuing from the practices of gift giving or of exchange have to do respectively with celebration of the other, compassion, and the affirmation of life or on the other hand with subjugation of the other, egotism, competition and the affirmation of "value-free objectivity". These two cultures co-exist at various levels, and, as I was saying, can also be found within the same person[10]. This already complex situation is further complicated by the fact that the two kinds of economic identities are not independent and unrelated but "male", and especially Patriarchal, economies and cultures are based on the denial and distortion of gift giving and the direction of the flow of gifts towards the dominators. For example, the Global North is now acting as an economic male, attempting to extract the gifts of the South, which it is forcing or manipulating into an economically female position.

The market, like the Patriarchal identity, is a social construction that is made to receive free gifts. Because in the 'developed' countries women have been assimilated as market agents and their gifts are now being taken not as direct free work only but also as surplus value, they have gained some equality with men as "economic males" and some "economic male" privileges. As the economy of Patriarchal Capitalism in the North has somewhat relinquished its hold on the gifts of women, and has been forced by the workers' movements to diminish some of its profits, it has displaced its gift-extracting mechanisms into other areas. The new gifts that come from the Global South to the North, are added to other gifts that for centuries have been flowing from women to men, indigenous peoples to colonial powers, from people of color to whites, and from the general public to corporations. Patriarchal Capitalism is commodifying previously free gift areas such as traditional knowledge, seeds, species, water, even blood and body parts. Women and children are being commodified and trafficked. The "female" economies of the South, and gifts of nature and tradition are being seized and transformed into new "food" for the hungry market mechanism.

By recognizing that the market is not an inevitable sui generis process however, and looking at it dispassionately as a transposition and incarnation of the concept formation process as it is used in sorting, particularly in the sorting and formulation of gender, we can approach it in a new way without fear, in order to peacefully dismantle it.

Subjectivities

The two logics, exchange and gift giving, also produce different kinds of subjectivities. The practice of exchange creates an ego-oriented ego according to its logic of self interest while the practice of gift giving promotes more other-orientation. Exchange is a gift turned back upon itself, doubled and made contingent. It requires quantification while gift giving is mainly qualitative. Exchange is ego oriented and gives value to the self, while gift giving is other-oriented and gives value mainly to the other. Exchange places the exchangers in adversarial positions as each tries to get more than the other out of the transaction. The values of Patriarchy are implicit in exchange, and drive Capitalism, as each contender struggles to reach the top of the hierarchy to own more and to become the Big Man. The kind of ego that is based on the exchange logic is necessary for the market, while the gift giving personality is eliminated, or is easily victimized and becomes the host of the exchange ego.

One superstructural consequence of this kind of ego formation is that consciousness itself is considered in the light of exchange as self reflecting, in a sort of equation of value with itself. The subconscious is thus placed in the gift giving position. We might say that our idea of consciousness in its capacity for self-evaluation is made in the image of preparation for exchange. It floats upon the gifts of the subconscious and of experience, without a clear indication of how those gifts come into the mind. Similarly the market floats on a sea of gifts without a clear indication of where they come from and how they constitute profit.

In individuals, the coexistence and conflict, as well as symbiosis of these two kinds of ego structures, can be seen as a result of the exchange paradigm, not its cause. That is, it is not that human beings are greedy and therefore create the market and Capitalism. Rather, the system has an existence that is over and above that of its individual participants. The market and Capitalism create the human ego structures that are well adapted to their needs. Greed is one of the human qualities that is functional to the maintenance and development of the market as such. Competition for narcissistic self aggrandizement and dominance are played out on the economic plane because otherwise the market would not "grow" and maintain its control over other possible ways of distributing goods i.e. gift giving. Patriarchy supplies the motivation that drives Capitalism and the individuals who embody the motivation, with the ego structures and belief systems that justify the embodiment. Capitalism supplies the tools and rewards with which individuals and now corporations carry out the Patriarchal agendas on the terrain of so called "distribution" of goods to needs through exchange[11].

Mothering, on the other hand, involves the unilateral free distribution of goods and services to young children and a consequent creation of human bonds between givers and receivers. Society has assigned this role to women. Although it may be characterized as the distribution of goods, mothering is usually not seen as an economic category. In fact by overvaluing exchange and making it dominant, the market devalues mothering, making it dependent and subservient. The gift paradigm allows us to see that the direct distribution of goods and services to needs that is present in mothering can be understood as an example of the practice of an alternative economy. As a mode of distribution, it is present in all societies because it is required, not by the biology of women, but by the biology of children. That is, for a very long period of time, children's biology does not allow them to independently satisfy most of their own or others' needs. It requires and elicits other-orientation and unilateral gift giving from their caregivers.

Children begin their lives with their mothers in a relation – creating communicative gift economy and they begin learning language at the same time. However binary gender categorizations in language and in society soon intervene and the boy child finds that he belongs to a category that is the opposite of that of his nurturing mother. That is, if her most salient characteristic for him is the unilateral satisfaction of needs, the fact that he belongs to a binarily opposite gender category implies that he will not unilaterally satisfy needs. There is very little for the boy at this early age that is not part of the gift giving and receiving economy. He learns to deny its importance, transform it into something else and even take categorization itself as part of the content of his identity. The father (who went through the same process when he was a child) becomes for the boy the exemplar of the human, taking the place of the mother who paradoxically gives more to the father and son than she does to herself or her daughter. That is, she gives and gives value preferentially to those whose gender identity requires that they NOT give. The displacement of the mother model and takeover by the father of the role of exemplar of the (not giving) human is the seed of the dominance of male over female, categorization over communication, and eventually exchange over gift giving. In fact the ego oriented relations of exchange are a socially created opposite of gift relations and they provide a way for society to distribute goods to needs without individual nurturing. The market is an area of life where, by exchanging, we can give without giving and receive without receiving. In fact, in the market we must "deserve" what we receive, that is, we must have previously "given" an equivalent for which the present "gift" is a payment. The equality of the commodities and money in exchange cancels out the gift. Since we necessarily get back the equivalent of what we gave, there is no visible transfer of value from one person to the other. The market is one of the solutions society has provided for the conundrums created by the imposition of binary gender categories upon its children. It is a part of life and a place where people can deny their other orientation and turn their production for others to their own advantage, a place where they will not be accused of direct mothering. The fact that women can participate equally with men in this ungiving area simply shows that its roots are not biological but social, located in a social, not biological, construction of gender.

The escalation towards dominance through competition can be done not only economically of course but also physically, psychologically, linguistically and institutionally, at the level of individuals and at the level of groups. One of the first non-nurturing human interactions that boys learn is *hitting*. In fact hitting may be seen as a transposed gift in that one reaches out and touches the other, transmitting physical energy, not to nurture but to hurt and to dominate. The fact that this is a transposed gift can be glimpsed in such linguistic expressions as "Take that!" and "You asked for it!". Such physical competition permits the one who can "give the most" harmful blows, to dominate.

As many women have noticed, there is a continuity in kind between the backyard brawl and war. The same principles seem to apply in both. The technology is different though symbolically concomitant. Since the penis is the identifying property of those in the non nurturing category, "male", it is not surprising that the individuals and the groups that are competing for dominance provide themselves with ever larger and more dangerous category markers, from sticks to swords and from guns to missiles. Moreover, competition between sons and fathers for dominance pits those with the smaller phallic properties against those with the larger. Thus in an attempt to achieve the position of the exemplar, the dominant father, groups supply themselves with ever larger instruments of death, which can destroy ever more people and goods. The aspect of size can then be substituted by the aspect of effect, in that WMDs whether biological or nuclear become the mark of the dominant male nation.

This collective striving to achieve the dominant male position can have the effect of confirming the masculine identity for the men who fight and even for those who are just members of the nation. Women can fight or give support to those who fight or participate in other ways, also just as members of the nation. Society thus provides a way for groups to achieve a collective male identity that is actually independent from individual biological gender in that both men and women can participate in it. Male dominance is then read as neuter objective *power*[12] over others and both women and men can achieve it as can, at a collective level, nations or corporate entities. Both women and men can also of course participate in a collective male dominant identity of their nation (or corporation) even if individually they are subservient. Such is the content of patriotism (or company loyalty). Racism is the participation in the collective male dominant identity of the supposed "exemplar" race. Classism is the participation in the collective male dominant identity of a supposed "exemplar" class.

Psychological competition for dominance can take the place of physical competition, and the categorization of others as inferior replays the gender distinction over and over, placing some people. who are usually also themselves the categorizers, in a "superior" category to which those in "inferior" categories must give. At the same time the positive gift giving and receiving that is actually continually being done in material and linguistic communication is unrecognized as such and disparaged – or over valued and made unreachable for ordinary people. In its place we have neuter and neutral [13] "objective" categories which reflect the neutral non giving market categories: exchange value, production, distribution (through exchange) consumption, supply and demand, monetized labor, commodities, money, capital, all of which are constructed on the back of the gift economy.

Gift giving is made arduous by its co existence with exchange. Since it is cooperative while exchange is competitive, it loses the competition by not competing. The context of adversarial exchange creates suspicion in the community and gift giving can appear to be a moral ego trip or a veiled bid for power and recognition. In fact, especially in a context where exchange relations are the norm, gift giving *can* become manipulative, and be used for ego oriented purposes, transforming away from its unilateral transitive path, and doubling back upon itself. The worst aspect of the competition between exchange and gift giving is that the exchange paradigm really cannot compete in a fair way with gift giving, because living according to the logic of the gift would be life enhancing, while living according to exchange is bio pathic. The exchange paradigm has therefore created a system that cripples gift giving and makes it dependent on the market for access to the means of giving. By diverting the flow of gifts into the hands of a few by wasting "excess" wealth on armaments, drugs and symbols of power (skyscrapers, monuments, jewels), as well as by privatizing the free gifts of nature and culture, Patriarchal Capitalism creates the scarcity that is necessary to keep gift giving from prevailing. In fact the flow of gifts to the wealthy must be regulated so that not too much will trickle back down. The tide must be kept low; otherwise all the ships would sail away.

Although girl children are not socialized to construct a gender identity that opposes that of their nurturing mothers, and many of them will have to do mothering themselves as adults, they can be encouraged to strive for inclusion in "superior" categories and to achieve the "male" exemplar position. In a context of scarcity, where categorization itself has become so important due to the binary categorization of gender, girls also strive to be included among the privileged group to whom others must give. Nevertheless, because children require unilateral gift giving to survive, women who have been socialized towards this work remain in the gift logic in many parts of their lives, even when they do not have children and even when they have been absorbed into the market and see the world mainly through the eye glasses of the exchange paradigm.

The practice of the gift logic at the material and at the verbal level can take place without our being conscious of it as such. In fact unilateral gift giving is transitive and gives value and attention to the other, while exchange requires quantification and measurement, reflecting back to the exchangers what they are doing. We in the North are accustomed to the exchange way of knowledge and self-reflecting consciousness and so we embrace what we see in that way, which is of course NOT the gift. Gratitude might make us conscious of the gifts we receive and give but if we make our gift contingent on the others' gratitude, the gift is no longer unilateral. In the context of exchange, even gratitude becomes problematic. There is a sort of scarcity of gratitude because "deserving" appears more honorable than receiving. What is necessary now is to see gift giving and exchange from a broader "meta" point of view that includes them both as paradigms, look at the way they interact, and deliberately restore the consciousness of the gift where it has been erased.

Communication

By looking at communication as unilateral need satisfaction we can view mothering as communication, and exchange as altered and distorted communication, that is, altered and distorted mothering. We can see unilateral need satisfaction as communication not only on the plane of signs and language but on the material plane. Gift giving creates not only minds and psychological subjectivities, but also bodies, material subjects and human relations. The relations created in this way are bonds of a possible community that is not based on exchange but on turn taking, participation in a gift circle or circulation that does not require equivalent paybacks by receivers to givers[14]. Such a communicative "female" economy continues to exist within some indigenous communities and in Capitalism within some families. However in families it is often altered and distorted internally by Patriarchy as well as externally by the context of the market and the exchange paradigm. Many

indigenous communities had positive "female" economies based on common ground and the circulations of gifts to needs without the intervention of exchange. The parasite of Patriarchal Capitalism has captured these economies whenever possible however, and on pain of death, made them its hosts.

Viewed from Patriarchy we usually only see the victimization of gift giving. From the point of view of the gift paradigm we go farther into the question and see the positive and creative root of the gift. Language itself can be viewed as an ideal abundant gift economy in which everyone possesses the means of production and a sufficient supply of the products of previous labor to be able to give again in turn. I want to include here at least a few indications of the steps I have taken in developing this perspective because I think that embracing this view can have far reaching consequences for the rest of one's worldview. By discovering gift giving in language, and characterizing language as gift giving at many levels, we can reclaim both language and linguistics for mothering. On the other hand, by extending mothering beyond gender and beyond economics to the pan human processes of linguistic communication, we situate mothering as one particularly intense moment of gift giving within a much wider context of gift processes. These processes are constitutive of the human in a way that Patriarchy, Capitalism, the market and exchange are not.

Recognizing the communicative relation-forming capacity of material gift giving allows us to find something that words and things have in common, which in turn allows us to consider words not only as abstract values of a combinatory mechanism, but as verbal gifts which take the place of material gifts. Words function as verbal gifts in their capacity for forming human relations among people in regard to parts of the world that are gifts or potentially gifts. Verbal gifts can take the place of material gifts in forming human relations but they do not supersede them altogether. Indeed material gifts continue to be given at all levels whether or not we are talking about them[15].

Material gift giving creates human relations and gifts can be given in order to create the relations (that is to satisfy the social and psychological need for relations) rather than primarily to satisfy material needs. Verbal gifts can perform this function as well and in fact, once the possibility of verbal communication is broached, a communicative need arises for verbal gifts regarding all the parts of the world with regard to which human relations can be formed. Words can thus be seen as verbal gifts which substitute for material gifts, satisfying communicative needs and thereby forming human relations regarding the interlocutors and regarding as well the gifts of the world that have been substituted. Words are verbal gifts originally given to us by other members of the community and we can give them again in turn. The question as to what words and things have in common is thus answered by the recognition of both words and things as relation-forming gifts. Would words or things have this capacity without the presence of human beings? No, any gift needs a receiver. However when members of a linguistic community are available to give and receive them, words and things do have this common gift character. Exchange causes problems, however, because it cancels the gift and so makes it appear that there is no connection between the verbal and the material or non-verbal levels.

Not only are words verbal gifts but they combine according to the gift principle as well in that they are given to each other. That is syntax, which is considered by linguists to be a *sui generis* rule-governed mental activity, is actually a construction of transposed gift giving.

From the gift perspective, adjectives combine with nouns for example because one word can satisfy the "need" of the other, a need arising from the relation of the referent to the word and to the human beings involved. If a human being wants to communicate about a red ball, she finds "ball" has a need for "red" in order to convey that idea, and she gives "red" to "ball". On the reality plane I believe that we can also make a case for the way we understand the "properties" of objects. That is, a ball is red because the "property" red has been given to it. Some words can receive some other words as gifts while others cannot. A plural ending prevents the word from receiving a singular indefinite article, an adverb cannot be given to a noun. Similarly humans can eat eggs but not elephants or mountains. That is, there are also constraints on the kinds of material gifts that can be given and received as well.

Even the noun-verb-complement structure can be understood as transposed giver-gift or service-receiver: "The girl hit the ball". Verb phrases are given to noun phrases with the help of transmitters like prepositions. Prefixes and suffixes determine what kinds of word gifts can be given and received by other word gifts. Moreover as each person satisfies the communicative needs of the other person, she also conveys her own ideas, feelings and intentions, stimulating and satisfying the others' needs to know. At a purely material level sound flows through air from the vocal chords and the breath of one to the ears of the other. Writing is inscribed upon the page and is perceived/received by the eyes of the other. Language is thus complex multi layered gift giving and receiving, and as such would require a treatment as thorough as giftless theories of language now provide from a much more mechanical viewpoint. For example, calling a sentence an "assertion" leaves aside its gift aspects under a neutral cover. Instead renaming a sentence as a gift made up of many gifts at different levels and itself contained within larger gifts such as the discourse, also made of many sentences and the text in turn made of many discourses, gives a radically different view of what we are doing when we communicate linguistically. We cannot even declare anything without satisfying communicative needs of the other, that is, giving word-gifts.

Perhaps it appears that language, considered as the giving and receiving of verbal gifts, cannot be hardwired in our brain circuitry. Yet we must also be able to satisfy needs on a material plane if we are to form communities, and that ability to give must be hard wired to some extent. Sex and mothering are two areas in which both human and non-human animals have to satisfy others' needs. Moreover the cry of the animal that perceives a danger satisfies the need of others to be warned – a situation analogous to the satisfaction of a human communicative need. Perhaps our brains themselves can be considered from the point of view of need satisfaction in that a neuron fires and satisfies the need of another neuron for stimulation. That neuron can then "pass it on". At another level brain cells even sometimes physically migrate from one area to another area where they are needed.

There is much more intentional and unintentional gift giving in the universe than we imagine due to our entanglement with exchange and Patriarchy. The possibility that humans are doing multi level gift giving when they communicate linguistically is therefore not as unlikely as it might seem. Nor does the hard wiring in this case diminish the social character of linguistic (or non linguistic) communication. Looking at language from the point of view of giftless brain mechanisms, like looking at life from the point of view of Patriarchy and the market, leaves meaning aside. Looking at language and life from the inside, from the receivership of a wide variety of gifts at different levels and the ability to give gifts again, as well as transpose them from one level to another, gives us a point of view from which we can look back at brain circuitry as possibly functioning also according to gift principles. If we see this as a projection of mothering, then we must certainly also see giftless brain circuitry as a projection of neuterizing Patriarchy and exchange. The fact that there is meaning both in language and in life speaks to the existence of gifts and gift giving everywhere. Meaninglessness is a result of Patriarchal Capitalism at both the level of life and the level of language. In fact exchange leaves everyone starving for the gift principle and for free gifts. This starvation for gifts could be seen as one main component of greed[16]. At the same time there are billions of people who are actually starving because their gifts have been taken away.

Meaning in language can be seen as the other-directedness of words and things, our ability to attribute a gift character to them as being potentially and/or actually for others, pertinent to them. That is, they are receivable by others, which implies that they can also be given, whether actually or only perceptually or experientially. Their receivability by others accounts for their significance. The fact that we can also use both words and things by ourselves alone conceals their other-direction from us especially when we are living in a society that validates self reflection and self interest. Meaning in life is the turning of goods towards needs, unilaterally giving to others that which is useful for them at whatever level. It is not the exemplar position that makes life meaningful in Patriarchy. In fact the satisfactions of that position as such are usually illusory except to extreme narcissists. Rather the capacity to satisfy numerous needs that the exemplar position could potentially bring, gives it the "meaning" we see in it.

The market, the law, the commons

The market and private property go hand in hand, because exchange allows private property to change proprietor. If property could not be transferred from one mutually exclusive owner to another, there would be paralysis. Commons have sometimes been left as gift sources, without a proprietor, or with a collective proprietor. In a context where gift giving and the gift paradigm are not recognized as valid, however, ownerless or collectively owned property can be seized and made the host of any parasitic corporate entity with the capacity to legally and materially enforce its ownership. In fact gifts are logically prior to the law because they are prior to exchange. The law regulates exchange from an exchange point of view, that is, by categorizing actions as crimes and making criminals pay for them. Gift giving does not require retribution but what we call in this case "compassion", the recognition and satisfaction of the social, psychological and material needs that cause people to commit crimes. The mercy movement, and the movement against the death penalty are gift-based initiatives but they rarely have a chance to generalize their values. The generalization of the gift paradigm would connect those issues to other issues such as the privatization of the commons.

Because gift giving is prior to exchange, it is not recognized by the law, and places where it can be done are usually considered as existing only inside private property, as happens in the home. Thus it seems that any free area can and perhaps even should be privatized, becoming the property of individuals, corporations, or the state, and thus regulated by law. As long as gifts continue to be unrecognized as such, not only by the law, but even by the very activists who are trying to defend the commons, the only appeal will be to the law itself, which is structurally based on Patriarchy and exchange. Even winning such battles brings the gift into the patriarchal capitalist camp and coopts, denatures and disqualifies it. The same might be said about the rights discourse, which legitimizes the law as arbiter, leaving needs in second place. Even morality can be seen as an attempt to mitigate some of the worst aspects of the exchange paradigm, while the gift paradigm (which actually motivates morality) is completely invisible.

At another more abstract level the law may be seen as a gift – to the patriarchal capitalist system itself. The needs that are satisfied by the law are the needs of the system to maintain itself and expand. As regards the perpetrators of personal crimes, these are systemic needs for the defense of property and proprietors. As regards the privatization of the commons[17] or the corporate commodification of the gifts of seeds, water, and genes, these are systemic needs for growth and expansion. They are not the human needs of individuals but the impersonal needs of collective entities to maintain the status quo and to make ever-larger profits. The corporate entities do have human "carriers" of course, and these carriers have human needs as well as points of view, which are typically based on the exchange paradigm and promote ego orientation and self-aggrandizement. They may also involve gift based abilities however, such as cooperation and teamwork within the corporation itself. As individuals they are presumably required to obey the law while as members of corporate categories or entities other rules apply.

Non-human corporate entities have many resources for protecting themselves from regulation by the law and from the protest of those they harm. However they are presently being undermined from within by the individual crimes of their CEO's who have stolen and pocketed the money of investors, as in the cases of ENRON and PARMALAT. Though a few of these persons are caught, since the market really *requires* the kind of greed and dishonesty that drives people to implement the expansion of the system, others soon replace them and try similar maneuvers. The law works to some extent to regulate the crimes of the individual, though it rarely works to regulate the corporations themselves. The more general, broader injustice usually remains even when some of the more particular ones are remedied. These considerations, while depressing, point to the fact that the most impelling need at present is for general, big picture social change. In order to create this change a paradigm shift is necessary. Without it, both individuals and corporate entities are continually validated in their parasitism. By reducing this validation at all levels of society we can create a new context where the need for systemic change can be more easily satisfied.

The paradigm of exchange justifies the spread of the market into ever new areas by occupying the top place in our individual hierarchical priority systems[18] and characterizing itself as the main or only need-satisfier. Not only does there appear to be no clear alternative to Capitalism but (apart from a few courageous attempts to choose sustainability or live in alternative communities) most of us, especially in Euro/America, cannot recognize any viable alternative to the market logic for our own lives, nor do we see what we might do to change things for the better. Although ethical systems, compassionate religions and simple human kindness continue to pull individuals away from the market logic, the values of self interest that the market promotes and the general scarcity for the many that is artificially created by Capitalism keep most people stuck in the exchange paradigm. Indeed everyone's survival is made to seem contingent upon accepting it. The overvaluing of the exchange paradigm by the culture of Capitalism focuses the attention of the entire society on exchange, distorting the perspective even of those who are practicing gift giving or who are on its margins. People who do not share the values of exchange are considered "failures" by those who do, and are often discounted and subjected to ridicule.

We can alter this negative picture if we realize that there is in each of us the core of an alternative paradigm that already exists and is based on the unilateral gift logic that we use to communicate as well as on our experience as mothered children. Bringing this paradigm to the foreground and understanding its logic as the basic human process rather than the logic of exchange, gives a leverage point with which we can reduce the hegemony of exchange over our thinking, and understand how and why our "creature" has taken over and turned against us. Whatever place in society we occupy, we can find the gift paradigm within ourselves if we can look beyond the exchange paradigm.

The devastating real world life and death consequences of the expansion of Patriarchal Capitalism hide the fact that even the people working for businesses and governments in the North and elsewhere have beliefs and value systems they are putting into practice, which they have learned growing up, in homes, religious institutions, schools and in universities which make learning those beliefs and value systems a point of pride. They have been educated to derive their self-esteem within the exchange paradigm framework and to consider gift giving, not as an economy or as an interpretative key, but as at most an ("unrealistic") moral stance.

Academic endeavor is not "value free". Indeed it usually promotes the exchange paradigm while appearing neutral and objective. The reason for this is not so much that academics are in bad faith, though some are, but that for centuries the exchange paradigm and Patriarchy have had free reign in defining the terrain upon which questions are addressed, and in determining the questions themselves. Perhaps we could say that misogyny and the devaluing of the gift paradigm are one and the same, at least they coincide to a great extent. Women were kept out of universities for centuries. When they were finally admitted, academic endeavor was already deeply and firmly patriarchal, allied with the exchange paradigm. The result is that the gift paradigm has been deleted from academic disciplines. Mothering has not been considered as having an economic character, but also gift giving has been deleted from epistemology. Yet humans are intensely mothered as children. Patriarchy and exchange have made us turn against that common legacy as a model for understanding, and deny its importance, as is typical when one is exploiting something or someone. Yet it is only by *projecting* mothering in terms of giving and receiving, onto the Universe that we can understand it in a way that does not leave us orphans among lifeless stars, ready to plunder and prey upon each other.

The gift paradigm needs to be reinstated throughout science, not only in economics, psychology, semiotics and linguistics, but also in biology and the "hard" sciences. We need to extend the metaphor or metaform[19] of giving and receiving to perception as the creative reception of experiential data, as well as to atomic-level electron "donation", and to the "transmission" of hormonal messages. The transmission of motion can be seen as a variation of the gift syllogism: "If A gives to B and B gives to C then A gives to C". However we need particularly to re vision signs, language and communication from the point of view of the gift paradigm. Otherwise a central aspect of the way we are human is invisible to us, and we misinterpret what we are doing in ways that validate both the suicide of 'mankind' and its matricide of mothers and of Mother Earth.

It is not that material gift giving, language and sign behavior are not to a certain extent brain functions as well as social gift constructions, but that brain functions should also be understood in terms of gift giving and receiving need-satisfying – eliciting and – educating impulses. The release of adrenaline in the bloodstream is a gift from the hormonal level to the human being as a whole, who needs to run away. The brain can be seen as organized according to giving and receiving, and capable of internalizing those patterns in consciousness when it encounters them in language and life. If language is based on gift giving, it serves as a model in that sense, as well as in the capacity for abstraction and concept formation. Mothering must take place for children to survive. Since mothering happens from our earliest moments, inside as well as outside the womb, the patterns of gift transmission must be at least as familiar to us as those of abstraction. Only because as a patriarchal and capitalist society we renounce our mothering heritage, do we cancel the deep metaform of mothering.

By extending our notion of gift giving to nature, revivifying it/her as the locus of multi-level processes of gifts to needs, from the atomic level to the level of centrifugal and centripetal swirls of galaxies[20], from the biological level where the heart sends blood with nutriments and oxygen to the cells, to the level in which the other-turning and-tending activity of our attention becomes the mind, we can find and restore our commonality with Mother Nature. It is by erasing the idea of the gift at all these levels instead of extending it to them that we have permitted the destruction of the environment by a non nurturing economy. Misogyny could be seen as an economic emotion, a hatred and devaluation of gift giving in women, which allies with a hatred and devaluation of the gift aspects of nature.

It is against the image of the mother, robbed of all these connections with gift giving in the rest of life, victimized and giving gifts to extenuation that the feminist movement has rebelled. However this is a false image. If we refocus and consider mothering and gift giving as the human norm, we can see that it is not mothering but Patriarchy-and-exchange that is the aberration and the cause of the problem. Mothers and other gift givers *are* often victimized, but this is not caused by their defects, weaknesses or masochistic tendencies. Even the image of their victimization distracts women (and men) from the truth, which is that it is the whole Patriarchal Capitalistic context of artificial scarcity and power-over that is responsible for the suffering of all and must be changed. Women cannot solve the problem by individually rejecting the image, though perhaps by refusing that model, they can become strong enough to do something about it.

Essentialism

Essentialism and anti essentialism come from the same matrix: the processes of abstraction by which males are sorted out from females, and commodities are sorted out from gifts[21]. These processes have deleted, concealed and manipulated the mother model, banishing it and replacing it with the model of the father, then replacing it again as a model in the market with the "neuter" object, money. The non nurturing models propagate in academic endeavor, religions, science, business and politics. The father is the exemplar of the category "human" while money is the exemplar of the category "value". Both of these categories are constructed by abstracting from gift giving. That is, they are categories with regard to which gift giving is seen as irrelevant, a discarded quality[22]. Money and the father (as well as the king, the general, the C.E.O. etc.) are "general equivalents", used to evaluate and sort the items relative to them. The "common quality" or "essence" of commodities is exchange value and it is expressed in a certain quantity of money, which is exchanged for the commodity. Every time we evaluate a commodity in money, buy and sell, we abstract from gift giving and affirm the common quality of exchange value. (The gift is always just beyond, as "the road not taken". In fact in every personal transaction, we could just decide to give the other person something instead of selling it to h/er.) We usually perform this operation of evaluation and abstraction daily in Patriarchal Capitalism, and at a number of different levels. The common quality of exchange value thus appears to be real and evident. Similarly every time we use the term "mankind" we abstract from mothering, leaving it aside as irrelevant to the formation of that concept[23].

The male identity leaves aside gift giving in a way that is somewhat different from the market abstraction, yet both are social sorting processes. For boys, manhood is a goal rather than an inherited property[24]. A metamorphosis must take place that turns the tiny child into a dominant male. In Euro/American Capitalist Patriarchy, males are expected to create the kind of personality and behavior that is identified as "masculine". That is, they have to sort their own behavior, abstracting from gift giving within themselves and replacing it with other behavior, engaging in hitting and competition with other males. Otherwise they are penalized, by being considered "sissies", "girls" and "soft". Since numerous "exemplar" positions have been invented in social hierarchies of all kinds, males have a chance to reach that position not only as exemplars of their gender but as exemplars of many other male-dominated categories, from the military to religion to government etc. Paradoxically the ability to be dominant and the "one" to whom the many relate, appears to be a *common* quality of the male gender. In fact it cannot be *common* because logically not all of them can be dominant or the "one". These are relational qualities, not properties. Manhood is a socially imposed agenda into which the sorting process itself has been absorbed. By sorting out and discarding his female qualities, a male hopes to become an exemplar of the non-mothering category. Sorting itself, in the sense of judging, naming and categorizing are seen as predominantly male "capacities". Hitting replaces gift giving as a way to interact with others, establishing relations of dominance rather than mutuality. This replacement of giving by hitting also appears to be a commonality of males, possibly a biologically determined characteristic. Exchange replaces gift giving, canceling the gift with an equivalent return

30

"gift" and creating a non-nurturing interaction. Similarly hitting provokes a return of hitting, an exchange of blows.

Those who do not relate in this way are seen as "acting like girls". That is they are acting like those people who are expected to be the second term in a dominance-submission relation. Empathy is seen as a female, not a male quality, I believe, because it is necessary for gift giving. That is, in order to identify needs we must respond emotionally to the other person. The "masculine disassociation" and refusal of empathy and emotion are thus part of the refusal of the gift economy, not just a defect that biological males are born with. The masculine "essence" is constructed as an artificial quality or group of qualities in opposition to gift giving. However gift giving does not begin as an abstraction but is itself a basic and necessary transitive process in which some give and other(s) receive many kinds of goods and services at different levels. In fact it is the process in which the child is deeply involved when he learns he is "other", something else, in an opposite gender category.

Because the socialization of the boy takes place so early, it is the mother with regard to whom he finds himself to be the opposite, not women generally. Moreover since the male identity is so difficult to achieve and so conflicted throughout men's lives, the mothering role is what continues to be identified (by men) as women's and not men's "nature". The childhood binary opposition with the mother (and gift giving) remains as the basis of the male identity and thus mothering is the most relevant aspect of the female identity for the male gender construction. In fact this renunciation of gift giving seems to give males the right to plunder those who remain gift givers. On the other hand the market provides the possibility for males to "make money" and maintain their families, becoming gift givers after the fact. That is at this level they can provide a kind of market-based neuter nurturing-without-nurturing that is even more necessary than the gifts of nurturing proper, as it has been made their pre requisite. Males can provide the money that gives access to the means of giving, though fortunately they no longer have a monopoly on this ability as women have obtained more equal status, though constructing that equality using the (now neuterized) male exemplar.

Processes not properties

Both female and male identities are based on processes, not properties. Mothering is a particularly intense moment of gift giving which is one of the major processes of life itself but which, however, appears to be a defect and a liability for "real" human beings who are those engaged in violent conflict, competition, and the market.

The process of gift giving requires and produces some human qualities and capacities that are different from those of exchange (which denies gift giving). I just mentioned empathy and I believe that the emotions create a kind of map that lets us identify needs. Sensitivity to what others are experiencing is an aspect of the gift mode. Other-orientation is not only a pre requisite for gift giving but is also its result. We care about those to whom we give, and we give value to them. The relation-creating capacity of giving and receiving, which confirms the existence and positive character of each for the other, with or without explicit gratitude, is an important aspect of gift giving which is often identified with women.

On the other hand the kinds of relations that are necessary for exchange and are created by it are more similar to those usually identified with masculinity: separation, competition, instrumentality of the other, ego orientation, adversarial behavior, acquisitiveness, growth to a large size. It is the comparison between the qualities coming from the "economic modes" in which we participate, as mothers on the one hand, and as (male and female) exchangers on the other, that makes us think we are looking at essences. Instead gift giving is not an essence but a process with emotional, psychological and material consequences. Exchange is also a process but it is the very process of abstraction (sorting) itself, transferred onto the material plane. The identification and the giving-without-giving of a socially created "essence", exchange value, is its reason for being. In investigating a female "nurturing essence", we are looking at women in the light of the market. We are trying to accept or reject the existence of a common quality that is a kind of reflection of exchange value, which itself is a quality artificially created by the aberrant *do ut des* exchange communication. Without a common essence, the members of a category, in this case women, would seem to fall into the reciprocal independence and indifference that is the common relation of (mutually exclusive) exchangers to each other. However women's commonality comes not from their membership in a category but from the practice of a process that is creative of subjectivities, of self as well as of others, as we have been saying. It comes from what women do, not from what they are[25].

Gift giving is the ground upon and against which both the process of the male identity and the process of exchange are constructed. What women have in common is that they have not been made men. They have not been estranged from the gift process early in childhood, and they can therefore practice it in a relatively straightforward way. This is changing to some extent as women take on the values of the market in order to survive and succeed there. However if they become mothers they still have to access the gift values and practice the gift processes at a personal level in that period of their lives, often maintaining the two paradigms internally at the same time. Moreover many women who do not become mothers nevertheless practice intense gift giving in other areas. Women can unite across all the patriarchal boundaries as those who continue to practice the human gift process outside the context of the market and often inside it as well. Though this process involves different kinds of gifts and has many cultural variations, women are similar because they make themselves by "making" others through satisfying their needs unilaterally, beyond the exchange process.

Mothering and gift giving are the thesis, the male and the market are the antithesis, and exploitation and parasitism are the synthesis. We need to go back and start a different dialectical progression, so that everyone can be included in the practice of the gift process and validate it.

The essence of profit

The market can be seen as a gigantic process of sorting products having the common quality of exchange value, using money as the exemplar. Gift processes and their free products, services and resources are sorted *out*, discarded as irrelevant. They are relegated to an area outside exchange but many of them are then turned towards that incarnated sorting process itself and made to support it, giving it value by implication, flowing into (and mixing with) exchange value. Thus there is a kind of *de facto*-essentialization, a kind of "reprocessing" of the gift which abstracts it (or extracts it) from its particular concrete transactions and channels it "upwards" towards the capitalists as profit. The value of the caring labor of housework passes invisibly and noiselessly through the surplus value created by the worker into the profit of the capitalist (even when the housewife is herself also the worker). Similarly the gifts of nature and of past and future generations flow into profit unrecognized. These are gifts of all the collective caregiving and maintenance of the past, which have preserved the environment and the (physical and spiritual) community up to the present, the gifts of traditional knowledge which have been handed down through generations, as well as the gifts of the people of the future who will not ever have access to the natural and cultural abundance that is now being used up, flowing to corporations and their investors and stockholders. These are also the gifts that the poorer nations are giving to the richer ones due to level of life. Not only is labor cheap (that is, a large part of it is a gift) but the population collectively receives fewer of the gifts of its environmental and cultural context and thus passes on more of them into the profit of the investors from the North. The goods that are consumed are cheaper to produce than those in the rich countries and of poorer quality. Access to natural and cultural gifts and resources is limited; even expectations of a good life are limited. By restricting the production and consumption available for local use and channeling money, products, work and resources out of the country, gifts for the local population are made scarce and the gifts of cheap goods, resources and labor are made to flow Northwards. This process of exploitation "refines" gifts making them invisible, "purified" of their local relevance, and "vital", essential to the functioning of the capitalist machine. *Pecunia non olet*, money doesn't smell, however, and we cannot tell the difference between the money that has come as a forced gift and money that has come from an "equal" exchange.

If we look at all the elements that go into profit: the surplus value of present and past labor, the value of gift labor such as housework and other free labor that flows unseen into value and surplus value, the gifts of free and cheap raw materials, the gifts leveraged from the public by high prices, gifts leveraged by inflation, and deflation, gifts given as interest on loans, gifts coming from differences in level of life in the country of origin and in the country of sale, gifts taken by appropriating species and knowledge through patenting, gifts of savings garnered by desecrating the gifts of the environment etc., we can see that profit is a gift made of many gifts. In profit the market abstracts again from concrete gift processes and re presents the gifts amalgamated, homogenized and sanitized under the name of "making money".

Any income above the cost of production and capital is free to the capitalist, who also may contribute free work, but whose "risk" is only that s/he will not be able to leverage these gifts through h/er exchange activities. The common quality of profit is that it is a free gift to the capitalist. That is indeed its essence[26].

Thus the gift of profit is the actual essential aspect of production for needs *and* for exchange that flows from the unpaid work of the many into the hands of the few in an economy based on exchange and Patriarchy. This gift essence is the ownable (common un-common) property of successful capitalists. It is passed on to others not as a gift however but as an exchange, when it is invested in order to extract the gift essence again from other labor. Far from being the identifying common property of women, the nurturing essence is the invisible motivator of the whole economy.

Conclusion

It is against the market and Patriarchy that we should direct our rage not against mothering. The context created by the market and Patriarchy is what makes mothering/gift giving difficult. Mothering is not per se a self-sacrificing role leading to victimization, but is a more positive human process than for example, the market, the law or the academic disciplines from which it has been deleted. Women (and some men) continue to do gift giving in the face of great obstacles because they are human, not because they are masochistic. Self-sacrifice is sometimes the only way to assert our humanity in the face of a corrosive and poisonous Patriarchal system.

If we stopped educating our boys not to be like their gift giving mothers, we could recreate humanity on the basis of the gift paradigm. However we would also need to change the institutions that have been made in the male image or with the neuter cover of the market. That change is what I am proposing. The first step in doing this is of course recognizing what needs to be changed and what to put in its place. Schools, governments, religions, media, corporations, the law, the market: all of these institutions can be changed from within, under the non patriarchal leadership of women, by promoting a paradigm shift in the minds of the individuals who implement them. As mothered children we all have the gift paradigm deep within us. As communicators we practice gift giving all the time and develop our subjectivities accordingly. As mothers we have to do intense gift giving in that period of our lives. As caring human beings we continue to satisfy needs of all kinds, without recognizing that is what we are doing. If we can re focus, we can shift our priorities. In the U.S. the discourse on "values" seems to be the province of the Right Wing. That is because values are identified with the Patriarchal values that denigrate gift giving and/or capture it in the kitchen and the nursery. It is time for a widespread affirmation of values based on the gift paradigm. Sharing the analysis of the gift and exchange can provide the rationale for the gift giving behavior of everyone in a new world beyond the exchange paradigm.

Notes

[1] Vygotsky and Marx were both investigating what Irrigaray and others would call Aristotelian "monologic". However this logic is not just descriptive but it is incarnated *in res* in the market and other patriarchal structures. This incarnation validates the monologic both as a description and as a concept forming practice.

[2] I mention this particularly because I want to distinguish myself from the French sociologists of the gift who publish in the *MAUSS Revue*. I did not read any of their work until sometime in the 1990's. This lacuna may seem strange but first I am not primarily an academic and secondly, I did search for other writers on the gift but always found they

had not made the distinction between gift and exchange. That was the case for a long time regarding the *MAUSS Revue* as well. Writers on gift giving also did not make a connection between mothering and gift giving. For one partial exception see Lewis Hyde (1979). A particular problem I see with the concept of Anti-Utilitarianism is that it links exchange and the utilitarian satisfaction of needs, as if gift giving could not satisfy basic "utilitarian" needs. Women's gifts are also invisible as such just for this reason – because they do so often satisfy basic needs. That does not mean that they do not also have psychological and spiritual or aesthetic aspects and consequences.

[3] Seeing the immense amount of free work that is performed by women made me realize that Marx's theory could only be a partial explanation of Capitalism, since he did not include it as a determining factor. For that reason I stopped considering myself a Marxist. I believe feminism is broader and deeper than Marxism because it includes free labor. Unfortunately attempts to create a better world have almost always been patriarchal and therefore unsuccessful. Women are a vanguard composed of more than half of the population and can create the necessary social change if they can let go of their patriarchal conditioning. In fact their free labor is a gift to the economic system, perhaps even a way of "communicating" with it and giving it importance.

[4] Unilateral gift giving thus appears not to exist or not to be human, and mothering, which is a large part of human experience, is cancelled or misread as defective exchange and also not human in the sense of being "merely natural".

[5] I was able also to draw on Jean Josef Goux's (1990) exploration of the different forms of the general equivalent in society: the king, the phallus, the head etc.

[6] Females could also be socialized in this way, away from mothering, and to some extent this is happening as we are absorbed into the market. However, without the gift logic and values, it becomes difficult to spend the time and attention that is required to do adequate mothering.

[7] In fact the exemplar used in forming concepts can be just any member of a category that is like the others. The exemplar position has been invested with privilege and power-over by Patriarchy. On its own it is just a moment in a process of thought.

[8] Slavery is a way of directing gifts into profit which are free to the receiver but imposed by force upon the giver. Slavery is typically seen as imposed by race rather than by gender and existed long before as well as during Capitalism. Together with the free gifts of the lands of the Native Americans, the constrained gifts of African slaves constituted the pool of capital upon which the U.S. economic system is based. As salaried labor replaced slavery the free aspects of labor became invisible. The hungry parasite began to cast about for ever new areas of gifts, ever new hosts.

[9] Perhaps they could be considered "economic mestizas", part of a "border culture" between one kind of economy and the other. See Mechthild Hart's paper in this volume.

[10] It is now fashionable to call gift and exchange within the same person, the masculine or the feminine "sides" of the individual. In this way of thinking, taking the initiative, even to give, appears to be "male" while receptivity appears to be "female". Privileging the male continues to be done surreptitiously by considering the male the active principle while considering the female the passive principle (see for example the *I Ching*, the Chinese Book of Changes where the Creative is male and the Receptive is female). Yet gift giving and mothering are certainly active and creative though they are rejected as part of the male identity in the West. Receiving is also creative in that the receiver must engage in the appropriate use of the gift in order to bring it to fruition.

[11] The ego orientation of exchange has had a liberating effect for women in many ways. On the other hand the logic of ego orientation is more limited and more narrowly focused than that of other orientation. Like the class consciousness of the workers' movement in the North, it has had the effect of improving the lives of some through the validation of profit-sharing while obscuring the sources of the gifts that constitute the profit. This has the effect that some feminist movements in the North are inward turning and localizing while not recognizing the source of gifts in the exploitation of the women and men of the South and their resources. When these gifts diminish, due to the depletion of the level of life and the machinations of finance, such feminisms find themselves losing the ground they had previously gained in terms of individual well being. Nor do they have any real possibility of regaining it. The problem is that extending ego orientation to more people (eg. a class or a gender) does not change the exploitative system. The logic of other orientation opens us to recognize gift sources (in solidarity against exploitation). This recognition reveals the parasitism of the system and thus the need to change it. Feminism needs to embrace the gift logic with an international perspective in order to effectively challenge and dismantle the totalizing system of Patriarchal Capitalism.

[12] Power-over can be described as the capacity to make others give gifts.

[13] We might say that the not giving area of the market is made to look neuter by Patriarchy to hide the gendered character of gift and exchange and to make the market an area where the gender relations can be played out again on a more neutral territory. It is a sort of acting out of an original change of models, from mother to father (see Vaughan 1997). The neuter character then extends into other areas as well, from which gender and gift giving are cancelled.

[14] See Lewis Hyde (1979) on community and Kaarina Kailo in this volume, on circulating gifts.

[15] Non-verbal gestures and signs can be considered gifts as well. They satisfy communicative needs and are non linguistic yet not completely material because they are received as located within sign systems.

[16] The desire for knowledge has been altered because whatever is new can potentially be sold for a high price. Thus "thirst" for knowledge is now profit driven and becomes greedy, as the huge profit-making (gift-garnering) capacities of new discoveries and new fields such as genetic engineering are revealed.

[17] The question is no longer just the ownership of means of production but of the means of giving. Collective access to the source of gifts contradicts the system based on private property and exchange.

[18] Perhaps the exchange paradigm is most firmly held by those who receive the most advantage from it. It contains mechanisms by which it validates itself however, with the consequence that even those who are exploited by it, believe in it. Ethnic traditions of family and culture often contain strong gift elements, which continue to create community in spite of the market. However they are also subject to erosion by the values of the system.

[19] See Danesi and Sebeok (2002) for the term "metaform".

[20] See on the extension of another life-based concept, autopoesis, to the universe Elizabet Sahtouris (2002; 43). She also discusses Walter Russell's "model of continual creation, through the inward and outward motions of contraction (gravity) and expansion (radiation)". I think these could also be seen as a physical template for receiving (gravity) and giving (radiation).

[21] Saying that set theory derives from Aristotelian metaphysics, Maya J. Goldenberg argues that anti-essentialism cannot be negotiated within that framework because it necessarily becomes a problem of inclusion according to a monologic. Her project is "to follow Irrigaray in theorizing difference instead of sameness to construct an independant and positive category of woman" (Goldenberg 2003: 2). My alternative solution is to consider the gift process as prior to categorization and especially to gender categorization. Thus it is a process practiced by both genders but denied and exploited by men whose gender identity has been constructed specifically according to Patriarchal monologic.

[22] While women's gift giving is irrelevant there is a way in which money and the father "provide". That is they take over the mother model and re propose it at a different level, since it is upon them that gift givers are made dependent for access to the means of giving. Thus the boy who gives up giving as his gender identity can paradoxically practice it again as an adult through participating in the market and supporting his family, "bringing home the bacon".

[23] The common quality of mankind, leaving the mother aside, is then identified in higher, more "spiritual" qualities, for example, "valor", the homonym of "value"– a homonymy that should give us pause.

[24] See Gilmore (1990) on the "manhood agenda".

[25] I am reminded of the Sinatra existentialism formula I saw on a tee shirt Do-be, do-be, do.

[26] Unions and worker's movements throughout the world have succeeded in regulating working conditions and pay scales to some extent. However much labor now has been taken out of the workplace and is done in the home without any guarantees and with irregular pay. This is what Maria Mies calls the 'housewifization' of work. If we look at it in gift terms we can see how more gifts are made to flow into profit by once again reducing the expenses for the capitalist. Because the house has substituted the factory, the actual care of the house flows directly into profit as a gift rather than going first to the children and adults and then through their work into profit as surplus value. Isolation in the home away from other workers, and irregular and low wages continue to leverage more surplus value as a gift and create a greater dependency of the worker on the capitalist. This precarious situation disempowers the worker and de facto essentializes work, as it makes more and more of it into a gift that nurtures the capitalist.

References

Caille, Alain and Jacques T. Godbout (1992). *L'Esprit du don*, Editions La Decouverte, Paris.

Chodorow, Nancy (1978). *The Reproduction of Mothering: Pscyhoanalysis and the Sociology of Gender*, University of California Press, Berkeley.

Danesi, Marcel and Thomas Sebeok (2000). *The Forms of Meaning, Modeling Systems Theory and Semiotic Analysis*, Berlin-New York. Mouton de Gruyter.

Derrida, Jacques (1992). *Given Time:1, Counterfeit Money*, Engl. trans. Peggy Kamuf, The University of Chicago Press, Chicago.

Gilligan, Carol (1982). *In a Different Voice*, Harvard University Press, Cambridge, Mass.

Gilmore, David G. (1990). *Manhood in the Making*, Yale University Press, New Haven.

Godbout, Jacques T. and Alain Caille (1992). *L'Esprit du don*, Editions La Decouverte, Paris.

Goux, Jean-Joseph (1994 [1984]). *The Coiners of Language*, Engl. trans. Jennifer Curtiss Gage, University of Oklahoma Press, Norman and London.

— (1990). *Symbolic Economies: After Marx and Freud*, Cornell University Press, Ithaca.

Hyde, Lewis (1979). *The Gift, Imagination and the Erotic Life of Property*, Random House, New York.

Malinowsky, Bronislaw (1922). *Argonauts of the Western Pacific*, Routledge, London.

Marx, Karl (1930 [1867]). *Capital in Two Volumes: Volume One*, Engl. trans. Eden and Cedar Paul London, J.M. Dent & Sons, London.

— *Grundrisse* (1939 [1857-1858]). Engl. trans. Martin Nicholaus, New York, Vintage Books, 1973.

Mauss, Marcel (1990 [1925]). *The Gift: The Form and Reason for Exchange in Archaic Societies*, Engl. trans. W. D. Halls, W W.W. Norton, New York.

Rossi-Landi, Ferruccio (1968). *Il linguaggio come lavoro e come mercato*, Bompiani, Milano. New ed. 2003.

— (1974). "Linguistics and Economics", *Current Trends in Linguistics*, vol. 12, ed. Thomas A. Sebeok.

Sahtouris, Elizabet (2002). "A Tentative Model for a Living Universe" from "Consciousness-based biology; Biology-based Science" presentation at Unified Science Conference, Los Angeles.

Saussure, Ferdinand de (1931). *Cours de linguistique generale*, Charles Bally and Albert Sechehaye (eds.), Payot, Paris.

Shiva, Vandana (1997). *Biopiracy, the Plunder of Nature and Knowledge,* South End Press, Boston.

Sohn-Rethel, Alfred (1965). "Historical Materialist Theory of Knowledge", *Marxism Today*, 114-122.

Vaughan, Genevieve (1980). "Communication and Exchange", *Semiotica* 29, 1-2.

— (1981). "Saussure and Vygotsky via Marx", *Exchange*, Plain View Press, Austin, Texas.

— (2002). "Mothering, Co-muni-cation, and the gifts of Language", *The Enigma of Gift and Sacrifice,* Edith Wyschogrod, Jean-Josef Goux and Eric Boynton (eds.), Fordham University Press, New York.

Vygotsky, L.S. (1962 [1934]). *Thought and Language*, Engl. trans. Eugenia Hanfmann and Gertrude Vakar, The M.I.T. Press, Cambridge, Mass.

Waring, Marilyn (1988). *If Women Counted, A New Feminist Economics*, Harper and Row, San Francisco.

By restoring gift giving to the many areas of life in which it has been unrecognised or concealed, we can begin to bring the gift paradigm to consciousness. Gift giving underlies the homonymy of "meaning in language" and the "meaning of life" (Vaughan 2002: 2).

The current world situation – the deepening of neo-liberal economic fundamentalism – represents the most threatening stage of human development. It may even be interpreted as the apex of the patriarchal and capitalistic exchange economy, with cynical self-interest at its ideological core. This is a moment in his-story when the gifts of the many, of the land, of nature, the caregivers in homes, hospitals and educational institutions are not only being taken for granted but exploited and appropriated to serve the market.

Women are 70 per cent of the world's poor, and they own one per cent of the world's wealth. In every country in the world, women are poorer than men, and their poverty and economic inequality affects every aspect of their lives – their basic survival and the survival of their children, their access to food and housing, their physical security, their sexual autonomy, their health, their access to education and literacy, their access to justice, their ability to participate in public life, their ability to influence and participate in decisions that affect them. Women's economic inequality is integrally connected to their sexual exploitation, and to their lack of political power. As long as women as a group do not have an equal share of the world's economic resources, they will not have an equal say in shaping the world's future (Day 2000: 12).

It is also worth considering that in 1994 the richest 20 percent of humanity garnered 83 percent of global income, while the poorest 20 percent of the world's people struggled to survive on just 1 percent of the global income (World Bank 1994). The situation appears to have only worsened. As the above references to the widening income gap suggest, women's lack of political and economic power translates into the devaluation and incorporation of their gift labour in all of its public and private forms – emotional domestic, public service[1]. Neo-liberal globalisation has extended its tentacles to the most remote regions from the overexploited South to the overdeveloped West and the marginalized Arctic, wreaking havoc on indigenous and mainstream communities, on men and women, but most particularly, on those women who, due to lack of resources and power are most vulnerable to economic sexploitation. Masculated[2] economic policies and the psycho-spiritual control of women by patriar-

39

chal religions have represented a major threat to women's self-determination and status throughout history. The new marriage of right-wing religious and economic fundamentalisms risks taking women back to the dark ages in terms of their economic, sexual and psychological self-determination and choices. As our basic rights to work, resources, water, security, peace and clean air are being traded for corporate entitlements and privatisation, global ethics, too, are being "outsourced" and "downsized". It is important, then, to take collective action against the new fundamentalisms threatening the historical achievements in the realm of woman/human rights and the politics of positive difference. It is equally urgent to theorize and research the underlying roots of the expanding dysfunction and loss of values.

Genevieve Vaughan's writings on the gift economy (1997) and the paradigm on which it is built, represent one much-needed and timely theoretical response to this crises. They represent a powerful naming and valorisation of women's traditions of circulating gifts. After all, it is thanks to the philosophy and worldview based on gift giving and circulation that communities hit hard by the market and the Bretton Woods (the unholy trinity of IMF, WTO and the World Bank) institutions have survived and may well continue to do so. Where the current neo-liberal politics is based on an unrecognised unilaterality of taking, the Gift Economy stresses the value of unilateral giving, when the gift recipients are not in a position to give back. In the exchange economy, profits motivate the unilaterality, in the latter, giving is a response to the satisfaction of needs – basic needs to which all are entitled.

In this article, I have chosen to focus on Vaughan's theories of the Gift, because I feel they promise renewal and "re-sourcement" to counter the scarcity of solidarity, the freezing over of social responsibility. They help analyse how "progress" could have led to this, and how we might best get out of the mess. The purpose of this article is twofold: first, to briefly situate Vaughan's work in the academic lineage addressing gift giving from the influential theories of Marcel Mauss to contemporary theorists of the gift. I also include feminist materialist theories as a lineage of theories on women's surplus labour, with which Vaughan has significant affinities. Second, I will give an example of my own adoption of the Gift Economy concept, which I term Gift Imaginary, and through which I address the need for new paradigms and practices of transformational politics. The members of the international group, Feminists for a Gift Economy, started by Vaughan in 2002, are committed to a politics of affinity and cross-cultural solidarity that values diversity and difference, while working towards common local/global goals of gift-based world renewal[3].

1. *Giving Back to the Gift Economy – Vaughan's Contribution to Theoretical Gift Circulation*

Genevieve Vaughan's theories (and the activism to which they are inextricably linked) could be analysed in the light of a number of theoretical schools and feminist theories from Feminist economics (eg. Folbre 2002; Mellor 2002) to cognitive psychology, semiotics, psychoanalytic feminist theories (object relations)[4] and Marxist or materialist Feminist theory. However, it seems most appropriate to situate her writings in the genealogy of anthropological theories on the gift while at the same time recognizing their broader applicability and their holistic, interdisciplinary gist.

40

1.1. *The Lineage of the Theories of the Gift*

Since Marcel Mauss' influential *Essai sur le don* or *the Gift* in 1924, gifts and gift exchange have been frequent topics of inquiry within the field of anthropology. For Alan D. Schrift, in addition to that, the theme of the gift can be located at the centre of current discussions of deconstruction, gender, ethics, philosophy and economics:

> Where commodity exchange is focused on a transfer in which objects of equivalent exchange value are reciprocally transacted, gift exchange seeks to establish a relationship between subjects in which the actual objects transferred are incidental to the value of the relationship established. Commodity exchange thus exhibits the values that, for example, Carol Gilligan associates with an ethic of rights based on abstract principles of reciprocity, while gift exchange exhibits the forming of and focus on relationships that she associates with an ethic of care, an ethic based on interpersonal needs and responsibilities, an ethic that speaks in a voice different from the one that has heretofore dominated the moral tradition (Schrift 1997: 2-3).

The theme has emerged also within the humanities and education from literature to Native (Kuokkanen 2004) and Women's studies or theories recognizing gender (Strathern 1988; Berking 1999: Cheal 1988). Lewis Hydes' *The Gift. Imagination and the Erotic Life of Property* (1979) traces the writings on the Gift by focusing on literary works and Jacques Godbout's *The World of the Gift* (1998) (in collaboration with Alain Caille) spans a number of fields in an interdisciplinary social science and anthropology perspective. Although the works of both Hyde and Godbout are quite extensive, bringing up new insights and knowledge on gift-circulating nations and authors, they also personify and role-model in their approach the ease with which male scholars neglect or trivialize women's historic role as nurturers and gift givers. In fact, Godbout's analysis of the writings as well as his own approach towards women's gift processes reproduce the values and biases of the exchange economy. At worst, Godbout misnames feminists' theoretical gifts and spreads the stereotypes about feminists being merely "recent converts to the market", out to disparage the "feminine" ways of giving without utilitarian interest (Kailo 2004d). The exchange economy refers to a worldview which according to Vaughan is more characteristic of men than of women, and which due to upbringing predisposes men to taking gift giving for granted while rendering them all the more attentive to the worldview based on exchanging: giving in order to receive the equivalent or more of what one has given. In contrast with Vaughan, as the above quotation reveals, Schrift labels even gift giving as a form of exchange. This is the prevalent attitude also of the other male theorists.

According to Schrift (1997), the contemporary focus on gifts and exchange can be traced to "two important developments". He identifies them as the writings of Jacques Derrida (1991, *Donner le temps, l. la fausse monnaie*, or *Given Time: l. Counterfeit Money*) and second, as the emergence of gender issues within critical theory[5]. Among the critical theories Schrift notes the writings of Helene Cixous. Without going into a detailed comparison of the research, it is obvious that few of the Gift analysts go into any length or depth regarding the contributions of women or mothers as primary gift givers and providers of non-monetized care, or as transmitters of a social contract not based on self-interest. The circulation of women among men as currency of exchange is in some cases even seen as desirable, far from it being analysed as a symptom of patriarchal power relations and ownership entitlements. It is significant and quite radical in the patriarchal context of academic theory that Schrift should give recognition to gender issues as belonging to the "important developments". However, the particular and concrete ways in which women contribute to the upkeep and reproduction of Patriarchy and the labour force as the unrecognised pillars of capitalism remains surprisingly absent or unfocussed. Unlike the purely theoretical, abstract and even elitist writings of Cixous, Vaughan's theoretical and real life activism is informed by concrete, pragmatic caring for social justice and transformation. She practices the philosophy of the gift, having also created many projects, founded a feminist foundation and an international network for women to share visions and strategies on gift circulation despite the obstacles to it created by neo-liberal politics. Vaughan's formulations of the tension between the gift and the exchange economy as gendered categories provide the theoretical lens through which the oversights and selective biases of the male writings can be exposed and situated. In light of the current world crises, it is most important to give weight to the lived, pragmatic dimensions of the gift paradigm. The world has never been transformed by theory and academic action alone. As a feminist writer and activist, Vaughan is both inside and outside of the academe, using her resources to help women devise ways of re-owning their gift ways, while also dismantling the Master's House (Lorde), undermining the market and its parasitical ways. Thanks to the act of naming women's gifts, Vaughan also helps us women come out of the closet as self-belittling gift givers or as the unconscious closet supporters of the patriarchal exchange economy.

The fact that Vaughan's writings are ignored by Schrift and Godbout,[6] among others, might well attest precisely to what is wrong with patriarchal attitudes towards the gift; their tendency to privilege even those gift-*analyzing* women, who have concretely done less for the transformative politics than those, whose concrete grassroots labour of caring might help undo the world's asymmetries of power. But this is the essence of patriarchal academic circulation of knowledge-as-a-gift; those gifts are recognized and circulated which best reinforce and uphold the status quo of the non-gift-giving manhood agenda; gifts that do not upset the balance of power favouring the masculated world view and order. Helene Cixous, for all her feminism and experimental feminine writing, is still part of the more hegemonic system of gendered power. Paradoxically, as a discursive rebel and feminist theorist of "the other bisexuality", she is still an accepted, near-canonical figure of the academic institution. In Europe as in North America, she is privileged over the sweaty, exhausted activist feminists, whose labour of love may be seen to rock the unsustainable patriarchal economics more concretely and tangibly. However, it is important to stress that this reservation I have about putting gift-theorizing scholars on a pedestal does not mean having to adopt the either/or politics of hierarchical patriarchy; of pitting the grassroots vs. the academic activists. In my holistic interpretation of Vaughan's theories[7] all levels of rebellion and theorizing are needed to bring about the long and short-term transformation of the patriarchal exchange economy. I do not question the gift of Cixous' "other bisexuality", her creative and transgressive feminine writing on the gift. I only question the elitist one-sidedness that has colluded with the appropriation and silencing of the concrete and pragmatic gift impulse. Academics tend to privilege the academic, at the expense of the "other" gift givers. In fact, one wonders whether the academic context lends itself to gift circulation at this neo-liberal stage of the knowledge society. In Europe as in North America, academic freedom is being watered down as corporate interests and the (market-oriented) "social mission" of universities is being strengthened. Knowledge is in the process of being turned into a marketable, profitable commodity. Knowledge creation is becoming merely knowledge trade, an academic variety of capital accumulation.

1.2. *The Exchange and the Gift Economies*

Unlike most of the theorists on the gift, Vaughan heeds the impact of gender on the very worldview and theoretical lens through which such theories have and should be approached. One of Vaughan's contributions is to bring home tangibly and convincingly that the scientific, academic approaches of Mauss and his followers bear the unavoidable imprint of the theorists' own sex – and I would add, even their culture and history. One's own understanding of the nature of humans as either *homo economicus* or as *homo donans* (Vaughan 1997) cannot but impact on how gift circulating societies are perceived and evaluated. A scholar who has himself naturalized human self-interest rather than the nurturing impulse thus ends up projecting such a negative assumption on the cultures he is studying. This bias is present in many theories on the Gift. Throughout history, male scholars have sought to naturalize women's difference from men, writing theories about women's alleged closeness to nature, nurture, intuition, and emotional leanings. Women have been kept out of politics with the pretext that politics is too cruel, hard and immoral for women – whose role is in stark contrast the upkeep of a nation's morals and more communal values. Curiously, many of the very same scholars have extended and projected the self-interest and less "moral" ways of the male sex to all of humanity, forgetting that they had considered the other half (of mankind) as more self-sacrificing and caring. Implicitly, Vaughan addresses this major contradiction within male philosophy, psychology and other academic theories.

Vaughan argues that two basic economic paradigms coexist in the world today, the *exchange paradigm* based on power over, a selfish mode of trading, competition, short-sighted and divisive self-interest and on the other hand, the unconditional *gift economy* which seeks to satisfy needs and consolidate communal life (Vaughan 1997; 2002). The two basic orientations in life, with their gendered roots, co-exist and compete: "These paradigms are logically contradictory, but also complementary. One is visible, the other invisible; one highly valued, the other undervalued" (Vaughan 1990: 84). For Vaughan, the former, based on unilateral need satisfaction and the creation of bonds between giver and receiver, is essentially connected with elite white men; the latter with women. Echoing the theories of Belenky et al. (1986), Gilligan (1982), Chodorow (1978), Noddings (1984) and others, for Vaughan, women have been assigned the role of caring unilaterally for children, which is why they are more likely to develop the logic of the gift (2002: 3, 7). Without dwelling on culture-specific sex/gender systems, Vaughan believes that

There is something else that all the societies have in common: the caregiving done by mothers. This social constant does not depend so much upon the biological nature of mothers as upon that of children, who are born completely dependent. If someone does not take care of their needs, they will suffer and die. The satisfaction of their needs must also take place without exchange, because infants cannot give back an equivalent of what they receive (Vaughan 1997: 35).

Vaughan explains that transforming the gift process into an equal exchange erases the other-orientation of both exchangers – making their equality only the equality of their self-interests. Exchange becomes a kind of magnetic template around which societies organize themselves. The thinking of both men and women gravitates towards the masculated "template", giving it a great deal of credit, perhaps because of its similarity with naming and definition (the linguistic processes from which it derives and which we continue to use at least in English). Giftgiving continues unabated, but remains invisible and does not become generalized as a model, which is validated by having conscious followers. In fact, the gift paradigm gives way: it does not complete with the exchange paradigm. It is thus in the situation of giving value and giving many gifts to exchange (Vaughan 1997: 49)[8]. Vaughan's insight is thus to consider the way in which the very notion of exchange comes to dominate a boy's and the adult man's cognitive maps. Because in most modern societies men have more power than women, they have the opportunity to project their own cognitive patterns and images into their work, politics, policies, beliefs and institutions. Vaughan looks at such similarities between patriarchal structures at different levels not as analogies, historical isomorphisms or homologies. Rather they are self-similar social patterns created by the reciprocal feedback of the form of the definition into the definition of gender (and vice versa, the definition of gender into form of the definition) at many different levels (Vaughan 1997: 51-52). In Vaughan's view, language and communication themselves need to be re-approached by divesting them of the cognitive and evaluative projections of the male theorists[9]. Hence, we need to realize the extent to which they have governed and directed our understanding of any number of social phenomena – not just theories of the gift. One might look upon the exchange economy as also a form of mind colonization – ideological imposition. Vaughan believes that language, for example, needs to be seen as a sort of free gift economy:

> We do not recognize it as such, because we do not validate gift giving in our economic lives and, in fact, we usually recognize the existence of nurturing specifically only in the mother-child relation. It, therefore, does not occur to us to use gift giving as a term of comparison for language. With language, we create the human bonds that we have stopped creating through material comuni-cation. Language gives us an experience of nurturing each other in abundance, which we no longer have – or do not yet have – on the material plane (Vaughan 1997: 36).

The social significance of the above theories in the neo-liberal modern context is obvious. The cut throat individualism and one-upmanship of the neo-liberal politics can be exposed as anything but "natural" and unavoidable, to defy the persistence with which its tenets are disseminated and imposed. As David Korten (1996) among others has discussed, neo-liberalism is projecting crude and divisive self-interest as the essence of human nature, arguing also that this is what, together with competitiveness and greed, best motivates humans and thus best guarantees economic growth and increasing prosperity. Vaughan's analysis adds a gender-sensitive dimension to the male discussions of economic fundamentalism, reminding us that macho-capitalism also has very obvious gendered roots.

In contrast with the worldview based on abundance and gift circulation, the ideologies of lack, of artificial scarcity, deficits, "inevitable" cutbacks coalesce in the masculated mind-set[10]:

> If we look at co-muni-cation as the material nurturing or free gift giving that forms the co-muni-ty, we can see the nurturing that women do as the basis of the co-muni-ty of the family unit. The nuclear family, especially the relation between mother and children, is just a vestige of what a community based on widespread gift giving may have been at some time in the past, or could be in the future. The isolation of pockets of community from each other keeps the gift model weak, while the scarcity in which most of us are forced to live makes gift giving difficult, even self-sacrificial and, therefore, "unrealistic" (Vaughan 1997: 35)[11].

In this regard Vaughan's writings echo also the views by Vandana Shiva and Maria Mies (1993) who find that deficit thinking and reductionism are inherent features in Western science:

> There seems to be a deception inherent in divided and fragmented knowledge, which treats non-specialist knowledge as ignorance and through the artificial divide, is able to conceal its own ignorance. I characterize modern, Western patriarchy's special epistemological tradition of the "scientific revolution" as "reductionist" because: 1) it reduced the capacity of humans to know nature both by excluding other knowers and other ways of knowing; and 2) by manipulating it as inert and fragmented matter, nature's capacity for creative regeneration and renewal was reduced. Reductionism has a set of distinctive characteristics which demarcates it from all other non-reductionist knowledge systems which it has subjugated and replaced. Primarily, the ontological and epistemological assumptions of reductionism are based on uniformity, perceiving all systems as comprising the same basic constituents, discrete, and atomistic, and assuming all basic processes to be mechanical. The mechanistic metaphors of reductionism have socially reconstituted nature and society. In contrast to the organic metaphors, in which concepts of order and power were based on interdependence and reciprocity, the metaphor of nature as a machine was based on the assumption of divisibility and manipulability (1993: 23).

Vaughan believes that despite the parasitism of the exchange economy, the gift paradigm is present everywhere in our lives, though we have become used to not seeing it[12]. Vaughan elaborates on the gendered aspects even of creativity by arguing that patriarchy has assigned "activity and creativity" to men and "passivity and receptivity" to women, because it has been blind to the creativity of gift giving and of receiving. However, Vaughan sees both gift giving and receiving as creative: "The use of what has been given to us is necessary to make what has been given into a gift. If we do not use it, it is wasted, lifeless. The fact that the capacity to receive is as important as the capacity to give is manifested in our ability to transform sentences from active to passive and from passive to active" (Vaughan 1997: 47). In Vaughan's view, reinstating the gift paradigm to its central place in the group of interpretive registers, through which we address the world, lets us see that most human "activity" is oriented towards the satisfaction of a need at some level[13].

As the above brief summary of Vaughan's theories suggests, gift giving by women is not just a concrete activity that we need to revalorise, to prevent it from being appropriated by patriarchy and capitalism as women's unpaid free labour. This appropriation of the gifts not just of women but also of the land and its free "resources" is a reflection of a scarcity-based and un-giving worldview with a particular gendered, masculated agenda. Vaughan has thus broadened the scope of the classical analyses of the gift by not limiting it to the gift, but showing how a non-giving worldview and cognitive bias affects all areas of human and non-human life. This is the perspective that also sets Vaughan's theories of "surplus labour" apart from the feminist analyses going back to the 1970s.

1.3. *On Materialist Feminism*

As Hennessy & Ingraham (1997) note in their anthology, *Materialist Feminism: A Reader in Class, Difference, and Women's Lives*, capturing the views also of the Feminists for a Gift Economy network, the strengthening and spreading of global capitalism since the 1990s has presented the women's movement with serious new challenges. The Left has had to reorganize in new ways, to address the failure or weakening of the power of socialism. The women's movement, too, following the political apathy of postmodernism and deconstruction, has gradually woken up to the radical challenges of neo-liberalism and the deepening backlash against women's rights. Commitment to social transformation, attention to the political economy of capitalism has had to be debated rather than taken for granted. Although many forms of feminist cultural politics dealing with gender, race, class, sexuality or their intersections have heeded issues of privilege and power politics, they have together tended to displace a systemic analysis that might engage feminism directly with the struggle against capitalism (Hennessy & Ingraham 1997). Feminist engagement with Marxism has adopted a perspective on social life and the sex/gender systems that considers together the materiality of meaning, identity, the body, the state, the nation, all of which are intimately linked with the division of labour benefiting patriarchal capitalism. Hennessy & Ingraham note that

> Women's labor continues to be a primary source of capital accumulation. Feeding and caring for children, attending to the sick and the elderly, and providing one of the main sources of cheap labor in waged work have been women's long-standing contributions to capital accumulation across the globe. Women perform most of the world's socially necessary labor, and yet they are far more vulnerable to poverty than men (1997: 2).

The authors remind us that white women earn 70 percent of white men's earnings, while black women earn only 64 percent of what white men earn (US Bureau of Census 1995). They stress that

> It is important to remember that poverty is not mainly a function of gender or race but a permanent feature of capitalism that affects children and men too. The socially produced differences of race, gender, and nationality are not distinct from class, but they play a crucial role – both directly and indirectly – in dividing the work force, ensuring and justifying the continued availability of cheap labor, and determining that certain social groups will be profoundly exploited while others will be somewhat cushioned (1997: 2).

46

I agree with the authors that the theory underlying feminist practice cannot afford to eclipse the material realities that bind race, gender, sexuality, and nationality to labour. For Hennessy & Ingraham, these, however, are the very connections that have been abandoned by western feminists in the past twenty years. They feel the oppressive construction of difference and identity connected to capitalism's drive to accumulate have no longer been sufficiently addressed by feminisms. When feminists have questioned visible differences as the basis for political movement, the alternatives proposed often appeal to abstract, ahistorical, or merely cultural categories like desire, matter, or performativity. In bracketing the relationship of visibility and bodies to capitalism as a class-based system, feminism has implicitly and at times even explicitly embraced capitalism – or, more commonly, ignored it (1997: 2). Hennessy & Ingraham thus call for a return to considerations of class and anticapitalist theorizing and practice.

What is Vaughan's contribution in light of these feminist needs? While Vaughan does not brand her theories as "materialist" or "feminist Marxist" or the like, together with her network and activist writings (eg. the pamphlet *36 Steps towards a Gift Economy*, 2002), her political, transformative engagement is both implicit and explicit[14]. "Feminists for a Gift Economy" produced a joint statement, which was circulated first at the World Social Forum in Porto Alegre (Jan. 2001), then at other feminist events from Uganda to Mumbai (2004). In this declaration of our goals and visions, as well as the critique of patriarchal capitalism, we refer to the class dimension of neo-liberal economic fundamentalism, and also point out the surplus value that women's labour represents to the capitalists.

As early as 1981, Heidi Hartman asked, in one of the early classical Marxist feminist articles, whether Marxism and feminism might be reconcilable as potential "marriage partners". She was of the opinion that such a union would have been as unequal and asymmetrical as that of men and women in matrimony: it is the women or the feminism that gets incorporated instead of the union being one of two partners with equal weight and power. In this regard, her theory echoes Vaughan's view of the gift as the "invisible" economy. Vaughan's theories address the burning issues that face the women's movement in the 21st century, and it is thus normal that the focus should differ from those worrying Hartman. While the collective feminist awareness of the roots of patriarchal and capitalistic abuses has deepened, the approaches – and particularly their intersectionality and interdisciplinary nature have also broadened. Feminist theorizing has expanded to include issues and perspectives that were unheard of at the time of early Marxist feminism. For all that, Hartman's article remains a classic in its own right, and was one of the early efforts to heed the role of class and capitalism rather than an ahistoric patriarchy as key foci of feminist theorizing.

According to Hennessy & Ingraham (1997) Annette Kuhn, Anne Marie Wolpe, Michele Barrett, Mary MacIntosh in Britain, and Christine Delphy in France were the initial promoters of materialist feminism. They favoured this term over "Marxist feminism" in order to emphasize the point that although Marxism had not adequately addressed women's exploitation and oppression, a historical materialist analysis might be developed that would account for the sexual division of labour and gendered formation of subjectivities. More than socialist feminism, materialist feminism was the conjuncture of several discourses – historical materialism, Marxist and radical feminism, as well as postmodern and psychoanalytic theories of meaning and subjectivity. In drawing on postmodern critiques of the humanist subject and neo-marxist theories of ideology, materialist feminism constituted a significant shift from the feminist debates of the early 70's, both radical and socialist alike (Hennessy & Ingraham 1997: 6-7)[15]. For all their differences, most materialist feminists share the view that an essential feature of capitalism's gendered division of labour is gender ideology – those knowledges, beliefs and values that present women's oppression as natural.

1.4. Surplus Labor and Marxist Feminist Theories

As regards the notion of domestic and emotional labour, Vaughan has affinities with the tradition of Marxist feminism that has theorized the implications of these forms of gendered "surplus labour" to capitalist profiteering. Vaughan also refers to the masculated biases of economics, with the gross national product being limited to "productive" work:

> Though communism may be seen as an attempt to satisfy needs, it has been undermined, like capitalism, by patriarchal structures. Marx and other male economists up to the present day, did not understand women's free labor as value-producing work. If women's work were counted (See Marilyn Waring, *If Women Counted, A New Feminist Economics*, Harper and Row, San Francisco, 1988), we would have to add on at least 40% to the GNP of most Western countries, more to Third World countries. Economists who leave aside such macroscopic elements must be skewing their analyses, as if a student of the solar system were to leave aside 40% of the planets. S/he would have to find other explanations for their effects – irregularities in orbits, for example, and would not be able to map an itinerary for successful space travel. Feminism is a more complete analysis, deeper and farther reaching, and a better basis for social planning than communism or capitalism, because unlike them it gives value to free labour (Vaughan 1997: 101).

Vaughan sums up that women's un-monetized gift labour has been invisible to economists until recently because those who were practicing the values of exchange were the only ones studying it (Vaughan 1997: 53)[16].

Against classical Marxism, Dalla Costa and James (1972) also argued that women's domestic labour is integral to the production of surplus values. They saw the entire domain outside the wage market as a "social factory" that is not strictly speaking outside capitalist production at all, but is the very source of surplus labour. Women's housework – feeding, laundering, cleaning, educating – is indispensable to wage work because in doing this unpaid labour women produce the living human beings who enter the wage sector. This position was shared by Benston (1969) and Gimenez (1978), who contended that the material base for women's oppression is their exploitation as domestic workers. As Benston explained it, women's reproductive labour in the home is necessary "if the entire system is to function", and it is therefore a crucial component in the class system. In this respect, women are potentially the central figures of subversion in the community. This view echoes the vision of the Feminists for a Gift Economy that reviving or making visible the already existing gift motivation and making women recognize their concealed economic value can have radical consequences for social transformation and the undermining of cutthroat capitalism. Swasti Mitter has elaborated this point by detailing as early as 1986 the role of women's labour in the global factories of late capitalism and outlining strategies for organizing women workers internationally (1998: 12). Vaughan's contribution, other than the added dimensions described above, is, however, to situate women's labour as a particular form of multidimensional Gift labour, which cannot be reduced to the Western understanding of economics as separate from spirituality, worldview and broader socio-psychological issues (Vaughan 2002). The early materialist or Marxist feminists have tended to operate from within an uncritically embraced Western paradigm that did not at the time realize the impact and importance of epistemic and ontological cultural differences of perspective and worldview. While Vaughan does not explicitly build the understanding of cultural variation in perception and interpretation into her own culturally-situated theory, she recognizes its relevance and has created a space for cross-cultural explorations of the gift and its many manifestations through the gift network. Furthermore, Vaughan feels that whereas materialist feminists look upon women as predominantly exploited victims[17], she prefers to foreground women's labour as a logic and worldview in its own right, something so basic to human survival that it should not be seen as the other of the male economy. In fact, she feels, together with many members of the Feminists for a Gift Economy network, that this logic of gift circulation should most importantly be extended also to boys and men. To raise boys as virtual soldiers or upholders of the national competitive economy also prepares them for power-over forms of object relations, predisposing them to replace giving with hitting (Vaughan 1997). Considering the fact that violence against women is the single most serious human rights issues today (Amnesty 2004), one cannot overestimate the transformative power mothers and fathers can exert through their educational values and methods.

2. The Gift Imaginary – Reuniting Politics and the Spirituality of Everyday Life

Ecofeminism challenges all relations of domination. Its goal is not just to change who wields power, but to transform the structure of power itself (Starhawk 1982: 77).

The Gift is an agent of social cohesion, and this again leads to the feeling that its passage increases its worth, for in social life, at least, the whole really is greater than the sum of its parts. It brings the group together; the gift increases in worth immediately upon its first circulation, and then, like a faithful lover, continues to grow through constancy (Hyde 1983: 35).

In this last section, I wish to create a third space between Vaughan's theories of the Gift and those of the socio-politically oriented (socialist, Marxist and other) feminisms that overlap but also part on points that I consider to be critical for the transformation of the neoliberal agenda. A recent comment I received from an organizer of a conference on Spirituality and Globalisation alerted me to the importance of highlighting certain aspects of the gift paradigms: what I myself call the Gift Imaginary. A selection committee member had expressed reservations about my participation at this event, since grassroots feminism is to his mind mostly, or even essentially secular rather than spiritual. I did get invited, but only after protests by some other members of committee that had precisely interpreted my articles as spiritual in nature. Are the Gift Economy and the network around it "spiritual"?

What is the very meaning of the term "material"? I suspect that the persistent stereotypes about feminism as "reverse sexism", as an agenda seeking to revert rather than transform the gendered power relations can be found behind such views. The dualisms of Western philosophy and enlightenment thought (spirituality vs. materiality, mind vs. matter, spirit vs. body, man vs. woman, nature vs. culture…) also give rise to the false dichotomies that pit spirituality against political or material dimensions of life and being.

2.1. *The Gift and Master Imaginary*

In order to perpetuate itself, every oppression must corrupt or distort those various sources of power within the culture of the oppressed that can provide energy for change (Audre Lorde 1984: 53).

I call the dominant Western paradigm and worldview to do with human identity and consciousness the "master imaginary". Not unlike the exchange economy, the concept condenses the artificial and arbitrary dichotomies that have allowed white heterosexual elite men to dominate nature, women, native populations and people of colour, as well as men defying the hegemonic gender contracts. Among the central elements of the master imaginary are assumptions and projections of non-egalitarian difference (eg. humans vs. animals, the civilized vs. primitives) which, upon closer scrutiny are merely the ideological tools through which the hegemonic class has sought to control, subjugate and label those it has placed in the periphery of its hierarchical order. Reason and emotion are among the gendered dimensions of being that have led to a most harmful gendered division of ethical and moral labour in the Western world. Rationality, as Max Weber among others has argued, is a highly valued feature of human (male) society, whereas the nurturing, emotional, empathetic qualities projected as the domain of women have not been even considered as "rational". Today, thanks to Hildur Ve and other feminists, the male interpretation of rationality has been exposed as limited and reductive and a more multilayered, complex understanding has emerged regarding the different varieties of rationality based on care, responsibility and productivity. It is crucial for us to grasp the gendered, historic and cultural interpretations of rationality, for many feminists, particularly of the socialist and Marxist orientation have embraced the cult of reason uncritically.

The Gift Imaginary is a world view, a projected fantasy of how I would like the world to be ordered, which has at its core the undoing, the dismantling, the blurring of the reductive dualisms within the master imaginary. The dualisms coalesce and overlap, reformat and fade as the assumption of spirit and matter, rationality and irrationality get approached via the lens of the Gift – the impulse to circulate care, solidarity, well-being. From the point of the view of the Gift, it is most irrational to exhaust the world's dwindling resources – all in the name of short-term profit and the increasing destruction of cultural and biological diversity. Neo-liberalism, from the point of view of the Gift imaginary is not only irrational but even suicidal. We cannot have the abundance needed for gift giving in a situation of artificial scarcity, created through wars and economic arrangements to benefit the few at the expense of the many. Likewise, it is not irrational to care about people rather than accumulate capital; to create utopias of gift circulating societies rather than spreading myths of the inevitability of neo-liberalism. Yet, even among feminists, the assumption of virile rationality reigns as a strong principle and ideal (Kailo 2004c). I call for the necessary, if not shot-gun union, of the spiritual and the political, claiming that the very opposition is artificial. I also call for sustained attempts to seduce men into the open marriage of spirituality, politics, economics, feminism. The "union" we need in the women's movement is not that of Marxism and feminism (Hartman), although that would help; we also need the gift of wisdom that consists in opening up to the other imaginaries and epistemologies, those of woman-identified women, Native people, people of color. We need the union of solidarity economics AND of spiritual and psycho-social wisdom and practice.

2.2. *"Opium for the Oppressed?"– on the Union of Ecospirituality and Material Feminism*
Historically, feminists of the Marxist or socialist orientation have been the most resistant to the spiritually or ecologically oriented feminisms with ecofeminism a case in point. Although this risks being itself a stereotype, for Marxist or socialist feminists anything smacking of religion or spirituality would be opium for the oppressed[18]. This is not true of them all, and indeed, the labelling of feminists as belonging to strict schools of their own is problematic and artificial. It might well be a symptom of what Mary Daly has called patriarchal methodolatry, an obsession with methods and categorization as ends in themselves, and as a means of controlling reality. Yet, Marxist feminists have tended to see spiritually oriented feminists as "irrational" or misguided – the energy spent on pining after lost matriarchies or the Golden Past where women were venerated is perceived as so much precious time wasted from the politics of here-and-now. Vandana Shiva's and Maria Mies' writings on ecofeminism and globalization (eg. 1993) have likewise drawn critical outpourings from feminists who have no patience for myths of the "female angel in the ecosystem", or who prefer to put their energies into the strengthening of women's paid wage-labour rather than the utopian discourses about a subsistence perspective. In light of the rise of cyberfeminism to embrace the marriage of humans and machines (Kailo 2003b), and considering the deepening digital and prosperity wedge between the privileged and less privileged women of the North and the South (Eisenstein 1998), I look upon feminist ecospirituality as all the more important, to help us restore the Gift Imaginary and to ensure an eco-social future for all. While it is easy to find something commendable and important in all feminist approaches (the essence of the Gift Gaze), including the critiques of the most utopian ecofeminisms, I prioritise today materialist/economic AND spiritual perspectives as the politics of social transformation. If the gifts of so many, and of nature and natural "resources" are being destroyed under neo-liberal globalisation, we simply cannot afford to promote an uncritical global relativism. Unfortunately, many women and feminists also embrace the values of the master imaginary, not hesitating to treat less privileged women and nature as the "other". What I appreciate about ecofeminism, when it is not rooted in or does not embrace the dualisms of the master imaginary, is the broadness and inclusivity of its tenets and values: the promotion and maintenance of diversity in all of its forms, not just in nature but among cultures, and among men and women. This is not just any open-ended and tolerant form of diversity, but one based on

the respect of human-woman rights, nature's inalienable rights and the rights of future generations to share in the riches of the planet.

Whereas many materialist feminists ignore or wilfully neglect the issues of ecology and sustainability, many ecofeminists do also ignore the concrete material differences of women around the world. Resurrecting the goddess religions and going back to nature may work for the chosen few; the majority of the poor in the world, however, are women in need of direct political and economic action, food, clean water, unpolluted surroundings and medicine. Yet, we also need the long-term transformation of values, away from profit-based greed towards the circulation of gifts and the reinforcement of all peoples' economic, basic self-sufficiency: the subsistence perspective (Mies & Shiva 1993). It is in this regard that I find it necessary to seek out and adopt alternative visionings of society – such as the gift circulating communal values of past ages. Subsistence has to do with being locally self-sufficient, not dependent on consumer goods imported from overexploited countries. Ecospirituality as part of the new Gift Imaginary is then not the luxury for the privileged; it is only by replacing the psycho-spiritual motors of consumer-based market ideologies that we can bring about lasting changes. Economic greed and consumerist behaviour rests on ideological-political rather than human premises; people are led to support the multinational corporations and an addictive patriarchy ruling the world by their consumerist choices because they are filling a deficiency at the heart of being. Capitalism thrives on all kinds of gaps, lacks and forms of inner emptiness. Goods are poured into the void produced by a worldview that has no space or appreciation for the free gifts of the soul, the spirit, nature, human bonding, and interspecies communication. According to Vaughan, the non-gift giving boys are brought up to compensate for the emptiness of not living according to the logic of nurturing and giving. Communion and communication – with gifts in the centre – are replaced by ammunition, violence, hitting, robbing[19]. With global warming (and freezing of values), we are in dire need of new social contracts – the marriage of ecospirituality and a form of material interconnectedness that does not misname the gifts of women, nature and many others. In archaic cultures, gifts of material and spiritual nature were circulated in the context of "world renewal ceremonies". The purpose was to ensure the collective survival base of communities that were interdependent (including humans and animals). The Native American are one expression of the early forms of economics that integrated spirituality and the distribution of the vital resources from water to food and healing (Kailo 2003, 2004a, 2004b; Kuokkanen 2003, 2004). Native literature and theory contains an abundance of examples of a relationship with the land and the extended family which bears limited resemblance to Western politics of hierarchy and mastery over the other:

> Europeans and their perception of land is based on the materialistic. They look upon land as "my land, I own that land". It is a commodity. Whereas Aboriginals look at something as part of the whole, a part of themselves, and they are part of that – the land. The land and they are one (One of seven Aboriginals speaking about Musgrave Park, Australia, qtd. In Wilson Schaef 1995: Oct. 3).

> When a rainbow gets constricted, it becomes one color – white (Wilson Schaef 1995: March 31).

2.3. *The Gift Imaginary as Visionwork*

The Gift Imaginary I advocate condenses and combines – ideally – the most *muni*ficient of ecospiritual writings, and of the concrete theories and activisms that aim at the radical transformation of the global village. When humans rediscover their interconnectedness and spiritual continuum with nature (of which indeed we are part), they may well find ways of filling the inner void beyond the materialist trappings of consumer hysteria and the tiring titillation of the rat race. Simultaneously, reowning the inner space means undermining the psycho-spiritual roots of neo-liberal commercial power. By providing fewer consumers, ecospirituality is a radical means of starving the market of its gift-robbing power. After all, women and men finding their inner power and authority are less vulnerable to the market seductions. For Iglehart, feminist meditation for example emphasizes practical uses of self-discovery and the development of each person as a whole being with integrated mind, body, and emotions. People who use meditation with these guidelines in mind take more control over their lives, are far less likely to give over their spiritual or political power, and are able to apply their own extensive inner wisdom to everyday life (Iglehart 1982: 297).

Not just any spiritual doctrine would bring about balance and interconnectedness, based on equality. History has proven that male-directed and "male-owned" religions have quickly appropriated the teachings to consolidate the manhood agenda, subjugating women and nature. The Gift Imaginary is gender-sensitive and recognizes that due to their different upbringing and socialization, women's "visionwork" differs in degree and contents from that of male spiritual practices. The Gift Imaginary involves meditative withdrawal rituals into one's inner being as a means of breaking, periodically, the hold of the negative forces, powers, authorities, and addictive images with which patriarchal capitalism overwhelms us. It helps keep the internalized patriarchs, labeled by Jungians as "animus" under control.

"Visionwork" is my umbrella term for all "visionary" strategies of self-help and the inner Gift Gaze that women in different communities across time and space have relied on to practice healing and realignment with their inner wisdom beyond patriarchal or external authorities' echoes in their souls. It comprises a variety of techniques such as visualization, guided imagery, dream interpretation, active imagination, individual and group meditation etc. It refers to whatever helps women connect with a Soul of their own. Most importantly, it is aimed at the periodic dissolution of dichotomous representations of self/other, Cartesian and enlightenment models of cognition with over reliance on "left brain" cognition (linear, rational thought, objectifying vision/the gaze, cerebral, analytical modes of thought). It is not based on the objectifying, detached Gaze – the epistemic first principle of Western thought and perception – but on a broader base of knowledge reception, on the recognition that knowledge comes through all of the senses (sight, hearing, touching, feeling). Visionwork privileges "vision" as a term only to the extent that it refers to psycho-spiritual and mental imagery and insights that result from the creative re-collection and re-membering of modes of knowledge, knowing that come from a variety of sources. Paradoxically, visionwork is often linked with in-Sights gained with closed eyes – it can also be referred to as the "third eye", "the third ear", "the inner eye". Thanks to these techniques women can seek to replace the negative, one-sided or polarized fantasies of femininity produced by androcentric sex/gender systems. Visionwork as a channel of the Gift Imaginary can be used to gain fresh new views on anything from new modes of solidarity to ways to dismantle patriarchal systems and structures of domination. We need such methods of self-resourcement because women's (and also men's) bodies have been represented almost exclusively within patriarchal signifying practices, leaving them with identifications based on male fantasy. Today, it would be more accurate to label these neo-liberal, market-oriented fantasies serving the exchange economy. Gearhart labels her concept of embodied self-recovery "re-sourcement":

> To re-source is to find another source in an entirely different and prior one, a source deeper than the patriarchy and one that allows us to stand in the path of continuous and cosmic energy. Re-sourcement is a fundamental departure because people using this strategy for change do not "fight" or "do battles": they see those modes as part of what has to change. We use destructive weapons at a great cost to our authenticity (Gearhart 1976: 16).

Vaughan feels that we need a peace and justice movement led by women; this is because of women's long tradition and experience in giving and circulating gifts as a response to the needs of those who are unable to reciprocate. Women have also had a different attitude toward power; as Starhawk's definition of power (see above) describes. Indeed, women's leadership is needed because, as feminism has noted, woman-identified power is not about seizing male power, but about transforming the very notion of power as *power over*[20]. Woman-identified women's leadership is also needed to guarantee that sustainable "development" does not increasingly mean ways of sustaining the consumer-dependent market, of adapting even sustainability to the logic of the exchange economy. In fact, I replace the very notion of development for an eco-social sustainable future. We do not need more development, we need more livelihoods, justice, rights, security, peace and balance.

2.4. *The Gift Imaginary and Epistemic Otherness*

While I cannot take up space here to elaborate on the cultural varieties of the Gift Imaginary, I would like to cite a few examples from cultures that do not embrace the "rationality" of harnessing everything for profit. A Mohawk two-spirited writer, Beth Brant is a good example of a tradition bearer giving expression to a worldview rooted in the recognition of humans' interconnectedness with other species – not the individualistic cult of independence that marks Western ways. In *This is History* (1991) she role models an attitude towards gender, heterosexuality, nature and difference that is rooted in a recognition of mutuality, equality and the cyclical processes of death, renewal, rebirth. Also her character – the primal ancestress of the Mohawks, literally gives thanks to creation for its abundance: "Sky Woman prayed, thanking the creatures for teaching her how to give birth. She touched the earth, thanking Mother for giving her this gift of a companion" (1991: 23). Many Native writers and theorists evoke their cultural tradition of "giving back" (Caffyn 1993) and we also owe "Thanksgiving" to North American Indian traditions[21]. However, such an apparently banal gesture as thanking is radically absent in the dominant Western ethos of development: nature is there for the taking, as are women and their taken-for-granted labours of love. Western male writers in particular tend to look upon nature and animals as mere hunting objects or resources. Brant's story is a reminder of values and a way of relating that is being outsourced and downsized fast in the neo-liberal context of fierce competition and musical chairs. It represents an eco-social cosmos not based on the Western dualisms, including that of a clearly demarcated good and evil. As in the Native trickster tradition, good and evil are not clearly demarcated or predictable oppositional categories; rather, they are shifting effects flowing from relationships and traits co-present in both those labelled good and those seen as "bad". To become familiar with such an alternative non-hierarchical worldview can mean becoming more tuned to the other imaginaries, a precondition also for creating or resurrecting an imaginary order based on one's own culture. The idea is not, of course, for white women to appropriate Native spirituality but to recover from their own cultural, colonial amnesia, the patriarchal overwriting of their stories and myths. The Gift Imaginary means being connected with one's own deepest roots – experiencing the healing impact of cultural, gendered continuity of being. Yet the local and global intersect and overlap, and it is also necessary to consider that not all humans have knowable roots (orphans, for example). The Gift Imaginary is therefore an adaptable, broad concept, an umbrella that shelters people of all backgrounds and seeks to provide us a globally valid, if locally colored container for images and values, rituals and practices beyond the master imaginary, the imperialist white mythology.

For Vaughan, women should be the leaders of the new gift-based order. According to the same logic, Native and/or women of color might be earmarked as the most appropriate leaders of a new consciousness. After all, more than white privileged women, they have centuries of experience of multilevel oppression, and simultaneously, of keeping sane and whole under inhuman pressures. Most importantly, however, they have retained more of the eco-socially sustainable worldview, the Gift Imaginary, than most white folks.

In the life celebrating worldview of ancient nature peoples, including the Finno-Ugric peoples to which I belong, gift relations determined socio-cosmic covenants and the strict, hierarchical dualisms of the West did not exist as such. Indigenous attitudes towards the land, for example, are very different from those characterizing the Western corporate mentality. For G.M. de Frane (Coast Salish):

All things of the land are sacred; this includes human people, non-human people and inanimate people as well [...]. All teachings are sacred; all teachings are stories; all stories are sacred. Sacred Teachings explain everyday life to Salish young and old. Salish people are taught from birth how to be with everything in the land [...]. The philosophy of Take No Photos, Leave No Footprints addresses the practice of being prepared before we enter the land. It is a way of being that presupposes that any human people would know how to be spiritually, physically and mentally, and employ reason to ensure that the intrusions are limited in duration and leave no evidence of having been there [...]. The Land is our host when we are on the Land. Being guests on the Land means working with the Land in a mutually respectful way (de Frane 2001: 135)[22].

For Indigenous people of the North, including the Finns and the Sami as Finno-Ugric peoples, giving back to nature may well have been based on a non-hierarchical and non-dualistic worldview where goods are circulated as gifts in the name of collective peace and balance, not horded for private consumption. Treating animals with respect as subjects with inherent, inalienable rights contrasts sharply with the commodification and subjugation of animals within agribusiness (Kailo 1998, 2003, 2004c). Also, in the distant times the notion of power – at least when attached to women – was not one of power over, but one of power within (Spretnak 1982). There is always the risk with these discussions of resurrecting the myth of the noble savage or of lending weight to the myths of women's nurture and Natives' nature gene. Therefore it is important to stress that women, as well as Native people, only risk being stereotyped in dualistic, idealising and denigrating ways through the Exchange Gaze. The concept of women being closer to nature than to culture is only possible from the perspective of the master imaginary or the exchange economy that values culture over nature, and thus cannot imagine men wanting to be part of it. However, evidence is strong that in the prehistoric worldview no such dualisms dominated. All were on the side of nature, with nature being part of culture. From the point of view of the Gift Gaze, there is no dualism of noble vs. shameful savage; individuals are what they are with their foibles, but a worldview based on Indigenous notions does not have either nobility or savages; its order consists of interdependent members of an extended family of humans and animals. Also, for the East Indian ecologist, Shiva, who has written much about East Indian Native traditions and attitudes towards nature, diversity is the basis of mutuality and reciprocity – the "law of return" must replace the logic of return on investments, if the planet is to survive (1997: 87). For Vaughan, reciprocity is itself a term that aligns itself with the exchange economy; therefore she privileges the term GIFT.

2.5. *On Combining the Individual and the Social*

The Gift Imaginary then as a concept is not in itself new, as is true of most ideas. It is a background notion in the feminist herstory and feminist or Native ways of ordering reality. I am selecting and combining feminist and other writings and my own perspective to create a narrative concept with a new focus. Dorothy Riddle for example has addressed the need to unite spirituality and politics in a collection of ecofeminist writings published in 1982 as *The Politics of Women's Spirituality. Essays on the Rise of Spiritual Power Within the Feminist Movement*. Riddle addresses similar issues of feminist theory as I have evoked above:

> Traditionally, we have tended to focus either on spirituality or on politics, either on process or on product; but they are interrelated. Spirituality focuses from society to the individual, emphasizing uniqueness and individuality. Politics focuses from the individual to society, emphasizing our membership in a group. At the same time, spirituality focuses on our interconnectedness and sense of oneness, while politics focuses on our differences, which result in our experience of separateness (Riddle 1982: 374)[23].

For Riddle, consensus revolution is an integration of the product focus of conquest revolution and the process focus of cultural feminism. As a model of change, it assumes that the need for change lies both within ourselves and in the society. She stresses that the vision is both a given and is continually in the process of change, being composed of a series of visions to help us move into a qualitatively new space which we cannot now envision:

Consensus revolution is a process of identifying and stating one's own needs and then releasing them to be met in ways never before imagined. It is a process of sharing one's vision with others and negotiating a gestalt which incorporates that vision without becoming attached to any one vision as better. It is the process of coming together to create a qualitatively different product than what each could create separately. It is working toward specific societal changes while remembering that ultimately one can change only oneself (Riddle 1982: 379).

The pragmatic version of the Gift imaginary stresses that democratic behaviour does not just happen. I agree with Riddle that "In developing our vision, we need to be continually learning about our process of working together. We tend to work best in small groups where we can develop mutual trust and have accountable leadership. [...] We need to remember that the creative process is non-rational and to experiment with various tools that will help us be in touch with intuitive knowledge" (Riddle 1982: 379). Riddle's sense of time also aligns itself with the Native and eco-spiritual view that time is ultimately non-linear and involves leaps of new awareness: "Probably the most crucial part of the cycle of change is that of being able to end or release a vision. Unless we are able to release or eliminate, we become constipated with old forms. The trick is that we need to be able to release or end without necessarily knowing what will come next" (1982: 379)[24]. For Riddle, the ingredients of any process of change include an awareness of the need for change, a belief or vision that change is possible, and a commitment to action. She views the first ingredient as primarily a political process-one of analysis and the second as primarily a spiritual process-of imaging a potential new synthesis. Riddle also echoes Starhawk's writings on the need to invent alternative forms of power as empowerment to benefit all:

Power-over relating, or the conquest model, is maintained by several myths. The first of these is the myth of the half-person. This myth states that we are each half-persons and that we need another person in order to make us whole [...]. The second myth is that of scarcity, i.e., that there is not enough to go around. If we believe that we must compete for scarce resources, then we will also believe that we must hoard whatever we have rather than sharing it (Riddle 1982: 377).

Judy Grahn has also written about power as an elemental form of inner power, which has been downgraded into patriarchal worship, not the woman-friendly worth-ship of olden days:

In the time of the societies that flourished before the rise of the doctrines of patriarchy, male supremacy, white supremacy, ownership supremacy, the world outside of THAT noisy world-power and control were one entity and vested in the same being. Power was greatly respected for what it is; the production of interlocking life, and it was given worth-ship. This word has come down to us as worship (Grahn 1982: 266).

From the perspective of the Gift Imaginary, even love needs to be rethought, for under the exchange gaze, it has also been associated with property, owning and control. The definition of the Lesbian theologist Carter Heyward's provides a great Gift-based interpretation of the concept:

To say I love you is to say that you are not mine, but rather your own. To love you is to advocate your rights, your space, your self, and to struggle with you, rather than against you, in our learning to claim our power in the world. To love you is to make love to you, and with you (Carter Heyward 1989: 4).

Echoing the Gift Imaginary, both spirituality and politics are combined since action contains both process (means) and product (end) components (Riddle 1982: 374-75). What I add is a more thorough, deep-delving, locally and globally relevant perspective on the imaginary as narrative and as a culturally embodied and spiced-up spiritual process. Instead of masculated existentialism, based on being and nothingness (Sartre), the lack and deficit cutting, the freefloating signifier (Lacan), ego-building as the drive toward aggressive individuality (Freud), I opt for abundance and the gifted state of beeing[25]. Instead of the psychopathology of everyday life (Freud), I stress the need for an imaginary recognizing the everyday eros of gift-based living.

The Gift Imaginary, then, is not first and foremost an academic concept but a creative process towards a radically other worldview, based on concrete action as well as innovative and grounded theory. Chrys Ingraham has coined the term "heterosexual imaginary" to reveal the extent to which the dominant imaginary is rooted in compulsory, if unavowed heterosexuality. For her, it is that way of thinking which conceals the operation of heterosexuality in structuring gender and closes off any critical analysis of heterosexuality as an organizing institution. The effect of this depiction of reality is that heterosexuality circulates as taken for granted, naturally occurring, and unquestioned, while gender is understood as socially constructed and central to the organization of everyday life (Ingraham 1997: 275). I agree that the exchange economy does contain this dimension of a particular heterosexist imaginary as well, which further exposes the particular and subtler operations within patriarchy. I also embrace a critique of heterosexism as yet another important dimension to be exposed and transformed. Seen through the lens of the Gift, heterosexism, however, is not just about male-female sexuality and power, it is about a whole worldview based on a dualistic rather than multifocal, multilevel lens – a kaleidoscopic mode of Seeing. Compulsory heterosexuality also reflects the obsession to see dualistically – through the filter of a naturalized male-female mode of organizing reality. It ignores the rainbow of colours and ways of being that better reflect life's infinite variety. Indeed, it is necessary also to interrupt the ways in which the heterosexual imaginary naturalizes heterosexuality and conceals its constructedness in the illusion of universality. The realization of a Gift imaginary also necessitates a systemic analysis of the ways in which compulsory heterosexuality (mostly a Western, historical manifestation of the cultural sex/gender systems) is historically implicated in the patriarchal distribution of economic resources, cultural power, and social control. Vaughan's theory of the gift economy can be complemented most fruitfully by a materialist feminist concept, Ingraham's "heterogender" which de-naturalizes the "sexual" as the starting point for understanding heterosexuality. In contrast, it connects institutionalised heterosexuality with the gender division of labour and the patriarchal relations of production (Ingraham 1997: 276). What holistic practices associated with the Gift Imaginary offer at best is the opportunity for women and men willing to espouse the other "conditioning", to recover and re-source their own sources of wisdom. It enables them to align themselves with new or newly re-discovered expanses of being and living. The political implication of self-healing includes not only the empowerment of the self, but also the creation of new definitions of our potential as members of human society. To heal is to become whole. To become whole means being able also to assess and act on collective, societal addictions through increased self-knowledge, critical consciousness, embodied spiritedness.

However, I have not answered whether gift circulation, care and emotional labour are really "spiritual". Who has the power and authority to define the "spiritual"? Since the dominant class – elite men – have had the privilege and power to define reality, they have also seized it to shroud spirituality in associations and definitions reinforcing their own self-reflections. Are the grass-roots feminists and academics within the Gift Economy group "spiritual"? While I do not wish to speak for and define spirituality on behalf of other women, I do seize the power to define it for myself. For me, based on my understanding, both intuitive and academic, of the worldview of archaic Finno-Ugric peoples, spirituality and materiality, the spiritual and the earthly, the mind of matter and the matter of which the spirit consists are not manifestations of duality. They are not essences, and what matters is not their inner core or unknowable reality. What matters – very concretely – is the attitude we bring to them. All created beings are by definition animate, they are alive, they grow, die, get recycled. To relate to them and the inherent nature that we are through the Gift perspective, is to respect their immanent sanctity. By aligning ourselves with the sanctity of all forms of life, we are also more likely to align ourselves with respectful attitudes that see value in giving back, or in passing on the gifts we have received for the benefit of the entire ecosystem, and all of its members.

Conclusion

We are at a crucial point. We must begin to make qualitative advances, evolutionary leaps, or we will stay in a holding pattern, moving in ever narrowing circles until we have, literally, nowhere to turn. One reason we have not been making these leaps is because we have not faced the problem of power: what it means in a masculinist world; what it could mean to us (Starrett 1982: 185).

As I have suggested, politically engaged materialist feminism and ecospirituality need not be strange bedfellows. "Virile" feminisms based on the master imaginary, a dualistic world view and the espousal of the cognicentric rationality, can be seen to reflect the master/slave identity, an imaginary based on the very notion of deficit which characterizes masculated thought and values; it is characterized by an either/or way of seeing life, an inability to flow with the rapids of spirituality and Marxism, expressing a fragmented, compartmentalized relatedness to the world, to mind and matter, the soul and the earth. At worst, it is intolerant of other ways of perceiving and evaluating life, denigrating other forms of rationality.

Vaughan exhorts us to restore the mother image as the human image, and gift giving as the human way. Many Western feminists, particularly of the "secular" Marxist trend, have more in common with the instrumental view of life than they may be willing to admit. It stresses material conditions and prioritizes economic issues at the expense of earth-centred spirituality and the interconnectedness of humans and nature in its diverse forms and manifestations. Seen from the Give back and Gift perspectives, however, economics and spirituality do not need to be mutually exclusive. Many women's and Indigenous peoples' traditional paradigms have, as proof, united the spirituality of care and giving with the "economics of Giving back" which are part and parcel of the holistic worldview. In such a perspective, politics and spirituality, spirituality and economics are not separate, compartmentalized realms: they form one unified whole. Spirituality is not reserved for particular sites or days but permeates one's approach and attitude toward self and another. While some places are considered particularly powerful and sacred, this does not translate into their "opposites" being secular. Rather, everything is spiritual, some sites merely more so. The secular as a category does not exist.

I will conclude with Vaughan's comments on the logic of motherhood as a nonessentialist process, for I agree with de Beauvoir that women are not born but become women. Boys, too, can be brought up on those care rational values that could make the difference we need in the world. It is worth remembering that according to many studies, girls as a group are more sensitive to the environment, they are less racist and also more collaborative in their working lives. The major challenge of the women's movement, then, is getting boys and men to embrace these same eco-socially sustainable values.

> Mother earth is not just a metaphor. Nature actually functions according to the gift way, not the exchange way. [...] If we project the non-nurturing perspective of exchange we will see nature as objectified. Our understanding of nature as alive or dead really depends on whether we project the gift giving way onto "her" or not. And very much the same for ourselves. The point of view of the ego created by exchange is very limited. Taking the point of view of the other, or of many others as having a need which we might satisfy, expands our perspective. [...] Create and believe in a women's culture with the economic base of gift giving now still burdened by the exchange economy, patriarchy and its values, but liberateable. [...] Act in accord with gift values while not self-destructing (2002: 5-6).

Vaughan stresses that mothering (gift giving) is not a state but a creative process (2002, 7). One need not be a biological mother to adopt the values and the logic of caring, catering to needs:

> Abstracting from a state [...] is different from abstracting from a process or different instances or levels of a process. Abstracting from states we may find an essence, attempting to abstract from a process at different levels and instances of a process gives us a common logic or series of interconnected behaviors. If mothering is a process which takes place at different levels, abstracting its commonalities does not give us an essence. It gives us the logic of the gift (Vaughan 2002: 7).

Vaughan's logic of motherhood as the new norm does not reside in the dualistic division of labour established by patriarchy to the benefit of elite nations and men, but in extending the role of nurturing and the ethics of care and responsibility to all. This logic of mothering as a way to meet the needs of all in society, and to extend thanks and respect to the entire ecosystem, also means becoming active rather than passive and unconscious recipients of care, of seeing concrete and political value in care taking, something that in patriarchy is only idolized and delegated to those of lesser prestige, not appreciated in terms of salaries, pensions or social values. We need to consider how we can pool our resources around the gift paradigm and economies, in order to formulate a strong practice of resistance to the mccolonial forces. This means that the global women's movement needs to also address its own robbery or "privatisation" of the gifts of the less privileged groups-foremost women of colour in the overexploited rather than the overdeveloped countries. It is undeniable that the appropriation of gifts has taken place not just between men and women, but between men and less privileged men, between privileged women in North and South and the less privileged women (and men) in all parts of the globe. As Vaughan sums it up, patriarchy is a societal disease, while gift giving creates alignment with nature (Vaughan 2002). The combined strategies may well undermine the patriarchal exchange economy within the academic world and its exchange-based disciplines, and also create positive resistance outside of the institutions, on grassroots levels. The strategies are not either/or ways of organizing and taking action, but philosophies and a worldview based on both/and visionings, rooted in embodied politics, politics with spirit bodies.

Notes

[1] On feminist perspectives on globalization, see for example Batra (1994); Ås (1999); Hale (1995); Kailo (2004e); Wichterich (2002); Pyle (2003); Sassen (2000); Goldsmith (2002); Day (2002). I also recommend a special issue of the *International Sociology Journal, Gender Matters: Studying Globalization and Social Change in the 21st Century* (2003) and *Canadian Woman Studies/Cahiers de la femme issue, Women, Globalization and International Trade* (2002).

[2] A term used by Vaughan (1997) to refer to the outcome of boys' upbringing to become the less giving sex; to identify with the masculated agenda.

[3] Where the activists participating at the world social forum have adopted the motto "Another world is possible", members of the Gift Economy Group, meeting recently in Mumbai, India, ask: "is another world view possible?".

[4] The psychofeminist and moral philosophical theories which Vaughan could also be related to include Belenky et al. (1986), Carol Gilligan (1982), Nel Noddings (1984); Nancy Chodorow (1978), Jean Baker Miller (1973) and Dorothy Dinnerstein (1976). At a first glance, Vaughan addresses similar key questions about the impact of parenting arrangements on the psychosocial and ethical values of boys and girls; yet she has consciously extended her theorizing a step deeper into concrete action and transformational politics. She also lays more emphasis on cognitive psychology, the impact of language, communication and semiotics. Her focus is less on parenting arrangements as such than on the role of the boy occupying the subject position of the "protohuman", the one who is in a category the opposite of the giving mother.

[5] Although it is of course possible that they had not come across Vaughan's book when doing their research, it is nevertheless symptomatic of the masculated lens to ignore the specific theories on women's surplus labour, on which feminists have written extensively since the 1970s. Also, Vaughan has since contacted Caille and others, whose attitudes to her notion of the gift have not been gender-sensitive (personal communication with Vaughan in 2002).

[6] The "imaginary" is a Lacanian term borrowed by many theorists from social science to literature and educational science. Among the many uses of the term, Louis Althusser defines ideology as "the imaginary relationship of individuals to their real conditions of existence" (1971: 52), Althusser argues that the imaginary is that image or representation of reality which masks the historical and material conditions of life.

[7] Many empirical studies confirm this insight; indeed, women's sense of space and bodily boundaries are marked by their education, upbringing and conditioning towards sacrifice and yielding. This gendered dimension of occupying space is even reflected in sports. In Finland, for example, boys and men occupy public spaces and the commons with their motorized vehicles from snowmobiles to water scooters. Where the typically male sports take space

not only spatially, but also in terms of noise and sound, women and the typical female hobbies and sports are marginalized. Horseback riding is a good example of a form of sports cherished by girls. Yet, girls on horseback are not allowed on public roads and must be restricted to enclosures away from the public. Horses and girls must not take space from motorized sports. Additionally, the restricted space has its corollary in the restriction of public funding mostly to male sports. The girls' culture of tending to horses beyond the hierarchical and rougher male sports is not given public funding.

[8] Her focus is most likely the Western context and the English language although this point is not fully clear.

[9] Vaughan calls the values attached to the exchange economy as part of and as resulting from the "manhood agenda". I use the term "masculinist" as referring to Vaughan's analysis of masculinity as a process of masculation. Not all men need to identify with this agenda; nor is it essentialist but open for transformation through consciousness-raising.

[10] For an analysis of the etymology of "gift", "exchange" and "munus", see Emile Benveniste (1973). The etymologies can be interpreted in many ways, and have not stressed Vaughan's interpretation. I agree with Vaughan, however, that etymological speculation is as fraught with subjective elements as any other scholarly undertaking. We cannot avoid projecting cultural and gendered biases. Vaughan's contribution is to "project" another interpretation, one foregrounding the possibilities of the gift circulating rather than self-interested assumptions. On Vaughan's view of "munus" see 1997: 30-31. Vaughan notes: "Exchange, with its requirement for measurement, is much more visible [than the gift economy] […] Even our greetings 'How are you?' is a way of asking, 'What are your needs?' 'Co-muni-cation' is giving gifts (from the Latin munus-gift) together. It is how we form the 'co-mu-ni-ty'" (Vaughan 1997: 31).

[11] Shiva argues that the Green Revolution held technology as a superior substitute for nature, viewing nature as a source of scarcity, and technology as a source of abundance. Instead, this leads to technologies that create new scarcities through ecological destruction by reducing availability of fertile land and through the genetic diversity of crops (1997: 108). The expansion of cyberculture and new technology into the most remote reaches of the North can, of course, bring unprecedented opportunities for Northern people. It can open new vistas for information sharing and networking. However, Eisenstein has shown that technology and the virtual democracy have been nothing but empty rhetoric for the vast majority of marginalized populations, and will continue to be so, unless we address the asymmetrical power relations that go along with the technological revolution. The current neoliberal agenda is based on creating false consumerist dependencies and addictions, and it has led to sharp increases in gendered violence, by making women even more vulnerable to economic, and hence, other forms of power. For Vaughan, masculated hierarchies are used to continually re-create scarcity around the world, by siphoning off surplus wealth. They thereby maintain exchange as the mode of distribution for all, imposing a multilevel monoculture globally. In contrast, gift-based societies do not separate economics and politics, economics and socio-cosmic relations, economics and spirituality. Their goal has been (and in part, continues to be) to create and sustain the conditions for fertility, abundance, self-sufficiency, and to circulate goods as a precondition for social justice, peace, prosperity, the good life for all.

[12] Language consequently appears not as a mechanical concatenation of (verbal) activities, but as a collection of gifts and of ways of giving and receiving, in alignment with communicative needs, which arise from experience and proliferate at many levels, given that there are abundant means available for their satisfaction (Vaughan 1997: 48).

[13] Vaughan does not call herself a Marxist because she thinks that feminism is deeper than that; any theory that did not include the consideration of women's free labor, with such a huge piece missing, has to be wrong. Reintroducing that huge piece alters everything, in her view of the totality. Even the notion of class has to be revisited once free labor is introduced.

[14] Many cultural materialists who have critiqued or distanced themselves from deconstruction's textual analysis, however, also make use of theoretical frameworks that tend to reduce social life to representation, albeit a much more socially grounded understanding of language as discourse. In contrast, historical materialist (Marxist) feminists see it as their aim to make visible the reasons why representations of identity are changing (see Hennessy & Ingraham 1997).

[15] Sandra Lee Bartky also addresses the gendered phenomenology of oppression by addressing women's emotional labor (1990). She refers to Ann Ferguson, for whom men's appropriation of women's emotional labor is a species of exploitation akin in important respects to the exploitation of workers under capitalism. Ferguson posits a sphere of "sex-affective production", parallel in certain respects to commodity production in the waged sector. According to Ferguson, four goods are produced in this system: domestic maintenance, children, nurturance (of both men and children), and sexuality (qtd. in Bartky: 100). According to Ferguson (in Bartky's paraphrase), economic domination of the household by men is analogous to capitalist ownership of the means of production. The relations of sex-affective production in a male-dominated society put women in a position of unequal exchange. Just as control of the means of production by capitalists allows them to appropriate "surplus value" from workers, i.e. the difference between the total value of the workers' output and that fraction of value produced that workers get

in return – so men's privileged position in the sphere of sex-affective production allows them to appropriate "surplus nurturance" from women. So, for example, the sexual division of labor whereby women are the primary child rearers requires a "'woman as nurturer' sex gender ideal". Girls learn "to find satisfaction in the satisfaction of others, and to place their needs second in the case of a conflict". Men, on the other hand, "learn such skills are women's work, learn to demand nurturance from women yet don't know how to nurture themselves". Women, like workers, are caught within a particular division of labor, which requires that they produce more of a good – here, nurturance – than they receive in return (Lee Bartky: 100). Ferguson's claim that both men and women are exploited in the same sense, i.e., that both are involved in relationships of unequal exchange in which the character of the exchange is itself disempowering (men bring the bacon, women the nurturance). Lee Bartky finds this claim problematical for in order for "surplus nurturance" to be parallel to "surplus value", the intimate exchanges of men and women will have to be shown not only to involve an imbalance in the provision of one kind of thing – here nurturance – but not to involve an exchange of equivalents of any sort. But this is just what conservatives deny. The emotional contributions of men and women to intimacy certainly differ, they admit, but their contributions to one another, looked at on a larger canvas, balance: he shows his love for her by bringing home the bacon, she by securing for him a certain quality of nurturance and concern. Lee Bartky asks a most provocative question, which I will not address: "Are they right?" (Bartky: 101-102). I let Vaughan's theory respond to that.

[16] My communication with Vaughan at the World Social Forum, during the Gift economy workshop, Jan. 18th, 2004, in Mumbai, India.

[17] Janet Biehl is a Green Party activist who is dismayed at the prevalence of Goddess-based rituals among the Greens. She rejects the use of mythic history in achieving socio-political change, and challenges Marija Gimbuta's findings (and their "incautious adoption by spiritual feminists") regarding matriarchal Old Europe and the assumption that worship of "the Goddess" always goes hand in hand with peace and democracy. In sum, she warns that paying homage to the Goddess infantilizes us (1989). Biehl (1990) is not opposed to eco-feminism per se, but she seeks to make eco-feminist thought more analytical, politically astute, and less dependent on what seems to be the fundamental irrationality (and anti-rationality) of Goddess thealogy and cultural feminism. To Biehl, woman does not equal nature and statement "The Earth is alive" is neither profound or true. She is particularly skeptical that any myth (e.g., of the Goddess or Gaia) can be a useful political image. Many Marxist scholars contend that women's spirituality does not challenge class society, and that forming an alternative women's culture merely allows women to drop out of the struggle for liberation for all. They reject theories of ancient matriarchy and the popular identification of woman with nature, but admit that the Left has failed to reach people's souls as effectively as spirituality has. The case of Biehl is illustrative of the internal contradictions within ecofeminist theorizing, for she embodies, in my view, the repressive and intolerant monocultural bias that ecofeminism seeks to deconstruct as the bedrock of patriarchal relations concerning nature and the feminine. See my article critiquing her "rationalist" mode (Kailo 2004c).

[18] As Mies pointed out at the WSF in Mumbai, India, 2004, the etymology of privatisation goes back to the Latin "privare", to rob. Do men around the globe now seek to rob the earth of its gifts – to private the commons – only because there is a primary lack in their heart of being, the masculated heart of darkness? Perhaps the reasons are more complex, more cultural, more materialist and to do with human psychology and biology.

[19] See the many alternative non-hierarchical definitions of power in Spretnak, ed. the Politics of Women's Spirituality (1982).

[20] For a detailed analysis of Native male and female interpretations of this Mohawk story (or herstory), see Kailo 1997.

[21] I have elaborated on these points in several other articles (see Kailo 2003a, 2003b, 2004a).

[22] Carol Christ (1982) refers to the union of the spiritual and political with her own terms: "I have made a distinction between the spiritual and social quests. In making this distinction, I do not intend to separate reality into the spiritual and the mundane, as has been typical in Western philosophy. I believe that women's spiritual and social quests are two dimensions of a single struggle and it is important for women to become aware of the ways in which spirituality can support and under gird women's quest for social equality. Women's *social quest* concerns women's struggle to gain respect, equality and freedom in society in work, in politics and in relationships with women, men and children. In the social quest a woman begins in alienation from the human community and seeks new modes of relationship and action in society. She searches to find non-oppressive sexual relationships, new visions of mothering, creative work, equal rights as a citizen. If a woman has experienced the grounding of her quest in powers of being that are larger than her own personal will, this knowledge can support her when her own personal determination falters (328, 329).

[23] The Gift imaginary and its variants are not limited to women's ways of reordering the world. Jurgen Kremer, a German Jewish psychotherapist and scholar has written many articles about his own quest for re-covering his "indigenous roots", which for him involves the painful medicine of facing one's collusion with colonialism, patriarchy, racism and a lot of other symptoms of the split Western consciousness and identity that he labels "dissociative schis-

mogenesis". Kremer's writings evoke a radically different sense of time and cosmic being, which he calls the participatory consciousness: "The knowing of the body, the knowing of the heart, the knowing which comes from states of shifted awareness (including the dialogue with the ancestors) are all valuable processes. Storytelling, star observation, conversations with plants, animals and ancestors are equally valuable. Even though every consensus will have to withstand the challenges posed in verbal, rational discourse, the words and stories of resolution will have to withstand the challenges from all other human dimensions of experience – somatic, sexual, emotional and spiritual as well as ancestral, historical and ecological. Such an embodiment of knowing can heal the various splits, such as between body and mind. Any resolution has to include the explicit, verbal expression of agreement as well as the felt sense of common understanding. Any resolution needs to be open not just to be questioned through the pragmatics of testing propositional truths; it also needs to be open to moral and aesthetic (in the Batesonian sense [1991]) investigations. Somatic knowledge and intuition need to see the light of the rational mind, while the mind needs to see the light which is in the body" (Kremer 1997: 40-41).

[24] I spell beeing consciously with two "ees" for I want to root it in the ontological hints contained in the Finnish pre-christian worldview with its world renewal ceremonies; in the sacred, spiritual sweats where the world order was being recreated, the shaman-as-a-bear may well have called upon divine bees to help with the process of rebirth and cyclical renewal. Beeing was created on the basis of the magic substance of renewal, of which the bees knew the secret, with their divine honey (Kailo 2004f). "Beeing" has to do with the plenitude, not existential emptiness of being, it refers to meady, cosmic longings and oneness with the sense of self-expansion more central than the recognition of the lack at the heart of being. It refers to an "oceanic state" beyond the existential Angst of questions such as to be or not to be.

References

Althusser, Louis (1971). *Lenin and Philosophy and Other Essays*, Ben Brewster, Engl. trans. Monthly Review, New York.

Baker Miller, Jean (ed.) (1973). *Psychoanalysis and Women*, Penguin, New York, N.Y.

Bartky, Sandra Lee (1990). *Femininity and Domination: Studies in the Phenomenology of Oppression*, Routledge, London.

Batra, Ravi (1994). *The Myth of Free Trade: the Pooring of America*, Simon & Schuster, New York.

Belenky, Mary et al. (ed.) (1986). *Womens' Ways of Knowing. The Development of Self, Voice and Mind*, Basic Books, New York.

Benveniste, Emile (1973). *Indo-European Language & Society*, Engl. trans. Elizabeth Palmer, Faber, London.

Berking, Helmuth (1999). *Sociology of Giving,* trans. Patrick Camiller, Sage, London.

Benston, Margaret (1998). "The Political Economy of Women's Liberation" [1969], Hennessy, Rosemary & Chrys Ingraham (eds.), *Materialist Feminism. A Reader in Class, Difference, and Women's Lives*, Routledge, New York, pp. 17-24.

Bianchi, Eugene C. and Rosemary R. Ruether (1977). *From Machismo to Mutuality: Essays on Sexism and Woman-Man Liberation*, Paulist Press, New York.

Biehl, Janet (1989). "Goddess Mythology in Ecological Politics", *New Politics,* Brooklyn, NY, Winter 2 (2), pp. 84-105.

Biehl, Janet (1990). *Rethinking Eco-Feminist Politics*, Boston, South End Press, (also published in a slightly more expensive edition as: *Finding Our Way: rethinking eco-feminist politics* [Black Rose Press, Montreal and New York, 1990]).

Brant, Beth (1991). "This is History" in *Food and Spirits*, Press Gang Publishers, Vancouver.

Cheal, David (1988). *The Gift Economy*, Routledge, London & New York.

Chodorow, Nancy (1978). *The Reproduction of Mothering*, University of California Press, Berkeley.

Dallacosta Mariarosa & Selma James (1998). "Women and the Subversion of the Community", (1972) in Hennessy, Rosemary & Chrys Ingraham (eds.), *Materialist Feminism. A Reader in Class, Difference, and Women's Live*, Routledge, New York, pp. 54-59.

Day, Shelagh (2000). *The Indivisibility of Women's Human Rights*, Canadian Woman Studies/les Cahiers de la Femme, Volume 20, Number 3.

Dinnerstein, Dorothy (1976). *The Mermaid and the Minotaur. Sexual Arrangement and Human Malaise*, Harper & Row Publishers, New York.

Eisenstein, Zillah (1998). *Global obscenities. Patriarchy, capitalism and the lure of cyberfantasy*, New York UP, New York.

de Frane, Gordon (2001). "Take No Photos; Leave No Footprints: A Salish Philosophy of Being in the Land", Rattray, Curtis and Tero Mustonen (eds.), *Dispatches from the Cold Seas. Indigenous Views on Selfgovernance, Ecology and Identity*, Tampere Polytechnic Publications Ser. C, Study Materials 3, pp. 134-138.

Ferguson, Ann (1979). "Women as a new revolutionary class", in *Between Labor and Capital*, ed. Pat Walker, South End, Boston.

Gearhart, Sally (1976). "Woman Power", *WomanSpirit*, vol 2. 8, p. 16.

Gilligan, Carol (1982). *In a Different Voice*, Cambridge, Harvard UP.

Glendinning, Chellis (1982). "The Healing Powers of Women", *The Politics of Women's Spirituality. Essays on the Rise of Spiritual Power Within the Feminist Movement*, Doubleday, New York.

Godbout, Jacques T. in collaboration with Alain Caillé (1998). Engl. trans. Donald Winkler, *The World of the Gift*, McGill-Queen's University Press, Montreal.

Golding, Peter (1996). "World Wide Wedge: Divisions and Contradictions in the Global Information Infrastructure", *Monthly Review*, vol. 48. 3 (July-August), p. 82.

Hale, A. (1995). *World Trade is a Women's Issue. Women Working Worldwide*, Briefing Paper, Manchester.

Hartman, Heidi (1981) [1976]. "The unhappy marriage of Marxism and feminism: Towards a more progressive union", in Lydia Sargent (ed.), *Women and revolution: a discussion of the unhappy marriage of Marxism and feminism*, South End Press, Boston.

Helander, Elina & Kaarina, Kailo (eds.) (1998). *No Beginning, No end – The Sami Speak Up*, Edmonton, Canadian Circumpolar Institute, Kautokeino.

Hennessy, Rosemary & Chrys Ingraham, (eds.) (1997). *Materialist Feminism. A Reader in Class, Difference, and Women's Lives*, Routledge, New York.

Hyde, Lewis (1983). *The Gift. Imagination and the Erotic Life of Property*, Vintage Books, New York [1979].

Iglehart, Hallie (1982). "Expanding Personal Power Through Meditation", in Spretnak, Charlene (1982) (ed.) *The Politics of Women's Spirituality. Essays on the Rise of Spiritual Power Within the Feminist Movement*, Doubleday, New York.

Kailo, Kaarina (1997)."Hemispheric Cross-Talk. Women Collaborating on Storytelling", Northern Parallels. 4th Circumpolar Universities Cooperation Conference Proceedings, Feb. 23-25, 1995, ed. Shauna McLarnon and Doublas Nord, UNBC Press, Prince George, pp. 102-116.

Kailo, Kaarina (1998). "Indigenous Women, Ecopolitics and Healing – 'Women who Marry Bears'", *Minorities and Women*, ed. Robert Jansson, Mariehamn: Åland Fredsinstitut, Åland Peace Institut, Åland, pp. 85-121.

Kailo Kaarina (2004). Ed. *The Gift Gaze. Wo/men and Bears. Transgressing back to Nature as Culture*, Inanna Press, Scarboro, Canada. Forthcoming.

Kailo, Kaarina (2004a). "Sexual Violence, Monoacculturation and the Mechanisms of Patriarchal Violence", Workshop on Sexual Abuse and the Heteropatriarchal Culture of Violence, *Women's Worlds Congress, Uganda. July 21-27*, Conference Proceedings. Forthcoming.

Kailo, Kaarina (2003b). "Cyber/ecofeminism – From Violence and Monoculture towards Eco-social Sustainability", *Gender and Power in the New Europe, the 5th European Feminist Research Conference, August 20-24, 2003 Lund University, Sweden*. Unpublished paper circulated on the conference website.

Kailo, Kaarina (2003d). "Honor, Shame, Culture and Violence. From the Hidden Gender Contract towards Ecosocial Sustainability and Intercultural Peace", *Unesco Conference on Intercultural Education, Jyväskylä, 15-18 June, 2003*. Conference Proceedings.

Kailo, Kaarina (2004a). "Gift and Give Back Economies. Cultural Sensitivity and Gender Awareness as Social Capital in the North", *2nd Northern Research Forum Open Meeting, Northern Veche, Veliky Novgorod, Northwest Russia, Sept. 19th-22nd, 2002*. Conference Proceedings.

Kailo, Kaarina (2004b). "From Sustainable Development to the Subsistence or Abundance Perspective – Back to the Gift and Give Back Paradigms in the North", *Women's Worlds Congress in Uganda. 21st-27th July, Session on Ecofeminism and the Patriarchal Culture of Violence*. Conference Proceedings.

Kailo, Kaarina (2004c). "From the Virile Dis-Course to Fertile Concourses – Globalization, Ecofeminism and Northern Women", *Ecofeminism Symposium. Madrid, 2000*. Conference Proceedings. Forthcoming.

Kailo, Kaarina (2004e). "Vaihtotalouden ja hoivaeetoksen rajapinnoilla. Globalisaation sukupuolivaikutukset ja naisliikkeen vastarinta", *Tasa-arvon haasteita globaalin ja lokaalin rajapinnoilla*. Kaarina Kailo, Vappu Sunnari ja Heli Vuori (eds.), Northern Gender Studies, Oulu University Press, Oulu.

Kailo, Kaarina (2004f). "From Give Back to the Gift Economy. The Return of the Ethical Repressed", *World Congress on Women, Conference Proceedings. Kampala, Uganda (July 2002)*. Forthcoming.

Kelley, Caffyn (eds.) (1992). *Give Back. First Nations Perspectives on Cultural Practice*, Gallerie Publications, Vancouver.

Korten, David (1996). *When Corporations Rule the World. Towards a Green Revolution*, Kumarian Press, San Francisco.

Kremer, Jürgen W. (1997). *Are There "Indigenous Epistemologies"?*, California Institute of Integral Studies, San Francisco.

Kuokkanen, Rauna (2000). "Towards an 'Indigenous Paradigm' from a Sami Perspective", *The Canadian Journal of Native Studies*, 20.1.

Kuokkanen, Rauna (2004). "Indigenous Gift Practices: A Critique of Globalization and Manifestation of Autonomy", Statement of post-doctoral Research for MacMaster University, Crossing Press, New York.

Lowe, Lana (2001). "Caring for the Land, Caring for the People. The Role of Canadian Resource Managers in the Realization of Aboriginal Rights", Rattray, Curtis and Tero Mustonen (eds.), Dispatches from the Cold Seas, *Indigenous Views on Selfgovernance, Ecology and Identity*, Tampere Polytechnic Publications Ser. C, Study Materials 3.

Mies, Maria and Vandana Shiva (1993). *Ecofeminism*, Fernwood Publications, Halifax.

Miller, Jean Baker (1976). *Toward a New Psychology of Women*, Beacon Press, Boston.

Mitter, Swasti (1998). "Women Working Worldwide" (1986). Hennessy, Rosemary & Chrys Ingraham, (eds.), *Materialist Feminism. A Reader in Class, Difference, and Women's Lives*, Routledge, New York, pp. 163-175.

Ngan-Ling Chow E. (2003). Guest Editor. "Gender Matters: Studying Globalization and Social Change in the 21st Century", *International Sociology*, 18. 3, pp. 443-461.

Noddings, Nel (1984). *Caring. A Feminine Approach to Ethics and Moral Education,* University of Calif. Press, London.

Plaskow, Judith and Carol P. Christ (eds.) (1989). *Weaving the Visions: New Patterns In Feminist Spirituality*, HarperCollins Publishers, San Francisco.

Pyle J. L. and Ward K. B. (2003). Recasting our Understanding of Gender and Word During Global Restructuring, *International Sociology*, 18. 3, pp. 461-491.

Rich, A. (1986). Compulsory Heterosexuality and Lesbian Existence, *Signs* 5, pp. 631-660.

Riddle, Dorothy I. (1982). "Politics, Spirituality, and Models of Change", *The Politics of Women's Spirituality. Essays on the Rise of Spiritual Power Within the Feminist Movement*, Doubleday, New York.

Sassen, S. (2000). "Women's Burden: Counter-Geographies of Globalization and the Feminization of Survival", *Journal of International Affairs*, 53(2), pp. 503-24.

Schrift, David (ed.) (1997). *The Logic of the Gift. Toward an Ethic of Generosity*, Routledge, New York & London.

Shiva, Vandana (1997). *Biopiracy. The Plunder of Nature and Knowledge*, South End Press, Boston.

Spretnak, Charlene (ed.) (1982). *The Politics of Women's Spirituality. Essays on the Rise of Spiritual Power Within the Feminist Movement*, Doubleday, New York.

Starhawik (1982). *Dreaming the Dark. Magic, Sex & Politics*, Beacon Press, Boston.

Barbara Starrett (1982). "The Metaphors of Power", *The Politics of Women's Spirituality. Essays on the Rise of Spiritual Power Within the Feminist Movement*, Charlene Spretnak (ed.), Doubleday, New York.

Strathern, Marilyn (1988). *The Gender of the Gift: Problems with Women and Problems with Society in Melanisia*, University of California Press, Berkeley.

Vaughan, Genevieve (1997). *For-Giving. A Feminist Criticism of Exchange*. Foreword by Robin Morgan, Plainview Press, Texas.

— (2002). *36 Steps Toward a Gift Economy*, Austin, Texas.

Wichterich, Christa (2002). *Globalized Woman. Reports from a Future of Inequality*, Engl. trans. Patrick Camiller, North Melbourne. Spinifex Press, Zed, London & New York, 2000.

Ås, Berit (1999). "Globalization as the Feminization of Poverty. What Whom and How do We Teach?", in *Globalization – On Whose Terms?*, ed. Birgit Brock-Utne and Gunnar Garbo, Institute for Educational Research, University.

Wilson Schaef, Anne (1995). *Native Wisdom for White Minds*, Ballantine, New York.

World Bank (1994). *Infrastructure for Development*, Oxford University Press, New York.

Introduction

The relationship between Modern Matriarchal Studies and the Gift Paradigm

There are important analogies between modern matriarchal studies and the gift paradigm.

The subject of matriarchal studies is the investigation and presentation of non-patriarchal societies of past and present. Even today there are enclaves of societies with matriarchal patterns in Asia, Africa, America and Oceania. None of these is a mere reversal of patriarchy where women rule – as it is often commonly believed – instead, they are all egalitarian societies, without exception. This means they do not know hierarchies, classes and the domination of one gender by the other. They are societies free of domination, but they still have their regulations. And this is the fact that makes them so attractive in any search for a new philosophy, to create a just society.

Equality does not merely mean a levelling of differences. The natural differences between the genders and the generations are respected and honoured, but they never serve to create hierarchies, as is common in patriarchy. The different genders and generations have their own honour and through complementary areas of activity, they are geared towards each other.

This can be observed on all levels of society: the economic level, the social level, the political level and the areas of their worldviews and faiths. More precisely matriarchies are societies with complementary equality, where great care is taken to provide a balance. This applies to the balance between genders, among generations, and between humans and nature.

The differentiated rules of matriarchal societies have been meticulously researched regarding existing societies of this type. Merely historical facts will not reveal how matriarchal people thought and felt, how they conducted their politics and how they lived their faith.To be able to research this is an advantage of anthropology. In my principal work *Das Matriarchat* I presented matriarchal societies throughout the world and was able to deduce from these examples their rules and functioning on all levels of society. I base my arguments on my research of thirty years.

In order to show up the analogies between matriarchal research and the gift paradigm, I will give you a brief overview of some of the rules and regulations of matriarchal economy. This economy is a subsistence economy. It is usually based on agriculture using animals for labour, (Mosuo in Yünnan/China, or the Minangkabau of Sumatra/Indonesia) although in some instances there are societies using animal husbandry (such as the Tuareg in Northern Africa). There is no private property and no territorial claims. The people simply have usage rights on the soil they till, or the pastures their animals graze, for "Mother Earth" can not be owned or cut up in pieces. She gives the fruits of the fields and the young animals to all people, and therefore the harvest and the flocks can not be owned privately. Parcels of land and a certain number of animals belong to the matriarchal clan (matrilineal and matrilocally organised clans) and are worked on communally. Parts of flocks can be united with other parts and land often changes hands within the peasant community as chosen by lot.

The women, and specifically the oldest women of the clan, the matriarchs, hold the most important goods in their hands, for they are responsible for the sustenance and the protection of all clan members. The women either work the land themselves or organise the work on the land; the fruits of the fields are given to them and the milk of the flocks as well. The big clan houses also belong to them or the tents in case of nomadic tribes.

Matriarchal women are managers and administrators who organise the economy not according to the profit principle, where an individual or a small group of people benefits; rather, the motivation behind their action is *motherliness*. The profit principle is an ego-centred principle, where individuals or a small minority take advantage of the majority of people. The principle of motherliness is the opposite, where altruism reigns and the well being of all is at the centre. It is at the same time a spiritual principle, which humans take from nature. Mother Nature cares for all beings, however different they may be. The same applies for the principle of motherliness: a good mother cares for all her children in spite of their diversity. For example with the Mosuo, the woman who is elected to be the clan mother from among her sisters, is the one who most clearly displays the attitude of care for the other clan members.

Motherliness, as an ethical principle pervades all areas of a matriarchal society, and this holds true for men as well. If a man of a matriarchal society desires to acquire status among his peers, or even become a representative of the clan to the outside world, the criterion is "He must be like a good mother" (Minangkabau).

On the economic level this principle prevented the development of the exchange economy as Genevieve Vaughan defines it:

Exchange is giving in order to receive. Here calculation and measurement are necessary, and an equation must be established between the products (Vaughan is talking here about the invention of money. HGA). In exchange there is a logical movement, which is ego-oriented rather than other-oriented. The giver uses the satisfaction of the other's need *as a means to the satisfaction of her own need*. [...] In capitalism, the exchange paradigm reigns unquestioned and is the mainstay of patriarchal reality (1997: 31).

Compared to this, matriarchal economy is exactly what Genevieve Vaughan defines as the gift economy:

It is a way of constructing and interpreting reality that derives from the practice of mothering and is therefore women-based. [...] The gift paradigm emphasizes the importance of *giving to satisfy needs*. It is need-oriented rather than profit-oriented (ivi: 30).

70

This is not a romantic idea of motherliness, however, as it has been portrayed so often in patriarchy, leading to the concept of motherliness being devalued and made to appear just sentimental. The portrayal is a systematic obscuring of the fact that motherliness is caring and nurturing work, which is still the basis of every society, including all patriarchies. In this respect it does not matter whether caring and nurturing work is done by mothers, who do it most often, or by other people. Without this work of daily care, there would be no help for the sick, for crisis situations of any kind, or for elderly people. In particular, there would be no children, which means any society would cease to exist in a short while. Motherly work is the most important work of all, work for life itself, work for our future. Because of its great importance this work is intentionally made invisible by patriarchy.

Matriarchies build their existence consciously on this work, which is why they are much more realistic than patriarchies, not to mention the fact that they have much more vitality. They are on principle need-oriented. Their regulations aim to meet everybody's needs with the greatest benefit.

This could be demonstrated in many different areas of matriarchal societies, but it would be beyond the scope of an introduction, so I will limit myself to a few aspects of matriarchal economy. In matriarchal economies, gift giving is not just a coincidental, arbitrary act, which is confined to the private sphere. Moreover, gift giving is not forced from all mothers and care-giving people, by the denial of recognition of their work. This forced giving is the pattern of patriarchal exploitation, in particular of women's work. The principle of matriarchal economy contrasts with that kind of "gift-giving". In the matriarchal economy goods circulate as presents. Generally money is not known, because it has no purpose. The seasonal folk festivals of the agricultural year are the main economic motor of matriarchal economies. Added to this are the lifecycle festivals of the individual clans, festivals that are also celebrated together with the whole village or town. In all these festivals the goods are being "moved around" not in the sense of exchange to make a profit, but as a gift. For example there is one rule that a clan that has had a bumper crop and is able to collect a great harvest will give this fortune away at the first opportunity. At the next festival this lucky clan will overextend itself by inviting everybody in the village or town or district and will entertain them all and give out presents. The clan will hold the festival and not hold back anything. Within a patriarchal society this would be suicidal behaviour and would ruin the giving clan. But in matriarchal societies it works according the maxim "Those who have shall give". And at the next big festival another clan, who is by comparison better off than the rest of the community, will take on this role. Now the others are invited and gifts are lavished upon them.

So round and round it goes in the community, and it is always the well-off clans who have the responsibility for the festivals. Individual clan festivals on the other hand, concern all clans, according to the lifecycles, such as birth, initiation, and funerals; they are held by the individual clans who are celebrating one of these events. Here again it is the rule that better-off clans support the clans who are not so well off, so that they too can invite the people of the community to a worthy festival.

It is apparent that in this economic system an accumulation of goods with a view to personal gain and enrichment is not possible. Matriarchal economy is not based on accumulation, as is patriarchy. The opposite is the case; the economic actions are geared towards a levelling of the differences in living standards, which achieves an *economy of balance*.

This matriarchal economy of balance is not a hidden exchange, where one gives goods in order to receive an equivalent amount. This would be a calculation but not a gift. Less fortunate clans could not give the same amount back even if they wanted to, but then the action of balancing out would be void and not achieve the equilibrium, which was intended. This is why the gift of the clan, which is temporarily wealthy, is always a present. This matriarchal economy of balance is not "primitive" because it does not know the symbolic instrument of money. Far from it, it is principally not interested; it has no need of money, for money would destroy the economy of balance.

A generous clan, which has overextended itself in the described manner, never gains any *demands* of goods from the other clans, but it wins honour. "Honour" in matriarchy means that the altruism and pro-social action of this clan gains great admiration from the other clans, and that this act verifies and strengthens the relationships between the clans. Honour is like a counter-value on a much higher level, for it is the priceless and invaluable value of friendship and human contact. Such a clan will always be supported by the other clans, should it have need of anything or even fall on hard times. This in turn is also a question of honour.

In matriarchal societies, in this sense, the economy of balance is also a mutual support system, but without being a billing institution. Economy of balance is a synonym of the gift economy and liberates the most honourable human feelings such as unreserved giving, true devotion, benevolence and friendship. It's intent is the care and deepening of human and societal relationships, by fulfilling needs free of ulterior motives. This enables love to grow. It is the principle of unreserved motherliness, in the physical as well as in the spiritual sense.

Genevieve Vaughan said it in her book *For-Giving* in this way:

Giving to needs creates bonds between givers and receivers. Recognizing someone's needs, and acting to satisfy it, convinces the giver of the existence of the other, while receiving something from someone else that satisfies a need proves the existence of the other to the receiver (1997: 30).

Modern matriarchal studies are adding an important step. The gift economy as presented by Genevieve Vaughan and called "gift paradigm" is not only a vision, but is of the highest value and a *practical reality of whole societies*, past and present. For this reason I would like to give a brief presentation of all areas of this new research, it's scope and the basic characteristics of matriarchal societies.

English translation: Jutta Ried

Matriarchal Society: Definition and Theory

Developing a new science
After I had completed my Ph.D. in philosophy at the University of Munich on the subject of the "Logic of Interpretation", I taught philosophy and theory of science there from

1973-1983. Then I left the university system, because I had found a much more important and socially relevant task. Ever since 1976, I had been doing pioneer work, along with my female colleagues, in founding Women's Studies in West Germany, and in this context I presented an outline of my "theory of matriarchal societies" for the first time. I had started to develop this theory as a young student of 25 years, using all the libraries of the different disciplines for my interdisciplinary research and traveling widely to visit many archaeological sites. These were my unofficial studies, in addition to the official ones in Analytical Philosophy, Theory of Science and Formal Logic. It was in 1976 that I first presented it in public, and in 1980 my first book in this field was published (See: *The Goddess and her Heros*, in German 1980, in English 1995). From 1983 on, I devoted myself completely to this task, one that was not acknowledged by any university in Germany. But another audience was very interested: my book marked the beginning of the discussion about women-centered societies and matriarchy in the New Feminist Movement in West Germany.

I was well aware that this discussion had a long tradition in German-speaking Europe (Switzerland, Austria, Germany), going back as far as the famous work of J. J. Bachofen: *Myth, Religion and Mother Right*, which came out in 1861. For more than a century, the discussion on "mother right" and "matriarchy" continued: the subject now was used and abused by all the intellectual schools of thought, and all political parties, each with its distinctly different point of view. What worried me most about this reception of Bachofen's ideas was the complete lack of a clear definition of the matter at hand, and furthermore, the huge amount of emotion and ideology that was involved in the discussion. This combination of unclear definitions and excessive emotionality already occurs in Bachofen's work itself.

Bachofen's work is in the field of history of cultures, and it represents a perfect parallel to the work of H. L. Morgan (in the field of anthropology/ethnology), who did research in the matriarchal society of the Iroquois of his time (1851, 1871/77). But the works of these scholars have been evaluated very differently: the differences cast light on just how political the subject of "matriarchy" is in the midst of our patriarchal society. Scholars of the humanities and social sciences, who should be extremely interested in Bachofen's findings, ignored or ridiculed the majority of them. Morgan was praised and called "the father of ethnology", because he founded the new science of anthropology/ethnology; meanwhile Bachofen, who also founded a new science: the "science of non-patriarchal societies", or "matriarchy-ology", was not honoured in the same way. The reason is simple: if his work had been taken seriously, it would have caused the beginning of the breakdown of patriarchal ideology and worldview. It marks the beginning of the development of a new paradigm of human history. That is why it is too dangerous to be acknowledged adequately!

After these insights, I decided – building on the foundation of my philosophical tools – to give the matriarchal studies, i.e., the research into all forms of non-patriarchal societies in both past and present, a modern scientific foundation. I value this field of research as too important to be neglected in this respect; furthermore I am involved as a researcher myself. "To give it a modern scientific foundation" means to formulate a definition, that integrates its vast material, and to develop a supporting theoretical framework. In the light of a theoretical framework, the many excellent special studies that have already been done in this field would more clearly exhibit their mutual interconnections, and future research could be inspired and guided by it. Developing such a universal theory does not at all mean to lock it into a closed system (a traditional philosophical attitude that has become obsolete), but rather it means to give it an open structure that is clarifying and helpful for each specific piece of research, including my own.

When I started to work on this task, I first spent ten years developing a research methodology for matriarchy, one that is basically interdisciplinary and relies on criticism of ideology. One part of the task was to relate the different disciplines used in this research to each other, and to do this systematically (and not only arbitrarily, as is often done). Another part was to develop a special method of ideological criticism to investigate all the different aspects of patriarchal ideology, and not just reproduce them unconsciously anew. Step by step, I developed the framework of a "theory of matriarchy"; I would like to present it now in a short outline. Then I want to give a sketch of the structural definition of "matriarchal society", which is the core of the "theory of matriarchy". Both sketches are the *result* of 30 years of research in the field of matriarchal societies, developed through a long process of trial and error. They are in no way presupposed deductive axioms, although I am presenting them here in a concentrated, abstract way.

Part 1

I want to begin with some notes concerning my use of the term "matriarchy". In spite of the difficult connotations of this word, I call all non-patriarchal societies "matriarchal" for several reasons:

1. The term "matriarchy" is well known from the discussion that has gone on since Bachofen (1861), and it is by now a popular term.

2. Philosophical and scientific re-definitions mostly refer to well-known words and redefine them. After that, scholars can work with them, but they do not lose contact with the language of the people. In this process, the word often takes on a new, clearer and broader meaning even in the popular language; this is also influenced by the re-defining activities of scholars. In the case of the term "matriarchy", this redefinition would be a great advantage, especially because for women, *reclaiming* this term means to reclaim the knowledge about cultures that have been created by women.

3. It is my opinion that it may not always be helpful to create new scientific terms like "matrifocal", "matricentric", "matristic", "gylanic", etc. Some of these terms, like "matrifocal" and "gylanic", are very artificial and have no connection to popular language. Others like "matricentric" and "matristic" are too weak, for they suggest that non-patriarchal societies have no more to them than just being centered around the mothers. The result can be a somewhat reduced view of these societies – by the researchers as well as the critics – a view that neglects the intricate network of relationships and the complex social networks that characterize these cultures.

4. We are not obliged to follow the current, male biased notion of the term "matriarchy" as meaning "domination by the mothers". The only reason to understand it in this way is that it sounds parallel to "patriarchy". The Greek word "arché" has a double meaning. It means "beginning" as well as "domination". Therefore, we can translate "matriarchy" accurately as "the mothers from the beginning". "Patriarchy", on the other hand, translates correctly as "domination by the fathers".

5.   To use the term "matriarchy" in its re-defined, clarified meaning is also of political relevance. It doesn't avoid the discussion with professional colleagues and the interested audience, which is urgently necessary. This might easily happen with the other terms, which have the tendency to conceal and to belittle. Researchers should not shy away from the provocative connotation of the term "matriarchy", both because research in this field is so important and because only continued political provocation will bring about a change of mind.

The Scope of Modern Research in Matriarchy

Following the argumentation of my main work *The Matriarchy*, which is in the process of being published in several consecutive volumes, I briefly want to present my *theory of matriarchal society*. It shows the scope of modern research in matriarchy. Important research, which already exists about the topic, has been, and will continue to be, included in this framework.

In the first step of developing this theory I give an overview of the previous research in matriarchy. Therein I follow the course the research has taken, using examples of the scientific as well as of the political discussion. What becomes obvious is the lack of a clear and complete definition of "matriarchy". Furthermore, in this book I put the method of ideological criticism in correct terms. This method is necessary in this area of study, because most of the early and contemporary writings about the topic contain a massive amount of patriarchal ideology (See: *Das Matriarchat I. Geschichte seiner Erforschung*, Kohlhammer 1988-1995).

In the second step of the development of this theory I therefore formulate the complete structural definition of "matriarchy", a definition we urgently need. This definition specifies the necessary and sufficient characteristics of this form of society. It is not formulated abstractly, but is arrived at by investigating an immense amount of ethnological material.

The systematic step of my ethnological research becomes visible now. I have dedicated the past ten years to this research, because we cannot get a complete definition of "matriarchy" from cultural history alone. There we are only dealing with the remains and fragments of former societies. That is not sufficient for an overall picture.

It remains without question that these fragments may well be very numerous, and that they may well be extremely important; still they can give us only scattered information. Through historical research alone we cannot know how matriarchal people thought or felt, or how they organized their social patterns or political events, that is, how their society was structured as a whole. In order to gain this knowledge, and consequently to achieve a complete definition of "matriarchy", we have to examine the still living examples of this form of society. Fortunately, they still exist on all continents except Europe.

I have considered these cultures in the second step of my theory, in which I present all of the world's extant matriarchal societies.

(See: *Das Matriarchat II,1. Stammesgesellschaften in Ostasien, Indonesien, Ozeanien*, Kohlhammer 1991/1999, and see: *Das Matriarchat II,2. Stammesgesellschaften in Amerika, Indien, Afrika*, Kohlhammer 2000).

In the third step of the development of my theory I use the complete definition of "matriarchy", which I have now extracted, as a scientific tool for a revision of the cultural history of humankind. This history is much longer than the four to five thousand years of patriarchal history. In its longest periods, non-patriarchal societies were developed, in which women created culture and embodied the integral center of society. Extant matriarchal societies are the last examples.

Fortunately, in this field some excellent research is already available. It has been developed recently. What is still lacking, however, is the systematic framework of connection, that is, the overall picture of the long history of matriarchy (Project: *Das Matriarchat III. Historische Stadtkulturen*, in the process of development).

It is obvious that such an immense task is impossible without a complete definition of "matriarchy". After it has been formulated in the ethnological part of my theory, we now have, for the very first time, the chance to adequately write the complete history of humankind, and to do so without the distortions of patriarchal prejudices. This new interpretation of history is urgently necessary today, because the patriarchal interpretation of history more and more turns out to be wrong and out-dated.

In the fourth step of the development of this theory I write about the problem of the rise of patriarchy. Two important questions have to be answered: 1. How could patriarchal patterns develop in the first place? 2. How could they spread all over the world? The latter is by no means obvious.

In my opinion neither question has been sufficiently answered yet. Instead, a lot of pseudo-explanations have been offered. If we want to explain the development of patriarchy we first of all need clear knowledge about the form of society that existed previously – and that was matriarchy. At present, this knowledge is in the process of being developed. It is the absolute precondition for explaining the development of patriarchy. Otherwise, we begin with false assumptions.

Secondly, a theory about the development of patriarchy has to explain why patriarchal patterns emerged in different places, on different continents, at different times and under different conditions. The answers will be very different for the different regions of the world. This task has not yet been done at all (Project: *Das Matriarchat IV. Entstehung des Patriarchats*, in the process of development).

In the fifth step of the development of this theory, I write about the analysis and history of patriarchy. Until now, the history of patriarchy has been written down as a history of domination, as a history "from the top". But there also exists the perspective of the history "at the bottom" which shows a completely different picture. It is the history of women, of the lower classes, of the marginalized and the sub-cultures. It shows that patriarchy did not succeed in destroying the ancient and long matriarchal traditions on all continents. In the end, it parasitically lives on these traditions.

The task is to show that these traditions (oral traditions, customs, myths, rites folklore, etc.) have their roots in preceding traditions, in matriarchy. But we can recognize this only with the help of the complete definition of matriarchy. If we can manage to follow the traces backwards through the history of patriarchy and to connect them, this means nothing less than *regaining our heritage*. (Project: *Das Matriarchat V. Matriarchale Traditionen in patriarchalen Gesellschaften*, in the process of development).

Part 2

Definition of the Matriarchal Society

Now I shall give the structural definition of "matriarchy", which means that not one criterion can be left out, if the definition is to be valid. I will present the criteria of matriarchal society on three levels: on the economic level, on the level of social patterns and on the cultural level.

On the economic level, matriarchies are most often agricultural societies. The technologies of agriculture they developed reach from simple gardening to full agriculture with plowing (at the beginning of the Neolithic Age, about 10.000 years before our time), and, finally, to the large irrigation systems of the earliest urban cultures. Simultaneously, the social forms of matriarchy continued to become more differentiated in the course of the millennia. The rise of matriarchy is directly connected with the development of these new technologies.

Goods are distributed according to a system that is identical with the lines of kinship and the patterns of marriage. This system prevents goods from being accumulated by one special person or one special group. Thus, the principles of equality are consciously kept up, and the society is egalitarian and non-accumulating. From a political point of view, matriarchies are societies with perfect mutuality. Every advantage or disadvantage concerning the acquisition of goods is mediated by social rules. For example, at the village festivals, wealthy clans are obliged to invite all inhabitants. They organize the banquet, at which they distribute their wealth to gain honor. Therefore, on the economic level I call matriarchies *societies of reciprocity*.

On the social level, matriarchies are based on a union of extended clan. The people live together in big clans, which are formed according to the principle of *matrilinearity*, i.e. the kinship is exclusively acknowledged in the female line. The clan's name and all social positions and political titles are passed on through the mother's line. Such a matri-clan consists at least of three generations of women: the clan-mother, her daughters, her granddaughters, and the directly related men: the brothers of the mother, her sons and grandsons. Generally, the matri-clan lives in one big clan-house, which holds from 10 to more than 100 persons, depending on size and architectural style. The women live permanently there, because daughters and granddaughters never leave the clan-house of their mother, when they marry. This is called *matrilocality*.

What is most important is the fact that women have the power of disposition over the goods of the clan, especially the power to control the sources of nourishment: fields and food. This characteristic feature, besides matrilinearity and matrilocality, grants women such a strong position that these societies are "matriarchal". (Anthropologists do not make a distinction between merely matrilineal and clearly matriarchal societies. This continues to produce great confusion).

These matri-clans in their clan-house on their clan-land are self-supporting groups. How are the people in such self-supporting groups connected to the other clans of the village? This is effected by the patterns of marriage, especially the system of mutual marriage between two clans. Mutual marriage between two clans is no individual marriage, but a communal marriage leading to communal matrimony. For example, the young men from clan-house A are married to the young women clan-house B, and the young men from clan-house B are married to the young women in clan-house A. This is called *mutual marriage between two clans* in a matriarchal village. The same takes place between fixed pairs of other clan-houses, for example the houses C and D, E and F. Due to additional patterns of marriage between all clans, finally everyone in a matriarchal village or a matriarchal town is related to everyone else by birth or by marriage. Therefore, I call matriarchies *societies of kinship*.

The young men, who have left the house of their mother after their marriage, do not have to go very far. Actually, in the evening they just go to the neighboring house, where their wives live, and they come back very early – at dawn. This form of marriage is called *visiting marriage*, and it is restricted to the night. It means that matriarchal men have no right to live in the house of their wives. The home of matriarchal men is the clan-house of their mothers. There, they take part in the work in the fields and gardens; they take part in the decisions of the clan. There, they have rights and duties.

In this system of clans a matriarchal man never regards the children of his wife as his children, because they do not share his clan-name. They are only related to the woman whose clan-name they have. A matriarchal man, however, is closely related to the children of his sister: his nieces and nephews. They have the same clan-name as he does. His attention, his care for their upbringing, the personal goods he passes on are all for his nieces and nephews. Biological fatherhood is not known, or no attention is paid to it. It is not a social factor. Matriarchal men care for their nieces and nephews in a kind of *social fatherhood*.

Even the process of *taking a political decision* is organized along the lines of matriarchal kinship. In the clan-house, women and men meet in a council where domestic matters are discussed. No member of the household is excluded. After thorough discussion, each decision is taken by consensus. The same is true for the entire village: delegates from every clan-house meet in the village council, if matters concerning the whole village have to be discussed. These delegates can be the oldest women of the clans (the matriarchs), or the brothers and sons they have chosen to represent the clan. No decision concerning the whole village may be taken without the consensus of all clan-houses. This means, the delegates, who are discussing the matter, are not the ones who make the decision. It is not in this council that the policy of the village is made, because the delegates function only as bearers of communication. If the council notices that the clan-houses do not yet agree, the delegates return to the clan-houses to discuss matters further. In this way, consensus is reached in the whole village step by step.

A people living in a certain region takes decisions in the same way: delegates from all villages meet to discuss the decisions of their communities. Again, the delegates function only as bearers of communication. In such cases, it is usually men who are elected by their villages, since the clan-mothers do not leave their clan's houses and land. In contrast to the frequent ethnological mistakes made about these men, they are not the "chiefs" and do not, in fact, decide. Every village, and in every village every clan-house, is involved in the process of making the decision, until consensus is reached on the regional level. Therefore, from the political point of view, I call matriarchies *egalitarian societies* or *societies of consensus*. These political patterns do not allow the accumulation of political power. In *exactly* this sense, they are free from domination: they have no class of rulers and no class of suppressed people, i.e., they do not know *enforcement bodies*, which are necessary to establish domination.

78

On the cultural level, these societies are not characterized by "fertility cults" – such a simplifying view distorts the fact that these cultures have a complex religious system. The fundamental concept matriarchal people have of the cosmos and life, the belief they express in many rites, myths and spiritual customs, is the belief in rebirth. It is not the abstract idea of the transmigration of souls, as it later appears in Hinduism and Buddhism, but the concept of rebirth in a very concrete sense: all members of a clan know that after death they will be re-birthed – by one of the women of their own clan, in their own clan-house, in their home village. Every dead person returns directly as a small child to the same clan. Women in matriarchal societies are greatly respected, because they grant rebirth. They renew and prolong the life of the clan. This concept is the basis of the matriarchal view of life. Matriarchal people have adopted it from the natural world they live in: in nature, the growing, flourishing, withering and the returning of the vegetation takes place every year. Matriarchal people are convinced that every plant that withers in fall is reborn next spring. Therefore, the Earth is the Great Mother granting rebirth and nurturing all beings.

In the sky, they observe the same cycle of coming and going: all celestial bodies rise, set and return every day and every night. They perceive the cosmos as the Great Goddess of Heaven and Creation. She is constantly creating everything, it is she who grants the ordering of time. She gives birth to all stars in the east, lets them move over the sky, until they die through her power in the west. A good example of this matriarchal concept of the cosmos is the Egyptian goddess Nut, the Goddess of Heaven. She gives birth to her son Ra, the sun, every morning, and devours him every evening, only to give birth to him again at the next sunrise.

In the cosmos and on the earth, matriarchal people observe this cycle of life, death and rebirth. According to the matriarchal principle of connection between macrocosm and microcosm, they see the same cycle in human life. Human existence is not different from the cycles of nature; it follows the same rules. Their concept of nature and of the human world lacks the dualistic, patriarchal way of thinking that separates "spirit" and "nature" or "society" and "nature".

Furthermore, it lacks the dualistic concept of morality that defines what is "good" and splits off what is "evil". From the matriarchal perspective, life brings forth death, and death brings forth life again – everything in its own time. If everything is necessary in its own time, the drastic opposition of "good" and "evil" makes no sense. In the same way, the female and the male also are a cosmic polarity. It would never occur to a matriarchal people to regard one sex as inferior or weaker than the other, as it is common in patriarchal societies.

The entire view of the world of matriarchal people is structured non-dualistically. They make no essential distinction between the profane and the sacred. The entire world with all "her" appearances is divine and, therefore, sacred to the people. They respect and venerate nature as holy, and they would never exploit and destroy it. For example, every house is sacred and has its holy hearth as a place where the living and the ancestors meet together. And each daily task and common gesture has a symbolic meaning, every action is ritualized. Therefore, on the cultural level, I call matriarchies *sacral societies* or *cultures of the Goddess*.

Summary of the criteria of the matriarchal society
– *Economic criteria*: societies with self-supporting gardening or agriculture; land and house are property of the clan: no private property; women have the power of disposition over the source of nourishment; constant adjustment of the level of wealth by the circulation of the vital goods in form of gifts at festivals – *societies of reciprocity.*

– *Social criteria*: matriarchal clans, which are held together by matrilinearity and matrilocality; mutual marriage between two clans; visiting marriage with additional sexual freedom for both sexes; social fatherhood – *non-hierarchical, horizontal societies of kinship.*

– *Political criteria*: principle of consensus in the clan-house, on the level of the village, and on the regional level; delegates as bearers of communication, not as decision-makers; absence of classes and structures of domination – *egalitarian societies of consensus.*

– *Cultural criteria*: concrete belief in rebirth into the same clan; cult of ancestresses and ancestors; worship of Mother Earth and the Goddess of Cosmos; divinity of the entire world; absence of dualistic world view and morality; everything in life is part of the symbolic system – *sacral societies as cultures of the Goddess.*

English translation: Solveig Göttner, Karen Smith

References

Bachofen, Johann Jakob (1861). *Das Mutterrecht* [Myth, Religion and Mother Right], Stuttgart.
Göttner-Abendroth, Heide (1995 [1980]). *The Goddess and her Heros*, Anthony Publishing Company, Stow, MA.
Göttner-Abendroth, Heide (1988). *Das Matriarchat I. Geschichte seiner Erforschung*, Kohlhammer, Stuttgart.
— (1991). *Das Matriarchat II, 1. Stammesgesellschaften in Ostasien, Indonesien, Ozeanien*, Kohlhammer, Stuttgart.
— (2000). *Das Matriarchat II, 2. Stammesgesellschaften in Amerika, Indien, Afrika*, Kohlhammer, Stuttgart.
Morgan, Henri Lewis (1901 [1851]). *League of the Ho-de-no-sau-nee or Iroquois*, H. M. Lloyd.

RAUNA KUOKKANEN

THE GIFT AS A WORLDVIEW
*IN INDIGENOUS THOUGHT**

For the most part, the gift is understood and approached either as a mode of economy (e.g., as part of informal local economies) or a form of exchange. While exchange can also be a form of economy, some literature discusses gift exchanges outside the economic realm, something that takes place between individuals particularly in contemporary society. Instead of viewing the gift as a form of exchange or having only an economic function, the gift in indigenous societies is a reflection of a particular world view characterized by a perception of the natural environment as a living entity which gives its gifts and abundance to people if it is treated with respect and gratitude (i.e., if certain responsibilities are observed)[1]. Central to this perception is that the world as a whole is constituted of an infinite web of relationships extended to and incorporated into the entire social condition of the individual. Social ties apply to everybody and everything, including the land. People are related to their physical and natural surroundings through genealogies, oral tradition and their personal and collective experiences pertaining to certain locations. Interrelatedness is reflected in indigenous systems of knowledge, which often are explained in terms of relations and arranged in a circular format consisting mostly or solely of sets of relationships seeking to explain phenomena. In many of these systems of knowledge, concepts do not stand alone, but are constituted of "the elements of other ideas to which they were related" (Deloria 1999: 48).

It is a well-established argument that the gift functions primarily as a system of social relations, that it forms alliances, solidarity and communities and "binds collectives together" (Berking 1999: 35)[2]. What is often ignored, however, is that the gift in indigenous worldviews extends beyond interpersonal relationships to "all my relations"[3]. In other words, according to this philosophy, giving is an active relationship between human and natural worlds based on a close interaction of sustaining and renewing the balance in the socio-cosmic order. The foundational principle of indigenous worldviews – the intimate and intricate relationships with the land and community – are established and affirmed by gifts. These relationships also form the ethical basis of indigenous worldviews, sustaining cultural and ecological survival (LaRocque 2001: 67; see also Deloria 1999, ch. 26).

In this article, I will discuss the gift philosophy in indigenous thought as a central manifestation of the special relationship that indigenous peoples have with their lands and territories. In this philosophy, the gifts are given back and shared with the larger cosmos as a means of recognizing and thanking the land and cosmos for its gifts. Through the act of giving, the kinship or relationships are actively recognized, not taken for granted or ignored. This creates a collective sense of respect, reciprocity and responsibility. In short, it could be suggested that in indigenous societies, the gift is one of the most important organizing principles around which values and perceptions of the world are attached.

While discussing some of the general, shared principles and aspects of indigenous peoples' worldview of the gift, I will draw my examples from the Sami people, the indigenous people of Northern Europe, who, in the course of colonial history, have been divided by the nation-states of Norway, Sweden, Finland and Russia[4]. My consideration is by no means a comprehensive study of the functions, philosophy or logic of the gift within indigenous systems of thinking – it is clear that anything like that would deserve and require a separate study. It also is beyond the scope of my inquiry to raise and address the vast array of issues in various anthropological and other analyses of the gift. What is, however, necessary is to explain what is meant when we discuss the relationship that indigenous peoples have with their lands.

Indigenous Peoples' Relationship with the Land

For indigenous peoples, the relationship with their homelands and territories is a fundamental issue, forming the basis of survival as a people. In this context, survival does not imply only physical sustenance and an ability or right to practice certain livelihoods, but that the very existence of a distinct people with a culture, language, worldview and value and knowledge systems is dependent on the land with which there has been a historical connection and continuity for generations. In other words, the collective identity of indigenous peoples are intricately and inseparably linked to their physical surroundings. The profound relationship indigenous peoples have to their lands has various social, cultural, spiritual, economic and political dimensions and responsibilities (Daes 1999). An indigenous people is connected to a certain location through its history and genealogies traditionally told and reflected in oral tradition – stories, songs, myths, legends, proverbs and other verbal expressions[5]. A common view among indigenous peoples is that stories tell who "we" are as a people. This includes stories of origin and of ancestors, worldview and values, knowledge for everyday and long-term survival. Various forms of oral tradition are rooted in and draw upon certain places and locations and they are used to explain and interpret experiences (Basso 1996, Cruikshank 1990). The connection relationship with a specific territory is also reflected in names of places and people: in many indigenous cultures including the Sami, families and also individuals are commonly identified by or named after places and locations.

The relationship that indigenous peoples have with their lands also has a spiritual dimension rooted in a specific worldview. This understanding of the cosmological order emphasizes relationships and interconnectedness instead of causality and separation of human from the rest of the world. Australian Aboriginal historian and activist Jaggie Huggins articulates this view as follows:

Like most Aboriginal people it is my spiritual and religious belief that we come from this land, hence the term "the land my mother". This land is our birthing place, our "cradle"; it offers us

82

connection with the creatures, the trees, the mountains, the rivers, and all living things. This is the place of my dreaming. There are no stories of migration in our Dreamtime stories. Our creation stories are linked intrinsically to the earth. This is why place and land are so important to us, regardless of where and when we were born (1998: 106).

Others have explained this understanding by comparing it to the dominant western perceptions of the human relationship with the phenomenal world which foreground the mastery and control over nature (Brody 2000, Vickers 1998: 142-3)[6]. In other words, it is necessary to understand that when we talk about indigenous peoples' relationship with their lands, we are not talking about a relationship on an individual level. The question is rather about a worldview – a specific way of knowing and being in the world which is transmitted through values and cultural practices. Naturally, it is important to distinguish between the indigenous philosophy and individual thinking and behaviour which may not always reflect or comply with the former. There is, therefore, a need for a different conceptual framework to understand this relationship as suggested by the UN Special Rapporteur Erica-Irene Daes (1999).

Classic Gift Theories on Giving to Nature

In Marcel Mauss's classic essay on the gift, *Essai sur le don, forme archaique de l'echange* (1967 [1924]), one of the themes in the economy and morality of the gift is gift giving to gods or nature. Mauss does not, however, advance a theory on this theme, partly because of the lack of facts in this area but also because of its "strongly marked mythological element, which we do not yet fully understand" (1967: 12). Similarly, most other considerations of the gift that address this aspect of giving at all only give meager attention to gift giving to the natural world, often imbued by assumptions of primitiveness, strangeness and antiquity[7]. One of the reasons many scholars do not give non-western systems of thought the serious and rigorous attention they do to western counterparts is the insistence, as Vine Deloria Jr. notes, that non-Western peoples represent an earlier stage of their own cultural evolution – often that tribal cultures represent failed efforts to understand natural world [...]. Non-Western knowledge is believed to originate from primitive efforts to explain mysterious universe. In this view, the alleged failure of primitive/tribal man [sic] to control nature mechanically is evidence of his ignorance and his inability to conceive of abstract general principles and concepts (1996: 37).

Classic gift theories are also usually characterized by serious misinterpretations simply because the analysis is informed by paradigms and thought of modernity which are incapable of adequately grasping the deeper meanings of gift giving to the natural world. In other words, there is a need for a theory of the gift that would focus on this largely neglected and misconstrued area. In this article, my intention is to discuss and reexamine some of the central aspects of the gift to the non-human realm, hoping to offer critical insights to previous gift theories.

Instead of viewing gift giving to gods and nature as a reflection of indigenous worldviews founded on active recognition of kinship relations that extend beyond human realm, Mauss explains it as a "theory of sacrifice" in which people have – they must make – exchange contracts with the spirits of the dead and the gods who are the real owners of the world's wealth. He gives the Toradja of the Celebes, Indonesia, as a classic example of people who believe that "one has to buy from the gods and that the gods know how to repay the price" (1967: 14). Moreover, for Mauss, "the idea of purchase from gods and spirits is universally understood" (*ibidem*). This is, however, a gross misinterpretation of the Toradja and other indigenous worldviews which are based on an understanding that the socio-cosmic order is maintained through the stability of various relations within that order, necessarily including the natural world and the ancestors. Following the teachings of her elders, a Toradja (or Toraja, as the correct spelling reads) woman explains that according to the understanding of her people, Deata ("God" or "Creator") provides the Toraja everything and that every creature has a spirit. The Toraja give gifts or "offerings" to thank Deata for everything that they have. After the harvest, for instance, the Toraja hold a ceremony to express gratitude for the season. These practices and this understanding are definitely not considered a purchase from the gods but a form of thanking and respecting the natural world (Sombolinggi, personal communication, 2004).

From this perspective, it is very peculiar indeed that Mauss, critical of the economic interpretations of the gift, has to resort to interpreting a practice reflecting a perception of the world that postulates a moral universe founded on respect and responsibility toward other forms of life by means of the terminology of economics (exchange contracts, purchase). In a similar fashion, Godbout analyzes the underlying philosophy of the "archaic" gift only cursorily and with a condescending tone, referring to gift practices as something "strange", "curious" and "primitive" (1998: 134).

While Godbout recognizes that "the gift represents the overall complex of relationships that brings together […] all the personalized powers that inhabit the primitive cosmos: human, animal, vegetable, mineral, or divine" (ivi: 135), he reduces it, however, into what he calls "the strange law of alternation" which rules that in archaic societies, giving is only possible by taking turns[8]. In his view, this might be "a primitive democratic requirement" motivated by the fear of revenge and destruction (ivi: 134). This kind of interpretation is reductionistic because it "consists of elements (values, structures, gender roles) which it has naturalized without heeding the animistic [sic] world's own attitudes towards life" (Kailo, forthcoming). It is also masculinist as Kaarina Kailo suggests, for this kind of giving "did not necessarily get organized along those dichotomous, conflictual lines that [many theorists] take for granted" (*ibidem*). In worldviews characterized by gift giving to the land and its various representatives or elements, the emphasis is not on apprehension or retaliation but on expressing gratitude for its gifts and kinship.

Starting with Mauss, most gift theories view the gift as a mode of exchange characterized by obligations, countergifts, pay-backs, debts, forced reciprocity and other mandatory acts. Mauss's central thesis was that the gift is constituted by three obligations of giving, receiving and paying back. Existing within distinctive social rules, the gift is both constrained and interested even if may first appear voluntary and disinterested. For Mauss the gift exchange represents a disguise and replacement for a deeper hostility, an alternative to war. In the same fashion, Claude Lévi-Strauss, though criticizing Mauss's analysis of ambiguity, has suggested that exchange is the primary structuring principle of society. In his view, all societies are founded on various forms – kinship, economy, culture – of exchange.

Building on Mauss's agonistic notion of the gift exchange as a substitute for hostility, Pierre Bourdieu has analyzed the gift as symbolic violence, which for him is "the most economical mode of domination" (1997: 218). In his view, the gift exchange ultimately leads to the accumulation of social capital of obligations and debts that are paid back, among other things, in the form of homage, respect and loyalty. Material capital thus produces symbolic capital, which is actively "misrecognized" as something else such as obligations, relationships and gratitude. In this system, the gift implies power acquired by giving (ivi: 217).

For Bourdieu, gift-giving is an observation of "moral obligations", an active denial and misrecognition of the embedded symbolic violence. He suggests that "the pre-capitalist economy is the site par excellence of symbolic violence" for in this system, the only way to establish and reinforce relations of domination is through strategies of which the true nature cannot be revealed – it would destroy them – but instead must be masked, transformed and euphemized. It is interesting that Bourdieu should want to interpret a social order constituted mostly of non-adversarial relationships observed through mutual responsibilities as a site par excellence of a form of violence. While there is no need to romanticize indigenous (or "pre-capitalist") communities as nostalgic examples of societies without violence, it hardly does any justice either to the complexity of the logic of the gift or the social order which largely depended on cooperation and nonaggression to reduce one of the central structuring principles, the gift, to a form of violence, however subtle and symbolic.

Violence has never been absent in any societies, including indigenous ones who have, like other nations, fought wars both among themselves as well as with and against various colonizers. Traditionally, however, violence has never characterized indigenous societies in the same way as it does the modern, western society which Pueblo Laguna scholar and writer Paula Gunn Allen calls a culture of death; culture where the presence of death is evident everywhere around us (Allen 1990: 30; see also Allen 1986: 127-35)[9]. Could it be possible that Bourdieu's interpretation is informed by his own cultural notions of adversarial, competitive and dominating relationships more than anything else, preventing him from seeing other functions and logic?

Bourdieu's and many others' analysis of the logic of the gift ignores giving and sharing that exist outside the restrained system of indebtedness in spite of countless examples that indicate otherwise. One such example is the Sami "grave gifts" in which the dead person is given a gift related to her or his livelihood while alive as well as food and tobacco[10]. Tobacco was also "put down in the earth to the departed" every time a person passed by a grave (Bäckman 1978: 35, 40)[11]. The function of these Sami grave gifts is not economic but preeminently social and spiritual, ensuring the continuance of a congenial relationship between the deceased and her or his living relatives (ivi: 36). This type of giving is often called an "offering" to the spirit world and thereby considered separate from (or perhaps a subcategory of) the gift proper.

As with other traditional livelihoods, Sami livelihoods of hunting, fishing and reindeer-herding are contingent upon a stable and continuous relationship between the human and natural worlds. Thus, knowledge of taking care of that relationship has traditionally been an integral part of social structures and practices, including spiritual practices (cf. Mulk 1994: 127-8).

The Sami cosmos consists of a complex, multilayered order of different realms and spheres inhabited by humans, animals, ancestors, spirits, deities and guardians, all of whom traditionally have had specific roles and functions in Sami cosmic order. An interesting, almost completely ignored aspect in the analyses of Sami cosmology and "religion" is the role of the female deities in giving the gift of life (both human and domestic animal, mainly reindeer) and the connection to the land. One could suggest that the Sami deity Máttáráhkká with her three daughters signified the very foundation in the Sami cosmic order for they were the deities of new life who conveyed the soul of a child, created its body and also assisted with menstruation, childbirth and protection of children (Ränk 1955: 31).

Thus the most significant gift or all, a new life, was the duty of these female deities that often in ethnographic literature have been relegated to a mere status of wives of male deities (reflecting the patriarchal bias of these interpretations). Moreover, Máttáráhkká could be translated as "Earthmother" (the root word máttár refers to earth and later also to ancestors). Initially, she could have also been an individual ancestress (ivi: 19). Moreover, words for "earth" and "mother" in the everyday Sami language also derive from the same root (eanan and eadni respectively). The role of women and female deities in Sami cosmology and the world order of giving and relations is a neglected area of study but should be noted here when considering Sami notions of giving[12].

The Sami view of the cosmos is reflected, for example, in the Sami drum. Traditionally, the main users of drums in Sami society have been noaidis who were spiritual leaders of siidas, the Sami self-governing units of extended families. They were also healers and visionaries and thus were the first ones to be exterminated amongst the Sami by church and state representatives (Paltto 1998: 28). Today, there are still noaidis but their knowledge and practice exist mostly in hiding. Noaidi used a drum depicting the Sami cosmos with its various elements and deities both to foresee future events and enter a trance which took him or her into journeys in other realms. In this way, a noaidi was able to communicate with animals and dead ancestors.

The goodwill of the deities, spirits and guardians who share the gifts of the land with humans plays a significant role in the well-being and survival of humans. In this system of thought and practice, relations with the spirit world and larger cosmos are secured by sharing the gifts of the land, returning the remains of an animal back to the land, and observing certain ceremonies and restrictions which guaranteed the continuance of the social and cosmic order, preventing serious, and often life-threatening ruptures.

Traditionally, one of the most important ways to maintain established relations and the socio-cosmic order has been the practice of giving to various sieidis. Sieidi, a sacred place of the gift, usually consists of a stone or wood to which the gift was directed. The common location for sieidis are in the vicinity of sacred places, camp grounds or fishing and hunting sites. Stone or rock sieidis is usually natural formations of unusual shapes, functioning as natural landmarks particularly in the mountains. Wooden sieidis are either trees with the lowest branches removed, carved stumps or fallen trunks. For the Sami, sieidis were considered alive although many ethnographers thought they represented merely inert stones and structures. This is well captured in the description by Sami reindeer herder John Turi in the early twentieth century:

> Some sieidis were satisfied if they received antlers, and others were content with all the bones, which meant every single bone, even the most wee ones. Fish sieidi did not demand less than a half of the catch but then it directed to the nets as much fish as people could collect. Some sieidis wanted a whole reindeer, which needed to be embellished with all kinds of decorations, cloth, threads, silver and gold (1987: 108)[13].

Sieidis require regular attention and if neglected, the consequences could be drastic: a loss of hunting, fishing or reindeer luck, illness or at worst, death. Although Christianity has severely eroded the Sami gift-giving to and sharing with the land by banning it as a pagan form of devil worshipping, there is a relatively large body of evidence that the practice of sieidi gifting is still practiced (Kjellström 1987; see also Juuso 1998: 137)[14]. These gifts are, particularly in ethnographic literature, almost invariably referred to as "sacrifice", usually defined as a gift (or gift exchange) to gods and nature. As a forfeiture of something for the sake of receiving something else, sacrifice is not voluntary but given under certain pressures or conditions. Jacques Derrida notes:

> Sacrifice will always be distinguished from the pure gift (if there is any). The sacrifice proposes an offering but only in the form of a destruction against which it exchanges, hopes for, or counts on a benefit, namely, a surplus-value or at least an amortization, a protection, and a security (1992a: 137).

I argue that giving to sieidis, however, cannot be completely understood through the concept of sacrifice. If sieidi gifts do have aspects of sacrifice, they are not, however, and should not be seen solely as such. They may have other dimensions that can be as significant – if not more so – than the aspect of sacrifice. Bones are given back, the catch shared and reindeer given to the gods and goddesses of hunting, fishing and reindeer luck represented by sieidi sites as an expression of gratitude for their goodwill and for ensuring abundance also in the future. In this sense, giving to sieidis appears involuntary as it is done for the protection and security of both the individual and the community. On the other hand, however, sieidis are considered an inseparable part of one's social order and thus it is an individual and collective responsibility to look after them. While it may appear that such a gift is an exchange and a mandatory forfeit (especially when interpreted from the framework of a foreign worldview), it is rather a voluntary expression of a particular worldview. Reflecting the Sami worldview of respect of and intimate relationship with the land, the practice of sieidi gifts is a manifestation of circular or loose reciprocity which should not be confused with restrained reciprocity present in systems of exchange.

It is, of course, possible to argue that any kind of giving is always a form of exchange – that even in the framework of indigenous worldviews gifts are exchanged for collective well-being. Discussing the bear ceremony in which the bones of the bear are ritually returned to nature and the spirit of the animal, Kailo notes that even if it might be "rooted in the exchange of gifts between hunters, the bear and the other actors of the bear drama [...], the attitudes, mood, values and philosophical context are very different"(forthcoming)[15]. She notes that while the ethnographic accounts on bear rituals do not explicitly discuss the underlying paradigms the interpretations are based upon, one can observe the implicit ideology of the nineteenth century nationalism and its unexamined assumptions of "primitive" cultures and male interpretations which stress the primacy of self-interest, guilt and aggression. In other words, these ethnographic interpretations are usually rooted in certain colonial, Eurocentric and patriarchal worldviews, ideologies and values (Kailo, personal communication 2004)[16].

To suggest that the gift necessarily extends beyond interpretations of exchange economy is not to deny the role of the gift also in the economic sphere of indigenous societies. There is a need, however, to question the economic bias that appears to inform the majority of interpretations of the archaic gift (Godbout 1998: 128). In this regard, Mauss's interpretation represents an exception for it recognizes how in archaic societies[17], the gift is a "total social phenomenon" with legal, economic, religious, aesthetic, morphological, political and domestic dimensions (1967: 76-7). Though recognizing the gift as representing various aspects and functions in society, Mauss's interpretation in many occasions tends, however, to emphasize the gift as an exchange economy which is a predecessor of the current market system and thereby implying evolutionary phases from primitivism to more civilized and highly developed forms of exchange. Writes Mauss: "We may then consider that the spirit of gift-exchange is characteric of societies which have passed the phase of 'total prestation' [...] but have not yet reached the stage of pure individual contract, the money market, sale proper, fixed price, and weighed and coined money" (ivi: 45)[18]. In spite of Mauss's ability to see the complexity of the gift in "archaic" societies, the western society and its models serve as the norm to which other societies and practices are inevitably compared.

Different Types of Reciprocity

The underlying logic of the exchange paradigm is that gifts cannot be given unless the receipt of countergifts is guaranteed. Reciprocity, usually defined as giving back in kind or quantity, is considered the condition of the gift by many theorists. In Bourdieu's view, the gift can remain unreciprocated only when one gives to an "ungrateful person" (1997: 190). This kind of constrained reciprocity – "a binary give-and-take" (Hyde 1983: 74) – emphasizes the movement inward and toward self, seeking to maintain the independence of the self. It requires that gifts be "paid off" by giving exact value back in order to remain self-contained and independent from others. In constrained reciprocity, based on the worldview of individualism and the notion of the Cartesian subject, dependency on others is considered a burden[19]. The desired norm of individualist subject views dependency on other people with trepidation – the common attitude of "no strings attached" or "even steven" supports the existence of separate, self-contained individuals with minimal responsibilities toward the other (cf. Tyler 2002: 78). In its extreme, receiving gifts in this model is considered a burden for it implies owing something of at least equal value to the giver:

Behind every gift lurks the ulterior motive of the giver who expects a return, and it is the recipient's perception of the giver's ulterior motive that impels him to "give as good as he gets" in order to be free of obligations or, conversely, to be locked into an ongoing relationship of reciprocal relationship of reciprocal exchanges over time (*ibidem*).

According to this thinking, dependency and responsibility are regarded as something negative – an obligation and a duty external to oneself imposed by others, whether individuals or society at large. According to such an understanding, responsibilities are no longer seen as necessary for the well-being of an individual or community (even if they are) – in other words, the connection between the self and the world has been weakened[20]. For Hélène Cixous (1981), this view is a reflection of the masculine economy characterized by uneasiness when confronted by generosity. As an alternative, she suggests feminist economies which do not imply a form of exchange but affirmation of generosity and establishment of relationships. This is also a central argument for Genevieve Vaughan who maintains that reciprocity is problematic for it is "a way of maintaining the self-interest of both of the parties involved in the interaction" (1997: 58). Others have also opposed the idea of strict reciprocity of the gift, viewing constrained reciprocity as opposed to direct giving and receiving. In Derrida's (1992a) view, it is the very reciprocity that makes the gift impossible. For him, the prerequisite of the gift is that it is neither recognized nor reciprocated. Once the gift is recognized as a gift, it ceases being a gift and becomes an object of exchange[21].

Hyde on the other hand suggests that there are two forms of giving, reciprocal and circular, which differ from one another in several ways. Reciprocal giving is a simplest form of gift exchange while in circular giving one has to give blindly, i.e., "to someone from whom I do not receive (and yet I do receive elsewhere)"(Hyde 1983, 16)[22]. For him, the condition of the gift is not constrained reciprocity but circulation and keeping the gift moving: "[a] gift that cannot move loses its gift properties" (1983: 8). The circulation of gifts is recognized also by Mauss who points out that "it is something other than utility which makes goods circulate in these multifarious and fairly enlightened societies" (1967: 70).

Reciprocity is commonly quoted as one of the central dimensions of indigenous thought. Stemming from world views and practices rooted in the close relationship with the natural world, it encompasses the aspects of sharing and giving back. This kind of reciprocity, however, goes beyond the reductionist "binary give-and-take" and more often takes the form of circular reciprocity and sharing, sometimes also called "ceremonial reciprocity" (cf. Kailo forthcoming, Richter 2001: 14-5)[23]. In this kind of reciprocity, gifts are not given first and foremost to ensure a countergift later on, but to actively acknowledge the sense of kinship and coexistence with the world without which survival (of human beings but also other living beings) would not be possible. The main function of circular or ceremonial reciprocity is to affirm the myriad relationships in the world from which stems the sense of collective and individual necessity "to act responsibly toward other forms of life" (Deloria 1999: 51).

This kind of reciprocity thus implies response-ability – ability to respond – ability to remain attuned to the world beyond self and willingness to recognize its existence by means of gifts. This sense of responsibility embedded in the gift is a result of living within an ecosystem and being dependent on it and as indigenous peoples continue to be culturally, socially, economically and spiritually more directly dependent on their lands and surrounding natural environments. It is quite obvious that this thinking remains a central part of indigenous philosophies while for many other peoples, this previously existing connection and relationship with the physical surroundings has started to erode generations ago as a result of modernization, urbanization and other developments since the Renaissance and Enlightenment which continue today in the form of neocolonialism, capitalism, consumerism and globalization[24].

In circular reciprocity, responsibility is commonly regarded as an integral part of being human and inseparable part of one's identity. Okanagan writer Jeannette Armstrong articulates this kind of understanding of responsibility in terms of her relationship to the surrounding environment:

> I know the mountains, and by birth, the river is my responsibility. They are part of me. I cannot be separated from my place or my land. When I introduce myself to my own people in my own language, I describe these things because it tells them what my responsibilities are and what my goal is (1996: 461).

Armstrong's notion of self is not limited to her as a individual but inseparably entails the connection to a certain place toward which she has certain responsibilities. By recognizing those responsibilities, she knows her location and her role; in short, she knows who she is (ivi: 462). A common way of carrying out these kinds of responsibilities, besides not treating them as taken-for-granted resources or commodities, is through acknowledging their existence with gifts, and acknowledging their gifts by sharing those gifts with them.

This understanding stems from a perception of the world in which the well-being of the mountains and river is related to her personal well-being and to the well-being of her community. In other words, it is an understanding which does not separate the self from the world to an extent that it would be possible to view human beings as independent from the rest of the creation. This understanding is embedded in the notion that personal and collective responsibility toward the natural environment is the foundation of society (Happynook 2000)[25]. Nuu-chah-nulth chair of the World Council of Whalers Tom Mexsis Happynook elaborates this understanding as follows:

> When we talk about indigenous cultural practices we are in fact talking about responsibilities that have evolved into unwritten tribal laws over millennia. These responsibilities and laws are directly tied to nature and are a product of the slow integration of cultures within their environment and the ecosystems. Thus, the environment is not a place of divisions but rather a place of relations, a place where cultural diversity and bio-diversity are not separate but in fact need each other (2000).

As with many classic interpretations of giving to nature in indigenous worldviews, analyses of indigenous understandings of responsibility are often characterized by assumptions grounded on different worldviews and values which remain blind to other ways of knowing and relating to the world. For instance, Bourdieu contends that the circulation of gifts is nothing more than "mechanical interlockings of obligatory practices" (1997: 198). While it is not incorrect to suggest that giving to nature is one of the many forms of socialization whereby the individual learns to conform to certain cultural norms and rules, it is however extremely reductionistic and dismissive to interpret indigenous (or any other) gift practices as merely rules which are blindly obeyed and conformed to only out of duty. Such views lack an understanding of different ethics and ways of being in the world and thus deny it from other peoples and cultures. Instead of being mechanically observed practices, giving to nature is the basis of the ethical behaviour and a concrete manifestation of worldviews which emphasize the primacy of relationships and balance in the world upon which the wellbeing of all is contingent.

Notes

* I would like to thank Dr. Kaarina Kailo for her helpful feedback and comments to this article. I would also like to acknowledge her long-standing, invaluable support and guidance in the vagaries of the academic world.

[1] By the term "indigenous peoples", I refer to those peoples and individuals who are considered indigenous as defined in ILO Convention No. 169 (1989) and the Cobo Report (1983). While there is no single, fixed definition of indigenous peoples, the ones in these two documents are widely accepted as informal working definitions. They emphasize the historical continuity in the territory later invaded or occupied by other people as well as the non-dominant status in society. It is important to distinguish between indigenous peoples and (ethnic) minorities, groups or populations. Indigenous peoples are often referred to as peoples who remain colonized or peoples without nation-states.

[2] Besides Mauss, other early work on this theme includes Durkheim (1964), Lévi-Strauss (1987) and Sahlins (1972).

[3] The expression "all my relations" (or "all my relatives") is commonly used by indigenous people in North America as an opening invocation and closing blessing of ceremonies and meetings (e.g., Deloria 1996: 41). Moreover, as Deloria contends, the phrase "describes the epistemology of the Indian worldview, providing the methodological basis for the gathering of information about the world" (1999: 52).

[4] Previously called the Lapps or Laplanders by outsiders, the Sami have claimed their right for their own collective term deriving from their own languages (*sápmelas* in Northern Sami). Moreover, the terms "Lapp" or "Laplander" is considered negative and derogative and today is used particularly by Finns living in Northern Finland (aka Lapland) to refer to themselves to further confuse the already complex and conflicting issue of Sami land rights.

[5] Oral traditions have often been referred to as "folklore". This however has been rejected by many non-Western people. Métis writer and critic Emma LaRocque for instance writes how "[o]ral traditions have been dismissed as savage or primitive folklore. Such dismissal has been based on the self-serving colonial cultural myth that Europeans (and descendants thereof) were/are more developed ("civilized") than Aboriginal peoples ('savage')" (1990: xvi). The common divisions of the Western paradigm between high and low culture, literature and folklore, history and story, oral and written, have been increasingly put under a critical, deconstructive light by more recent theories of poststructuralism, postmodern and feminist discourses, and of course, by growing critique of indigenous (and other non-Western) peoples themselves.

[6] For instance in Genesis (1: 28), human beings are commanded to "Be fruitful and multiply, and replenish the earth, and subdue it". Later this understanding was secularized by the Cartesian epistemology characterized by dualism, mechanistic worldview and detachment (assumptions which emanated from classical Greek philosophy, particularly Plato's articulations). As Susan Bordo notes, the separation of the self and the world (human/nature) was not an innocent exercise but was characterized with explicit attachment of value and hierarchy to those categories. Mind was elevated to possess godly qualities such as freedom, will and consciousness, whereas body and nature represented "res extensa", unconscious, brute materiality, "totally devoid of mind and thought" (Bordo 1987: 99). This thinking continues today in neoliberal corporate ideologies and practices which regard nature as a potential for economic profit, posing serious risks on the survival of indigenous peoples, communities, cultures and livelihoods. See, for instance, the International Cancun Declaration of Indigenous Peoples (2003) which states that the economic globalization and neoliberal agenda and policies have resulted in a situation where indigenous peoples rights to self-determination, to land, their knowledge, culture and identities are grossly violated.

[7] For instance, Sahlins considers the gift as "the social contract for the primitives" (1972: 169).

[8] Also Berking argues that in "archaic" societies, nobody is free to escape the duty of giving which "cannot simply be equated with the reproduction cycle of social community", including the dead and gods (1999: 34).

[9] On violence in contemporary indigenous communities, see, for example, LaRocque (1993). She indicates, like many others, that the main cause for the present-day social problems and violence in Native communities is the ongoing process of colonization. LaRocque argues: "There are indications of violence against women in Aboriginal societies prior to European contact. [...] It should not be assumed that matriarchies necessarily prevented men from exhibiting oppressive behaviour toward women. [...] There is little question, however, that European invasion exacerbated whatever the extent, nature or potential violence there was in original cultures" (75).

[10] Hyde calls this type of gifts as "threshold gifts" or "gifts of passage" (1983: 40, 41).

[11] Sami scholar of religion Louise Bäckman notes that "In pre-Christian times the dead were buried in individual graves in the wilderness" (1978: 30).

[12] It would be worthwhile to pursue this line of thought further but such an undertaking is, however, beyond the scope of this inquiry.

[13] My English translation.

[14] The Sami "religion" has drawn the attention of outsiders for centuries and it has been the subject of innumerable ethnographic, anthropological and religious studies around the world. See, for instance, Ahlbäck (1987), Bäckman and Hultkrantz (1978), Holmberg (1987), Karsten (1952), Manker (1938, 1950), Pentikäinen (1995), Scheffer (1751), Sommarström (1991) and Vorren (1962).

[15] According to Kailo (forthcoming), the bear ritual is "an effort to give back and pay tribute to the totem animal [who is] also venerated as half relative". Traditionally, the Sami have also conducted bear ceremonies.

[16] Kailo also questions the often taken-for-granted view that the western assumptions of human nature, for instance, are somehow more correct and legitimate than those of indigenous peoples and that such considerations are always necessarily interpretations as humanity or human nature cannot be scientifically measured.

[17] The term "archaic societies" is used by Mauss to refer to indigenous and other non-western societies that maintain a vital and active link to their social and cultural practices. To discuss the logic of the gift in indigenous societies and thought does not imply that similar values do not exist in other societies and cultures. Values of giving and sharing as well as the sense of responsibility for the other are present in many other cultures and religions, including Christianity (see, for example, analyses in Derrida 1992b and 1997).

[18] Bataille (1988) is, however, critical of this view, demonstrating the shortcomings of mechanistic model in analyzing human existence which seeks to reduce all of its aspects to classical economic balance between production and consumption.

[19] Here I refer to individualism as rooted particularly in Renaissance humanism and characterized by a strong emphasis on unique, self-sufficient, independent individuals whose possibilities and freedoms are viewed as limitless. This does not imply that the notion of individual is nonexistent in indigenous communities. Emma LaRocque asserts that the question of collective vs. individual is more complex than generally perceived by many non-Natives and Natives alike. She argues that "The issue of 'individual' versus 'collective' rights is a perfect example of Natives resorting to a cultural framework when boxed in by western liberal democratic tradition that are associated with individualism. Perhaps unavoidably, Native leaders have had to overemphasize collective rights to make the point that such rights are even culturally feasible. However, the fact that native cultures were egalitarian in organization does not mean Native peoples acted on some instinct akin to a buffalo herd with no regard for the well-being of individuals!" (1997: 87).

[20] Radical exclusion and hierarchization of realms of the self and the world has a long history in the intellectual tradition of the West, starting from the Greek philosophers and further articulated by Descartes. Though it is beyond the scope of my inquiry to delve into this in detail at this point, it would be good to point out that this is one of the cardinal differences between philosophical traditions of the western and indigenous societies (cf. e.g. Silko 1996: 37 and Mander 1991: 212-24). Armstrong has also pointed out how the traditional Okanagan teachings and prophesies caution "that we are cutting ourselves off from the ability to live well by distancing ourselves from the natural world. This is what my generation has been told by our elders. We are cutting off the abilities that we previously had that gave us the best chance to be in a healthy relationship with ourselves as people and with the rest of the world" (2000: 7).

[21] It is beyond the scope of this article to discuss Derrida's argument in detail. In my doctoral dissertation, I suggest along the lines of Derrida's (and others') thought that due to commonplace, often sanctioned ignorance in the academy, indigenous epistemes remain an impossible gift (Kuokkanen 2004). A longer version of this article can also be found in my dissertation.

[22] As examples of circular giving, Hyde mentions the *kula* circuit of the Trobriand Islanders in Papua New Guinea, one of the best-known circular gift practices, as well as several stories from European folklore tradition. For the *kula*, see particularly Malinowski (1922, esp. ch 3).

[23] This is not to assume, however, that circulation of gifts (or goods) exists only in indigenous or "pre-capitalist" societies. As Rodolphe Gasché notes, modern economy is also characterized by circulation. Yet the circulation of the modern economy "seems to be somehow deficient because a certain privilege of accumulation tends to produce absolute impoverishment. The privilege of accumulation makes closure of the circle of circulation as well as its compensatory action simply impossible" (1997: 107).

[24] These differences are not, of course, absolute between the different systems of thought. Many modern concepts, for example, are imbued with a Christian tradition of hospitality.

[25] Happynook observes how in the colonial context, these cultural responsibilities have been forced into a framework of "Aboriginal rights" to be defended usually "in an adversarial system of justice". These rights are, however, at their root first and foremost responsibilities (2000: 11).

References

Ahlbäck, Tore, (ed.) (1987). *Saami Religion*, Almqvist & Wiksell, Stockholm.

Allen, Paula Gunn (1986). *The Sacred Hoop: Recovering the Feminine in American Indian Traditions*, Beacon Press, Boston.

— (1990). "Interview". *Winged Words. American Indian Writers Speak*, ed. Laura Coltelli, University of Nebraska Press, Lincoln and London, pp. 11-40.

Armstrong, Jeannette (1996). "Sharing One Skin". *Okanagan Community. The Case Against the Global Economy. And for a Turn Toward the Local*, eds. Jerry Mander & Edward Goldsmith, Sierra Club Books, San Francisco, pp. 460-470.

— (2000). "The Ones from the Land Who Dream: An Interview with Jeannette Armstrong". With Mary E. Gomez, ReVision, 23. 2, pp. 3-9.

Basso, Keith (1996). *Wisdom Sits in Places, Landscape and Language Among the Western Apache*, University of New Mexico Press, Albuquerque.

Bataille, Georges (1988). *An Accused Share: An Essay on General Economy*, Engl. trans. Robert Hurley, Zone, New York.

Berking, Helmut (1999). *Sociology of Giving*, Sage, London.

Bordo, Susan R. (1987). *The Flight to Objectivity. Essays on Cartesianism and Culture*, State University of New York Press, New York.

Bourdieu, Pierre (1997). "Selections from The Logic of Practice", in *The Logic of the Gift. Toward and Ethic of Generosity*, ed. Alan D. Schrift, Routledge, New York & London, pp. 190-230.

Brody, Hugh (2000). *The Other Side of Eden. Hunters, Farmers and the Shaping of the World*, Douglas & McIntyre, Vancouver & Toronto.

Bäckman, Louise (1978). "The Dead as Helpers? Conceptions of Death Among the Saamit (Lapps)", *Temenos* 14, pp. 25-53.

— (1978). & Åke Hultkrantz, eds., "Studies in Lapp Shamanism". Acta Universitatis Stockholmiensis. Stockholm Studies in Comparative Religion, 16, Almqvist & Wiksell, Stockholm.

Cixous, Hélène (1981). "The Laugh of the Medusa", *New French Feminisms*, ed. Elaine Marks and Isabelle de Courtivron, Engl. trans. K. Cohen & P. Cohen, Harvester, Brighton, pp. 245-264.

Cobo, Jose R. Martinez (1983). "Cobo Report. Study of the Problem of Discrimination Against Indigenous Peoples" by Jose R. Martinez Cobo, Special Rapporteur of the Sub-Commission on Prevention of Discrimination and Protection of Minorities, United Nations.

Cruikshank, Julie with Angela Sidney, Kitty Smith and Annie Ned (1990). *Life Lived Like a Story: Life Stories of Three Yukon Native Elders*, UBC Press, Vancouver.

Daes, Erica-Irene A. (1999). "Indigenous people and their relationship to land". Second Progress Report on the Working Paper prepared for the UN Commission on Human Rights, UN Official Reports no. E/CN.4/Sub.2/1999/18.

Deloria, Vine, Jr. (1996). "If You Think About It, You Will See That It Is True", *ReVision* 18. 3, pp. 37-44.

— (1999) *Spirit & Reason. The Vine Deloria, Jr., Reader*, eds. Barbara Deloria, Kristen Foehner and Sam Scinta, Golden, CO, Fulcrum.

Derrida, Jacques (1992a). *Given Time: I. Counterfeit Money*, trans. Peggy Kamuf, Chicago University Press, Chicago & London.

— (1992b). *The Gift of Death*, Engl. trans. David Wills, University of Chicago Press, Chicago.

— (1997). *Adieu to Emmanuel Levinas*, Engl. trans. Pascale-Anne Brault and Michael Naas, Stanford University Press, Stanford.

Durkheim, Emile (1964). *The Division of Labour in Society*, Engl. trans. W. D. Halls, London.

Gasché, Rodolphe (1997). *"Heliocentric Exchange", The Logic of the Gift. Toward and Ethic of Generosity*, ed. Alan D. Schrift, Routledge, New York & London, pp. 100-120.

Godbout, Jacques T. (1998). *The World of the Gift*, trans. Donald Winkler, McGill-Queen's University Press, Montreal.

Goux, Jean-Joseph (2002). "Seneca against Derrida: Gift and Alterity", in *The Enigma of Gift and Sacrifice*, ed. Edith Wyschogrod, Jean-Joseph Goux and Eric Boynton, Fordham U P, New York, pp. 148-160.

Happynook, Tom Mexsis (2000). "Indigenous Relationships with Their Environment", Paper presented at a conference hosted by the International Institute of Fisheries Economics and Trade, Corvalis, Oregon, July 11-14. Available at: <http://oregonstate.edu/dept/IIFET/2000/abstracts/-happynook2.html>

Holmberg, Uno (1987). Lapparnas Religion, Uppsala Multiethnic Papers 10.

Huggins, Jackie (1998). *Sister Girl*, University of Queensland Press, St. Lucia.

Hyde, Lewis (1983). *The Gift: Imagination and the Erotic Life of Property*, Random House, New York.

ILO Convention no. 169 Concerning Indigenous and Tribal Peoples in Independent Countries. International Labour Organization (1989).

International Cancun Declaration of Indigenous Peoples (2003), 5th WTO Ministerial Conference – Cancun, Quintana Roo, Mexico, 12 September 2003, <http://www.radiofeminista.net/sept03/notas/declaration_indegenous.htm>.

Juuso, Inga (1998). "Yoiking Acts as Medicine for Me". *No Beginning, No End. The Sami Speak Up*, eds. Kaarina Kailo & Elina Helander, Canadian Circumpolar Institute/Nordic Sami Institute, Edmonton, pp. 132-146.

Kailo, Kaarina. "From the Unbearable Bond to the Gift Gaze – Women, Bears and Blood Rituals". *The Gift Gaze. Wo/Men & Bears. Transgressing Back Into Nature as Culture*, Inanna, Toronto. Forthcoming.

— (2004) Personal communication, Oulu, Finland, Feb. 19.

Karsten, Rafael (1952). *Samefolkets Religion: De Nordiska Lapparnas Hedniska Tro och Kult i Religionshistorisk Belysning*, Söderström, Helsingfors.

Kjellström, Rolf (1984). "On the Continuity of Old Saami Religion". Saami Religion: Based on Papers at the Symposium on Saami Religion held in Turku, Finland 16-18 August, ed. Tore Ahlbäck, The Donner Institute for Research in Religious and Cultural History, Abo, pp. 24-33.

Kuokkanen, Rauna (2004). "Toward the Hospitality of Academia: The (Im)Possible Gift of Indigenous Epistemes", Ph.D. Dissertation, University of British Columbia. Forthcoming.

LaRocque, Emma (1993). "Violence in Aboriginal Communities". The Path to Healing. Report of the National Round Table of Aboriginal Health and Social Issues, Royal Commission on Aboriginal Peoples, Ottawa, pp. 72-89.

— (1997). "Re-examining Culturally Appropriate Models in Criminal Justice Applications", *Aboriginal and Treaty Rights in Canada: Essays on Law, Equity and Respect for Difference*, ed. Michael Asch, University of British Columbia Press, Vancouver, pp. 75-96.

— (2001). "From the Land to the Classroom: Broadening Epistemology", *Pushing the Margins. Native and Northern Studies*, eds. Jill Oakes, Rick Riewe, Marlyn Bennett and Brenda Chrishold, Native Studies Press, Winnipeg, pp. 62-75.

Lévi-Strauss, Claude (1987). *Introduction to the Work of Marcell Mauss*, Engl. trans. Felicity Baker, Routledge & Kegan Paul, London.

Malinowski, Bronislaw (1922). *Argonauts of the Western Pacific: An Account of Native Enterprise and Adventure in the Archipelagoes of Melanesian New Guinea*, Routledge, London.

Mander, Jerry (1991). *In the Absence of the Sacred: The Failure of Technology and the Survival of the Indian Nations*, Sierra Club, San Francisco.

Manker, Ernst (1938). *Die Lappische Zaubertrommel 1*, Acta Lapponica I, Stockholm.

— (1950) Die Lappische Zaubertrommel 2, Acta Lapponica VI, Uppsala.

Mauss, Marcel (1967). *The Gift. Forms and Functions of Exchange in Archaic Societies*, Engl. trans. Ian Cunnison, W. W. Norton & Co., New York.

Mulk, Inga-Maria (1994). "Sacrificial Places and their Meaning in Saami Society", *Sacred Sites, Sacred Places*, eds. David L. Carmichael, Jane Hubert, Brian Reeves & Audhild Schanche, Routledge, London & New York, pp. 121-131.

Paltto, Kirsti (1998). "One Cannot Leave One's Soul by a Tree Trunk", *No Beginning, No End. The Sami Speak Up*, eds. Kaarina Kailo & Elina Helander, Canadian Circumpolar Institute/Nordic Sami Institute, Edmonton, pp. 23-42.

Pentikäinen, Juha (1995). *Saamelaiset – Pohjoisen Kansan Mytologia*, SKS, Helsinki.

Richter, Daniel K. (2001). *Facing East from Indian Country. A Native History of Early America*, Harvard University Press, Cambridge, MA & London.

Ränk, Gustav (1955). "Lapp Female Deities of the Madder-akka Group", Studia Septentrionalia VI, pp. 7-79.

Sahlins, Marshall (1972). *Stone Age Economics*, Aldine-Atherton, Chicago.

Scheffer, Johannes (1751). *The history of Lapland: Shewing the Original, Manner, Habits, Religion and Trade of that People: with a Particular Account of their Gods and Sacrifices, Marriage Ceremonies, Conjurations, Diabolical Rites*, R. Griffiths, London.

Silko, Leslie Marmon (1996). *Yellow Woman and a Beauty of the Spirit: Essays on Native American Life Today*, Simon & Schuster, New York.

Sombolinggi, Rukka (2004). *Personal e-mail communication*, 3 Feb.

Sommarström, Bo (1991) *The Saami Shaman's Drum and the Star Horizon*, Scripta Instituti Donneriani XVI, Stockholm.

Turi, Johan (1987 [1910]). Muitalus sámiid birra. Sámi Girjjit, Jokkmokk.

Tyler, Stephen A. (2002). "'Even Steven,' or 'No Strings Attached'". *The Enigma of Gift and Sacrifice*, eds. Edith Wyschogrod, Jean-Joseph Goux and Eric Boynton, Fordham U.P., New York, pp. 77-90.

Vaughan, Genevieve (1997). *For-Giving. A Feminist Criticism of Exchange*, Austin, Plain View Press & Anomaly Press.

Vorren, Ørnulf (1962). *Lapp Life And Customs*, Oxford University Press, London and New York.

I intend to discuss the gift paradigm in education. I must start by admitting that it was only about a year ago that I first heard about the gift paradigm. I was finishing my doctoral thesis about relational morals in teachers' stories when professor Kaarina Kailo gave me Genevieve Vaughan's book *"For-Giving, a Feminist Criticism of Exchange"* (1997) and encouraged me to read it. While reading this book, I felt I had found the missing piece to my "thesis puzzle". And it was not only the missing piece but actually provided a name to the picture in my puzzle. The gift paradigm helped me to make deeper sense out of my interpretations.

When I learned about the gift paradigm, I had been working several years in a research project titled "Teachers in Change – A Narrative-Biographical Approach to Teachers' Life and Work" funded by the Academy of Finland. Whenever I refer to teachers' stories, I am talking about the stories analysed by myself and my colleagues in our earlier studies, on which my doctoral thesis was based. We used a collection of autobiographical stories produced by a group of 65 Finnish teachers (including 35 student teachers). There were only five men among these autobiographers, and all the others were women (Estola 2003: 34).

The project was based on the assumption that teachers' voices in education were not heard, although they play the key roles in the educational practice. Trying to hear these silenced voices, the members of our research group listened to even young teachers talk about love, caring, and teachers' close relationships with children and adolescents. However, this discourse was not heard publicly, and even the informant teachers seemed apologetic when talking about these themes (Estola 2002). After these experiences, it was easy to agree with Genevieve Vaughan's (1997: 31) claim: "I believe that the gift paradigm is everywhere in our lives, though we have become used to not seeing it".

The effort to find out something that is not obvious or is downright ignored, such as the gift paradigm, is a challenge for the researcher. According to Vaughan, the main reason for the general ignorance of the gift paradigm is that the gift paradigm emerges from motherhood. For this reason, it does not have the power and privilege to become heard. Many researchers (Noddings 1984; Bowden 1997; Ruddick 1995) have pointed out that the practices of motherhood almost force mothers towards a morality pivoting on human relationships. These researchers also emphasize that motherhood is not connected with biological sex. Instead, the mother is the person who takes care of the infant, though in the western countries this caregiver is, in most instances, the woman who has given birth to the baby.

When reading about the gift paradigm, I noticed that it had many similarities to the teachers' stories analyzed in our project. We had written about such words as "love", "hope" and "calling" in teachers' narrative identities (e.g. Estola & Syrjälä 2002; Estola 2003; Estola, Erkkilä & Syrjälä 2004). According to our inquiries, teachers use these words in a special, other-oriented way. Still, not even researchers have been interested in them. Because Genevieve Vaughan (1997: 30) herself mentions that the gift paradigm is very close to the caring and nurturing implicit in mothering, I thought that the manifestations of the gift paradigm in teachers' stories would be worth closer study.

In this article, I base my reflections about the gift paradigm on Genevieve Vaughan's (1997) book. I will first briefly introduce the gift paradigm and the exchange paradigm in the (Finnish) educational context. After that, I will analyze teachers' stories in the context of the gift paradigm from two perspectives. First, I will discuss the gift paradigm as a part of teachers' general view of teaching, which I call "narrative identity". Second, I will make some observations on the gift paradigm in educational practices.

The concepts of "gift paradigm" and "exchange paradigm" in educational contexts

"Classrooms are places where many voices meet", write Freema Elbaz-Luwisch, Torill Moen and Sigrun Gudmundsdottir (2002: 197). There are voices from different times, places and people. The loudest public voice is heard from the administration, and it speaks more and more often with the words of business and the marketplace. The "marketplace discourse" is close to what Genevieve Vaughan calls the "exchange paradigm". Education, day care centres and schools are expected to be efficient and economical with children as their clients. Schools compete with each other, the best schools are ranked; children, pupils and students are said to be trained for the future and for the needs of the labor market. In brief, in this discourse, the human being is only an instrument of exchange, and the highest value is offered for the extraordinary, the winner, the best performance. The biggest investment is made in those who will pay back most, i.e. will be most productive in the future. This discourse is highly individualistic, encouraging people to search for their own good (see also Estola & Syrjälä 2002). The "marketplace discourse" consists of the authoritative discourse of fathers, "who are felt to be hierarchically higher" (Bakhtin 1981: 342).

As I mentioned, Genevieve Vaughan's descriptions of the gift paradigm sounded familiar to me against the background of teachers' stories. Generally speaking, the gift paradigm is opposed to the exchange paradigm. The gift paradigm does not expect any "pay back". A similar viewpoint has been presented by Hélène Cixous (1997), who claims that the gift is also described by Marcel Mauss and Jacques Derrida in the context of the masculine economy, which does not talk about generosity. Instead, the gift in feminine economy allows giving without expectation of anything in return. The gift paradigm is oriented towards satisfying the needs of others and towards providing well-being to others. It is qualitatively rather than quantitatively based, and it therefore easily remains invisible, not being countable or quantifiable (Vaughan 1997: 30-32).

As far I have understood, Genevieve Vaughan developed the gift paradigm especially for language and economics. Despite this economic background, the main features of the gift paradigm are compatible with the relational moral in teachers' stories. For them, the "internally persuasive" discourse speaks about relations of love, trust, and caring. It talks about listening to children's voices and needs. Education is not seen as an efficient project but rather as a long and slow process. In contemporary society, this discourse is often silent, and if it is heard, it is often considered old-fashioned. For me, this "relational discourse" is a manifestation of the gift paradigm.

In classrooms, teachers simultaneously hear both voices of the "marketplace discourse" and voices of the "relational discourse". The former tempts them towards effective teaching and good results and the latter towards considering the children's needs.

The following quotation is from Tiina, a student math teacher who is struggling between these discourses:

> There are many things that make you feel good. They are not necessarily directly related to pupils' learning. Rather, I think they are more closely related to attitudes. There was a ninth-grader who improved his mark by two units. I thought to myself that this was probably the first time he had ever had a positive learning experience at school. I was really happy about that.

Calling as the expression of the gift paradigm in teachers' narrative identities

I use the term "narrative identity" to refer to identity as a constantly told and retold story about "who am I as a teacher?" (Ricouer 1984). In addition, I refer to Charles Taylor's (1989: 47-48) concept of identity as a moral horizon, from which teachers find their solutions by trying to orient towards goodness and to provide an insight into the meaning of one's life.

"Calling" for me is the moral voice in teachers' narrative identities that basically determines the way in which teachers approach their work. Although some teachers recall their memories about a sense of calling from their childhood, the calling manifests and develops through practice. Calling neither implies an inborn ability to accomplish a specific task nor is it something self-evident. Rather, teachers often develop a sense of calling through highly strenuous and contradictory life experiences (Estola, Erkkilä & Syrjälä 2004).

Calling can be described as two-dimensional: a teacher feels that she or he is serving others and also derives personal satisfaction from teaching (Hansen 1995). The next quotation describes one teacher's development of calling. Tiina writes:

> I decided to become a teacher after some eventful episodes [...] So, this idea to become a teacher was really not a youthful dream. The more I think about it and the more time I spend at school, the more I feel that this will be my calling. It must be the greatest change that has ever happened in me – the feeling that I am heading in the right direction.

When we think of female teachers' lives and their connections with calling, there are also stages related to motherhood, such as pregnancies, deliveries and maternity leaves, which might support the sense of serving others' cause. The experiences of pregnancy may be one reason why women learn that neither their bodies nor their minds are only for themselves. Vaughan (1997, p. 36) describes this process:

> I believe that women are socialized to be mothers. Since babies cannot "pay back" for what they receive, someone must satisfy their needs free, without exchange. This functional Other orientation is made necessary not by the nature of women but by the nature of babies who cannot satisfy their own needs...

Although I hesitate to emphasize the experiences of motherhood when talking about teachers' calling, motherhood should not be underestimated, either (Sikes 1997). Learning to be a mother can be a very demanding and even frustrating process, which makes the mother learn the lesson about giving without expecting the other to "pay back". One of our informant teachers, Helena, told of how the birth of her babies forced her to reflect on her own role as a mother and a teacher. She told of how, during her first pregnancy, she did not have any "*maternal feelings*", and after giving birth to her first baby, she often felt tired with the small, constantly crying, colicky baby. She wrote: "The first baby was a hard lesson for us and made us grow in a short time more than any other thing could have". Helena recalls the experience of feeling like a failure as a mother after admitting she found it "awful to be a mother" (Estola & Syrjälä 2002).

We should not draw a parallel between gender and biological sex. Many male teachers are sensitive to the voices of relational discourse, although such sensitivity might come more easily to women. The multi-voiced educational practice is complicated: both women and men hear diverse, often contradictory voices, and they need continuously to make decisions as to which voices they listen to. There are many female teachers who do not listen to the voices of relational discourse. From my own history, I can retrospectively recognize the time when I served as the principal of a college for kindergarten teachers, when my sensitivity to relational voices was quite weak. This reminds me of Genevieve Vaughan (1997: 28-29), who warns that joining the work force has somehow made many women speak in the voice of the patriarchy.

From the male teachers' stories, I have picked one short quotation from a young student teacher writing about his dreams as a teacher. "In a short and busy period of time, I want to become both a mother and a father figure that these kids from such different backgrounds can really trust. I know this could prove to be emotionally trying, but it could also be very rewarding". (Estola 2003: 188). This brief statement can be taken as an example of the gift paradigm and Other-oriented relational discourse without the expectation of return. It also tells us about the emotional vulnerability and hardness of the work. The quote reminds us of "trustful hope": a teacher who never gives up (van Manen 1991).

In my thinking, calling as a way of serving others is a concrete manifestation of the gift paradigm in teachers' stories. It emerges in practice when teachers find the children calling them. This metaphor of Max van Manen (1991) about children's call fascinates me in its concrete imagery and reminds me about the power of children. This image is easy to connect with motherhood: when the child calls, the mother has to answer. Answering to this call, however, may be harder now than ever. In our educational institutions, the loudest discourse is more and more often the exchange-oriented "marketplace discourse", which speaks in the voice of the patriarchy. For this reason, all efforts towards strengthening the gift paradigm in narrative identities are welcome. I would like to claim that "calling" is teachers' own word to talk about the gift paradigm. We should revitalize that concept. It would help to make the gift paradigm more visible.

Gift paradigm in embodied educational practices

Until recently, the body has been a taboo in the discussion of educational practices. It has been either totally ignored or referred to indirectly. On the other hand, at least in sociology, anthropology and feminist research, the body has been a topic of active interest (Featherstone, Hepworth & Turner 1991; Jacobus, Keller & Shuttleword 1990; Jokinen 1997).

The silenced voices of the gift paradigm and the body seem to me something that would be worth of looking at together. In educational research, the body has been written between the lines by using such words as "manners" or "tact", or by describing the ways in which teachers move, talk, or smile (Hansen 2001). Max van Manen, when talking about teachers' style, refers to the body explicitly (1991: 121), pointing out that style is "the outward embodiment of the person".

Teachers' stories are, however, full of references to the body that seem to bear resemblance to the gift paradigm: touching, happiness or exhaustion, gentle and hostile bodily contacts, hugs, looks, and many others. Feminist research has indicated that body writing is especially explicit in women's stories (Bleakley 2000). George Lakoff & Mark Johnson (1999) have conclusively argued that our language has a material basis. The language talks about the body with words and metaphors, as does the next quotation from Liisa, a Finnish primary school teacher:

> The most difficult thing in this demanding job of teaching is the perpetual presence. You cannot hide your own being, feelings, and attitudes behind the subjects you are teaching. Every moment, no matter what kind of a phase of life you are living in, you have to be there. You have to be present in the very situation where learning takes place and where the developing individuals, your pupils, are watching you. At the same time, they are modeling themselves on you and also need guidance and encouragement.

When I analyzed teachers' stories of this kind with my Israeli colleague, Freema Elbaz-Luwisch, we suggested that teaching could be seen as embodied physical labor (Estola & Elbaz-Luwisch 2004). We were, however, advised to drop the concept "physical labor" because physical labor was said to involve hard and heavy work that requires muscles and strength. The notion of physical labor has notably masculine connotations: it speaks with the voice of a man in authoritative discourse, "which demands that we acknowledge it [...]" (Bakhtin 1981: 342). Yet, teachers' stories tell about different aspects of physical labor.

Those voices make teachers' work physical because the body is the main vehicle toward children (Mitchell & Weber 1999: 124). Using the vocabulary of the gift paradigm: the gifts in educational practices are given through and by the body.

Silva Tedre's (1999) views encourage us to read this concept of "physical labor" in a more polyphonic "Bakhtinian" way, assuming that the collective voice of women would be heard in this discourse against another voice, that of the father, because teachers' stories include frequent references not only to the physical heaviness of teaching, but also to affectionate looks, hugs and touching. Tedre points out that there are very many different bodily activities that have remained totally unspoken because they have traditionally belonged to women and to privacy.

Liisa, a Finnish primary school teacher, middle-aged and mid-career, writes about the concrete physical demands of teaching.

> The teacher's work requires surprisingly good physical fitness. To be standing on your feet all day, going from one pupil to another in the class, to prepare schoolwork, and possibly even to teach physical education require strength and good health. But even more strength can be required by factors taxing the mind, such as work-related stress, the noise filling your ears from all around you, the settling of quarrels between pupils, the imbalance of personal relationships in the school community, and other such factors.

In educational practice, such words as "love", "hope" and "care", which are used by teachers when talking about their moral horizons, have embodied material backgrounds. They refer to certain practices rather than emotions (see also Ruddick 1995). When we connect this idea with the gift paradigm, it is obvious that an important part of for-giving consists of concrete, material gifts in the world of nurturing. Genevieve Vaughan (1997: 37) describes the development of nurturing the child first with goods and services and later with words. In this interaction, the mother is not the only giving person because the child participates in turn-taking with the mother. Genevieve Vaughan (1997: 37) distinguishes turn-taking from exchange: "The motivation in turn-taking is not constrained reciprocity, but sharing, alternating giving and receiving, and communication".

The next quotation from a teacher' story is an impressive example about the "for-giving" face of the child. It is also an example about the importance of the body in for-giving practices in general. "I shook hands with my future pupils and wished them a happy summer. A small girl came and hugged me hard, pressed her cheek against my breast and looked round-eyed into my eyes, trustfully. Let that look give me light, strength and love with these 'last ones' of mine".

In educational practices, gift giving takes place through bodies both symbolically and concretely. The smaller the children, the more the teacher's body has to be concretely close to them. The older the children, the more diverse gifts are given by their teachers. Teachers give gifts by providing knowledge in different subjects, manners, cultural traditions, arts, etc. In that sense, teachers' work, similarly to mothers', reaches far into the future. And although teachers do this without being justified to expect any "payment back", there are, at least from time to time, situations where they experience a strong sense of turn taking.   102

Maybe those episodes especially support teachers to continue their work. Let us listen to how a student teacher wrote about teaching. "I was impressed by the aspects of the teachers' stories which made it clear that, even in the most modest conditions, the teachers did the most dedicated work, developed new solutions, and turned down general beliefs to which they did not adhere".

Conclusions

I started by arguing that, similarly to the generally neglected gift paradigm, there are silent voices in teachers' stories that should become heard. In this paper, I have talked about calling and embodiment as voices that reveal the Other orientation in teachers' work. This Other orientation is what connects teaching with the gift paradigm.

We could help to make the Other orientation more visible and louder by revitalizing the words that are spoken in its voice. In addition to the words "calling", "gift", "love", "hope", and "care", we could also include "generosity" (La Caze 2002) and especially "gift". It is, however, not enough to use these words but we must be careful that they are used in an Other-oriented sense. For instance, "hope" also has a male voice, which speaks about a concept that can be measured and tested by using "hope scales" (Snyder 1994). As far as I understand, "gift" has an extra benefit compared to the other words mentioned above: it brings economic and global questions into play. For that reason, it should become part of teachers' vocabulary not only implicitly but also quite explicitly.

As concluding remarks, I want to mention two probable reasons why the voices of the gift paradigm in education have become silenced.

First, in the project of professionalizing teaching, it is problematic that the overwhelming majority of teachers are women, who tend to approach their work based on the paradigm of motherhood. The tendency to respond to other people's needs and to approach people as individuals is considered "an obstacle to professionalization, a deficiency, or a disorder" (Henriksson 2000: 86-88). This attitude ignores the societal significance of women's practices and implicitly assumes women's experiences and ways of thinking to be inferior to those of men; they are self-evident in the home context, but lack any wider significance (cf. Vaughan 1997: 51, 239; Freedman 1987: 78-79).

Second, teachers' voices are not heard because the female identity has remained silenced. The discourse of autonomous identity has been so loud that the different relational identity of women has not even been recognized (Enoranta 1996, p. 132, referring to Nicole Brossard). Female subjectivity has never been able to develop into the kind of autonomous individuality that is characteristic of modern (male) identities. The ideal of autonomous identity is an element of the exchange paradigm. If we want to make the gift paradigm flourish, we should not encourage women to adopt this autonomous identity. Instead, it is important, as Vaughan points out, to encourage "women and men with caring values to stop nurturing the patriarchy" (Vaughan 1997: 29). Finally, it makes sense to remind ourselves that the entire ideal of autonomous identity is a fantasy: "Each human is a part of the collective because her/his identity is formed by using the collective's material, cultural and linguistic gifts, which are given to each of us by others, and are given by each of us to others" (ivi: 107). Charles Taylor (1989: 35-37) writes about the same topic it by saying that every person can only be as individualistic as the cultural context allows her/him to be.

I want to close with a quotation from a female student teacher. It summarizes what I have written about Other-oriented teacher identities and educational practices.

I want to recognize and overcome the problems of being a student, a child, a person. This sounds wonderful on paper, which is why I want to see myself achieve this goal over and over again, time after time, tirelessly and with tenacity. I hope that I possess flexibility and openness, I hope that I have wise eyes and a warm heart, I hope that I can be a person for people. I really hope that this is not merely fictitious prose and an overused cliché.

References

Bakhtin, Mikhail (1981/1990). *The Dialogic Imagination. Four Essays*, ed. Michael Holquist, University of Texas Press, Austin.

Bleakley, Alan (2000). "Writing with invisible ink: narrative, confessionalism and reflective practice", *Reflective Practice*, 1 (1), pp. 11-24.

Bowden, Peta (1997). *Caring. Gender-Sensitive Ethics*, Routledge, London and New York.

Cixous Hélène (1997). "Sorties: Out and Out: Attacks/ways Out/Forays", in Schrift A.D., (ed.), *The Logic of the Gift. Toward an Ethic of Generosity*, Routledge, London, pp. 148-173.

Elbaz-Luwisch, Freema, Moen, Torill & Gudmundsdottir, Sigrun (2002). "The multivoicedness of classrooms. Bakhtin and narratives of teaching", in Huttunen R., Heikkinen H.L.T. & Syrjälä, L. (eds.), *Narrative Research. Voices of Teachers and Philosophers*, SoPhi 67, University of Jyväskylä, pp. 197-218.

Enoranta, Teija (1996). "Satumainen subjekti. Nicole Brossardin integraali ilman nainen" [Fantastic subject, in Finnish] in Kosonen P. (ed.), *Naissubjekti ja postmoderni* [Female subject and post modernism, in Finnish], Gaudeamus, Tampere, pp. 131-150.

Estola Eila (2003a). "Hope as work – student teachers constructing their narrative identities", *Scandinavian Journal of Educational Research*, 47 (2), pp. 181-203.

— (2003b). In the language of the mother – re-storying the relational moral in teachers' stories. Acta Universitatis Ouluensis E 62, University of Oulu.

Estola Eila & Syrjälä Leena (2002a). "Love, body and change. A teacher's narrative reflections", *Reflective Practice* 3 (1), pp. 53-69.

— (2002b). "Whose reform? Teachers' voices from silence", in Huttunen R., Heikkinen H.L.T. & Syrjälä L. (eds.), *Narrative Research. Voices of Teachers and Philosophers*, SoPhi 67, University of Jyväskylä, pp. 177-195.

Estola Eila & Elbaz-Luwisch Freema (2003). "Teaching Bodies at Work", *Journal of Curriculum Studies*, 35 (6), pp. 697-719.

Estola Eila, Erkkilä Raija & Syrjälä Leena (2003). "A moral voice of vocation in teachers' narratives", *Teachers and Teaching: theory and* practice, 9 (3), pp. 239-256.

Featherstone, Mike, Hepworth, Mike, Turner, S. Bryan (eds.) (1991). *The Body. Social Process and Cultural Theory*, Sage Publications, London.

Freedman, Sara (1987). "Teachers' knowledge from the feminist perspective", .in Smyth J. (ed.), *Educating Teachers. Changing the Nature of Pedagogical Knowledge*, The Falmer Press, London and New York, pp. 73-80.

Hansen, David T. (1995). *The Call to Teach*, Teachers College Press, New York.

— (2001). "Teaching as a Moral Activity", in Richardsson, V. (ed.), *Handbook of Research on Teaching. Fourth Edition*, American Educational Research Association, Washington, pp. 826-857.

Henriksson, Lea (2000). "Professiot ja sukupuolten välinen työnjako terveystyössä" ["Professions and division of labour between the sexes"] In Kangas, I. Karvonen, S. & Lillrank, A. (eds.), *Terveyssosiologian suuntauksia* [Trends in Health Sociology, in Finnish], Gaudeamus, Helsinki, pp. 85-103.

Jacobus, Mary, Keller Evelyn & Shuttleworth, Sally (1990)."Introduction", in Jacobus, M., Keller, E. & Shuttleworth, S. (eds.), *Body/Politics. Women and the Discourses of Science*, Routledge, New York, London, pp. 1-10.

Jokinen, Eeva (ed.) (1997). *Ruumiin siteet. Tekstejä erosta, järjestyksestä ja sukupuolesta* [Bondage of the Body. Texts about Separation, Order and Gender, in Finnish], Tampere, Vastapaino.

Johnson, Mark (1987). *The Body in the Mind. The Bodily Basis of Meaning, Imagination, and Reason*, The University Chicago Press, Chicago.

La Caze, Marguerite (2002). "The Encounter between Wonder and Generosity", "*Hypatia*", 17 (3), pp. 2-19.

Lakoff, George & Johnson, Mark (1999). *Philosophy in the Flesh. The Embodied Mind and its Challenge to Western Thought*, Basic Books, New York.

Mitchell, C. & Weber, Sandra (1999). *Reinventing Ourselves as Teachers: Beyond Nostalgia*, The Falmer Press, London.

Noddings, Nel (1984). *Caring: A Feminine Approach to Ethics and Moral Education*, University of California Press, Berkeley.

Ricoeur, Paul (1984). *Time and Narrative.* Volume I. Engl. trans. McLaughlin K. & Pellauer D., The University of Chicago Press, Chicago.

Ruddick, Sara (1995). *Maternal Thinking. Toward a Politics of Peace*, Beacon Press, Boston.

Sikes, Patricia (1997). *Parents Who Teach. Stories from Home and from School*, Cassell, London.

Snyder, C. R. (1994). *The Psychology of Hope*, The Free Press, New York.

Taylor, Charles (1989). *Sources of the Self. The Making of the Modern Identity*, Cambridge University Press, Cambridge.

Tedre, Silva (1999). *Hoivan sanattomat sopimukset. Tutkimus vanhusten kotipalvelun työntekijöiden työstä* [The Unspoken Contracts in Social Care. A Case Study of Paid Workers in Finnish Municipal Home Help Services for the Elderly, in Finnish]. Publications in Social Sciences 40, University of Joensuu.

Van Manen, Max (1991). *The Tact of Teaching. The Meaning of Pedagogical Thoughtfulness*, The Althouse Press, Ontario.

Vaughan, Genevieve (1997). *For-Giving. A Feminist Criticism of Exchange*, Plain View Press, Austin.

BHANUMATHI NATARAJAN

> The forest is a peculiar organism of unlimited kindness and benevolence that makes no demand for its sustenance and extends generously the products of its life activity; it affords protection to all beings, offering shade even to
> the axeman who destroys it.
>
> *Gauthama Buddha*

Introduction

The world around us is surrounded with biodiversity. Biodiversity is the sum of organisms that include plants, animals, microorganisms and the ecosystems they live in (CBD 1998). These natural resources are gifts of nature that are important for humans and for the functioning of ecosystems. The local/indigenous peoples have been custodians of diversity so far. Through an understanding of the natural processes they have been able to use and share the natural resources wisely. Gift giving and receiving, however, are thwarted by the exchange value system.

In the dominant exchange system, goods are created for the market, with the sole objective of bringing profit. Gift giving is considered unnatural unless the resources are processed into goods for the market (Vaughan 1998). Today transnational corporations (TNCs) are the main actors of the dominant exchange system. They acquire profits by commodifying gifts they receive. These gifts include for instance women's care work, natural resources and traditional knowledge.

Patriarchy has established power structures and created a consumer society; biodiversity is converted into goods for consumption without regard for the environment and the interactions of species within the ecosystems. A degraded environment is the result, and it may further result in endangering the rights of people to their traditional ways i.e. nurturing, respecting, using and protecting the ecosystem. To quote Posey (1999), human beings are an integral part of biodiversity, not merely observers and users of the "components of biodiversity". For the indigenous and traditional peoples nature is not a commodity to be bought and sold, patented or preserved apart from society, precisely because nature is what defines humanity. The earth is their (our) mother and cannot be compromised, sold or monopolised. Thus there is an inextricable link between nature, society and culture.

In this paper, I will present examples and discuss the importance of the traditional knowledge of biodiversity that local/indigenous peoples possess. New varieties of crops cultivated by local/indigenous women and the knowledge of how to use wild plants that has been acquired for centuries, are gifts that are shared and freely available. The market regards these gifts purely as profit elements to be privatised, whereas the gift aspect is ignored. The danger, however, is that essential biodiversity and traditional knowledge may disappear forever.

107

The status of biodiversity and traditional knowledge

Nature has provided us with bountiful gifts in the form of biodiversity, with which humans have experimented. Local/indigenous peoples' lives are based on the resources found in their local environment. They have experimented and learnt to use these gifts of nature: for instance plants and animals, as food. Through a keen sense of observation of the ecosystem they have cultivated new varieties of crops. In addition they have also used wild biota in health care. The traditional knowledge has been passed on from one generation to another by word of mouth. This oral tradition is alive even today. According to the World Health Organisation (WHO) about 80% of the world's people rely on traditional medicine for their primary health care needs (Farnsworth 1985). Furthermore, local/indigenous peoples have used fibres for clothing and ropes and wood and leaves for providing shelter and for making boats or canoes.

The manifold use of plants is probably the reason for their veneration by local/indigenous peoples. This can be seen, for instance, by the spiritual role that forests play in the lives of these peoples. Their respect for nature has prevented indiscriminate use and secured protection of diversity. Therefore, the reverence for biodiversity by local/indigenous peoples cannot be ignored. The existence of sacred groves in many parts of the world is a living example of the spiritual aspect in the conservation of biodiversity. Thus knowledge of biodiversity and its use are intertwined with traditional, cultural, spiritual practices of a large number of peoples.

Due to the disappearance of biodiversity, local traditions are forgotten and eventually disappearing from communities. Knowledge and biodiversity get further eroded due to industrialisation, modernisation of agriculture, such as monoculture cultivation, pollution, and migration of people to cities, due to war and population pressures. Wilson (1988) and Lovejoy (1992) estimate that there are somewhere between 30 and 100 million species on earth. This diversity is being lost at the rate of 27,000 species each year, 74 each day or 3 each hour (Wilson 1992).

Development projects such as dam construction, mining and cash crop cultivation have resulted in people moving away from rural areas. This not only results in loss of income for local people but also a loss of healthy diets based on local diversity. So traditional crops are either lost or not cultivated, and this has led to malnourishment of the local people, especially the children.

Agrobiodiversity

Several varieties of crops have been and are cultivated and maintained by local/indigenous peoples. Their knowledge of the local gene pool is a gift to all, and forms the base for new varieties. For example, potatoes cultivated by the peoples of the Andes for thousands of years form the base for new varieties cultivated today (Ugent 1970). The Cochabamba people of the Andes have maintained 70 varieties of potato. Some single families maintained up to 31 varieties. Women play a very important role in cultivation. They are involved in seed selection, production, harvest, storage, processing, and last but not least cooking (GRAIN 2000). Arawakan women of the Guainia-Negro region of the Venezuelan Amazon cultivate more than 70 varieties of bitter manioc (Hoffmann 2003). In one of the many villages of Liberia, Kpelle women maintained 112 varieties of rice (Thomasson 1991).

Besides crop species a large number of wild plants including seasonal vegetables and fruits form part of the diets of local/indigenous peoples. In Kenya a considerable amount of wild biodiversity is used by women during the rainy season for food, medicine and other products. In Bangladesh stagnation of water is common during the monsoons. Women collect seeds of jack fruit, fry them and keep them ready before the onset of the monsoon, as it may be difficult to prepare elaborate meals due to water logging. The seeds are stored in pots and hung outside their dwellings to prevent them from being damaged by water. Local people have cultivated crops for their nutrition value and for their taste too. Several other crops, legumes, tropical fruits and other wild species form part of nutritious diet in a small area. Of course the art of preserving and pickling based on local biodiversity is well known to women.

Women are also involved in cultivating vegetables, greens and other herbs in kitchen or home gardens. These home gardens also harbour many indigenous varieties that are very often taken care of by women. In rural Bangladesh for example, women select seeds of vine and gourd species, chiefly indigenous varieties that are to be grown the following year (Wilson 2003).

Medicinal diversity

Local/indigenous peoples also use a wide variety of local biodiversity for medicinal purposes. Samoan women healers use about 100 different plant species, and an antiviral drug prostratin from the plant Holmanthus nutans was discovered after verifying traditional claims (Cox 1995, Cox 2000). In India indigenous women from the State of Madhya Pradesh use a combination of plants as birth control agents (Citizen's Report 1982). A medicinal plant Pelargonium reniforme that grows wild and is endemic to Eastern Cape of South Africa is used by the Khoi/San descendents and Xhosa traditional healers against stomach ailments, dysentery and blood in stools (Limson 2002). All these plants come from the tropics and have been used by indigenous people. 74% of the 119 chemical substances extracted from higher plants that are used in medicine have the same or related uses and have been used by the local/indigenous populations or in ethnomedicine (Farnsworth 1988). Tropical plants are used as direct therapeutic agents. They are, among others, sources of information for deriving new synthetic constituents and for the discovery of novel compounds (Oldfield 1984). Qunine and quinidine are only two chemical compounds extracted from the bark of cinchona tree (Cinchona officinalis), and are used as anti-malarial drugs and in the treatment for cardiac arrhythmia, respectively. There are many other chemical compounds that are used for various health conditions. It is estimated that two-thirds of 35,000 species of plants in the tropics have medicinal value.

Socio-cultural or spiritual aspects

Sustainable use and protection of biodiversity can be seen in various cultural practices. Religious legitimation is also given to plants and animals. As a means of sharing biodiversity one can see hunting in specially protected areas in local communities, where animals and birds are captured during festivals and the meat shared. In other places game meat is used to celebrate the dead. Special areas are allotted for hunting game meat for such occasions.

In India and Sri Lanka, some of the richest sites of medicinal plants are the sacred groves that are scattered throughout the country. They are a concept and practice of in-situ conservation and protection of biodiversity. In Sri Lanka they are under the care of the Buddhist monasteries and in South India under the care of various deities. Sacred groves in India such as the aurans of Rajasthan, devaranyas (God's groves) of the Western Ghats, nagaranya (serpent's groves) and kavus of Kerala are also symbols of the maintenance of diversity. These are traditional mechanisms of management and protection of diversity. Sacred groves are a feature across different continents too. Today, these are protected by the local people, who only at times are allowed to go and get medicinal plants for their own treatment of ailments. The groves have stood the test of time due to socio-cultural traditions. These reserves are a "local insurance" – not being taken care of by governments but by the people themselves who use them.

Even in temples and homes in cities, plants and leaves are used for religious purposes and during festivals. According to Ghate (1998) at least 45 species used in different religious ceremonies from Pune city have been enumerated. These species are both cultivated and available as wild plants. Many grow as weeds and are easily available and many are rare and not easily available. These plants provide economic benefits as fruit trees, or ornamentals or are used as medicine locally. Thus the spiritual aspects show us that there is more than the utility value of a genetic resource. These species are used in a sustainable manner and protected as well.

The spiritual aspects also include the celebration of diversity by local/indigenous peoples. Harvest festivals and local fairs are some of the ways through which diversity is celebrated and knowledge of biodiversity is shared with others. Sharing of biodiversity not only enhances the diversity of the gene pool but also the knowledge of these through communication. This strengthens the cultural and traditional base of local/indigenous peoples' practices related to farming and the use of biodiversity as medicine. The relationship that local/indigenous peoples have built up with their local ecosystems enhances the gifts of nature, both in the form of biodiversity and traditional knowledge. It is through such interaction and understanding of interconnectedness that they have been and still are able to protect and make sustainable use of diversity. These elements are lost in the exchange system, which leads to the alienation of nature and people, and the regard for the resources is lost.

Commodification of the skills of traditional knowledge

In the free market society, nature's gifts are converted into commodities by the market for its use in the accumulation of profits. Traditional varieties of crops and knowledge of biodiversity have been increasingly commodified in the past couple of decades and have benefitted the countries of the North. For example, a wild tomato variety was estimated to be worth ca. 8 million dollars a year to the U.S. (Iltis 1988). An Ethiopian barley gene protects crops in California from lethal dwarf virus and is worth $150 million in the U.S. (RAFI 1994). Many of the crops have been selected and cultivated by local/indigenous peoples. When it comes to medicinal plants, the rosy periwinkle (Catharanthus roseus) has been used by local/indigenous peoples as an oral hypoglycaemic agent. The most useful alkaloids isolated from this plant are used to treat childhood leukaemia and Hodgkin's disease in modern medicine. The market sales in 1980 were in the range of $100 million (see Plotkin 1991). The value of the pharmaceutical industry has more than quadrupled between 1981 and 2000. The top 10 corporations control 48% of the $317 billion market. When it comes to the seed industry, the top 10 corporations control about 30% of the $24 billion market (ETC 2001, ETC 2003).

Women's free services are gifts that the exchange based economic system needs for profit making. Similarly the biodiversity and traditional knowledge that are available gratis are beneficial for the market. During the colonial times the colonisers cultivated and transferred exotic species for trade and established a market for these. Very often cultivation was based on monocultures. Each colonial power grew plantations from which it could profit most. In Sri Lanka cocoa, coffee, cinchona, quinine, rubber and tea were grown in succession. (Dixon 1990, NRC 1975). Today trade agreements such as the World Trade Organisation (WTO) have replaced the colonial system, but with the same winners and losers as before.

Biodiversity and traditional knowledge are threatened as a result of privatisation and monopoly rights that corporations want to impose. Patriarchal institutions such as the WTO, which cater to the market's needs, help corporations to take out patent rights on biodiversity and traditional knowledge. Private property rights may endanger the rights of women and local/indigenous peoples in using and sharing their resources as they have done. Biodiversity and traditional knowledge together with the embedded gifts may be lost forever as a result.

TNCs have realised that the use of ethnobotanical tools can give them a quicker and cheaper way of exploiting drugs for their benefit. So the study of ethnobotany is now beginning to be taken up by modern scientists for exploring new chemical substances and for cost effective research. In modern scientific terms ethnobotany is the study of how plants and animals are used by local/indigenous peoples. It is an interdisciplinary study and includes fields such as botany, zoology, pharmacy, ecology, anthropology, sociology and politics. According to Balick (1985), an ethnobotanical approach would increase the chance of drug discovery by 400 times. Ethnomedical or ethnobotanical approach by Shaman pharmaceuticals has shown to be 125-630 times more efficient in the drug discovery processes when compared to searching for compounds in the wild (Carlson 1998). Many other pharmaceuticals have started to incorporate the local traditional or ethnobotanical knowledge of species in their drug discovery processess. Discussions are taking place as to how people can be compensated for the resources and knowledge they part with, for instance in the case of the discovery of a drug, with no regard being given to the holistic perspective of biodiversity.

Patents on biodiversity and traditional knowledge

Several private and public enterprises and institutions are engaged in collecting, sampling and acquiring biodiversity and traditional knowledge for development of foods, nutraceuticals, pharmaceuticals and other industrial products. But knowledge that comes from industrial countries is well protected by intellectual property rights. For example, article 27 (b) of the Trade Related Intellectual Property Rights (TRIPs) agreement, which comes under the purview of the WTO agreement, allows countries to patent processes and products. Countries that have signed the WTO agreement must adhere to these Intellectual property laws (IPR). The current IPR system does not protect the interests of communities, and ultimately threatens conservation and the further development of biodiversity. It only serves the interests of the corporations. The market does not recognise the gifts that these people have in the form of traditional knowledge, unless the gifts are transformed into commodities that can make money. In fact the gift economy of the local peoples is replaced by a theft economy, the TNCs being a parasite on local biodiversity and traditional knowledge. Patents on basmati, turmeric, jasmine rice, chick peas and Mexican beans are all well known. These patents only serve the corporations and not the local people.

According to Human Development Report (1999) industrialised countries own 97% of the patents, which are in turn owned by TNCs. Citizens of the North own over 80% of the patents granted by the developing countries. Once patenting has occurred it may be difficult for the local communities to fight the patents as the corporations have enormous resources, both in the form of money and legal personnel. Furthermore, the language used in the agreements is not easy to understand. The indigenous communities may finally lose their control over their resources.

The Western paradigm claims to bring development to the world's people, especially in the third world, while what we see is an opposite outcome. The models of development as portrayed by the International Monetary Fund (IMF) and World Bank and now the WTO are mechanisms created to serve the colonisers, as discussed in the examples above. Countries may have become independent, but in reality the same policies continue.

Women's actions in fostering the gifts (diversity)

In the past decade we have seen women as victims of development and environmental degradation. But what we increasingly realise is that they play a crucial role in the cultivation and the management of diversity. Their contribution to food production is large. In Africa women produce 80% of the food, in Asia 60% and in Latin America 40%. In addition to food production as discussed above women use a number of species to cater to their daily needs, such as wild and domesticated species, trees, shrubs, roots, leaves, bark and animals as food and medicines. Thus they rely on a diverse range of species and preserve the same.

The chipko or hug-the-tree movement was staged by women in India to protect the trees in the area, as it is they who realised the importance of the forest. In Kenya the Green Belt Movement mobilised more than 80,000 women to plant trees. Indeed we can see women resisting the destruction of the environment in countries of both the North and the South as it is they who have seen the connections between ecology, health and survival all along.

Biodiversity management in South India clearly shows how tradition and culture are carefully applied in cultivation and protection of diversity. In areas where finger millet is grown women are involved in seed selection and storage. Seed selection starts with the celebration of diversity in the form of performing rituals, and takes place continuously through field observation, which they do when they work. Thus they have keen eyes for selection and perform scientific experiments to choose seeds in their own way. When the crops are harvested a gift of grain is given to those who have helped with the harvest and also shared among the poor. Seed storage also involves rituals. The leaves of Lakki-Vitex negundo or neem are used in seed storage as they have insecticidal properties (Ramprasad 1999). Thus we see the cultivation and the protection of biodiversity where both traditional and spiritual practices play an important role. These connections therefore cannot be separated.

The appreciation of nature's gifts and management initiatives go hand in hand with culture. Natural resources are given respect and treated with dignity. They are also appreciated and shared. These aspects are taught and practiced by women of indigenous societies of Northwest America for sustainable development and to fight consumerism (Turner 1992, Turner and Atleo 1998). As Mahatma Gandhi put it, there is plenty in the world for everyone's needs but not for everyone's greed.

Towards a feminist gift perspective

Patriarchal institutions of capitalism have expanded more than ever due to the mantra of globalisation, which goes beyond privatisation, taking control of biodiversity and knowledge for control of peoples lives, just as colonisation has done in the past 500 years. The current actors of globalisation – the TNCs – claim that they are bringing culture and prosperity to all peoples, whereas they are the colonizers.

A feminist approach towards a gift economy would be to learn ways and means from local culture and traditions in the use of biodiversity instead of dismissing them as uncivilised ways of doing things. Thereby diversity could be appreciated. Small self-reliant entities, with diverse traditions and cultures, would pave the way for respecting diversity. Furthermore, we may be able to understand the vulnerabilities of associating with the global market and the threat this can be for present as well as future generations. By identifying and continuing traditional practices we can better protect and use biodiversity in a sustainable manner. This may in turn strengthen the diverse bases and lead to protection and the sustainable use of biodiversity. A synthesis of the old and new may further be important for a better management of biodiversity and traditional knowledge. And women can pave the path towards achieving this.

Last but not least; we are part of a bigger society based on the dominant exchange systems, so our minds are tuned to that way of thinking. A starting point would be for each one of us to start to recognise the gifts we give and receive at an individual level. That may be a step towards understanding the gift aspect embedded in biodiversity. This in turn could foster a society that appreciates gift giving and receiving; in other words it would be a move towards a gift society.

References

Balick, M. J. (1990). "Ethnobotany and the identification of therapeutic agents from the rainforest. Bioactive compounds from plants", Ciba Foundation Symposium 154, John Wiley & Sons, Chichester, UK.

Carlson, T. J., Cooper, R., King, S. R. and Rozlon, E. J. (1996). "Modern science and traditional healing", in S. Wrigley et al. (eds.), *Phytochemical Diversity, A Source of New Industrial Products*, The Royal Society of Chemistry, Cambridge, UK.

CBD (Convention on Biological Diversity) (1998). *Convention on biological diversity*, Text and annexes, ICAO, Canada.

Cox, P. A. (1995). "Shaman as scientist: indigenous knowledge systems in pharmacological research and conservation", in K. Hostettmann et al. (eds.), *Phytochemistry of plants used in traditional medicine*, Clarendon Press, Oxford.

— (2000). "Will tribal knowledge survive the millennium?", *Science*, vol. 287, pp. 44-45.

CSE (Centre for Science and Environment) (1982).*The state of India's environment 1982. A Citizens report*, CSE, New Delhi.

Dixon, C. (1990). *Rural development in the third world*, Routledge, London.

ETC (Action Group on Erosion, Technology, and Concentration) (2001). "Globalization, Inc. Concentration in corporate power: The unmentioned agenda", *Communique*, # 71.

— (2003). "Oligopoly, Inc. Concentration in corporate power 2003", *Communique*, # 82.

Farnsworth, N. R. (1988). "Screening plants for new medicines", in *Biodiversity*, eds. E. O. Wilson and Frances M. Peter, National Academy Press, Washington, D.C.

Farnsworth, N. R. and Morris, R. W. (1976). "Higher plants: the sleeping giants of drug development", *American Journal of Pharmacy*, 148, pp. 46-52.

Farnsworth, N. R., Akerele, O., Bingen, A. S. et al. (1985). "Medicinal plants in therapy", *Bulletin of the World Health Organisation*, 63, pp. 965-981.

Ghate, V.S. (1998). "Plants in patra-pooja: Notes on their identity and Utilization", *Ethnobotany*, Vol. 10, # 1 & 2, pp. 6-15.

GRAIN (2000). "Potato: A fragile gift from the Andes", September 2000.

HDR (Human Development Report) (1999). United Nations Development Programme, Oxford University Press, Oxford.

Hoffmann, S. (2003). "Arawakan women and the erosion of traditional food production in Amazon Venezuela", in *Women and Plants, Gender relations in biodiversity management and conservation*, ed. Patricia L. Howard, Zed Books, London & New York.

Iltis, H. L. (1988). "Serendipity in the exploration of biodiversity. What good are weedy tomatoes?", in E. O. Wilson and F. M. Peter (eds.), *Biodiversity*, National Academy Press, Washington D.C.

Limson, J. (2002). "The rape of the pelargoniums", *Science in Africa*, Africa's first on-line science magazine.http://www.scienceinafrica.co.za/2002/june/pelarg.htm.

Lovejoy, T. E. (1997). "Biodiversity: What is it?", in *Biodiversity II: understanding and protecting our biological resources*, eds. M. L. Reaka-Kudla, D. E. Wilson and E. O. Wilson, Joseph Henry Press, Washington, D.C.

NAS (National Academy of Sciences) (1975). *Underexploited tropical plants with promising economic value*, NAS, Washington, D.C.

Oldfield, M. L. (1989*). The value of conserving genetic resources*, Sinauer Associates Inc., Sunderland, Massachusetts.

Plotkin, M. J. (1991). "Traditional knowledge of medicinal plants, the search for new jungle medicines", in *Conservation of medicinal plants*, eds. O. Akerele, V. Heywood and H. Synge, Cambridge University Press, Cambridge.

Posey, D. (1999). "Preface", in *Cultural and Spiritual values of Biodiversity. A complementary contribution to the Global Biodiversity Assessment*, UNEP, Intermediate Technology Publications, London, UK, p. XVII.

RAFI (Rural Advancement Foundation International) (1994). "Conserving indigenous knowledge, Integration two systems of innovation", Study commissioned by the United Nations Development Program.

Ramprasad, V. (1999). "Women and biodiversity conservation", *COMPAS Newsletter*, October.

Thomasson, G. C. (1991). "Libera's seeds of knowledge", *Cultural Survival Quarterly*, Summer 1991.

Turner, N. (2003). "Passing on the News: Women's work, traditional knowledge and plant resource management in indigenous societies of North-western North America", in *Women and Plants, Gender relations in biodiversity management and conservation*, ed. Patricia L. Howard, Zed Books, London & New York.

Turner, N. J. (1992). "The earth's blanket: traditional aboriginal attitudes towards nature", *Canadian Biodiversity*, Vol. 2, No. 4, pp. 5-7.

Turner, N. J. and Atleo, E. R. (1998). "Pacific North American first peoples and the environment", in *Traditional and modern approaches to the environment on the Pacific Rim, tensions and values*, ed. H. Coward, Centre for studies in religion and society, State University of New York Press, Albany, pp. 105-124.

Ugent, D. (1970). "The potato", *Science*, No. 3963, vol. 1979, pp. 1161-1166.

Vaughan, G. (1998). "Jacob wrestles with the angel. Exchange and giftgiving. The struggle between two paradigms – and why it matters", *Crone Chronicles*, Summer Solstice.

Vietmeyer, D. N. (1986). "Lesser known plants of potential use in agriculture and forestry", *Science*, vol. 232, pp. 1379-1384.

Wilson, E. O. (1992*). The diversity of life*, Harvard University Press, Cambridge, MA.

Wilson, E. O. and Peter M. Frances (1988). *Biodiversity*, National Academy Press, Washington, D.C., 5.

Wilson, M. (2003). "Exchange, patriarchy and status: Women's homegardens in Bangladesh", in *Traditional and modern approaches to the environment on the Pacific Rim, tensions and values*, ed. H. Coward, Centre for studies in religion and society, State University of New York Press, Albany, pp. 105-124.

Introduction

When, at a seminar at the Women's University in Løten, Norway, in the summer of 2001, I was introduced to the idea of a gift economy, I found it both interesting and challenging, but also unsettling. I thoroughly agreed with Genevieve Vaughan's critique of exchange economy (Vaughan 1997) and its devastating effect on the world economy, but I found it difficult to imagine how a complex, modern society might organise itself according to the idea of the gift. Then gradually, while learning about the many examples of various untraditional solutions to economic problems of communities, i.e. on how, on Barbados, as co participant Peggy Antrobus said, the economy of the society for a great part depends on gifts from immigrant workers in the USA, my understanding of economy widened. Also, becoming more closely acquainted with some of Genevieve Vaughan's thoughts about what women as mothers contribute to the economy by their free giving of services to their families (*ibidem*), I was reminded of the Norwegian feminist discussions in the 70ties about the number of hours per week women spent on unpaid production, i.e. housework, and how, if paid according to an average industrial worker's wage, their income would amount to an important part of the gross national product (Wærness 1980).

I was also reminded of how, in the late 70ties and early 80ties in Norway, one of our leading feminists, Bjørg Åse Sørensen, introduced a paradigm shift within women's research. She proposed that instead of discussing and doing research on women's difficult and oppressed position, we should go in for presenting positive data on women and develop theories of women's importance for society. Sørensen (1982) created a kind of revolution by claiming that instead of stressing the adverse situation of women, we should rather emphasise the dignity of women's lives. She herself had done very interesting research on how female industrial workers empathised with their fellow workers in difficult situations. She developed the two concepts of responsible and technically limited rationality respectively, in order to analyse differences in men and women's reactions in the workplace. For me this approach meant a new, and some times totally different interpretation of male and female teachers' situations and action patterns in schools, and for some of my colleagues, it meant new inspiration in their research on the situation of health-personnel.

Initially, in our various theorising on women's responsible rationality, we equated this with their ability to care for others and show empathy, and we took as our point of departure women's experience as mothers. For a while, within the Nordic countries, Norwegian women's research enjoyed a certain recognition and had a fairly productive period. All this changed however, when, in the beginning of the 90's, postmodernism entered the scene, and we were accused by other feminists of working from an illusion of a women's essence.

Farewell to postmodernism

In revisiting the various research reports from the epoch mentioned above I was reminded of the old saying that "development moves in waves". Learning more and more about the ideas of a gift economy, I began to experience a new sense of freedom similar to the one Bjørg Aase Sørensen had initiated 20 years earlier (Sørensen 1982). Already, due to the post-structuralist discourse, the respect in relation to many of our Western civilisation's theories and concepts within sociology, psychology, pedagogy and other social sciences, and even within the natural sciences, had somehow begun to wither away. In relation to the theme in this article, however, it is interesting to find that ideas basic to market economy, i.e. the necessity of competition and the freedom of the market, to my knowledge, for some reason have not been deconstructed, but are constantly gaining new ground. Neither has the utilitarian conception of the human actor, as someone who constantly seeks to increase his own winnings, been contested by postmodernists.

In discussing my experience of a widening of insight and new ways of understanding world problems, I find it necessary to emphasise that it is NOT related to the extreme relativism advocated by many poststructuralist feminists, which has resulted in the eroding of the platforms on which criticism of exploitation and oppression, regarding gender, class and race has been founded. Quite to the contrary, the new sense of freedom is related to Vaughan's approach to knowledge based on women's work as mothers in combination with her Marxist based criticism of exchange economy (Vaughan 1997). It was especially stimulating to read her arguments after having been exposed to the above mentioned poststructuralist discourse which has effectively silenced debates on the possibility of a special women's epistemology. The catchword, which has had this devastating effect, has been "difference", meaning that differences within groups of women and men respectively are as important as those between the two groups. The idea of women as a special category and of a special women's essence has for a time been anathema.

A new theory of knowledge

However, at the beginning of our new century, this poststructuralist position has been effectively challenged, and in many milieus it is again becoming legitimate to debate phenomena from a women's standpoint. In an instructive article, Norwegian postdoctoral candidate, Cathrine Egeland, discusses, among others, Gayatri Spivac's analysis of strategic essentialism (Egeland 2003). Especially, Egeland refers to Spivac's approach to Marxism and her analysis of how Marx de-essentialised the concept of class.

Without arguing for a special women's essence, I find it important to take as a point of departure the experience and learning that result from the bearing of, giving birth to and nurturing of children. It has been both disappointing and alarming that in all the different sciences referred to above very few theories or concepts have been developed that may throw light upon, or fathom this experience and learning so close to life itself. From the perspectives of medicine and psychology we have learned about various types of risks, and about how to take care of pregnant women, women giving birth, how to care for the health of babies etc. Of course, this has been of very great importance but within these disciplines, the focus is often on how to prevent or eliminate danger. The sheer joy and wonder of conceiving, carrying, giving birth to and nurturing a living human being, is seldom made a point of. Within family sociology, the literature on women's roles has been of great importance regarding how society shapes both our acting patterns and our ideas about ourselves. But the theoretical approach is to a great degree created by men, first and foremost Talcott Parsons (1951). Reading Dorothy Smith (1987) (see below) makes it clear that we have not written very much about the everyday world of women from women's point of view. In an article on "Sociology and the Conceptualisation of Women" (Ve 1992), in order to challenge the remote or depersonalised way in which the phenomenon of motherhood was generally treated within the discipline, i.e. by mostly discussing the norms constituting the mother role, I once introduced a calculation of how many litres of milk I might have "produced" for my three babies, and found that it must at least amount to 500 litres. While this fact, at the time of publishing, which coincided with the onslaught of postmodernism, got very few comments, maybe now, within a perspective of gift-giving, it may become relevant, again?

I have been especially inspired to think along these lines by reading chapter 10 in Genevieve Vaughan's book *For-Giving* (1997), with the sub-title "Gracias a la Vida". Here she writes: "A theory of knowledge could be developed which identifies knowledge with the gratitude experienced by the individual as the recipient of the gifts given by life, nature, culture and other individuals". In order to develop such a theory of knowledge, in my mind one would have to basically challenge traditional approaches within the various disciplines.

Below, after presenting the central themes of my article, I shall introduce two women scientists who, in my mind, have made some steps in the direction of a new theory of knowledge: geneticist Barbara McKlintock and sociologist Dorothy Smith.

I shall then present some new knowledge about matriarchal societies, presented in African journals, which has some relevance to the question of a gift economy.

A paradigm of life

In a Swedish television program, in which some of the winners of the year 2002 Nobel Prizes within the natural sciences took part, as a final question the participants were asked to state what were their wishes within their respective fields for future scientific development. The participants pointed to various fascinating intra-disciplinary challenges within medicine, chemistry, physics and economics respectively. The biologist, however, said that his most ardent wish was that they should all join in an interdisciplinary effort to try to solve the secret of the phenomenon of life. What his comment discloses is the really astounding fact that with all the progress within the natural sciences about important questions regarding the world around us, life as a phenomenon in itself is still a challenging puzzle.

For me, this served as a kind of revelation which awakened some dormant but very crucial memories: I relived – with extraordinary clarity – the totally unnerving and at the same time totally joyful experience of feeling my first baby stirring inside me. Suddenly I realized that I had never been able to talk about this enormously important moment when I felt that I was carrying a new life, because I had lacked the right words. In those days, back in the fifties, at least in Norwegian culture, to have a baby was a "natural" thing. One was not supposed to get excited about this first sign of the new being, and much less describe it as what it is: a wonder.

A very challenging thought presented by Vaughan is to equate knowledge and gratitude (1997:155). Such insight may be exactly what women need in order to be able to put words to our strongest experiences.

I have started to question whether the natural scientists, while looking for the beginning of life, all the time have been going further and further in dividing matter into ever smaller particles, maybe have started from the wrong end. We have learned from physics that a scientist must dig ever deeper in order to get closer to this "beginning", from molecules to atoms to quarks etc., etc. But given a new approach to knowledge, what about studying the first stirring of life in a foetus?

Somehow, I think that this way of reasoning corresponds to other themes in Genevieve Vaughan's book referred to above (*ibidem*). Among other themes, she writes about how, if we take gift giving seriously, we can perceive apples as round, red apples, which we can eat, not as a collection of atoms. The idea intimated in these remarks may be thought to be related to a discussion in a book about "The Ethic and the Universe"(1997) by the Danish dr. theol. Jakob Wolf. Here the author explains how the natural sciences in the last decades have taught us that when we look around us and see colours, for example, the beautiful, blue summer sky, what "really" happens is that certain light waves hit our retina. Likewise, when we experience a wonderful concert by Beethoven, what "really" happens is that certain sound waves hit our hearing organs. The author's point is that by making us deny that the messages of our senses have anything to do with "reality", and making no embrace this objectified understanding of the world (what the Germans call *Weltanschauung*), this interpretation at the same time makes us come to believe that the world is a neutral place, where all ethical questions are superfluous and irrelevant.

In my view, a new theory of knowledge shall have to challenge some of the crucial ideas of the natural scientists. One of their aims has been to control the forces of nature. We have to accept that by doing this, even if they have had some devastating effects on nature, they have made life on earth infinitely easier for many of us. Most importantly, science has made it possible to eliminate hunger and poverty. At the same time however, scientists have developed ever more dangerous weapons, which today make it possible to end all life on earth.

A new theory of knowledge might have as its aim both to transform and transcend the products of the natural sciences in order to make them into better tools in shaping a world, which may be a good place to live in for all mankind.

Women and a new theory of knowledge

Happily, among important natural scientists and philosophers there are some women who question many of the ideas imbedded in the assumptions about the world that have developed within the natural sciences during the last decades. Evelyn Fox Keller in *Reflections on Gender and Science* (Fox Keller 1985) points to the history of science, and criticizes any claims to universal truth that the various scientists may have, while she argues for a gender-free science. More concretely, she is preoccupied with transcending the androcentric bias in science. In connection with the theme of this article, of special interest is her discussion of the Nobel Price winner, geneticist Barbara McClintock's research. In relation to the phenomenon of life, McClintock argues (in an interview with Fox Keller) that "[…] Nature is characterized by an a priory complexity that vastly exceeds the capacities of the human imagination". Her major criticism of contemporary genetic research is based on what she sees as inadequate humility. "They have the answer ready and they know what they want the material to tell them, so anything it doesn't tell them they […] throw out". Fox Keller gives a gripping description of how McClintock went about her research. In the biography: *A Feeling for the Organism* (Fox Keller 1936), Fox Keller quotes some of McKlintock's sayings:

No two plants are exactly alike [...]. I start with the seedling, and I don't want to leave it. I don't feel I really know the story if I don't watch the plant all the way along. So I know every plant in the field. I know them intimately, and I feel a great pleasure in knowing them.

Her approach is very different from that of male natural scientists, many of whom considered her eccentric and with ideas that made very little sense. However, after 40 years of very important scientific work, she finally became recognized as one of the most significant figures in twentieth century science.

I find two aspects of McKlintock's work especially fascinating. Firstly, she seems to look upon the plants she is investigating in an unusually personal way – as if she cares for them and identifies with them. She doesn't relate to them in the traditionally detached way of male scientists. This approach seems to be an important reason why many of her male colleagues found her strange. Fox Keller, on the other hand, thinks that it is exactly this strong identification with her plants, which made it possible for McKlintock to grasp some of the vast complexity of nature that she writes about. To me, it seems that she is grappling with problems that have to do with the question the above mentioned Nobel Prize winner in biology is proposing, i.e.: "What is life?".

Secondly, and just as crucial: It seems that some of McKlintock's discoveries have to do with Darwin's ideas about random selection. Not being a biologist or geneticist, I may only hint at the possibility that emerges from McKlintock's work: the theory of the survival of the fittest is challenged by McKlintock for being too simplistic.

There are, in my mind, two reasons why this is of importance to our discussion on the Gift Economy. A: In the last decade, within biology, scientists are increasingly explaining the behavioural patterns of human beings within the neo-Darwinist frame of reference, to a degree that for some, the concepts and theories of the social sciences are appearing irrelevant. Any ideas about action and choice seem to disappear along with questions about ethics. "It is all in our genes". According to this view, the idea of the gift is without meaning. B: There is an important affinity between NeoDarwinism and NeoLiberalism, which seems to support the various theories of the latter regarding the "natural" inclination of humans to compete, and the idea that society's interests are best served by arrangements that let the "fittest" survive in the market.

Referring to Genevieve Vaughan's remark about the need for a new type of knowledge, I imagine that Barbara McClintock has made some important steps in this direction in a field which is of great importance regarding the situation of women: She has presented a new idea of what a natural scientist may be like: firstly, not to have an objective and detached attitude towards her/his work, but looking upon her data in a caring and engaged way. And secondly, looking without preconceived ideas about the world, but with a free and open mind.

The everyday world of women

Within another discipline, sociologist Dorothy Smith writes about a feminist sociology of knowledge (Smith 1987, 1990), She wants to investigate a situation known to many women: "The experience of a split relationship to language, of the under nurtured woman's voice outside the 'man's world'". Especially she examines the properties of patriarchal sociology from the standpoint of women's experience. She criticises sociology for not being concerned with "the everyday world", i.e. the world of women in households.

In her various analyses she reveals how sociological concepts and models are developed in order to make sense of men's experience. In the world of male sociologists it is assumed that

[...] the power to act and co-ordinate in a planned and rational manner and to exercise control as an individual over conditions and means is taken for granted. [...] The rational actor choosing and calculating is the abstract model of organisational and bureaucratic man, whose motives, and ego structure are organised by the formal rationality structuring his work role. At work his feelings have no place [...] (Smith1987).

Smith describes how for a long time she struggled within this paradigm of rational action, until she realised that if she wanted to understand the life of women, she would have to break out. She decided that she would try to make use of a Marxist approach, and she started by taking as her point of departure her own lived experience or praxis. She found that characteristically, for women, their daily routines to a great extent "are determined and ordered by processes external to and beyond our everyday world". She began to see her past not so much as a career but as a series of contingencies or accidents, and she realised that 122 this would be a good description of the lives of most women. Even though she had succeeded as an academic, she felt that she had become who she was almost by chance.

However, Dorothy Smith has done more than criticise the male approach to sociology. She describes how together with other women she has worked to change sociology into a tool that lets women speak about themselves and their own experience (*ibidem*). In order to do this, she conducted a very fascinating study of how mothers organise their daily life together with their children in a way that has the intellectual growth of the child as its aim. Smith captures "mothering" in a way that few researchers had done before her. From her research she is able to show that mothering is work. Also, she makes explicit the implicit ways in which school influences the lives of mothers and children, and how in this respect, social class serves to create different patterns in the interaction of mother and child. When reading the account of this project, one becomes very indignant, and angry at the authorities who would not grant her funding for a centre so that she might continue this very important work.

Smith has wanted to create a discourse that can expand women's grasp of their experience and increase the power of their speech by disclosing the relations organising their oppression in their "everyday world". In her work, like Barbara McClintock, she has created new knowledge by challenging the work of male members of her discipline, both through developing a new theoretical approach, and through her research, which has meant opening up an entirely new world, i.e. "the everyday world".

Even though neither of the two women scientists described above has discussed the economy as such, one might imagine that both of them might have felt related to many of the reflections in Vaughan's book (1997) about a gift economy and gift giving, especially those which deal with mothering.

Until now the discussion in this article has been on various aspects and dimensions of women's lives in the Western world. Recently, we are beginning to learn about societies in other parts of the world, and how they are organising women's lives. From this knowledge a new way of understanding motherhood is developing.

A New Paradigm

A Conference on Matriarchies

In Genevieve Vaughan's very interesting report from a conference in Luxembourg in the autumn of 2003 she refers to a discussion about various matriarchal societies, both in prehistory and in the present. She writes:

> The reason I want to write you about it is that if this kind of validation of the existence of matriarchies can be spread, and if the connection between matriarchies and peaceful, abundant and egalitarian ways of living can be made, we can have an alternative "vision" ready for our use, that will help in diminishing the hegemony of patriarchy (Vaughan 2003).

She goes on to underline that she learned from the many presentations is that mothering is the principle of matriarchy, and she lists the values of mothering as being: food and care for all, respect for the other, collective decision making and problem solving. Another important point that was made is that in the history of mankind, patriarchy as a societal system is a derivative, not an originary system.

Vaughan pays much attention to a discussion on the saying: "making the weaker the stronger", that originally came from the Minangkabau people whose society is matriarchal. She wonders about how it might be possible to make mothering stronger, without turning the motherers into dominators, and she reasons that theory might be a useful tool.

Finally she refers to an important discussion on the concepts of equality, reciprocity and exchange. She maintains that among other things the concept of reciprocity contains a dangerous ambiguity because it may disrupt the gift logic, making it seem as if it were really "the same thing" as the exchange logic. This is because giving without getting anything back is one face of exploitation. However it is also the positive basis of the gift. Here, in my opinion, Vaughan touches upon a very important problem, which she has also discussed in her book *For-Giving* (Vaughan 1997). In chapter 3, among other things, she poses a challenging question: "Is Reciprocity Exchange or Turn taking?". In further discussions on the gift giving problematic, I presume that also Marx' maxim about justice may be relevant, in which he argues: "From each according to ability, to each according to need [...]".

Interestingly, at the same time as Genevieve Vaughan introduced the concept of matriarchy into the debate on gift giving, a new journal appeared at the Centre for Women Studies and Gender Research in Bergen. It was *'Jenda', A Journal of Culture and African Women Studies* (2002). From this journal I shall present and discuss two articles. The first one is written by Oyeronke Oyewumi, and is called: "Conceptualizing Gender: The Eurocentric Foundations of Feminist Concepts and the Challenge of African Epistemologies".

Some African perspectives on motherhood

The article opens with a short presentation of the last 500 years, which the author mentions, have been described as the age of modernity. Among a number of historical processes of this age, the author starts by mentioning the Atlantic Slave Trade, the attendant institutions of slavery, and European colonisation of Africa, Asia and Latin America. She goes on to present a number of historical happenings and ends with mentioning that gender and racial categories emerged during this period as two fundamental axes along which people were exploited and societies stratified.

In the next paragraph the author describes how in the modern era the hegemony of Euro/American culture was established throughout the world. Among the many results of this development, one of the most important was how this culture came to influence strongly the production of knowledge about human behaviour, history, societies and cultures. One effect of Eurocentrism is the racialisation of knowledge in that Europe and Europeans become the centre of knowledge and the knowers respectively. Male gender privileges are an essential element in modernity. When trying to comprehend African realities, one must take these facts into account.

The author then goes on to state that her objective is to "Interrogate gender and allied concepts based on African cultural experiences and epistemologies" (Oyewumi 2002: 1). She wants both to make it possible for African research to build on local concerns and interpretations, and at the same time – being well aware of the global system's racism – that African experiences shall be taken seriously when and where general theory-building occurs.

In my opinion, the knowledge that Oyewumi is presenting is of great interest, and it would mean a serious loss to general theory building if it is not brought to the attention of scholars on every continent. For the theme of this article however, I shall have to concentrate on only a small part of her information.

One of her main contentions is that Anglophone/American feminists have used the concepts "woman" and "gender" as universal concepts, overlooking that they are first and foremost socio-cultural constructs. She especially underlines the critique put forward by many African American scholars that in the States there is no way that gender can be considered outside of race and class.

Furthermore, in a very important paragraph Oyewumi argues that feminist concepts are rooted in the nuclear family, and that despite many feminists' maintaining that their goal is to destabilise this institution, it constitutes the very basis of feminist values. All the three main concepts of feminism, Woman, Gender and Sisterhood, emerged from the nuclear family. She then goes on to define the nuclear family, and emphasises that it is gendered, in that as a single-family household it "is centred on a subordinated wife, a patriarchal husband and children". Very important for her argumentation is this sentence: "The structure of the family conceived as having a conjugal unit at the centre lends itself to the promotion of gender as a natural and inevitable category because within this family there are no cross-cutting categories devoid of it" (ivi: 2). She then points to patterns within African families, where the most important category is seniority. Also she argues that many of the concepts regarding family members which in Western social science often are gendered, like husband-wife, sister-brother, within African discourse are gender neutral, and she points to concepts like spouses and siblings.

Then Oyewumi presents her central theme: "The nuclear family, however is a specifically Euro/American form, it is not universal" (ivi: 3). And in spite of all the various agencies and organisations striving to introduce and promote it, it remains an alien form in Africa.

It is truly fascinating, but also in a way alarming, to follow her line of discussion in which she puts forward her analysis of the Western conception of "wife". She argues that when methodologically, the unit of analysis is the nuclear family household, then theoretically such a practice reduces woman to wife. "The woman at the heart of feminist theory, the wife, never gets out of the household. Like a snail she carries the house around with her" (ivi: 3).

Oyewumi argues that it follows from this that [...] "There seem to be no understanding of the role of mother independent of her sexual ties to a father. Mothers are first and foremost wives" (ivi: 3). She contrasts this reasoning to the African one by introducing the concept "single mother", which from an African point of view is an oxymoron, or an impossibility. Motherhood in African, as in most cultures, is defined as a relationship between a woman and her child/children. From this contention, Oyewumi develops a very illuminating discussion on what it means in American/European culture regarding the understanding of the gendered division of labour, that woman is to be understood as synonymous with wife. She reasons that this may explain why procreation and lactation in the gender literature (both traditional and feminist) are usually presented as part of the sexual division of labour. "Marital coupling is thus constituted as the base of societal division of labour" (ivi: 4). In my opinion, Oyewumi to a certain extent presents an explanation of why these practices, so fundamental for women, i e. giving birth to and nurturing one's baby, have not been considered topics for theoretical analysis from a feminist standpoint.

In the final paragraphs of Oyewumi's article, the author describes various African family patterns which serve to make us aware of the great possibility for flexibility concerning family relationship that exists throughout the world. Running through her descriptions from many African cultures is the importance of the tie between mother and child. One of her conclusions is that a central challenge to African gender studies is the difficulty of applying feminist concepts to understand African realities. This is due to the incommensurability of social categories and institutions. For the problems raised in this article, it is especially important that Oyewumi challenges Western feminist concepts about woman and mother. Furthermore, even more important is that as a consequence of her knowledge of African family patterns, she challenges Western feminist thinking regarding the universality of women's oppression.

The second article is written by the Danish sociologist Signe Arnfred, who has for many years worked in Africa. It is titled: "Simone de Beauvoir in Africa: Woman=The Second Sex? Issues of African Feminist Thought". Arnfred outlines the purpose of her article by stating: "The point is to open the mind to different ways of thinking about gender [....]. Freeing ourselves from old mindsets will allow us to envision new kinds of gender relations as we look forward to the future – both the future of Africa and the future of ourselves as Western (men and) women" (Arnfred 2002: 1). The old mindset that she wants to free us from is the idea of "woman as the other". And the point of doing this "is to open the imagination for different and more liveable feminist futures than the ones now on offer, which are embedded in the notions of modernity and development" (ivi: 1). I shall return to this point in my discussion on how to understand progress within a women's perspective.

I consider Arnfred's article to be of major importance for feminist discourse. She is taking it upon herself to deconstruct Simone de Beauvoir's famous work on women as the second sex. She argues that she does this because in the last years this work has again become important in feminist discourse, and this she finds most undue. Arnfred underlines that Beauvoir's work in 1949 was both brave and pioneering, but now, fifty years later, it is time to question from which context and with which concepts she developed her analysis. Doing this, we must take into account that very much has happened during these fifty years, both in the world and in feminist thought. Arnfred especially points to the importance of non-Western thinking becoming known in various milieus in the West. For my purpose, I shall concentrate on those parts of the article most relevant to our understanding of motherhood.

For Arnfred, it is an aim to show that Simone de Beauvoir is firmly rooted in the modern, and that she thinks that women's chance to become emancipated has mainly to do with getting control over procreation and becoming economically independent. Moreover, women must strive for transcendence, which according to de Beauvoir is "all that is fun and

126

worthwhile, creative, productive and essentially human" and "distinguishes humans from animals as culture from nature" (ivi: 3). Here she is influenced by Jean-Paul Sartre, and both of them see transcendence as inherently male. Then, for women, to become more like men means becoming emancipated.

The opposite of transcendence is immanence, which de Beauvoir describes as "passivity and repetition, the drudgery of daily housework in which giving birth, breastfeeding and motherhood are included" (ivi: 3). Important in this connection is de Beauvoir's view that having, and taking care of children are not to be considered as activities because no project is involved. They are to be looked upon as natural functions. A woman submits passively to these tasks, and in no way may she find in them "[...] a lofty affirmation of her existence" (ivi: 4). Regarding the degree to which de Beauvoir identifies with masculine ideology, and the value hierarchy of male modernity, one quotation is especially illuminating: "It is not in giving birth but in risking life that man is raised above the animal; that is why superiority has been accorded not to the sex that brings forth but to that which kills" (ivi: 4). Within the perspective of this article, it is difficult to understand how this argument could be accepted, or at least not severely criticised.

Arnfred also presents other parts of de Beauvoir's work, and discusses among others the one in which she has presented her famous dictum: "one is not born but rather becomes a woman" (ivi: 4). To Arnfred it appears that as to this opinion, her work is in contradiction with itself: de Beauvoir both believes and demonstrates that the conditions of women are socially determined. But all through her work it appears that women are slaves of their bodies, and there is always this conflict between women's own interests and the reproductive forces.

In the middle of her article, Arnfred sums up three main themes within mainstream modern thinking on gender: "a, Man is posed as subject and woman as other. b, Development is conceived as a unilinear move from 'tradition' towards 'modernity' – the measure for achievement being the Western world. c, Third world women are conceived of as subordinated and oppressed" (ivi: 7). In order to discuss these theses, Arnfred introduces concepts and lines of thinking which she considers especially important in African feminist literature. For her it is crucial that African feminist thinkers refuse to see woman as "other", and they deny that in their own societies the patterns of behaviour in any way support such ideas.

In order to make African family life understandable to feminists from other parts of the world, it is important to get some knowledge about kinship terminology. Here I shall only mention a few examples: it is possible to state that often in matrilineal societies there are no fathers and no mothers i.e. there are no words or concepts comparable to those developed in our societies in the West, and patterns of parenting are different. An important fact to bear in mind is that often in these societies seniority is more important than gender.

Arnfred quotes the author of the article I have referred to above, Oyewumi, and emphasises the fact that in Africa, the most crucial position of a woman is that of mother. Arnfred also mentions that in part of her work, Oyewumi has introduced the concept "the patriarchalising gaze" in order to warn against influence from Western social science. This gaze invents – women as other –, and introduces what she calls "body-reasoning" where "the cultural logic [...] is based on an ideology of biological determinism". She argues that a mind/body hierarchy is deeply embedded in Western thinking. Here I find it relevant to quote Descartes' maxim "I think, therefore I am".

Arnfred then goes on to present themes from another African author, Ifi Amadiume (1987). One key point of this social anthropologist's work is her analysis of power in African society. She argues that many societal positions may be taken up by either man or woman, and maintains that there is: "in African gender systems a flexibility which allows neuter construct for men and women to share roles and status" (ivi: 10). She strongly underlines that power is not masculine per se.

Arnfred has a very interesting paragraph on motherhood. Based on Amadiume's research she argues that the structural status of motherhood in Africa is very different from that in Europe. She goes on to explain this by outlining two systems that Amadiume has studied in the Nnoby society, the female mother focused, matricentric unit, and the male focused, ancestral house. These systems co-exist, and if one tries to understand the relationship between them by introducing a patriarchal paradigm, one might lose important aspects of how this society functions.

Amadiume refers to her study in which she finds that "[...] the traditional power of African women had an economic and ideological basis, and derived from the sacred and almost divine importance accorded to motherhood" (ivi: 11). This means that motherhood is in itself empowering. Amadiume realises that "the very thought of women's power being based on the logic of motherhood has proved offensive to many Western feminists" (ivi: 11). She argues that it is easy to see why this is so since in the European system, wifehood and motherhood represented a means of enslavement for women.

In her work it is important for Amadiume to raise awareness of the often implicit patriarchal paradigm in the social sciences. She is deeply engaged in crafting concepts that are fitted to deal with motherhood – not abstract motherhood – but with the concrete sociological phenomenon of "the mother-focused, matri-centric unit." Arnfred explains how Amadiume introduces the term "matriarchy" in order to strengthen the awareness of the centrality of motherhood. She wants to make "the matriarchy paradigm" into a useful concept. In her writing about matriarchy, she refers to the concept's long and complicated history in European social science. She maintains that she is not interested in creating "a total rule governing a society", but discusses how in her studies of the Nnobi society, as mentioned above, it appears that the female mother-focused, matricentric unit, and the male- focused ancestral house coexist. Amadiume argues that the matricentric unit is a female gendered, paradigmatical cultural construct, which goes against the generalising theory that man is culture and woman is nature.

In Vaughan's letter from the conference on matriarchy mentioned above (Vaughan 2003), she refers to an article written by the German social anthropologist Heide G. Abendroth (now in this volume) "Matriarchal Society: Definition and Theory". Here Abendroth seems to be interested in constructing the type of "total rule governing a society", that Amadiume seeks to avoid, and lists 4 criteria for such a society. In the future discussion on gift economy, it may be productive to compare these two somewhat different approaches to matriarchy.

In her concluding remarks, Arnfred comments that she has enjoyed presenting these two brave feminist scholars "who have the courage to go against established power structures in feminist thought". But more importantly she looks at these African contributions as a source of inspiration for Western feminists to think differently about gender. Finally – and this is a crucial point – she has learned through the African perspective that Western patriarchal thought has managed to naturalise and trivialise motherhood to an appalling degree, and that very little protest has come from the feminist camp.

Regarding the discourse on motherhood in what Arnfred defines as the feminist camp, some interesting contributions have come from France, where especially Julia Kristeva has worked with the different images of "the mother" and of "woman" found in Greek and Christian tradition (Kristeva 1989). In both places the story is deeply ambiguous. In Christianity, on one hand we have woman as virgin in man's conscious thought, on the other hand woman as whore in man's unconscious thought. This woman is capable of feeling "*jouissance*". Kristeva argues that between these two one finds the mother, and that this is the virgin-mother. One of Kristeva's main contentions is that the woman's body, which is capable of feeling "*jouissance*", can have nothing to do with the mother.

In the US, two feminist theorists who have had great influence on feminist thinking in the Nordic countries, Nancy Chodorow and Carol Gilligan, have contributed to the discourse on motherhood in a somewhat different way. Chodorow has been especially interested in the mother's influence on the identity development of her son and daughter respectively (Chodorow 1978), while Gilligan has studied differences in girls' and boys' approach to ethical questions, especially regarding relationship to the other (Gilligan 1982). While these various contributions to our understanding of motherhood in Western feminist thought are important, they are all – though in somewhat different ways – engaged in a patriarchal discourse in that they are in one way or another involved in a discussion with Freud and his followers, to a great degree on Freudian premises.

Regarding arguing for the gift paradigm, it shall become necessary to challenge the fundamental ideas of this discourse if we want to tear away from the tendency towards the trivialization and naturalisation of motherhood. In doing this, we shall have to question one of the most cherished ideas of our Western culture, i.e. that modernity means enlightenment and progress.

The gift economy and the idea of modernity

To my mind, one of the most illuminating aspects of Oyeronke Oyewumi's article (2002) is her analysis of the last 500 years, which she defines as the modern epoch of the Western world. She maintains that from an African perspective, both gender and racial categories emerged during this epoch along with exploitation and stratification based on these two fundamental axes. Arnfred goes further in her deconstruction of one of the crucial idea of modern social science, i.e. that modernity has offered more liveable futures for women than have non-Western or pre-modern societies. Drawing on her experience from working for several years in Mozambique, she emphasises that modernity has many faces, but lists three of its basic assumptions: "1, a human being is a man, and the male position is believed to be gender-neutral. 2, In this context development has been a unilinear motion from tradition to modernity with the Western 'developed world' serving as the model for achievement.

3, African and third world women are being particularly oppressed, and are hopefully and gratefully awaiting the blessings of modernity".

Before elaborating further on the relationship between modernity and motherhood, I shall, because I find that there are certain similar traits, comment shortly on how some important male sociologists have evaluated tendencies within the epoch we call modernity. Already at the beginning of the 20th century, Max Weber was warning against certain development trends following the capitalist bureaucratisation of the world (Weber 1920). He used very colourful expressions, writing about demystification (*entzauberung*) of the world, and the iron cage of rationality. Nearly a century later the Polish-British sociologist Zygmunt Bauman, while analysing the development in Nazi-Germany in order to try to understand how the phenomenon of the Holocaust could be possible, intimates that typical aspects of late modernity are lack of social responsibility and empathy (Bauman 1998). Like Weber, he blames these development trends on tendencies within capitalist bureaucratisation where the aim of the civilising process is to foster rationality. Bauman maintains that this modern rationality in a way "frees" people when it comes to morality. For the purpose of this article, his analysis of sociology, and his focusing on the conceptualisation in this discipline of what it means to be human are of great interest. Bauman emphasises that the idea of "the other" is lacking in sociology at the same time as he argues that "To be with others" and "Responsibility for the other" are basic traits in human existence and human subjectivity. He qualifies what he means by referring to Martin Buber's ideas about how we may relate to other people as either "you" or "it" (Buber 1958).

Arnfred's message to women is that it is imperative to analyse how the strengthening of male gendered privileges have been the goal of most of the political endeavours in modernity, and how these goals have been reached to a great extent at the cost of women. Regarding modernity's idea of a good life for women, let us take as our point of departure the extracts of the writings of Simone de Beauvoir quoted above. From them it appears as obvious that for a woman, the best way to create a good life for herself is to get control over procreation and becoming economically independent. To become a mother is to be caught in the drudgery of daily housework, including various aspects of motherhood. In other words, if women can model their lives more or less along the same lines as men, they will be successful.

One may ask by what standards this type of woman is being measured and found to be successful? The importance of introducing the gift paradigm is, among other things, that it renders a new model for interpreting the way we lead our lives, and what will be the consequences of latter day development trends within modernity. Looking at Dorothy Smith's description of "the rational actor" one gets the impression of a person in a strait-jacket. Recently, when reading or looking at many successful women's descriptions in newspapers, magazines, TV discussions etc. of "life on the job", the feeling of stress becomes overwhelming. Lately, one of the strongest arguments I have ever heard against the way business firms are organising work was presented in a TV interview by a women leader: "They do not take into consideration that the workers have children. In our society, there is little understanding of the necessity of having children at all".

From another angle the situation concerning motherhood is also threatened by some alarming trends. It seems that the possibility of cloning ones babies is coming within reach.

We already have the technology available to program our babies; we may rent women who will bear our babies, women may sell their eggs at a high price in the market; young women are taught to look like young boys: tall, thin, flat stomach and narrow hips etc etc.

It seems that Aldous Huxley's famous and coldly frightening future fantasy epos, "Brave New World", is no longer to be considered a wild nightmare (Huxley 1932). It is of importance to remember that the ugliest and most feared word in his Utopia was "mother". There was absolutely no place for the feelings between mothers and children in the thoroughly commercialised society Huxley imagined. The message is that in this society there is no room for warm feelings since they cannot be controlled. The contrast between Huxley's horror picture of a future society and the image of a matriarchal society evoked by Genevieve Vaughan in her article in this book is dramatic indeed.

Society, gift giving and motherhood

Interestingly, in France, a group built around the studies of social anthropologist Marcel Mauss works with some of the same ideas of gift giving as Vaughan, being inspired both by Marxist thought and by research among Kwakiutl Indians in British Columbia. A main difference between this group's approach and that of Vaughan, however, is that the concept of motherhood doesn't seem to have influenced the thinking of Marcel Mauss or that of his followers. It may be productive to learn more about their reflections, but it seems that to concentrate on gift giving from the perspective of motherhood is infinitely more promising, but at the same time also more challenging.

We are socialised within the patriarchal paradigm to a degree that is difficult to comprehend. In order to break out, we shall need courage because we shall have to learn to enter theoretically totally new territory, while at the same time there will be a strong temptation to use the familiar, old "rational" maps. At the same time, however, to many of us it may become a great joy to take into consideration what this new territory has to offer regarding new knowledge. Looking at Genevieve Vaughan's listing of the values of mothering mentioned in the Conference on Matriarchies as being: food and care for all, respect for the other and collective decision making and problem solving, the fascinating thing is that it sounds at the same time both new – regarding theory making – and well known regarding experience. I think we are lucky in that to join these to theory and experience, into new knowledge about gift giving, the job shall be easier with the help of our African feminist sisters.

References

Abendroth, Heide Gottner. "Matriarchal Society: Definition and Theory"(this volume).
Amadiume, Ifi (1997). *Reinventing Africa. Matriarchy, Religion and Culture*, Zed Books, London.
Arnfred, Signe (2002). "Simone de Beauvoir in Africa: Woman = The Second Sex? Issues of African feminist thought", *Jenda: A Journal of Culture and African Women Studies*, 2, 1.

Bauman, Zygmunt (1999). *Modernity and the Holocaust*, Polity Press, Cambridge.

de Beauvoir, Simone (1997 [1949]). *The Second Sex, Vintage Classics*, New York.

Buber, Martin (1958). *Ich und Du (I and Thou)*, Verlag Lambert Schneider, Heidelberg.

Chodorow, Nancy (1978). *The Reproduction of Mothering: Psychoanalysis and the Sociology of Gender*, University of California Press, Berkeley.

Gilligan, Carol (1982). *In a Different Voice*, Harvard University Press, Cambridge, Mass.

Huxley, Aldous (1958 [1932]). *Brave New World*, Chatto and Windus, London.

Keller, Evelyn Fox (1983*). A Feeling for the Organism. The Life and Work of Barbara McClintock*, W.H. Freeman and Company, New York.

— (1985). *Reflections on Gender and Science*, Yale University Press, New Haven and London.

Oyewumi, Oyeronke (2002). "Conceptualising Gender: The Eurocentric Foundation of Feminist Concepts and the Challenge of African Epistemologies", *Jenda: A Journal of Culture and African Women Studies*, vol. 2, 1.

Parsons, Talcott (1951). *The Social System*, The Free Press, Glencoe, Illinois.

Smith, Dorothy (1987). *The Everyday World as Problematic, A Feminist Sociology*, North Eastern University Press, Boston.

— (1990). *The Conceptual Practices of Power A Feminist Sociology of Knowledge*, North Eastern University Press, Boston.

Sørensen, Bjørg Aase (1982). "Ansvarsrasjonalitet" (Responsible Rationality), in H. Holter (ed.), *Kvinner i Fellesskap (Women in Collectivities)*, Oslo University Press, Oslo.

Vaughan, Genevieve (1997). *For-Giving, A Feminist Criticism of Exchange*, Plain View Press, Austin.

— (2003). "Matriarchy Conference report" (Personal communication).

Ve, Hildur (1992). "Sosiologi og forståelse av kjønn" (Sociology and Conceptualisations of Gender), in Taksdal A. and K. Widerberg (eds.), *Forståelser av kjønn i samfunnsvitenskapenes fag og kvinneforskning (Conceptualisations of gender in the subjects and women's research in the social sciences)*, ad Notam Gyldendal A/S.

Weber, Max (1947 [1920]). *The Theory of Social and Economic Organization* (Parts of Wissenschaft und Gesellschaft), New York.

Wolf, Jakob (1997). *Etikken & Universet (Ethics and the Universe)*, Forlaget ANIS, De-1820, Frederiksberg C.

Wærness, Kari (1980). "Kvinners omsorgsarbeid i den ulønnede produksjonen" (Women's caring work in unpaid prduction), in Halvorsen, K. (ed.), Arbeid og sysselsetting foran 80åra (Work and employment before the 80's), Pax, Oslo.

The Gift

how light spins out of stars
and falls into the ravenous caw of life,
the way a parent feeds a child, coaches children's soccer,
runs for office, works for the Sierra Club,
a Dispute Resolution Center –
the way one finds the quiet revolution of a Quaker meeting,
the free salvation of a twelve step program,
social action follows need.

Women, like the essential spin of gravity,
form in circles, say our names, name
our expertise, no one greater than the other, we come –
not for profit, or out of fear, but to create relationship,
community, to become the change we seek.
This is how we do things – a circle, not a ladder,
a seed, not a patent, many truths instead of one.

Our truths are diverse, contradictory, and non-linear.
One has the gift of science, one of art, one of native plants,
one organized the World Courts of Women,
one says the million people who marched peacefully
through the open air museum of Florence
demanded corporate accountability.
There is a better way.
The gift informs it.

But it's been plundered –
See how the resource gifts of Africa,
for instance, or South America

by limited liability giant corporations.
Half the labor gifts of the world, women's work,
are unpaid, marginalized, or invisible,
even in movements for social change –
which is unfortunate, because
there is a better
way and women are the map of it.

We rise as if from sleep.
Have you noticed how many people
know the logic of the warrior/robber barons is false?

How often does a parent, seeing children squabble,
encourage them to kill each other? For profit?

There is a better way
and women are the map of it.

Introduction

Throughout history, the providers of nursing and caring have been female. Women have been married, and persuaded or forced to adopt the role of a nurse and a carer. The power of authority has been wielded by the patriarchy, appealing to tradition, natural disposition or the "law of God". The few women who have refused subordination have been labeled as "unnatural" (Noddings 2001). Nursing and caring have been part of the necessary but anonymous domain of society, which in spite of its obvious lack of value has been considered both an obligation and a source of satisfaction. Most women still work in such fields, and most holders of such occupations are female. Are women still working subordinate to authority? Is acquiescence the sole justification of nursing and caring?

I will approach the justifiability of nursing and caring from the frame of reference of Max Weber's (1864-1920) classical definition of rationality of action. I will analyze, from a feminist perspective, the applicability of both Weber's thinking and the related concept of responsible rationality as explanations of the foundation of nursing and care.

Max Weber and instrumental rationality

According to Max Weber (1978 [1904-1905]), the actions of Western people are characterized by instrumental rationality. This means that maximally effective means are used to reach the goals (Niiniluoto 2001). According to Weber, the goal of Western[3] societal action is continuously and endlessly increasing affluence. One of the major factors contributing to this is the Protestant ethic. The Protestant ethic lays the foundation for western instrumental rationality and its manifestation in social interaction.

Religion at the background of western rationality

According to Weber, all religions in the world have their religious motives, which do not only affect religious actions, but also influence the actions of the economic world within the religion's sphere of influence. Each economic system is thus consistently oriented towards certain religious values. In the Western countries, the values of Christianity prevail (Hietaniemi 1987: 44, Weber 1978).

In order to understand the Protestant ethic and Western rationality, according to Weber, we must understand the difference between religion and magic. Magical thinking is only possible in a one-level world. Religion, on the other hand, is divided into a "background world" (*Hinterwelt*) and a visible or manifest world. The manifest world conceals behind it the background world, where religious actions take place. The religious actions taking place in the background world define both our relations to the manifest world and the valuation of things within the manifest world.

According to Weber, the reciprocity between the background and manifest worlds can be presented as two ideal models. In Asian religions, for example, the human being is a container of divinity. The person must be filled with divinity and get rid of evil by becoming part of the prevailing cosmic order and, hence, the divine. In Europe and the Near East, on the other hand, divinity is something personal and distinct from the evil world. The human being in the world is God's tool. Weber points out that the Judeo-Christian faith in salvation was the first pronouncement of a God radically separate from the world. This God is as far from the world as possible, on a high mountain or in heaven. He rules as a personal power and orders people to make the world accord with his ethical principles. The tension between the world and God is most consistent in Puritanism: humans are alone in front of the mighty and hidden God, who poses quite impossible demands upon them. For a Judeo-Christian, the world is merely a means of salvation. For a Puritan, the world is a tool just as, for God, the Puritan is a tool. This explains Weber's practice of life: adequately capitalistic actions precede the rise of capitalism.

The fact that the background and manifest worlds are so sharply demarcated in Europe and the Near East has two paradoxical consequences. Firstly, rationalization (*Versachlichung*) of the world occurs: the world begins to operate in accordance with its own logic, and all things become instrumentalized. This ultimately leads to secularization and the Western process of rationalization. Secondly, the demarcation also has paradoxical consequences for working ethics. The goal of Puritanism was to withdraw from the world and to practise ascetic frugality, but the hard-working and frugal Puritan ended up accumulating capital, which, in the long run, made the world much more secular than the papal worldliness originally opposed by Protestantism (*ibidem*).

Western instrumental rationality

Modern capitalism was thus considered by Weber as one particular manifestation of Western rationality. Rationality is not a feature unique to Western culture. Still, the Western countries differ crucially from the Eastern countries in terms of which aspects of life are rationalized and in what direction (Gronow & Töttö 1996). According to Weber, western rationality is reflected in market behaviour, the law, administration and professional ethics. By market behaviour, Weber refers to the tendency of even the law and institutions to promote computability and efficiency. At the same time, the possibilities of steering the economy on grounds other than mere efficiency diminish: human actions are guided by instrumentality and speculation. This eliminates the possibility of fostering substantial types of economy that would aim to satisfy collective needs. The legal system, in turn, encourages actions parallel to market behaviour. This means that appreciation of content is completely alien to the administration of justice, and cases are settled with strict abstract and formal rules. In this way, Western rationality becomes alienated from the principles of substantial justice (Hietaniemi 1987, Gronow & Töttö 1996).

Increasing rationalization results in growing administrative bureaucracy; matters are solved in line with formal judicial rules, and practices based on the "ethics of fraternity"are inapplicable. The ultimate manifestation of Western rationality is professional ethics. Professional ethics is a religious impulse of Protestant asceticism. Professional ethics brings market behaviour, justice and bureaucracy into practice. Work becomes an end in itself (Weber 1978, Hietaniemi 1987, Gronow & Töttö 1996).

According to Weber, non-rational actions remain outside instrumental rationality. He describes non-rational actions in terms of traditional, affective and value-rational actions. Weber points out that traditional rational action resembles reactive imitation or blind repetition: traditional action is based on uncritical, internalized habits. Affective rational action is guided by emotional states and rarely involves conscious reactions. Value-rational action is oriented by absolute value goals of, for example, aesthetic, ethical and religious actions. A certain line of action must be followed regardless of all consequences. Value-rational actions are more systematic and consistent than affect-driven actions. They comply with the orders and demands posed by the actors to themselves (Weber 1978, Gronow & Töttö 1996).

According to Weber, however, the ideal type of social action is goal-rational action. It prioritizes the optimally effective choice of tools to reach any goal. This means that both objects and expectations concerning other people's behaviour are used as prerequisites or means to attain a certain rationally desirable outcome or an intentional personal goal. The climax of goal-rational thinking is monetary cost-benefit analysis based on a comparison of quantitative costs and benefits (*ibidem*).

Weber's constraints

According to Nätkin (1986: 156), the only relevant criterion of action in Weber's definitions is the maximization of personal benefit. This rationality of modern business is pivotally based on resource planning, calculation of financial resources and, specifically, male power (Ve 1994: 44). Such limited rationality is actually only materialized in public institutions consisting of male citizens. It inevitably defines women's actions as being part of the private domain, or family life. Private action is a necessary prerequisite for public life, although it fails to obey the same laws of rationality as public life (Nätkin 1986: 160).

Weber's analysis ignores the role of work outside the public economy because it does not fit the definition of rationality (Ve 1994: 44). The values of capitalism based on Western ra-

137

tionality do not include nursing and care, which focus on persons and interpersonal relations. When working with people, we cannot talk about efficiency or productivity, and the principle of profit-making free trade cannot be applied to nursing and care (Held 2002, Nelson & England 2002). As Hietaniemi (1987: 43) pointed out, in Weber's thinking "caritas" and modern rationality are just as incompatible as fire and water.

When considering the premises of Weber's definitions of action, we must also allow for the temporal distance. Weber wrote his books at the turn of the 19th century, when the first signs of the recognition of women and women's actions and work were barely visible. Weber himself, however, was not aware of these signs, but considered women and the work done by women quite invisible and insignificant. Weber's subject was man: "a man of honour", "an honest man" and "a business associate". Still, the book also contains verbal imagery related to women. According to Weber, "money is of the prolific" and "its offspring can beget more" (Weber 1978: 49-50.) Money is hence gendered. Money is a means of exchange, it changes hands, and it is the most instrumental instrument – and female. Weber also concludes that the modern organization of capitalist enterprises would not have been possible without accountancy and the differentiation of the household from the company. Having thus set apart housework, Weber continues to advocate rationality as a basis of action merely as one dimension of economic life (Weber 1978).

Responsible rationality

According to Nätkin (1986), however, underlying reasons for action can also be approached from perspectives other than instrumental rationality. The term "responsible rationality" (*omsorgsrasjonalitet*) proposed by Norwegian sociologists refers to action justified by conscious responsibility. Such action maintains and sustains, and its consequences and significance are recognized widely and over long time spans.

According to Ve (1994: 46-47), responsible rationality differs from western instrumental rationality even in its view of humanity. Western instrumental rationality views human beings as means to maximize profit. In responsible rationality, the human being is an authentic subject and a goal in him/herself. The human being's intrinsic value characterizes interpersonal relations in both the private and the public domain. Interpersonal relations are unique and cannot be exchanged or replaced by other interpersonal relations. In actions motivated by responsible rationality, the actors try to take into account totality and continuity, while goal-rational action focuses on partial accomplishments. Responsible rationality is interested in other people's wellbeing and the consequences of one's actions and activities. It includes responsibility for the consequences of one's actions and willingness to modify one's behaviour in view of its possible consequences. Acceptance of unilaterality (non-reciprocity) is also central to responsible rationality (see also Meyer 1986).

The ways of gaining knowledge by instrumental and responsible rational actions are also different. The knowledge desirable from the viewpoint of instrumental rationality is objective and procured with the best scientific methods. From the viewpoint of responsible rationality, theoretical knowledge is important and essential, but practical knowledge is still

138

the priority. In responsible rationality, actions gain depth and significance through tacit knowledge based on trust, understanding or experience (Ve 1994).

In Ve's view the types of rationality shown by women and men are not biologically determined, but socially constructed, gender differences. She believes the actions of women have been restricted to nursing and caring, and their experiences have hence reflected this reality. Since experience is of crucial importance, the gendered division of tasks has merely enhanced the difference between the experiences of women and men and hence also the difference in what is called rationality. All in all, instrumental western rationality is specifically a manifestation of male rationality.

According to Meyer (1986: 150), caring actors do not only produce and reproduce concrete care, but also social relations and the reciprocal ability to grow and renew. Caring is not merely maintenance of reproductive resources, but also a mode of interpersonal, social communality. Caring thus has the same potential to cross boundaries as does any social relationship. Meyer further underlines the special feature that care is based on personal interpersonal bonds. It consists of reciprocal giving and taking between social actors. In Nätkin's (1986: 157) opinion also, responsible rationality combines the different aspects of social life. It blurs the line between work and other social interaction. Responsible rationality as the underlying justification of work implicitly includes a sense of the importance, justification and moral obligation of work.

Responsible rationality also prefers to view things as both-and instead of either-or. This helps to avoid extreme and absolute alternatives. Instead, solutions which are satisfactory from the holistic viewpoint are sought. Responsible rationality is capable of empathy, reciprocity and self-reflection. It also involves avoidance of risks and a sense of responsibility. Näre and Lähteenmaa (1992) invite attention to the relationship between responsible rationality and altruism. They believe it is possible to differentiate between responsible rationality and altruism, which they call altruistic individuality. According to Näre and Lähteenmaa, altruism is close to responsible rationality, but highlights the recognition of others, even at the cost of one's own wellbeing.

Responsible rationality has broken out of the straitjacket of gendered thinking. Women as nurses and carers have been considered subordinate to authoritarian expectations and norms, not social actors capable of reasoning, choosing and assuming responsibility for their actions. According to Ve (1994), rational responsibility also deals in a positive way with the bonding of women with other people: for a person with responsible rationality, people are really subjects who cannot be considered mere instruments to maximize one's benefit. As Ve points out, female researchers have moved a *good* distance away from Weber's typology.

The tottering foundation of the patriarchy

Genevieve Vaughan (1997: 23, 28) views critically the entire foundation of Western rationality. According to Vaughan, Western rationality is patriarchal. Rationality presently consists of the patriarchal domination of the global economy by white men, whose activities are enabled by white women, who do the nursing and caring and all other tasks that are not part of the patriarchy. According to Vaughan, the self-justified actions of patriarchal Western capitalism are questionable. She believes that the Western rationality-based capitalism involves distortions and subordination, which can be approached through the concepts of exchange and giving.

Vaughan believes that western rationality and capitalism are based on profit-oriented exchange: one gives in order to get something in exchange. In exchange, givers use other people's needs and their satisfaction as means to satisfy their own needs, and this is considered by Patriarchy as intrinsic to humanity. Exchange is pivotally based on speculation and profit, self-centred and ego-oriented. According to Vaughan, however, exchange is not the characteristic human way to act, but giving is more primary. Giving consists of responding to another person's needs. According to Vaughan, freedom to respond to needs is a matter of quality rather than quantity: no effort is made to quantify or control the giving. Giving is a quality that cannot be constrained. Because giving is qualitative, it has not been conceived of as the basic factor underlying interpersonal relations. The dimension of giving is present in all people and in all domains of social actions, but it is not easily seen because it is difficult to measure and define. The process of responding to needs establishes a bond between the giver and the receiver. This bond is unique and involves two subjects: the actions of recognizing a person's needs and responding to them affect both the giver and the receiver (Vaughan 1997: 30-34).

Discussion

If we use the Weberian frame of reference, the legitimacy of nursing and caring ranges through a spectrum from non-existence to altruism. Weber does not acknowledge "caritas" as a justifiable or rational activity. Responsible rationality labels nursing and caring as a conscious choice, which involves deliberate, selective responsibility. When we use the concept of responsible rationality, we accept "rationality" as a word, but assign to it a meaning notably different from Weberian instrumental rationality. Still, the basis remains rooted in the ideal of patriarchal rationality. Altruism as a foundation of nursing and caring consists of unselfishness, benevolence, sacrifice and charity. Underlying that is an attempt, or ethical imperative to improve the welfare of others. Altruistic individualism, in its extreme form, verges on martyrdom.

Vaughanian thinking, however, does not accept the approach based exclusively on patriarchal terms. Seen from this viewpoint, nursing and caring consist of "mothering" that is parallel to responsible rationality, non-gendered and present in all domains of life. It is conscious, responsible and aware of long-term consequences. Nursing and caring are holistic and interested in others.

From Vaughan's viewpoint, it is not intrinsically important whether nursing and caring are defined as rational or non-rational. The more interesting issue is to analyze the logic of the action. The "reciprocity" of responsible rationality can be specified from this perspective: nursing and caring are not *symmetrically* reciprocal. This means that their reciprocity is not based on patriarchal exchange of instrumental rationality, but on qualitative giving. This is not, however, altruism in the sense that the giving would require one to sacrifice one's own person. What is given in nursing and caring is not immediately returned, but may be given further to a second or third person or possibly even to someone quite unknown to the carer.

Western instrumental rationality would naturally also instrumentalize nursing and caring. The instruments have included the Son, bread, wine, the woman and one's fellows as well as money and machines. The most important thing, however, is that it is not even desirable to bring the giving in nursing and caring anywhere close to the concept of exchange of instrumental rationality. Firstly, the giving in nursing and caring is qualitative and therefore difficult to define with the concepts of exchange. Secondly, the giving in nursing and caring pertains to human beings and human values, which is incompatible with instrumental thinking. Thirdly, nursing and caring do not, generally speaking, aim to quantify their practices. Maybe Weber was perceptive enough to anticipate this: caritas is not rational as the kind of patriarchal ideal he considered it to be.

There is, however, some parallelism between Weber's and Vaughan's thinking. In the Weberian framework, the gift would be equally desirable for giving would "beget". The "reproduction" of exchange based on Weber's instrumental rationality takes place between the parties to the exchange A and B: A gives something to B and expects B to give the same or preferably even more in exchange, i.e. A expects his giving to "reproduce". In Vaughanian thinking, "reproduction" is equally desirable, but in a different sense. "Reproduction" takes place away from the giver, and the giver is not necessarily even aware of this "reproduction". Giving is going on. Therefore, nursing and caring are not an instance of exchange based on patriarchal instrumental rationality.

References

Gilligan, Carol (1982). *In a different voice: Psychological theory and women's development*, Harvard University Press, Cambridge, Massachusetts.

Gronow J. & Töttö P. (1996). "Max Weber – kapitalismi, byrokratia ja länsimainen rationaalisuus", Gronow J., Noro A. & Töttö P. (eds.), *Sosiologian klassikot*, Tammer-Paino Oy, Tampere.

Held, Virginia (2002). "Care and the Extension of Markets", *Hypatia* 17 (2), pp. 19-33.

Hietaniemi T. (1987). "Uskonto maailmanhistoriallisen rationalisoitumisprosessin kätilönä. Weberin uskonnonhistorian ajankohtaisuudesta", in Hietaniemi T. (ed.), *Aiheita Weberistä*, Tutkijaliitto, Gummerus Oy, Jyväskylä.

Meyer C. (1986). "Naissosialisaatio ja huolenpitotyö – muutoksen mahdollisuuksia etsimässä", in Rantalaiho L. (ed.), *Miesten tiede, naisten puuhat*, Gummerus Oy, Jyväskylä, s. 143-155.

Nelson A. & England P. (2002). "Feminist Philosophies of Love and Work", *Hypatia* 17 (2), pp. 1-18.

Niiniluoto I. (2001). *Järki, arvot ja välineet*, 2. ed., Otavan kirjapaino, Keuruu.

Noddings Nell (2001). "The Care Tradition: Beyond 'Add Women and Stir'", *Theory in the Practice*, 4 (1), pp. 29-34.

Näre S. & Lähteenmaa J. (1992). "Yhteenveto. Moderni suomalainen tyttöys: altruistista individualismia", in Näre S. & Lähteenmaa J. (eds.), *Letit liehumaan. Tyttökulttuuri murroksessa*, Tammer-Paino Oy, Tampere.

Nätkin R. (1986). "Naisten vastuun ja kotien ylläpitämisen ristiriidoista", in Rantalaiho L. (ed.), *Miesten tiede, naisten puuhat*, Gummerus Oy, Jyväskylä.

Vaughan, Genevieve (1997). *For-Giving. A Feminist Criticism of Exchange*, Plain View Press, Austin.

Ve, Hildur (1992). "Sosiologi og fortåelse av kjønn", in Taksdal A. & Widerberg K. (eds.), *Forståelser av kjønn*, Engers Boktrykkeri, Otta.

— (1994). "Gender Differences in Rationality, the Concept of Praxis Knowledge and Future Trends", in Gunnarson E. & Trojer L. (eds.), *Feminist Voices on Gender, Technology and Ethics*, Printing office at Luleå University of Technology, Luleå.

Weber, Max (1978 [1904-1905]). *The protestant ethic and the spirit of capitalism*, II ed., George Allen & Unwin, London.

When we talk about global feminist politics we open a Pandora's box of discourses on "globalization". Many writers from a host of different academic disciplines describe what they consider core meanings and main economic, political, social or cultural structures and characteristics underlying the term globalisation. This term is mostly used to summarize the operations of advanced global capitalism and its concomitant processes of social and ecological exploitation and destruction, of growing disparities between the rich and the poor within one particular nation, or between entire regions or parts of the world. In other writings the emphasis on global pillage shifts to the cultural side of globalization, as proclaimed by terms such as "global village". Some of these writings emphasize how the world market has a tendency to homogenize the cultural landscape in a troublesome, imperialist way. Others accuse the market of playing with and exploiting regional and cultural differences by turning specific cultural insignia into marketable consumer items.

Another growing body of literature addresses the issue of migration. In the wake of continued and growing economic and social globalization a number of academic discussions have begun to take a careful look at corresponding terminology, such as "international" or "multicultural", by unpacking the various meanings of these terms, and by introducing others, such as "multi-national" or "transnational" (Pries 2002, Kivisto 2001). These terms are inseparable from notions of dislocation, or of voluntary, semi-voluntary or enforced moves or displacements, and they signify a multi-layered, complex history of colonialism, neocolonialism (Mohanty 1997) or global capitalism, the force behind, for instance, labor export propagated by the IMF or Worldbank (see Chang 2000). Immigrants may therefore be refugees, in involuntary exile, or people who seek new opportunities for themselves and their families in the U.S., their host country. Others may be return migrants, or transmigrants (Pries 2002). Depending on the writer's disciplinary academic background and political concern, however, notions of economic livelihood at times only provide the political-economic background for analyses that focus on migrants' different relations to their homeland (or home country), and on shifting or multiplying cultural, linguistic and political identities.

Explicitly feminist writers deplore the absence of the category of gender not only in debates of globalization, but also in what is generally referred to as the anti-globalization

143

movement. Despite their critical intent, both are seen as at least in part mirroring the continued power of primarily masculinist, hierarchical, that is, Western frameworks of interpreting and responding to what is characterized as the global capitalist "crisis". At the same time, feminist criticism does not necessarily spare women's own attempts to establish international, global connections or networks, as class-privileged or Western women may be quite blind to the neo/colonial tendrils that ensnare their efforts to build global connections (see, for instance, Mindry 2001). Feminist writers are also critical of globalization theories because they tend to ignore the concrete, lived experience of people who have to move, or decide to move, to different places or countries. More recent ethnographic studies of populations affected by moves of the global market are welcomed, although they are also criticized for tending to screen out the powerful transnational, global mechanisms and forces that underpin the specificity of particular populations' everyday struggles[1].

In this paper I address what I see as the biggest challenge confronting a global feminist movement. Not only do we have to take into account the ever-increasing physical and mental mobility of individuals or large groups of people across places, countries or continents. We also have to reckon with the other side of translocal or transnational mobility: of leaving one's home or home country, of being dis-placed. We all need a homeplace of some sort that provides an anchor for our sense of belonging and our need for safety and protection. Moreover, we are also creatures of the earth, and we do have a body that comes out of another body, that grows and dies. Earth and body are separate as well as connected, "mobile" and place-bound. How we live on and with the earth affects how we live in and with our bodies. The physical, biological, ecological foundation of life is shaped, worked on by the culture in which it is embedded. Cultural interpretations of body and soil flow out of and return to this separateness/connectedness. They influence or guide their use, which may be in an exploitative and destructive, or in a respectful, giving way that allows to unfold its abundance. The title of my essay is to bring together these multiple connections and disconnections.

Home

"Home" is a complex, ambiguous, conflict-ridden, if not paradoxical notion and reality. It can be experienced in culturally and individually different ways, and with multiple connections to place and time. It can metaphorically demarcate individual and social or national identities that are embedded in personal or social-political relations of power. There has been a growing interest in the meaning of home as evidenced by numerous books and articles on the subject. The definitions or meanings of home that emerge from these texts are as diverse and multifaceted as the particular disciplinary as well as social-political frameworks within which they operate. These writings can, however, be grouped into those that address issues related to the "Big Home" and those that focus on the "Little Home" (Magat 2000).

Writers in the first group describe the anguish associated with national relocations or displacements, living in exile or in a diaspora, or transnational migration. A homeplace, homeland, or home country may be real or figurative, and these terms may refer to a place one was forced to leave and longs to go back to, or to a place of ultimate return. Questions

144

relating to national, social, and individual identities are particularly prominent in these writings. Analyses of the "Little Home", on the other hand, are more likely to address the presumably mundane tasks and experiences associated with daily living, but they reveal how these experiences are fully embedded in problematic normative assumptions and larger social power relations. "Doing home", for instance, has strong patriarchal underpinnings (Bowlby, Gregory and McKie 1997). Other writers emphasize how a physical homeplace provides safety, especially in a hostile social environment, and how doing home therefore includes work that benefits the well-being of an entire community (Hooks 1990). Another group of writers describes how the homeplace can be a public, and mostly exploitative as well as abusive workplace. Writers from the black diaspora, such as Patricia Hill Collins (1998), investigate how race, class and gender interlace in the lives of domestic workers. Others discuss how labor migration also has this other, private, hidden side of the public world of global finance, production, trade and telecommunications. Kimberley Chang and H. M. N. Ling (2000) describe how being employed as domestic workers, or as sexual commodities in the entertainment industry, makes Filipinas the "intimate other" (ivi: 27).

There are many hidden social, cultural and political connections between analyses and descriptions of the Big Home and the Little Home, and there are some rather obvious ones. In this paper I join the two homes by linking "the turbulence of migration" (Papastergiadis 2000) to the universal need for a homeplace, and a critique of the social and ecological devastations resulting from the predatory moves of global capital to the concern for nondestructive, life-affirming ways of being in the world.

Regardless of the local and cultural specificity of many different political struggles, all share a rather solid common ground: our physical, material, bodily rootedness in nature, the earth, and all her gifts and challenges. And this is also my main question, one I propose to place at the center of a locally specific but also translocal, transnational feminist politics: Can we be at home in the world and on the earth, can we create such a home that is place-bound and moving, socially (culturally) and geographically specific and all-encompassing at the same time?

The gift paradigm

Globalization is an abstraction. It abstracts from the concrete specificity of people's lives and chances for survival due to the global restructurings of the capitalist market economy. As Katz (2001) writes, this abstraction is not altogether wrong. It illuminates the encompassing, all-inclusive power of the market imperative whose tentacles reach deeply into all forms of life and living. At the same time, she suggests that feminists create a counter-abstraction, one that provides points of connection between the many different struggles feminists, women, people, are engaged in all over the world. Katz sees such a counter-abstraction as being rooted in people's struggles for escaping, or changing, the devastating consequences of economic-political upheavals. These struggles are taking place in specific places and under historically and culturally specific circumstances that include equally specific social and economic power relations. However, they are also always answers to overarching political-economic neo/colonial relations of power, dominance, exploitation and destruc-

145

tion. In terms of conscious political work, they are therefore grounded in a common, shared interest in not only resisting these power relations but also stopping their move toward global destruction, countering them with alternative ways of living and acting in the world.

I want to move Katz's suggestions a bit further by giving a specific name to this counter-abstraction, and by presenting it as a specific paradigm. A paradigm refers to the perceptions, values and thoughts that form a particular world view, and it determines which questions we ask regarding what is true or right, which ones we don't, and how we propose answers and put them into action.

Here I want to take up Genevieve Vaughan's notion of the gift paradigm. In *For-Giving* (1997) Vaughan develops this complex and highly intricate but tremendously powerful paradigm for thinking and acting, resisting and creating in a world that operates according to the individualistic, competitive and hierarchical exchange structure of the global market. She describes how both the exchange paradigm and what she calls "the gift paradigm" shape the predominant, globally and imperialistically imposed world view that structures, or seeps into, our language and culture, and how people live and survive in this world.

In Vaughan's framework the gift-paradigm is an unfolding of the principle of the Mother. However, the Mother is not understood "as biological or instinctual, but as conscious creative human practice" (ivi: 367). A mother's direct, non-calculated response to her child's needs is paradigmatic for what Vaughan describes as the essence of gift-giving, putting into action the "female value" of unilaterally providing the satisfaction of the other's needs. The good of others is the ultimate life premise of the mothering model. Vaughan describes many different dimensions of a mutually inclusive gift-giving and gift-receiving process where "I give so that you may give". This turn-taking is characterized by attributing value to the other and creating community bonds, since "the true continuing source of ourselves is interactive and comes from other-orientation" (ivi: 283).

"Male values" such as self-interest, self-aggrandizement, competition, dominance and hierarchy represent the ego structure of the predominant, all-encompassing exchange paradigm. The logic of exchange indulges in the freedom from other-orientation. It is "availability-driven", not "need-driven" (ivi: 286). It is ruled by effective demand, not the need of the other. The macro economy artificially creates scarcity by backgrounding the human needs of the many and by exercising the "destructive power of acquisition by force" (ivi: 172). Mother Earth becomes an endless resource where the few privatize her gifts and supplement them or bring them into forced interaction with the gift of free and cheap labor of the many.

Giving and sustaining life's quality is not only pushed aside. It is also incorporated, constrained, absorbed by the cultural, linguistic and psychological rules and dominance of exchange. Because exchange is dependent on the gift, gift labor is necessary for profit where the many give to the "one", not to each other (ivi: 294). Capitalism needs the hidden gift and corrals free nurturing into the exchange paradigm. Vaughan describes many different psycho-social and linguistic mechanisms that result from the forced coexistence of the two logics where giftgiving is coopted, instrumentalized, distorted.

Vaughan's analyses are rooted in a passionate call for unburying the giftgiving principle of life, culture and language, and for re-discovering the logic of a paradigm that is older and more fundamental than the exchange paradigm. Where the latter creates the un-community of competing, warring and killing "masculated" egos, the gift paradigm entails the possibility of creating and maintaining peaceful and abundant communities. Vaughan has a clear political-pragmatic agenda. She stresses the importance of collectively re-constructing and building a gift economy because gift-giving subverts the economic structure of exchange and calls for a collective rather than individual solution. The hope for such a solution lies in global, transnational feminist movements that find and practice a commonly shared "approach to problems and solutions that proves the validity of the assertion of the caring values of women everywhere across all the patriarchal boundaries" (1998).

Vaughan's analysis is of groundbreaking importance for such a feminist movement. At the same time, I also believe that we not only need to explore the manifold practical implications of gift-giving in our daily lives, work and political struggles but also enlarge and strengthen the paradigm's tapestry by continuously weaving and re-weaving it with new colors and new threads. Here I want to take up what I see as a particularly powerful aspect of the gift-giving paradigm: to provide a counter-abstraction to the notion of globalization, thus serving as an intellectual and emotional-spiritual bridge across vast social, cultural and geographic distances. I interweave this major thread with what I also see as a fundamental, universal reality. Global economic restructurings instigate or bring about new kinds of movements, trans/migrations, displacements and diasporic ways of living. The contradictions and conflicts they harbor are the result of new constellations that affect an old, omnipresent aspect of human living: the universal need for a safe homeplace. This is also the place where the mothering principle Vaughan describes is often most directly and most forcefully acted out, especially by women, and especially with respect to children.

In my own work I have only recently begun to make connections between motherwork (the focus of my writing) and the experience of "mobile motherhood" (Hoving 2001, 44) in the lives of many migrant workers. My recent study of the conditions of motherwork in Chicago's inner-city racial and economic ghettos (Hart 2002) has therefore taken on new meanings, moving my thinking into new directions. In this study I had conversations with mothers who lived in a place of social and physical isolation, a place shot through with direct violent responses to the structural violence of racial and economic segregation (of which the City of Chicago is one of the nation's most glaring examples). Earlier generations of Chicago's public housing residents were part of the Great Southern Migration to northern cities that promised more economic and cultural freedom. Slavery had combined the violent removal of millions of Africans from their original homelands via the gruesome Middle Passage with being bound to a particular place and being mobile capital that could be bought and sold according to their owner's purely economic motives. Later institutional practices established a variation of this violent mix by linking freedom from slavery to physical-geographical, economic and social segregation.

The relocation of the steel and automobile industry – originally the main job providers for inner-city residents – to cheap labor countries, and the subsequent move of new businesses or corporations to suburban areas trapped the inner-city poor in their place of residence. Many, if not most of the children thus became part of a growing economically superfluous population (Wilson 1996). Consequently, the mothers' stories were marked by hopelessness and despair. At the same time, the stories I heard from inner-city mothers were also replete with the theme of giving, not only to their own but also to the children of other mothers whose neglect at times bordered on abuse.

Mobile capital produces, however, not only locally confined and economically superfluous populations. It also produces mobile motherhood. Within the context of this paper I can only give an outline of the challenges this poses to the gift paradigm: How is/can the mothering principle be practiced by women, or people in general, who are migrating all over the globe? How can bridges be built across transnational geographies based on an abstraction that is grounded in a homeplace, the land, the body?

My attempt to start answering these questions moves into several directions simultaneously. Irrespective of specific social and cultural circumstances the migratory experience contains seeds for a new global nomadic consciousness, and such a consciousness enables us to make intense interconnections among people who may be dispersed over large geographical distances but with whom we share a political interest in building a better, livable world for all. Such a concern is not only lodged in the everyday need to survive or provide a living to oneself, one's family, or one's community. It is also lodged in the commonness of the physical foundations of life, the land and the body. It therefore simultaneously transcends the place-bound rootedness in a specific locale and a specific body by being voiced as a concern to preserve and sustain the physical foundation of all life in the most peaceful and dignified way.

Vaughan's call for a gift-economy is not entirely new. As I discussed in previous writings (1991, 2002), motherwork represents a prime example of the vital necessity as well as overall social devaluation of what in a different theoretical-analytical framework is referred to as "subsistence work". This concept was at the center of the "Bielefeld Approach", where in the 70s a number of feminist sociologists and political economists started challenging Marxist critiques of capitalism and related theories of development. These feminist critics were themselves involved in various international "development" efforts, primarily in Venezuela, Mexico and India. They pointed out that both, mainstream and Marxist theoreticians alike, ascribe to a masculinist Western notion of progress and development by couching capitalism's direct material dependence on unpaid, unremunerated, non-commodified subsistence labor in terms of "pre-capitalist", "not-yet-developed" kinds of economic structures. With the advance of capitalism these economies, and corresponding forms of labor, would thus all wither away.

As critics of this perspective point out, it is grounded in erroneous assumptions about the true workings of a capitalist economy, dismissing, or hiding, subsistence labor's – or in Vaughan's terms "gift labor's" – essential role in sustaining an exploitative commodity economy. Assuming a "subsistence perspective" would not only reveal this dependency, it would also valorize subsistence work (or gift labor). Moreover, such a perspective would reveal how the capitalist appropriation of subsistence work not only exploits its availability but also deforms, distorts, or destroys its very conditions. Above all, subsistence labor provides the fertile ground for a subsistence orientation that guides people's culturally specific practices. Very similar to the gift-giving paradigm's main characteristics, a subsistence orientation intricately interlaces the economic and the cultural, the physical-material and the spiritual-psychological[2].

Within the context of this paper I want to claim that the reality and imaginary of migration (in all its manifold variations) not only challenges such a place-bound economic-cultural paradigm. It also opens up "zones of possibilities" (Gloria Anzaldúa 2002, 544) for de-

148

veloping a translocal subsistence orientation and correspondingly complex, multiple, intersecting individual and collective identities. It is precisely the non-material dimensions of a nomadic consciousness that allow us to see and analytically-spiritually connect the various "points of elevation" Katz metaphorically describes in her call for constructing "countertopographies" to the topographies of power (2001, 1229). As I will describe later in the essay, such countertopographies can also provide the "contour lines" of a global home whose construction depends on a subsistence orientation, and on various kinds of physical and ideological subsistence labor that mutually influence or define each other.

Nomadic journeying and nomadic consciousness

The nomad, and the mobile mother, are the two images that bring together the way place-boundedness and displacement, homeplace and homelessness, rootedness and mobility are fully intertwined and define each other by their simultaneous presence and absence. A homeland, or a homeplace, takes on a different meaning when its absence is acutely felt in a host country that does not house one's children, and where people speak a foreign language.

According to Rosi Braidotti (1994) a nomad is a construct, a myth, a figuration that trespasses, blurs or transgresses boundaries between experiences, categories and identities, and that syncretizes them in a nomadic consciousness. The latter term is similar to Gloria Anzaldúa's (1987) "mestiza consciousness". In both cases a synthetic whole results from an ongoing process of understanding difference within the framework of divisive and hierarchical post/colonial global market relations while simultaneously seeing intense interconnections.

Anzaldúa is of Mexican and Indian descent, and she is surrounded by the Anglo culture. Thus, the mestiza "learns to be an Indian in Mexican culture, to be Mexican from an Anglo point of view. She learns to juggle cultures. She has a plural personality, she operates in a pluralistic mode – nothing is thrust out, the good the bad and the ugly, nothing rejected, nothing abandoned. Not only does she sustain contradictions, she turns ambivalence into something else" (1987: 79). This something else is the mestiza consciousness that has the ability to unite "all that is separate" (ivi: 79). It is the result of the continuous, ongoing effort of syncretizing into a synthetic whole the different pieces and fragments of different loyalties and affinities, of externally imposed or self-given categorical attributes. Such a synthetic whole does, however, live in constant movement, does not lose track of contesting or conflicting voices associated with loyalties or affinities. Complexity and heterogeneity are preserved, as the mestiza tolerates ambiguity and contradictions. Anzaldúa's writings are exemplary for a discussion of hybridity that does not get lost in "difference-talk" (Friedman 1998: 91), nor does it de-politicize or romanticize the multi-locality of people moving across the global landscape – a conceptual trap clearly laid out for the privileged few.

Anzaldúa's descriptions of "nepantla" strongly resonate with my own moving back and forth between different worlds, always living in an in-between place. The nepantla signifies the painful as well as transformative experiences of being "torn between ways" or "pulled between opposing realities". Above all, the notion of nepantla refers to the experience of living between cultures which "results in 'seeing' double, first from the perspective of one culture, then from the perspective of another" (2002: 547-549). This makes one live in a "zone of possibility", because in nepantla

> you experience reality as fluid, expanding and contracting. In nepantla you are exposed, open to other perspectives, more readily able to access knowledge derived from inner feelings, imaginal states, and outer events, and to "see through" them with a mindful, holistic awareness. Seeing through human acts both individual and collective allows you to examine the ways you construct knowledge, identity, and reality; and explore how some of your/others' constructions violate other people's ways of knowing and living (ivi: 544).

Living in an in-between place, inhabiting an existential juncture is difficult – to say the least – but it is also a method that "provides passage to that unfastened, differential juncture of being – la conciencia de la mestiza". It holds the promise of allowing "an evolutionary seeing, interpreting, and changing of the planet" (Sandoval 2002: 24).

The black diaspora also contains elements that can be syncretized into a new, future-oriented nomadic consciousness. Living in the black diaspora means, however, living within historical and geographical parameters that are quite different for Mexican-Indian return migrants. They remain in physical contact with their home country and with the cultures of the country (or countries) they migrate to. The very notion and reality of a black diaspora speaks, however, of a homeland, a land of origin, that is geographically somewhere else. It is absent as well as thoroughly present. As Hall writes, for the Caribbean culture Africa "is the groundbass of every rhythm and bodily movement. This was – is – the 'Africa' that 'is alive and well in the diaspora'" (ivi: 230). By being present and absent at the same time "Africa must at last be reckoned with by Caribbean people, but it cannot in any simple sense be merely recovered" (ivi: 231). The Africa of the diaspora is no longer the original Africa. Rather, it is a "spiritual, cultural and political metaphor" which is the "result of a long and discontinuous series of transformations" (ivi: 231). Hall describes how Africa creates a sense of belonging to a past to which all access originally had been cut off. Thus, Afro-Caribbeans can make no "final and absolute Return" (ivi: 226) to an original homeland which is continuously re-told "through politics, memory and desire" (ivi: 225). As an integral part of cultural identity and imaginary it is the destination of symbolic homeward journeys of the displaced[3].

Being born of dispersal and fragmentation the Afro-Caribbean cultural identity is not simply of one piece but moves along two intersecting vectors: the vector of similarity and continuity, and the vector of difference and rupture (ivi: 226). Hall places this "'doubleness' of similarity and difference" at the center of his notion of hybridity: "The diaspora experience as I intend it here is defined, not by essence or purity, but by the recognition of a necessary heterogeneity and diversity; by a conception of 'identity' which lives with and through, not despite of difference; by hybridity". It is especially the sentence following this quote that contains visions of a promising future: "Diaspora identities are those which are constantly producing and reproducing themselves anew, through transformation and difference" (ivi: 235). A cultural identity that is forged at points where similarity and difference intersect is therefore "a matter of 'becoming' as well as of 'being.' It belongs to the future as much as to the past" (ivi: 225)[4].

Isabel Hoving's (2001) analysis of texts written by Caribbean women moves Hall's discussion of the intersection of transformation and difference to another level. Hoving elaborates on the hybrid and diasporic nature of Caribbean literature. She describes how the "miraculously multiple writing by Caribbean women" illustrates "a diasporic, transatlantic, multilinguistic practice" (ivi: 2) and a strong transnational orientation (ivi: 12). Throughout her scholarly investigation Hoving keeps questioning the traditional masculinist interpretations of journey and home, and she describes how the texts she examines give examples of specifically feminine discourses of mobility. Women's sexuality, and particularly their link to motherhood, makes women relate to home, exile and movement according to quite different patterns (ivi: 15). Mothering makes women certainly "less enchanted by promises of experiences of travel". Nevertheless, Caribbean women's diasporic, transatlantic, multilinguistic experience underlies the development of new concepts such as "bound motion" (ivi: 15), or "mobile motherhood" (ivi: 44). These notions break with the gender-specific character of travel metaphors, and with the concomitant association of femininity with inactive, immobile space (ivi: 42). Moreover, they hold the promise of integrating the importance of place with the mobility of a transformative space, a space where life can take roots and unfold freely, unencumbered by cultural-patriarchal constraints.

In her study of Barbadian migrants to England Mary Chamberlain (1994) frequently refers to a "culture of migration" where most families include a model of immigration that has its roots in economic necessity and in the mobility and freedom it gives to individual family members. Family loyalty is, however, of prime importance for making intergenerational migratory moves possible while at the same time keeping intact a relatively stable sense of identity. Migration stories are often stories of children left behind, "back home", in the care of a relative who provides steady care and attention, and a relatively stable physical environment, that is, a homeplace. Chamberlain tells the stories of several adults, women as well as men, and she remarks that mothers who decide to migrate to another country mostly leave their children in the care of a grandmother. In other words, the children are not considered, and treated, as equally mobile as their parents. Thus, mobile motherhood cannot simply be equated with mobile childhood.

Chamberlain focuses on migratory moves and only mentions in passing that children were left back home, or in what Bell Hooks would refer to a homeplace. Hooks specifically addresses the importance of a homeplace for diasporic living because it is the place "where black people could affirm one another and by so doing heal many of the wounds inflicted by racist domination" (1990: 42). She stresses the primary role of women in creating and sustaining such a place. Home is the place where all women, especially mothers, are expected to care for and give to others, and where they are socialized into perceiving and responding to the needs of others. Regardless of the oppressive, patriarchal undercurrent of these expectations, home is the place where identities are shaped and children are nurtured. As Lemke-Santangelo (1996) points out, children are "the freshest link in the web of reciprocal obligation" (ivi: 146). Their universal need for being cared for can therefore provide the concrete, physical-spiritual foundation for making connections between people and places separated by vast geographical, geopolitical and cultural distances, and for translating these connections into reciprocal obligations to safeguard, repair, or rebuild the conditions of life, that is, our future.

Vaughan's writings here connect with Hooks' description of black women's primary role in creating a safe and nurturing homeplace, and in carrying that work into the community. Hooks rightfully chides those men who practice one of the mainstays of Western masculinity: subordinating women. Not only do they therefore threaten collective black solidarity and, consequently, the "survival as a people" (1990: 48), they also diminish, or deny, the general, all-encompassing importance of the work black women do for their families, communities, and society at large. Hooks describes how it is black women who make and live the political agenda for collective struggles, and who give the home, and the work performed in it, its radical political dimension. African-American history is replete with stories of women who constructed homeplaces under the most difficult circumstances, and who took care of "all that truly mattered in life [...] the warmth and comfort of shelter, the feeding of our bodies, the nurturing of our souls. There we learned dignity, integrity of being; there we learned to have faith. The folks who made this life possible, who were our primary guides and teachers, were black women" (ivi: 41-42). Patricia Hill Collins (1990) uses the term "community othermothers" to describe the tremendous individual and collective struggles involved in this other-orientation that Vaughan considers the core of the mothering principle[5]. In my own life the experience of having and being a mother has been at the center of my political agenda to create with others a mothering society, and to make gift-giving the paradigm for local and global practical working and living.

I have been moving between cultures, urban and rural landscapes, languages, sexualities and classes. Nevertheless, what home means to me essentially keeps me moving between two different spaces. One is the political space occupied by my critical awareness of the difficult, terrifying political history of Germany, my home country. I therefore keep returning to my own cultural and political heritage, each time with a new perception and understanding of its history. I fully embrace the lived experience of my place of origin, my home culture, as the constant standard of reference. Although I do revisit my home country, it is not my place of final return, the homeland I long to go back to. The other meaning of home derives from my autobiographical beginnings. It is space I inherited from my mother and have carried with me, inside me, during my journey through various cultural or political landscapes. My mother is home to me, whether I am with her or far away. She lives home for me, I am rooted in her. I came out of her body. She gives home the physical, bodily, place-bound resonance of all its multiple meanings. My mother also anchors this experience in the necessity and importance of everyday living and care. Since my parents were very poor my mother had to work extremely hard to get her family nourished and clothed. All the tasks and responsibilities she had to perform on a daily and nightly basis blended into each other. They were a necessary and meaningful part of caring for the lives of her children and her husband.

My mother provides the spiritual space of unconditional love and acceptance. She teaches me that the mobility of being a nomad does not mean being homeless. Rather, it means carrying home with me as my "essential belonging" (Braidotti 1994: 16), thus being capable of re-creating it in diverse places, anywhere. At the same time, this new home has to be more than a resting place for the individual traveler. It also has to be, or become, a practicing   152 ground for gift-giving and receiving, in the fundamental, deeply rooted personal and political sense of these words.

Writing this section of the essay brought to life my most poignant and most painful memory of feeling lost, without a home. I remember sitting on my bed in my comfortable apartment, in a country that was no longer alien to me, sobbing "I want to go home". I was separated from my child, and although I did not want to go where she lived, I wanted to be united with her, look at her, cook for her, brush her hair. Leaving her felt like crossing a bridge over a precipice, a bridge that was leading nowhere. I felt desolate, physically mutilated.

My child did not want to leave her "green house" because in her soul, in her body and mind, house and home were inseparable. Although I tried to persuade her I did not want to force her to come along with me, and only many years later did I realize that my leaving made my child feel homeless, disoriented, and alone, despite her father's presence and care. Only many years later did I dare tell my adult daughter about my pain, my sense of homelessness, did I dare face her pain when she said "It was you who made the green house my home. When you left, I no longer had one".

Before I had left the green house I had a disturbing and telling dream. I dreamed that there were two of me in the same room, one packing her suitcase, the other embracing her child. My packing the suitcase was the result of a clear decision, an absolute necessity. And I became a mobile mother who for a long time lived in an in-between space, who kept crossing bridges that led over precipices, raging rivers and traffic-jammed highways. I also knew that once crossed I could never uncross them and remain the person I left behind. The new person would have wounds that took a long time to heal and left big scars. But she would also be enriched by new visions, orientations, desires, projects. Anzaldúa (2002) vividly describes how such crossing of a life threshold affects one's entire being:

> To pass over the bridge to something else, you'll have to give up partial organizations of self, erroneous bits of knowledge, outmoded beliefs of who you are, your comfortable identities (your story of self, tu autohistoria). […] The bridge (boundary between the world you've just left and the one ahead) is both a barrier and a point of transformation (ivi: 557).

Because crossing thresholds is such an integral part of life Anzaldúa reaches the powerful conclusion that "'home' is that bridge, the in-between place of nepantla, and constant transition, the most unsafe of all spaces" (ivi: 574). What makes it unsafe and a homeplace at the same time is the fact that "a decision made in the in-between place becomes a turning point initiating psychological and spiritual transformation, making other kinds of experiences possible" (ivi: 569).

Anzaldúa's understanding of home is tied to her multiple identities. They are the result of being born to parents from different cultural origins, and of living and moving in between different cultures, thus transcending the place-bound notion of home or home country. She forges the pain caused by geographically, culturally, and psychologically mobile and conflicting affinities and loyalties into a source of personal and collective empowerment, as represented by the term "mestiza consciousness".

153

When Paula Gunn Allen speaks of a migration-conscious Pueblo mind (1998) her words resonate with the core meanings of a mestiza consciousness. However, American Indians were forcefully displaced from their homeland. Although they may still live on what used to be their original homeland, it has become a parcel grudgingly allotted to their nation by the rulers of their home country.

The stories of American Indians are similar to the stories of mobile mothers, where movement and living in place do not cancel each other out. They speak of nomadic, migratory moves of body and soul that transcend the enforced moves and dislocations brought about by encounters with the Western "discoverers". Traditionally, American Indians were at home on the Earth, where the land, the sky, animate and inanimate beings were all interrelated in highly complex and fragile ways (Silko 1999: 33). By living on a homeland that was stolen by their home country American Indians are entangled in numerous contradictions and conflicts. Deborah Miranda (2002) therefore urges non-Indians to listen to "what it's like to be an indigenous person alive in her contemporary, colonized homeland" (ivi: 194). And as she writes, "Our bodies and hearts carry a deep sting, an engulfing shame, and a contrary assertion of survivance, which sprang from this land, from a place stolen, defiled, yet still present beneath our feet every day of our lives. There is no metaphor for such pain" (ivi: 193)[6].

Indians never had a country in the political sense of a nation state. This sealed their fate of being declared non-existent and their homelands empty. The actual inhabitants who interfered with white settlers' claims to their land were therefore considered worthy of being driven out or killed. Aside from systematic attempts by settlers to annihilate entire Indian tribes, those who survived suffered multiple displacements and enforced movements across the entire continent. In 1924 when Native Americans were officially given the rights of U.S. citizens, they became citizens of a country that had stolen the very land on which they now allegedly enjoyed tribal, state, and federal rights (Chauduri 1992)[7]. At the same time, the criminal act of colonization never came to an end. Not only are American Indians the only Americans who are legally required to carry an ID card that recognizes their membership in a federally recognized tribe (Miranda 2002: 195), being ethnicized or racialized as "Indians" also seriously undermines their claim to political sovereignty and cultural autonomy (Barker 2002: 324).

Here nomadic existence takes on very different connotations. It is less rooted in geopolitical realities that involve the crossing of physically marked national borders or military checkpoints. The borders that are crossed, or the boundaries that are busted, are the fences, the material and rhetorical corrals constructed by Western (American) categorizations. Not only do these fences directly violate the freedom to move, to self-determine, to live according to one's cultural values, but their very existence also contradicts the essence of American Indian culture and tradition. As Allen writes,

> [...] as our traditions have always been about liminality, about voyages between this world and many other realms of being, perhaps crossing boundaries is the first and foremost basis of our tradition and the key to human freedom and its necessary governmental accomplice, democracy" (1998: 12).

154

Allen describes herself as a half-breed, hybrid, mixed-blood woman, a typical representative of a people that carries "every variety of blood that has found its way to our ancient continent" (ivi: 6). Her writings in *Off the Reservation* (1998) portray boundary-busting and bordercrossing on many levels that together clearly become the fertile ground for developing and tending to the growth of a planetary mestiza consciousness. Allen sees this as the result of being colonized and dispossessed, and of retaining "'indianness' while participating in a global society" (ivi: 6). Indianness signifies "the profound knowledge of the true nature of earth, the land, and all that exists upon and within it". This knowledge is "the true site of conflict. The differing definitions of reality and the accompanying values those definitions imply are what is at stake. And the outcome is the fate of the planet and multitudinous forms of life thereon" (ivi: 9). Allen here articulates the "indianness" of the notion of home and homeland. She places the earth, the land, at the very center of its core meaning. Earth, or Mother Earth, signifies the material, bodily grounding of the spiritual meaning of home. Without such grounding the very foundation of our physical and spiritual being gets lost or destroyed.

The global market system cannot afford such earth-bound values. The earth continues to be considered, and treated, as a freely available, cheap natural resource that can be used in whatever way contributes to the bottom line. This is the neo/colonial side of nomadism, bordercrossings, or boundary-busting where the nomadic capital of borderless corporations tethers powerful scientific knowledge and discoveries to its ruthless plunder of the ecosystem. Not only are natural resources such as land, air, or water for the taking. So are living organisms. They can be hybridized or technologically engineered without the slightest "consideration of their existence as integrated beings" (Anzaldúa 2002: 561). Modifying organisms by genetically crossing species boundaries means moving into and altering the interior of fundamental life processes. The ability to electromechanically shoot a foreign gene into a living organism makes living material itself quite mobile. What is now referred to as "life sciences" plays directly into the hands of agribusiness giants that restructure and control global agriculture. Above all, by patenting life mega-corporations are introducing a new version of colonialism. As Vandana Shiva remarked in an interview with *In Motion Magazine* (July 18, 1998), "Contemporary patents on life […] are pieces of paper issued by patent offices of the world that basically are telling corporations that if there's knowledge or living material, plants, seeds, medicines which the white man has not known about before, claim it on our behalf, and make profits of it". Not only are people robbed of their land, but also of their indigenous knowledge. The logic of control and use of this knowledge has been pushed even further by robbing seeds of their very ability to propagate. "Terminator seeds" make the farmer entirely dependent on buying future seeds from an agricultural giant such as Monsanto (Lappé and Bailey 1998).

Purely financial imperatives are behind biotechnology industry's welcoming of the fact that food crops can be genetically altered. Ecological biodiversity is replaced by large monocultures resistant to massive amounts of herbicides and pesticides. When the soil has become too poisonous to continue the mass production of food crops, nomadic capital moves somewhere else. The agbiotech industry therefore uproots local farmers and destroys the conditions for local food production. Borderless corporations don't create communities. Instead, they leave behind communities that are burdened with toxic wastes and embittered, disposable farmers or workers[8].

Transnational corporations also need a limitless supply of workers willing to cross multi-national borders in search of livelihood. Filipina domestic workers represent a striking example of such transnational bordercrossings. They have been uprooted from their home country and are being dispersed over vast geographical spaces (Europe, Asia, the Middle East, the United States). Their employment as domestic workers in foreign countries also makes them live with contradictions where the absence of their original home is stacked upon the presence of working in someone else's home. However, parts of their stories also resonate with the voices of a future transnational community and a new global consciousness. Many workers develop a dual loyalty to their home and their host country. They create "imagined communities" where they share experiences related to their work and to their separation from their family. Above all, they develop "transcontinental bonds" or "transnational family ties", and they create "multinational households in various forms" (Parreñas 2001: 1143, 1151, 1144; see also Chang 2000).

Constructing a nomadic home

The stories of trans/migrants, of people living on land stolen by their home country, or in a cultural diaspora, all contribute to the construction of topographies that counter the topographies of power. They remind us of the possibility of engaging in the political effort of constructing metaphorical countertopographies even if we do not share a common language or place of origin. In Katz's words, the metaphorical sense of topography "refers to a central aspect of most topographical maps – the contour lines. Contour lines are lines of constant elevation, connecting places at precisely the same altitude to reveal a terrain's three-dimensional shape" (2001: 1229). Translated into concrete political action, it is therefore possible to "imagine a politics that maintains the distinctness of a place while recognizing that it is connected analytically to other places along contour lines that represent not elevation but particular relations to a process (e.g., globalizing capitalist relations of production)" (ivi: 1129). The political impetus behind the construction of countertopographies is to connect different, specific places based on a common interest, and to "enhance struggles" in the name of such interests (ivi: 1130).

Constructing a nomadic home is strongly related to the construction of countertopographies. Not only is the place-bound bodiliness of one's origin experientially, autobiographically linked with the locality of one's however transitory current physical dwelling. The two are, or can become, analytically connected as well. It is therefore the primary goal of the political project of nomadic becoming to "connect partiality and discontinuity with the construction of new forms of interrelatedness and collective projects" (Braidotti 1994: 5). These new forms, accompanied by an awareness of the "deeper relatedness" that lies "beneath individual separateness" (Anzaldúa 2002: 569), need to be grounded in a concrete, tangible substance that combines mobility and rootedness.

Moving across different transnational, geopolitical and cultural spaces does not only mean gaining a critical distance to one's own location on the power map. It also means being engaged in the process of a nomadic becoming that translates into deeply felt interrelatedness with others who share the concern for creating a mothering society. My conversations with black inner-city mothers, and the fact that they welcomed my presence with freely giving me an abundance of stories, established one of those strongly felt connections between "friendly strangers" – a friendliness that was carried by our shared, deeply felt concern for the current and future well-being of children[9].

I have come full circle with the notion of nomad, this time by returning to its older cultural meaning. Nomadic "people of the land", such as the Maori in New Zealand, the tangata whenua, live on the land and regularly return to it. The land is sacred, it is the foundation of material and spiritual life, the fountain of life, where all life is one. As Anna Voigt and Nevill Drury remark in *Wisdom from the Earth* (1998) with respect to Australian Aboriginal peoples, they "have a complex and extraordinarily rich spiritual and social life, all of which is interwoven with the land. Because of this intimate connection to the land and all of its features, Aboriginal groups probably retain the most detailed knowledge of all the diverse regions on the Australian continent" (ivi: 128). To be a nomad therefore implies a purposeful motion that is guided by a thorough, profound knowledge of the land. To participate in the global challenge to sustain the complex, fragile web of life therefore also means to reclaim the gifts of Mother Earth, the great giver of life (Vaughan).

In its most complex and elaborate form, a global nomadic consciousness is rooted in a world that cherishes its richness by continually giving back to the great giver, allowing, enabling her to continually give back to us. However, such turn-taking cannot ignore, or bypass the actual physical labor that gets us in touch with the earth, with dirt and excrement, with the bodily needs of growing, sick, or dying bodies. A feminist global movement needs to place at its very center the actual support of such labor, raising it to points of elevation, and turning it into the contour lines of genuine countertopographies.

Being at home in the world means building bridges across vastly different landscapes. These bridges are, however, not erected to avoid contact with the landscape they allow us to cross. Moreover, building them is not the act (or responsibility) of a single individual. It is a common, collective endeavor where the workers tell each other stories from their lives and struggles in different cultural landscapes. They tell of the intimate knowledge of these landscapes, of forests, rivers and mountains, and of paths, dwellings and cultivated fields, and of the labor associated with them, the "deep earthly wisdom" that is necessary to live in a place without destroying it (Berry 1999: 49). They also tell of different struggles that are grounded in the common concern of stemming the global tide of destruction. It is this shared concern that makes the building of bridges necessary as well as possible. Both, intimate, specific knowledge and common concern provide the material, the colors, the shapes, and the architectural designs of sturdy bridges that are solidly anchored in specific places, thus establishing a relationship across spaces and between places, between past, present and future.

Notes

[1] For an overview and discussion of various theoretical frameworks as regards globalization and corresponding shifting boundaries between the global and the local see the summer 2001 issue of *Signs*, in particular the essays by Suzanne Bergeron and Carla Freeman.

[2] See Maria Mies and Veronika Bennholdt-Thomsen (1999), for a discussion of the main point of this approach.

[3] The declaration "Next year in Jerusalem" made at the end of the Passover seder echoes this relationship between the Jewish diasporic experience and its spiritual anchor in a place that was left ages ago.

[4] The term "diaspora" connotes a host of different historical and cultural events and meanings. The meaning of black diaspora, for instance, shifts between a "victim diaspora" and a "cultural diaspora", and it also touches on core meanings of a "labor diaspora". For a detailed discussion of the term see Robin (1997).

[5] There exists a large body of related literature on "community othermothers", "activist mothers", or "mother-activists". See, for instance, Collins (1993, 1994); James (1993); Jetter, Orleck, and Taylor (1997); Naples (1998). These writers describe how different groups of poor and working-class women placed the concerns and principles of making life possible at the center of their political struggles for better life conditions for their children, their community, and society at large. For a summary of these writings see chapter five in *The Poverty of Life-Affirming Work* (Hart 2002).

[6] Palestinian experience is very similar to that of American Indians. The loss of a homeland is, however, also tied to stories of transnational migration, and thus to the power of "back home", and these notions are currently mired in the experience of a particularly painful, violent encounter with the State of Israel. See Abdelhadi and Abdulhadi (2002).

[7] Before, in 1916, the Secretary of the Interior Fran,klin Lane had developed "citizenship ceremonies" where he "made the delivery of land patents and commensurate status of U.S. citizenship under the provision of the General Allotment Act of 1887 a ceremonial event" (Barker 2002, 322).

[8] Lappé and Bailey (1998) cover most of the arguments that speak for and against transgenic food production. There are numerous websites that monitor corresponding scientific and economic-political developments. See, for instance, <http://www.panna.org>, or <http://www.bio-integrity.org>.

[9] I take the notion of "friendly stranger" from Pamela Cotterill's (1992) discussion of the problems and pitfalls of ethnographic research.

References

Abdelhadi, Reem, and Rabab Abdulhadi (2002). "Nomadic existence: Exile, gender, and Palestine" (an e-mail conversation between sisters), in *This bridge we call home*, eds. G. Anzaldúa and A. Keating, Routledge, New York and London.

Allen, Paula Gunn (1998). *Off the reservation: Reflections on boundary-busting, border-crossing loose canons*, Beacon Press, Boston.

Anzaldúa, Gloria (1987). *Borderlands, la frontera: The New mestiza*, Aunt Lute Books, San Francisco.

— ed. (1990). *Making face, making soul: Haciendo caras*, Aunt Lute Foundation, San Francisco.

— (2002). "Now let us shift … The path of conocimiento … Inner work, public acts", in *This bridge we call home*, eds. G. Anzaldúa and A. Keating, Routledge, New York and London.

Barker, Joann (2002). "Looking for warrier woman (beyond Pocahontas)", in *This bridge we call home*, eds. G. Anzaldúa and A. Keating, Routledge, New York and London.

Bennholdt-Thomsen, Veronika, and Maria Mies (1999). *The subsistence perspective: Beyond the globalised economy*, Zed Press, London and New York.

Bergeron, Suzanne (2001). "Political economy discourses of globalization and feminist politics", *Signs: Journal of Women in Culture and Society*, 25 (4), pp. 983-1006.

Berry, Wendell (1999). "From a native hill", in *At home on the earth: Becoming native to our place*, ed. D. L. Barnhill, University of California Press, Berkeley.

Bowlby, Sophie, Susan Gregory, and Linda McKie (1997). "Doing home", *Women's Studies International Forum*, 20 (3), pp. 343-50.

Braidotti, Rosi (1994). *Nomadic subjects: Embodiment and sexual difference in contemporary feminist theory*, Columbia University, New York.

Chamberlain, Mary (1994). "Family and identity: Barbadian migrants to Britain", in *Migration and identity*, eds. R. Benmayor and A. Skotnes, Oxford University Press, Oxford, UK.

Chang, Grace (2000). *Disposable domestics: Immigrant women workers in the global economy*, South End Press, Cambridge, Massachusetts.

Chang, Kimberly A., and L. H. M. Ling (2000). "Globalization and its intimate other: Filipina domestic workers in Hong Kong", in *Gender and global restructuring: Sightings, sites and resistance*, eds. M. H. Marchand and A. S. Runyan, Routledge, London and New York.

Chaudhuri, Joyotpaul (1985). "American Indian policy: An overview", in *American indian policy in the twentieth century*, ed. V. J. Deloria, University of Oklahoma Press, Norman and London.

Cohen, Robin (1997). *Global diasporas: An introduction*, UCL, London.

Collins, Patricia Hill (1990). *Black feminist thought: Knowledge, consciousness, and the politics of empowerment*, Unwin Hyman, Boston.

— Hill (1993). "The meaning of motherhood and black mother-daughter relationships", in *Double stitch: Black women write about mothers & daughters*, eds. P. Bell-Scott, B. Guy-Sheftall, J. J. Royster, J. Sims-Wood, M. DeCosta-Willis and L. P. Fultz.

— (1994). "Shifting the center: Race, class, and feminist theorizing about motherhood", in *Mothering: Ideology, experience, and agency*, eds. E. N. Glenn, G. Chang and L. R. Forcey, New York and London, New York University Press.

— (1998). *Fighting words. Black women and the search for justice*, Minneapolis and London, University of Minnesota Press.

Cotterill, Pamela (1992). "Interviewing women: Issues of friendship, vulnerability, and power" *Women's Studies International Forum*, 15 (5-6), pp. 593-606.

Freeman, Carla (2001). "Is local: Global as feminine: Masculine? Rethinking the gender of globalization", *Signs: Journal of Women in Culture and Society*, 26 (4), pp. 1007-1037.

Friedman, Susan Stanford (1995). "Beyond white and other: Relationality and narratives of race in feminist discourse", *Signs: Journal of Women in Culture and Society*, 21 (1), pp. 1-49.

Hall, Stuart (1990). "Cultural identity and diaspora", in *Identity: Community, culture, difference*, edited by J. Rutherford, London, Lawrence and Wishart.

Hart, Mechthild U. (1992). *Working and educating for life: Feminist and international perspectives on adult education*, Routledge, New York and London.

— (2001). "Transforming boundaries of power in the classroom: Learning from *la mestiza*", in *Power in practice: Adult education and the struggle for knowledge and power*, eds. R. Cervero and A. Wilson, Jossey-Bass, San Francisco.

— (2002). *The poverty of life-affirming work: Motherwork, education, and social change*, Greenwood Press, Westport, CT.

Hernández-Ávila, Inés (1995). "Relocations upon relocations", *American Indian Quarterly*, 19 (4), pp. 491-508.

Hooks, Bell (1990). *Yearning: Race, gender, and cultural politics*, South End Press, Boston.

Hoving, Isabel (2001). *In praise of new travelers: Reading Caribbean migrant women's writing*, Stanford University Press, Palo Alto.

James, Stanlie M. (1993). "Mothering: A possible black feminist link to social transformation", in *Theorizing black feminisms: The visionary pragmatism of black women*, eds. S. M. James and A. P. A. Busia, New York and London, Routledge.

Jetter, Alexis, Anneliese Orleck, and Diana Taylor, eds. (1997). *The politics of motherhood: Activist voices from left to right*, University Press of New England, Hanover, NH.

Katz, Cindi (2001). "On the grounds of globalization: A topography for feminist political engagement", *Signs: Journal of Women in Culture and Society*, 26 (24), pp. 1213-1234.

Kivisto, Peter (2001). "Theorizing transnational immigration: A critical review of current efforts", *Ethnic and Racial Studies*, 24 (4), pp. 549-577.

Lappé, Marc, and Britt Bailey (1998). *Against the grain: Biotechnology and the corporate takeover of your food*, Monroe, Common Courage Press, Monroe, Maine.

Lemke-Santangelo, Gretchen (1996). *Abiding courage: African American migrant women and the East Bay community*, The University of North Carolina Press, Chapel Hill.

Magat, Ilan N. (1999). "Israeli and Japanese immigrants to Canada: Home, belonging, and the territorialization of identity", *Ethos*, 27 (2), pp. 119-44.

Mindry, Deborah (2001). "Nongovernmental organizations, 'grassroots', and the politics of virtue", *Signs: Journal of Women in Culture and Society*, 26 (4), pp. 1187-1211.

Miranda, Deborah A. (2002). "What's wrong with a little fantasy?", Storytelling from the (still) ivory tower", in *This bridge we call home*, eds. G. Anzaldúa and A. Keating, Routledge, New York and London.

Mohanty, Chandra Talpade (1997). "Women workers and capitalist scripts: Ideologies of domination, common interests, and the politics of solidarity", in *Feminist genealogies, colonial legacies, democratic futures*, eds. J. M. Alexander and C. T. Mohanty, Routledge, New York and London.

Naples, Nancy A. (1998). *Grassroots warriors: Activist mothering, community work, and the war on poverty*, Routledge, New York and London.

Papastergiadis, Nikos (2000). *The turbulence of migration*, Polity Press, Cambridge.

Parreñas, Rhacel Salazar (2001). "Transgressing the nation-state: The partial citizenship and 'imagined (global) community' of migrant Filipina domestic workers", *Signs: Journal of Women in Culture and Society*, 26 (4), pp. 1129-1154.

Pries, Ludger (2001). "The disruption of social and geographic spaces", *International Sociology*, 16 (1), pp. 54-74.

Sandoval, Chela (2002). "AfterBridge: Technologies of crossing", in *This bridge we call home*, eds. G. Anzaldúa and A. Keating, Routledge, New York and London.

Silko, Leslie Marmon (1999). "Landscape, history, and the Pueblo imagination", in *At home on the earth: Becoming native to our place*, ed. D. L. Barnhill, University of California Press, Berkeley.

Vaughan, Genevieve (1997). *For-giving: A feminist criticism of exchange*, Austin, Texas, Plain View Press.

— (1998). "Jacob wrestles with the angel", *Crone Chronicles*, Summer Solstice.

Voigt, Anna, and Nevill Drury (1997). *Wisdom from the earth*, Shambhala Publications, Inc., Boston.

Wilson, William Julius (1996). *When work disappears: The world of the new urban poor*, Harvard University Press, Cambridge, MA.

Introduction

In general, the Commons are the social (cultural heritage, housing, schools, hospitals, state pension) and natural (land, biodiversity, genetic material, oceans, rivers, mountain) conditions of life which are available for universal access by all members of the community. The notion of the Commons is central to understanding gender, domination and imperialism, and exploitation of humans and nature. The Commons debate is essential in explaining the new forms of social and territorial control that are leading to intensified dispossession – both of human and non-human lives in the indebted periphery. The commons discussion, in this paper, brings a Marxist, World System, feminist subsistence perspective that uncovers new gift giving areas for dispossession. These are; women's household labour, peasant and Indigenous Peoples' subsistence production, and Third World nature. Mies (1986, 1996), Mies and Bennholt-Thomsen (1978, 1999), Shiva (1989, 1993, 1994, 1998) and Salleh (1994, 1997) argue that women activists have no choice but to join the indigenous/subsistence movement because women's and indigenous peoples' situations are similar as a result of the conditions in which they live – poverty – and the physical work they do (protecting life and being in charge of the most highly productive work of society).

To reflect on these Commons, I use the concept "accumulation by dispossession" coined by David Harvey in his book, *The New Imperialism* (2003). He argues that Marx's general theory of capital accumulation was constructed under assumptions which exclude primitive accumulation processes or the living infrastructure of the commons. Marx's assumptions erroneously relegated accumulation backed up by depredation, fraudulence, and violence "outside of" the capitalist system, a matter of the past. Despite this, according to Harvey, Marx's primitive accumulation remains powerful within our present globalized capitalism. Thus, accumulation by dispossession includes the commodification and privatization of land and the forceful expulsion of peasant and indigenous populations; conversion of various forms of property rights (common, collective, state, etc.) into private property rights; suppression of rights to the commons; commodification of feminized labour and the suppression of indigenous forms of production and consumption; monetarization of exchange and taxation, slave trade and usury. In this way a full circle of violence and war is externalized against the "other". Thus, to accumulate by dispossessing means to devalue the "oth-

161

er" in order to buy local assets and labour cheaply. This is done through the use of the debt and the environmental crises.

Here, I see dispossession of the Commons by credit. I am concerned with how the socially constructed global credit markets (financial system) are systematically subordinating the non-human and human environment of indebted Latin America. Three questions are addressed in this paper. First, how is credit used to dispossess the Nature Commons? Second, how is debt used to dispossess the Social Commons? Third, how have the dispossessed begun to reclaim the Commons?

I begin with a brief treatment of credit, within which I pose these questions. In the 1970s, credit set in motion a capitalist dynamic which brought a situation in which producers were subjected to market imperatives. In 1982, the debt crisis that blew up in Mexico had two origins: the decline in the manufacturing rate of profit across the advanced capitalist economies (Brenner 2002), and the Vietnam War was expensive for the U.S. and gave rise to a large deficit (Gatt-Fly, 1985) that created a fiscal crisis on the developmental state. As the manufacturing industry and the Vietnam War crises escalated, the U.S. continued to print more dollars. Since the U.S. dollar was linked to gold, it caused global inflation and led to what came to be called the "Euromarket", as international banks dealing in American dollars began to open up shop in Europe. These dollars were recycled to Third World countries at relatively low, but floating, interest rates. At the time that Latin American countries had obtained the credits, the Euromarket operated on the basis of medium – and long-term credit with interest ranging between 2% and 4%. After 1978, these credits were replaced by short-term floating-interest rates which left the borrowers with most of the risk. By 1982, the short term credits were linked with the increase of interest rates up to 16.6% in the U.S. (Roddick, 1988). Since then, the U.S. interest has been using the International Monetary Fund (IMF) stabilization, and the World Bank (WB) Structural Adjustment Policies (SAP) to reorganize internal social production and reproduction of the indebted world to favor penetration of transnational capital.

Using the debt crisis, by the end of the 1980s, most foreign direct investment in Latin America was the result of debt/equity swaps. Under the Brady's debt-restructuring plan established in 1989 and the Washington Consensus in 1995, Latin American bank loans were transformed into bonds that could be easily traded on the financial market. An active market in trading these bonds quickly developed as a key source of capital. The U.S. Enterprise Americas Initiative (EAI), under President George Bush Sr., proposed debt swaps[1] using public funds to transfer indebted countries' public enterprises to U.S. private corporations. Through debt swaps, countries privatized their public infrastructure and placed the transnational corporation as the main player in their economy/ecology.

By the end of the 1980s, the debt (social) crisis was entangled with the environmental crisis. Recognition of the environmental crisis was precipitated with the publication of the 1987 Report of the United Nations' World Commission on the Environment and Development (UNWCED), "Our Common Future", often referred to as the Brundtland Report. In 1992, at the Earth Summit, northern experts of the development agencies and global resource managers (GRMs) encountered each other and merged their differing perspectives into what has been called "sustainable development"[2]. Sustainable development discourse argues that the tensions between poverty and ecology will be resolved in the indebted countries by rec-

162

onciling global economic interests and ecological interests (Asiedu-Akrofi, 1991; UNESCO 1995) through economic growth. In these frameworks, the solution to the debt and environmental crises is proposed by expanding the market system. One mechanism to expand the market system is using debt-for-nature swap funds, which will be referred to as debt-for-nature investments to highlight their nature. A debt-for-nature investment is a financial mechanism that repays loans held by creditors such as commercial banks or governments in return for natural resources. Debt-for-nature investments are core mechanisms of sustainable development which prevent the entry of new money into the country, since it is the indebted country that pays with local currency for bonds on a foreign debt that was contracted in dollars. The debtor country's "obligation" is to allocate domestic resources for financing ecological projects in exchange for extinguishing a limited portion of the country's foreign debt. Debt-for-nature investments are based on a negative assessment of the debt country, meaning that the debt must be considered unpayable, so the debt titles can be sold at a fraction of their value in the secondary market. Supported by the Global Environmental Facility (GEF) program of the World Bank and assistance through AID, debt-for-nature investments insist upon structural adjustment measures to stimulate economic growth.

In the late 1990s, I wrote my doctoral thesis in the rainforest of Costa Rica on one of the first exchanges of debt-for-nature between Canada and Costa Rica. Two events were important in this picture: indebtedness pressured Costa Rican local powers to share commercial interests with transnational corporations over its natural richness, and particularly its potential for genetic material; while, at the same time, corporate environmentalism emerged as the new ideology of modernization and environmental protection. The discourse of "protecting" land, air and water through private property for capital accumulation has played a key part in the neo-liberal agenda of private appropriation. In this paper, debt-for-nature is a "new program of common management" that represents the expansion of commodification as a new accumulation by dispossession. This paper shows that the debt crisis and the environmental crisis have become rationales for a continuation of the enclosure of rural women's household work, peasant and Indigenous Peoples' subsistence production and nature Commons.

In what follows, first, I attempt to articulate the Global and the Local Commons argument. Second, I unpack nature dispossession – in Costa Rica, and social dispossession – in the Latin America region, produced by credit. And third, I bring the issue of reclaiming the Commons by Bolivian commoners.

In conclusion, credit has legalized the expansion of commodification and the social and nature dispossession of indebted countries' people. The fight against commodification is unifying the struggle of rural women, peasants and Indigenous People. Pushed to the corner they are fighting back and reclaiming their Commons.

Enclosure: Global Commons vs Local Commons

Commons, in this paper, is the natural, social and political space that provides sustenance, security and independence, yet typically does not produce commodities for profit.

They have been subjected to enclosure. Enclosure means physical fencing of land, extinction of common and customary rights of use on which many people depended for their livelihood. Enclosure movements in 18th century England took place by acts of Parliament (Wood 2002). Early enclosure occurred when larger landowners sought to drive commoners off lands that could be profitably used for sheep farming. Locke takes a firm stand that most of the value inherent in land comes not from nature, but from labour and improvement. Instead, Marx (1977) identifies the early enclosure as the process of expropriation of direct producers; once dispossessed they were forced into markets. According to Polanyi (1967), a market is not an act of nature; society creates markets for accumulation purposes. Historically, the market economy fosters enclosures of the land to mobilize and produce rural proletariat for industry. With the expansion of the market the motive of natural action of subsistence was substituted by the motive of profit. The expansion of the market produces a conflict between the market and the subsistence production, as more and more means of direct reproduction are included in the market. Thus, the Commons are what still remains of gift economies when the market is the dominant system.

The Commons debate has become heated since 1968, when Garret Hardin, a biologist, put forward the argument that any Commons regime will result in degradation, since an individual user will gain more from overusing the commons than the individual loss he or she will sustain from its resulting ruin. He hopes for the expansion of private property, and the free market, because freedom of a commons brings ruin to all. According to Goldman (1998: 21), Hardin's discourse applied to the local commons is now utilized for the global commons striving to direct supranational decision-making on the Amazon biodiversity and forest, the earth's ozone, deep seas and so on (Goldman 1998: 21).

Since the Earth Summit, in 1992, a contemporary enclosure is taking place as a result of a policy which relies largely on economic/market-based instruments to achieve environmental protection. This agenda is implemented by professionals, developers and environmentalists. For instance, the WB, through the Global Environmental Facility (GEF), initiated a program of financing Global Resource Managers (GRMs), which will be referred to as Corporate Environmental Non-Governmental Organizations (CENGOs)[3], and defined the entire planet as the Global Commons. In the framework of the World Bank, the Commons are the areas of expansion of natural and social capital. The Global Commons "is a nation's portfolio of assets which includes built infrastructure, natural resources (minerals, energy, agricultural land, forest), human capital, and social capital" (Hamilton, 2001). Smith and Simmard (2001) of Statistics Canada have expanded the concept of Natural Capital into the Global Commons to include: natural resource stocks, the source of raw priced or unpriced materials used in the production of manufactured goods; land, essential for the provision of space for economic activity to take place; and environmental systems or ecosystems necessary for the services that they provide directly and indirectly to the economy, including purifying the air and water, providing biodiversity, stable climate, protection from solar radiation, and provision of stable flows of renewable natural resources. In sum, the Global Commons' rhetoric of universality makes the claim that it is acting in the general interest of "human kind". Using Geographic Information Systems (GIS), the Global Commons includes the Local Commons for the purpose of intervention.   164

As a result, the Local Commons (genetic material, land, water, forest, mountains etc.) are being handled by global actors and local concerns no longer matter. In effect, the Global Commons framework has revived colonization and dispossession particularly around indebted countries that still conserve their rain forest.

An example of this dispute is provided by the hidden debate on the Amazon. The Felix Varela Center of Germany (Santos 2004) cites a young Brazilian woman, resident in the U.S., informing that a Geography book, used in grade 6, shows the amputation of the Brazilian Amazon and El Pantanal from the Brazilian map. The book in reference is *Introduction to Geography* written by David Norman. Page 76 reads that the Amazon is the first international reserve, the most important forest reserve under U.S. and the United Nations' responsibility since the 1980s. The reason, according to Norman, is that the Amazon is one of the poorest area of the world and it is surrounded by irresponsible, barbarous and authoritarian countries. Norman also argues that the Amazon involves 8 different and strange countries in which violence, drug trafficking, ignorance, lack of intelligence and primitivism rule. Another paragraph remarks the Amazon is big in biodiversity, with variety of specimens of animals and vegetables. Such valuables in the hands of primitive populations and countries would condemn the world to total disappearance and destruction in few years. Since the Amazon's value is incalculable, the planet should be sure that U.S. won't allow these Latinos to exploit and destroy this property of humanity (Calloni 2004; Santos 2004).

A response from the Local Commons has been articulated by Brazil's Education Minister, Cristóvno Buarque, on January 09, 2004. During a debate in a U.S. University, a young fellow interrogated the Minister's thoughts surrounding the possible internationalization of the Amazon, declaring the Amazon region as part of the Global Commons. The student introduced the internationalization question conditioning his response as a humanist and not as a Brazilian. Here I summarize Mr. Cristóvno Buarque's answer, because of its importance:

> In fact, as a Brazilian I would simply speak against the internationalization of the Amazon. Despite the fact that our governments do not take appropriated care of this patrimony, it is ours. As humanist, knowing about the risk of environmental degradation that the Amazon suffers, I can imagine its internationalization, as much as the internationalization of whatever is important to humanity. If the Amazon, from the view of human ethics, must be internationalized, we must also internationalize the world oil reserves. Oil is as important as the Amazon for the welfare of humanity. However, the owners of the oil reserves feel that they have the right to increase or decrease oil prospecting and prices. On the same matter, the financial capital of rich countries must be internationalized. If the Amazon is a reserve for all humanity, it cannot be burned by the free will of its owner, or the needs of one country. Burning the Amazonia is as vicious as the provoked unemployment by the arbitrary decisions of global speculators. We cannot allow the financial system to burn out entire countries because of its speculation. During this encounter, the United Nations is having the Millennium Forum, but many presidents had difficulties in attending due to restrictions in the U.S. border. Because of that, I think that New York, as the central location of the United Nations must be internationalized. At least Manhattan should belong to humanity. Also Paris, Venice, Rome, London, Rio de Janeiro, Brasilia, Recife… Every city of the world, with its specific beauty, and history, should belong to humanity. If the U.S. wants to internationalize the Amazon, due to risks of leaving it in the hands of Brazilians, we have to inter-

nationalize the U.S. nuclear arsenal, because it has been provoking destruction a million times more than the regrettablel burnings done in the Amazon forest. In actual debates, U.S. presidential candidates are defending the idea of internationalization of the world forest reserves using debt-for-nature. We should start using that debt to guarantee that every child in the world has the possibility to eat and go to school. Let's internationalize the children, by treating them as a world patrimony that needs care, no matter were they were born. This is more important than the attention to Amazon. When the leaders treat poor children of the world as patrimony of humanity, they won't allow the children to work when they should be studying, to die when they should be living. As a humanist, I accept to defend the internationalization of the world. But as long as the world treats me as a Brazilian, I will struggle for the Amazon to be ours... ONLY OURS! (Personal communication, January 10, 2003).

Global Commons focuses in a narrow way on the physical nature of the forest, and evades the web of social relationships and processes in which rain forest and forest people are embedded. Further the agenda is mobilizing racism and preparing public opinion among its population to support the expropriation of the Amazon territory (Santos, 2004).

In what follow, we will see how credit has been articulating dispossession of rural women household, peasant and Indigenous Peoples and the nature of the Latin America Commons which provided their material means of subsistence. To address this issue, I will use a feminist understanding of the Commons provided by Maria Mies (1986). She abandons capital vs wage relation as the sole source of capitalist exploitation on the basis of reading of Rosa Luxemburg's theory of exploitation. With Luxemburg, two aspects of capitalist accumulation were linked: one aspect regards surplus value as a purely economic process, between capitalist and wage laborer; the other concerns the relations between capitalism and the non-capitalist modes of production. Mies inferred that the basic pre-condition for economic growth or capital accumulation continued to be the colonies, here treated as Commons. These colonies are women's housework, peasant and Indigenous Peoples' subsistence economies and nature. She argued that the strategy of dividing the economy into "visible" wage-labour and "invisible" non-wage labour allowed the exclusion of the invisible part from the real economy. Mies and Bennholt-Thomsen (1999) stated that the dominant theories about the functioning of the capitalist economy, including Marxism, were only concerned with capital and wage labour relations, the "visible" wage-labour, the tip of the iceberg. This sphere is regulated by law and exploited through wages. Most of the invisible proverbial iceberg consists of such things as the provenance of life, caring, nurturing, housework and subsistence production consisting of colonized peoples work, their territories, and nature. Women's household work is unpaid and often not recognized as work; peasant and Indigenous Peoples' subsistence production is subjected to underpayment, discrimination and exploitation, while nature is destroyed. These colonized areas are ruled by violence (Mies 1999), such as rape, domestic violence, genocide and ecocide, imperialism. Mies and Bennholt-Thomsen (1996; 1999) argued that women and colonies were over-exploited because their exploitation was not based on capitalistic appropriation of surplus labour, but of that which was necessary for their own subsistence production, or, indeed, their very survival. Most women's households and Third World peasants and Indigenous Peoples had combined their income from various sources, one of which was "subsistence" activity.   166

Therefore, according to Mies and Bennholt-Thomsen (1996; 1999), and Salleh (1994), both are producers directly concerned with the production and maintenance of food and life and are exploited by capital, not through wages, but through their product, which was taken from them free or at very low compensation. They are the gift economies and the Commons that provides continuity to capital accumulation.

Dispossessing the Nature Commons

Since the Earth Summit, the extension of the price system was expanded. Using the neoliberal agenda, all non-market structures that placed limits on the accumulation have started to be eliminated in order to commodify every part of nature. In the indebted Costa Rica, expansion of "natural and human capital" through the market economy was offered as the highest organizing principle for dealing with social (debt) and environment (natural) crises. A partnership between corporations and nation/states was established to accomplish enclosure, that is, to drive direct producers off the land. This scheme engenders a particular role for corporate environmental NGOs (CENGOs) and national states. On the one hand, CENGOs are engaged in genetic and species research; while at the same time they have become the managers of the IMF, the WB and developed states' projects of integrating local governments and communities into the global economy. On the other hand, "national states" are required to exercise a more complex intervention in the affairs of local communities. To fit their economic aspirations and activities into the world-system, states are now directly responsible for oppression and destitution of their citizens. Both CENGOs and "national states" have created the conditions for material expansion and a technically more intense mode of ecological dispossession in the indebted countries.

Thus, the sustainable development of the Global Commons movement has initiated a state-led management of the Conservation Areas for extraction of genetic material for research purposes, and appropriation of local knowledge for commodification; communities are losing their natural commons and becoming less able to adapt their local economies to local needs and conditions.

An example of designing Global Commons and partnership can be seen in debt-for-nature swaps between Canada and Costa Rica. The Canada-Costa Rica debt-for nature had 2 stages:

In 1991, a first Canada-Costa Rica debt-for-nature agreement organized the Arenal Project, under the management of the World Wildlife Fund (WWF-C), Canadian International Development Agency (CIDA) and the Ministry of Environment and Energy (MINAE). They elaborated the first step of a management plan, *El Plan General de Uso de la Tierra* (hereafter referred to as the Land Plan). The Land Plan regulated land access and use in the Arenal-Tilaran Conservation Area (ACA). The Arenal-Tilaran Conservation Area involves 250,561.5 hectares (ha.) of land. From this total, the Land Plan document recommended the protection of 116,690.2 ha. of which 76,707 ha. (37.54 percent of ACA) were selected for a research program and declared "nucleus areas" (*area nuclei*). The selected research areas function on the basis of inter-institutional agreements (Tremblay and Malenfant, 1996).

The Land Plan's biology section identified 4,283 species of flora and fauna in the nucleus area which represent 36% of the natural wealth of Costa Rica (ACA, 1993).

The natural commons of genetic material was privatized and used as the new frontier for capital accumulation. By 1994, INBio (Instituto Nacional de Biodiversidad), a Costa Rican NGO, established a partnership with the Ministry of Environment and Energy (MINAE) to collect samples for interested industries from the Conservation Areas. It searched for new pharmaceutical and agricultural products from plants, insects and other biological samples in three biological stations of Arenal Conservation Area (ACA). ACA-MINAE, in partnership with INBio, are involved in two research projects: 1) Biodiversity Resources of the ACA Development Project, financed jointly by the World Bank and INBio; and, 2) Development Knowledge and Sustainable Use of Costa Rica's Biodiversity, ECOMAPAS, financed by The Netherlands (Mora, 1998).

By 1996, the World Wildlife Fund-Canada (WWF-C), a Canadian NGO, in partnership with the Asociación Conservacionista Monteverde (ACM) collected material and researched flora and fauna (PROACA, 1996). The partners are bio-prospecting in 10 areas of the ACA territory.

As research centres are organized in the so-called nucleus areas, these areas are off-limits to rural communities unless they are part of the taxonomist program[4]. The Land Plan (ACA 1993) affected the resources of 108 communities, which were neither informed of nor included in the decision-making that changed their lives and livelihoods. The secretive approach of the Land Plan eliminated the communities' rights to use the land biomass included in the nucleus areas, and undermined local livelihoods. Enclosed reserves of genetic material and forested people are put under pressure by the commercial interests.

Land enclosure has transformed community members into criminal intruders. In ACA, the newly declared private areas land is patrolled by seven park guards who are organized in one Police Control Unit. When the Police Control Unit finds community members breaking regulations specified in the Land Plan (that is, not paying fees or intruding on designated research areas), the park guards confiscate anything the individual may have obtained on the land (eg., fish or game) and whatever tools were used, and then reports the offence to the office of the public prosecutor.

Biodiversity is a relational category, ecologically and culturally embedded, and local communities have worked as the keepers of nature for centuries. However, CENGO's, or large environmental corporations, manipulate the ecosystems to maximize the single component of genetic exploitation, which has undermined the integrity of nature and the rights of local communities to use their environment, and has plundered local community members' means of livelihood.

In Biodiversity Prospecting, the only process that adds value is the appropriation of nature's power and potential. It is only when nature is modified in the laboratory that nature's productivity counts or has any value in the sustainable development paradigm. However, CENGOs bioprospecting begins in the conservation areas with the biological samples brought by parataxonomists. They appropriate local knowledge about some of the attributes of the native plants and animals by hiring the daughters and sons in the rural communities as parataxonomists who initiate the collection. It is important to note that a parataxonomist is rural because there are many adverse factors, such as walking at night under heavy downpours to visit the incubator, with the added risk of falling branches and snake-bites. As a rural person, the parataxonomist brings intimate knowledge of the eco-system. In the work process, she/he acquires information about the protected area and becomes an information generator.

In Biodiversity Prospecting, NGOs working with business (pharmaceutical, odour industry) have virtually a monopoly on nature, knowledge and profits. In this framework, peasants and Indigenous People's labour has no economic value, while "scientific labour" is perceived to add value.

CENGOs cheapened local community knowledge in order to appropriate it through local parataxonomists. They initiated their collection with local knowledge, through the parataxonomist, and passed it on to the international and national business community. Medicinal plants for instance, sustained the health of all members of the community and forms the common knowledge of rural women. Through centuries of interaction rural women have created a rich and elaborate culture – a culture of the medicinal plants whose biological value is intrinsically linked to social, ethical and cultural values. There is a social/cultural structure governing their use. Medicinal plants were traditionally produced for a family's consumption, that is, they had use value not exchange value. Rural women were the keepers of medicinal plants and knowledge, and, as such, they prepared *cocimientos*, which are combinations of plants used for healing purposes. Most rural women grew medicinal plants surrounding their homes as part of the inter-cropping system and having grown medicinal plants for centuries, they acquired the knowledge of seeds and soils and the skills to prepare them. However, the social and cultural significance of the medicinal plants remained unrecognized, because 1) it was linked to women's work – something seen as non-work and non-knowledge despite the fact that women's work and knowledge has been central to biodiversity conservation and utilization; and 2) it was considered free because it was associated with wilderness and poor countries.

CENGOs devalued local communities as ecological authorities. "Scientific" knowledge undermines customary knowledge on the grounds that living knowledge is linked to sensuous knowledge and experience and thus is unauthoritative. In that way, the knowledge taken from local communities and Indigenous Peoples is unpaid. However, biodiversity is not just product created by nature, the activity of the Indigenous People and peasants has bred and improved traditional plants and medicines throughout the ages. Third World, local agriculturalists through millennia have made changes in genetics and continue to produce genetic material of great value. Genes are selected, improved and developed by agriculturalists which reflect their creativity, inventiveness and genius. Despite the fact that they are the providers and selectors of the biotechnology, their work is not recognized as labour (Cabrera 1993).

CENGOs also have monopoly of profits. INBio has agreements with Bristol Myers Squibb Company, Recombinant Biocatalysts, Analyticom ag, Merck, INDENA (phytopharmaceutical company Milan, Italy), Givaudan-Roure Fragrances of New Jersey (to identify and collect interesting odours from forest organisms), British Technology Group, Strathclyde Institute for Drug Research (Scotland) and many others (Mateo, 1996; Gudynas, 1998). In INBio's first agreement (1991), Merck and Co. awarded INBio a US$1 million dollar research budget to carry out a two-year, non-exclusive collaboration.

According to Goldman (1998), CENGOs

> have replaced the barefoot peasants as the "experts" on the commons; now, within the new discourse, it is their knowledge, rules and sciences and definitions that have become paramount for explaining ecological degradation and sustainability (p. 35).

> [...] as long as the commons is perceived as only existing within a particular mode of knowing, called development, with its unacknowledged structures of dominance, this community [CENGOs] will continue to serve the institution of development, whose raison d'être is restructuring Third World capacities and social-natural relations to accommodate transnational capital expansion (p. 47).

CENGOs are more concerned about the expansionary demands of the Northern industrial base than about the health of the ecology. They will make sure that industry gets what it needs because industrial expansionist projects require more raw materials extracted from the earth, rivers, forests, aquifers and cheap labour.

Dispossessing the Social Commons

Previous to the environmental crisis (1992), even previous to the debt crisis (1982), peasants and Indigenous Peoples were allowed to survive as "ecosystem people" (Guha and Martinez-Alier 1993), meaning the majority of the rural population lived from non-monetized biodiversity, particularly in the rain forest of the Amazon. With the increase in interest rates in 1982, the Mexican crisis marked the beginning of the generalized debt crisis and credit was shaped to become the best instrument for dispossession. How does the neoliberal-state dispossess the social Commons? There are several mechanisms in place with which to conduct this pillage. These are:

– a combination of powers in which Latin American governments (state), in combination with the U.S. treasury and the IMF, agreed to socialize the private debt of local and international business, while allowing the private sector to continue accumulating debts;

– to pay these debts, the state privatizes public enterprises in order to generate financial profits for private corporations and corrupt international organizations and local politicians;

– to intimidate and accept salary reduction, cutbacks in services and social investment to produce financial surplus, the powers use military enforcement (read killing, disappearances).

Between the IMF and the WB, governments are swamped with policy conditions that devalue the whole region in order to accumulate by dispossessing, that is, to buy local assets and labour cheaply. Cheapening assets and labour has been the result of reorganizing Latin American economies around the priority of regularly servicing their commercial

170

debts. During the 1990s, increasingly, the WB policy of privatization was taking precedence over other principles and other claims to property in order to promote economic "growth". In the 1990s, the direct investment of U.S. transnational corporations obtained 14%[5], the highest rate of profit in the world.

The growth proclaimed by the WB increases the monetary transactions while it destroys life systems and dispossesses millions. The imposition of the export-oriented growth of neoliberalism shifted the peasant and Indigenous People from:

– subsistence agriculture to export oriented agriculture with a focus on exports of meat, marine products (eg., shrimp), flowers, medicinal plants and vegetables. This has diverted land and water from production of staple foods for local consumption;

– control over resources from small farmers to agribusiness corporations. This has destroyed the natural resource base and people's livelihoods; and,

– agriculture from a peasant occupation of millions to a handful of agribusiness corporations, creating an industrial reserve army of unemployed workers.

In this environment of land dispossession, the sexual division of labour in the family provides a pool of cheap labour. The pattern of gender relations, in this context, is constituted by an articulation of capitalism with patriarchy, in which women are socially constructed as cheap labour. In cases where poor peasants get to maintain their lands, their daughters are tangled in micro-enterprises[6]. Rural women became the preferred work force in organic agriculture for a number of reasons: their mothers and grandmothers have the knowledge of traditional ecological agriculture methods; they are located in strategic zones; and the devaluation of women's work provides cheap labour.

When peasants families are evicted, women become the wage labour in order to find resources to assure subsistence and emotional support for the dispossessed family members. At the AWID[7] conference, in Guadalajara 2002, the consequences of the change of production from subsistence agriculture to export oriented agriculture were seen as responsible for converting peasant's daughters into maquiladoras workers. A new social structure of exploitation of wage labour has been layered in Mexico, Guatemala, Honduras, El Salvador, Costa Rica and Panama using women's labour, first, since the debt crisis and later the North American Free Trade Agreement. TNCs are allowed to send products to the maquiladoras for assembly where costs are lowest and then to be sent to the U.S. while exploiting the country and its people. At AWID (2002, a), women denounced that their low wages in maquiladoras[8] and tax exemptions in the export manufacture zones are considered another advantage that the elites of Latin Americans can offer to the global economy. 85% of the workers in maquiladoras are young rural women. Integration into the global system underlies the breakup of the rural families and forced mobility of women meanwhile; their labour power is threatened with physical disintegration. Girls from rural areas are becoming adults faster in order to get jobs in maquiladoras. As these women are from rural areas, they rent small apartments together, close to the factories, for sleeping and cooking. These places usually have no running water or electricity. The room usually has space only for four bodies. Their living and working conditions in the factory are not much different. In the maquiladoras, humiliating sexual exploitation begins with the hiring process. Applicants are required to submit information about the type of birth control they use, as well as if they are sexually active or not; further, employers ensure through pregnancy test that the applicants are not pregnant. Women work an average of 14 hours a day, in slave labour conditions. Regularly, workers are forced by the managers to take amphetamines to work longer schedules with wages that average only $100.00 monthly. They do not receive overtime payments. In the factory, there is no air circulation in the room and no time allowed for going to the bathroom. These conditions are producing countless occupational illnesses among women that are not recognized in the legislation of any of these countries. Generations of women are becoming ill due to repetitive movements in the work. Operations that take 10 seconds are forced to be done in 5 seconds. But the most affected are women producing computer chips for the electronics industry. There are chemical hazards that affect the health of these women. In general, after a period of 10 years of work, these women become blind. When rural women return to their homes, they usually go with health problems, as single mothers and poorer than they were before. In addition, women workers are surrounded by armed guards patrolling the Free Trade Zone, and women advocates are seen by these governments as interfering with corporate matters.

To expropriate the social Commons, the neoliberal policies of the state use organized violence from which no one can hide. Those governments persecute peasant and indigenous communities, sometimes with armed helicopters, paramilitaries, bomber planes, tanks, soldiers, police, sometimes with strident declarations, expectant silences, impotent silences. During 1970s-1990s, communities that organized themselves to defend themselves from the neoliberal agenda's attack were called "subversive". In the 2000s, despite United Nations recognition of Peoples human rights, when communities defend their rights and do not want to be submitted to dispossession, paramilitary[9] organizations are built in alliance with rich land owners, narcotrafico (Sandoval and Salazar 2002) and the regular army. In Colombia, important members of society have been implicated in counter-insurgence practices, stirring up paramilitaries; in Mexico, armed civilians have attacked the Zapatista municipalities and rural women; in Guatemala, assault and murder has been vicious and, in Bolivia, repression is genocidal. At the AWID conference (2002, b), Indigenous women from Chiapas and Oaxaca reported that women are now unable to work and are forced to be inside the household and/or leave the land in order to avoid rape by the soldiers who are allowed to use it as weapon; they also reported that fifty per cent of rural women suffer depression due to the low intensity war against women, men and children. Mexican women also raised the issue of the massive assassination of women in Ciudad Juarez, on the Mexican-U.S. border (AWID 2002, c). Over 800 female maquiladora workers have been kidnapped, raped and murdered with seeming impunity. These women were from rural areas, without family members, earning low wages and already suffering rampant sexual violence in the work place. A documentary video, *Senorita Extraviada*, by Lourdes Portillo, records in detail the disappearance of the first 200 women.

Hand in hand with violence against women, violence against their children has multiplied. Millions of children have taken to living on the streets ("The Madrid Declaration", 1994). Street children are at the mercy of police actions that are heavily implicated in the disappearances, tortures and deaths of suspected "subversives". These children are the children of impoverished and often single or abandoned women. The boys who live on the streets usually die on the street, while the girls live and die in violence selling the only valuable thing they possess: their bodies (Scheper and Hoffman, 1994). Furthermore, according to the International Labour Organization (ILO), in 1996 there were 17.5 million working children between the ages of 5 and 14. Most child workers operate in the urban informal sector or in agriculture, especially on peasant farms.

> The informal sector's most visible child members are the street workers, but those most at risk are household workers – the invisible multitudes, mainly girls, shut away from scrutiny behind the front doors of Latin America's family homes. Many more millions of girls work in their homes, caring for younger siblings, or maintaining the household so that their mothers can go out to work (Green 1999: 22).

In sum, before 1970s, the majority of Latin America population was still rural and outside the market, but with means of life infrastructure, land/game, water/fish, local education, health care and housing systems in place. But, since the 1980s, the unwaged subsistence poor have been joined by an outpouring of urban population victimized by privatization and growing unemployment, devaluation of currency/inflation, drops in real wages and loss of purchasing power, budget austerity, reduction of social expenditures and user fees in education, health care, housing, erosion of retirement pensions and basic justice, trade liberalization, removal of state subsidies, deregulation of grain markets, elimination of minimum wage legislation, further erosion of wages and salaries, liberalization of prices, and further polarization of income. This loss of control of means of survival and the pricing of their productive capacity have brought dispossession to masses of people (Debt Treaty[10], 1992; The Madrid Declaration, 1994; UNESCO, 1995, 1999). In 1990, in Latin American countries, the number of poor people living with $1.08 a day were 48.4 millions; by 2000, the entire region has been devalued and wages have dropped significantly, and the number of the poor increased to 55.6 millions. Those living with 2.15 a day also increased from 121.1 millions, in 1990, to 135.7 millions, in 2000 (WB, 2003). As a result of the continual increase, poverty in 2002 affects 62.1% of the population.

Francisco de Oliveira, at the opening of a Conferencia General del Consejo Latinamericano in Cuba, described how neo-liberalism has transformed the nation/states in exceptional states, in double ways, to protect the financial capital while condemning entire populations to impoverishment in the name of capital accumulation (CLACSO, 2003).

Reclaiming the Commons: Views of autonomy

A theoretical categorisation of the centrality of the Local Commons in emancipation from exploitation is crucial. Autonomy is only possible within a gift and Common-centered political economy. Ancestral communities are united in their opposition to commodification of their lives. In October 2003, a celebrated example of defending the Local Commons took place in Bolivia. A revolution involving Indigenous People, peasant cocaleros, the central union (Central Obrera Boliviana) and civil society rose up. This uprising intended to defend existing Commons against enclosure of hydrocarbon and natural resources which are in the hands of Transnational Corporations and the U.S. respectively. From the beginning, the popular movement clarified their rejection of the neo-liberal policies that have impoverished them and the Free Trade of the Americas. Pedro Fuentes (2003) argues that Bolivia is a country where historically the biggest contradictions are connected. Robbed first by Spain, British and U.S. imperialism, Bolivians now refused to sell gas to U.S. and Mexico, based on the argument that they themselves have been deprived of gas in order to export. According to Mamani (2003) the Indigenous People's identity politics paralysed Bolivia. Their identity is based on daily experiences such as family kinship, language (Aimara) and cultural links. The Indigenous People of Bolivia have constructed collective social and cultural forms of self-affirmation that allow them to take social and territorial space to defend themselves against government aggression. A peaceful demonstration was followed by a massacre of 6 adults protesters and a child. This terrible crime encouraged their self-determination to defend themselves, which was manifested in collective actions, such as a blocking avenues, street closures, clashing with the army, in addition to massive demonstrations, hunger strikes and political discourses. As the killings of Indigenous People and mine workers continued, the gas struggle was transformed from a struggle for gas into a battle to vanquish the government. In the end, the popular movement guided by mining workers ousted president Sanchez de Lozada.

For the Indigenous People and Campesinos of Bolivia the immediate issue, after expelling "their president", was reclaiming the Commons that had been enclosed by the elite and the U.S. corporations. Led by Mallka, leader of *Confederacion Sindical Unica de Trabajadores Campesinos de Bolivia* (CSUTCB), they organized direct land occupation to ensure people's control over their own lives, to rebuild what has worked in the past (*Correspondencia de Prensa 79*). They are looking toward their traditional practices for inspiration in restoring their ancient system: "*El Qullasuyu*" (Ortuzar, 2003). Firmly grounded in the culture of the Commons, Indigenous People are rising up against the historical racism and ethnic domination that has encouraged extreme violence against them. Following the defeat of the government, some 100 landless families occupied the "property" of the ex-minister of defence while others reclaimed 2,000 hectares property of the ex-president (both of them fugitives, now living in the U.S.) (*Econoticias 2003*). They vindicated this action as a "community justice" against two criminals, the first commanded the recent massacres (80 were killed and 400 were injured) and the second supported U.S. neo-liberal policies to dispossess the population. Bolivia is calling now for a new threshold of democracy, and a redefinition of the Commons and in defence of livelihood (*Correspondencia de Prensa Nos*, 66 and 85).

Conclusion

Since the debt crisis, 1982, indebtedness has created the conditions for massive dispossession through homogenized policies of the financial institutions, particularly stabilization

(IMF) and structural adjustments (WB). Since the Earth Summit, 1992, indebtedness has been used as the framework to fulfill the Global Commons in opposition to Local Commons. In this paper, I have evidenced that the credit system (finance capital), in Latin America, exhibits all the features of primitive accumulation that Marx mentions in *Capital*: fraudulence, thievery and dispossession. I have also dug into Marxist feminists arguments that capitalism depends on the free or cheaply paid work of rural women, on the un-paid peasant and Indigenous People's assets and work, as well as the gifts of nature. As a result of these approaches, three winners have been identified: commercial banks that have made record profits on their loans; transnational corporations that took control of Latin American cheap labour and privatized the social Commons; and large environmental NGOs that enclosed the nature Commons in the name of conservation.

However, dispossession and the creation of social exclusion are serious problems even for international finance, as a result they have determined to militarize its treatment. Since September 11, 2001, U.S. and the Latin American elites started to criminalize the acts of reclaiming justice and protesting intimidation. When communities defend themselves, they are called "terrorists" and genocidal policies are utilized. But accumulation by dispossession produces radicalization among Commoners.

Notes

[1] Debt swaps are financial mechanisms which exchange debt for ownership in national industries, public enterprises, bank assets, and nature.

[2] What is sustainable development? For UNWCED, it is development that meets the needs and aspirations of the present without compromising the ability to meet those of the future.

[3] CENGOs refer to the large environmental organizations that manage and supervise the process of socialization of capital. They are a special category of functionaries subordinated to the ruling class in which the managers are involved in the process of corporate globalization, economic restructuring and colonial practices. In the past, the main objectives of the corporate environmental organizations have been to identify and gain access to ecologically sensitive areas for use as sites for research and scientific data collection (Dawkins, 1992).

[4] Non-government Organization (NGO) initiates its collection with local knowledge, through the parataxonomist, and it passes it on to the international and national business community. In their conservation schemes, a parataxonomist's work does not add value. Parataxonomists are considered non-specialists because they have no formal degree, although they use the parataxonomist's knowledge to initiate every process.

[5] "Survey of Current Business", various issues from Doug Henwood in the *Free Flow of Money*, in *NACLA Report on the Americas*, 1996: 15.

[6] For a case study of the Abanico Medicinal Plant and Organic Agriculture please refer to Isla, Ana (2003) "Women and Biodiversity as Capital Accumulation: En Eco-feminist View", *Socialist Studies Bulletin*, No. 69, Winter.

[7] What is AWID? Association for Women's Rights in Development is an international membership organization connecting, informing and mobilizing people and organizations committed to achieving gender equality, sustainable development and women's human rights. AWID's goal is to cause policy, institutional and individual change that will improve the lives of women and girls everywhere.

[8] The maquiladora industry produces clothing and textiles, electronics, car parts, furniture, chemical products, processed food, toys and leather goods [Abell, Hilary (1999) "Endangering women's health for profit: health and safety in Mexico's maquiladoras", *Development in Practice*, 9 (5), p. 595].

[9] Paramilitary organizations are designated to break the protests coming from social exclusion.

[10] The Debt Treaty was elaborated and signed during the Global Forum of the Earth Summit, in 1992.

References

(ACA) Area de Conservacion Arenal (1993). *Plan General de Uso de la Tierra, Tomo III, Propuesta y Lineamientos Estrategicos*. Costa Rican Ministry of Natural Resources, Energy and Mines (MINAE), with the support of the Canadian International Development Agency (CIDA) and the World Wildlife Fund-Canada (WWF-C), Costa Rica.

AWID (2002 a). Workshop: Protecting the Labour Rights of Women Workers: The Maquila Situation in the Globalized Economy. Presented by Kichin Konojel, from Guatemala; Condicion de la Mujer en la Maquila, OIT, El Salvador; Center for Legal Action on Human Rights (CALGH), Guatemala; Honduran Women's Collective (CODEMUH), Honduras; Las Melidas-MAM, El Salvador.

— (2002 b). Workshop: In Solidarity with the Independent Movement of Women in Chiapas: Resistance to Neoliberal Globalization. Presented by COLEM, Mexico; FEMINARIO, Mexico; Formacion y Capacitacion A.C., Mexico; Red de Defensoras populares en Chiapas, Mexico.

— (2002 c). Workshop: Globalizing Actions Against Impunity of Feminicides in Ciudad Juarez was presented by ELIGE Youth Network on Reproductive and Sexual Rights, Mexico; Comision Mexicana de Defensa y Promocion de los Derechos Humanos en Mexico; Coordinacion de Organismos Civiles por un Milenio Feminista D.F. Mexico and AFL/CIO, Mexico.

Brenner, R. (2002). *The Boom and the Bubble: the U.S. in the World Economy*, Verso, London.

Correspondencia de Prensa (2003). "Bolivia. Gobierno de la Mesa promete lealtad al FMI", No. 66 October 22, ed. Ernesto Herrera: germain@chasque.net

— (2003). "Bolivia Despues de la Batalla. Parlamento Europeo pide depurar responsabilidades y negar asilo a ex-gobernanates", No. 79, October 24, ed. Ernesto Herrera: germain@chasque.net

— (2003). "Discurso Completo de Evo Morales", No. 85, October 26, ed. Ernesto Herrera: germain@chasque.net

— (2003). "La lucha contra la globalization es cuestion de sobrevivencia. Sub-Comandante Marcos", No. 86, October 26, ed. Ernesto Herrera: germain@chasque.net

Cabrera, Jorge (1993). "Derechos de Propiedad Intelectual y Recursos Geneticos", in *Diversidad Biologica y Desarrollo Sostenible*, Fundacion AMBIO, Euroamericana de Ediciones S.A., Costa Rica.

Calloni, Stella (2004). "U.S. Troops in the Guarani Nation. The Empire in Paraguay", Argen press 10/1/2004, Argentina.

CLACSO (2003). "Conferencia General del Consejo Latinoamericano de Ciencias Sociales in Cuba", October, 2003.

Econoticias, Bolivia.com "Gobierno de Mesa defiende a bala propiedades de Goni y sus amigos", Cochabamba, October 27, 2003.

Fuentes Pedro (2003). "La Insurreccion Boliviana. Cincuenta Años despues de la primera revolucion obrera boliviana", *Correspondencia de Prensa*, No. 69, October 23.

Gatt-Fly Report (1985). "Debt Bondage or Self-Reliance: A Popular Perspective on the Global Debt Crisis", Gatt-Fly, Toronto.

— (1987). "To Pay is to Die: We Want to Live", Gatt-Fly, Vol. VIII, No. 4, Toronto.

George, Susan (1988). *A Fate Worse Than Debt*, Grove Press, New York.

— (1992). *The Debt Boomerang: How the Third World Debt Harms Us All*, Pluto Press with the Transnational Institute, London.

Goldie, Mark (editor) (1997). "Second Tract on Government" and "An Essay on the Poor Law", in Locke, *Political Essays*, Cambridge Texts in the History of Political Thought, Cambridge University Press.

Green, Duncan (1999). "Child workers of the Americas", *Nacla, Report on the Americas*, Vol. 32 (4), pp. 21-27.

Gudynas, Eduardo (1997). "La Naturaleza ante el doctor Fausto. Apropiacion o conservacion de la Bodiversidad", *Ciencias Ambientales* 13 (November), pp. 55-63, Costa Rica.

— (1998). "Conservacion, Sustentabilidad ecologica y la Articulacion entre Comercio y Ambiente", *Ciencias Ambientales*, Costa Rica, 14 (June), pp. 49-57.

Guha, Ramachandra and J. Martinez-lier (1998). *Varieties of Environmentalism: Essays North and South*, Delhi, Oxford University Press, UK.

Hamilton, Kirk (2001). "Genuine Savings, population growth and sustaining economic welfare", Paper presented at the Natural Capital, Poverty and Development Conference, 5-8 September.

Hardin, Garret (1968). "The Tragedy of the Commons", *Science*, 162 (3859), pp. 1243-1248, dec. 13.

Harvey, David (2003). *The New Imperialism*, Oxford University Press, New York.

Mamani, Pablo (2003). "El Rugir de la Multitud", in Eco-noticias Bolivia.com special for Argenpress.info, October 27, Bolivia.

Mateo, Nicolas (1996). "Wild Biodiversity: The Last Frontier? The Case of Costa Rica", in *Globalization of Science: The Place of Agricultural Research*, eds. C. Bonte-Friedheim and K. Sheridan, International Service for National Agricultural Research, The Hague.

Marx, Karl (1977). "So-Called Primitive Accumulation", in *Capital*, Volume One, Vintage Books, A Division of Random House, New York, pp. 871-940.

Mies, Maria (1986). *Patriarchy and Accumulation on a World Scale. Women in the International Division of Labour*, Zed Books Ltd, London.

— (1996). "Globalization of the Economy and Women's Work in a Sustainable Society", Paper presented at the Sixth International Interdisciplinary Congress on Women, Australia.

Mies, Maria, Claudia von Werlhof and Virginia Bennholdt-Thomsen (1978*). Women: The Last Colony*, Zed Books, London.

— (1999). *The Subsistence Economy*, Zed Books, London

Mora, Maria Elena (1998). "Arenal, Corazon Energetico de Costa Rica", *aca en accion*, Edicion Especial. Magazine published by Arenal Conservation Area, Costa Rica, pp. 1-3.

Ortuzar Ximena (2003). "Bolivia despues de la batalla. Entrevista a Felipe 'Mallku' Quispe", *La Jornada newspaper*, October 25, 2003, Mexico.

— (2003). "Los Indigenas dan 90 dias de plazo al nuevo president, al que no auguran mucha vida", La Jornada, October 27, Mexico.

PROACA (1996). "Biodiversity-Programa de Investigation para el Uso Rational de la Biodiversity en el Area de Conservacion Arenal", World Wildlife Fund-Canada (wwfBc) and Asociacion Conservacionista Monteverde (acm), Costa Rica.

Polanyi, Karl (1967). *The Great Transformation*, Beaçon Press, Boston.

Robinson, William I. (1996). "Globalization: nine thesis of our epoch", *Race & Class*, 38, 2, pp. 13-31.

Roddick, Jackie (1988). *The Dance of the Millions. Latin America and the Debt Crisis*, Latin America Bureau (Research and Action), London.

Rowe, Jonathan (2001). "The Hidden Commons", *YES! A Journal of Positive Futures*, Summer.

Scheper-Hughes, Nancy and Daniel Hoffman (1994). "Kids Out of Place", *NACLA, Report on the Americas*, 27 (6), May/June, pp. 16-23.

Salleh, Ariel (1994). "Nature, Women, Labor, Capital: Living the Deepest Contradiction", *Is Capitalism Sustainable? Political Economy and the Politics of Ecology*, ed. Martin O'Connor, The Guildford Press, New York.

— (1997). *Ecofeminism as Politics. Nature, Marx and the Post-modern*, Zed Books, Ltd. London & New York.

Santos, Celso, Editora Abril S/A, Revista Casa Claudia "Estadno" de Brasil, "INDIGNACIÓN. LI-BROS DE USA DIFUNDEN BRASIL SIN EL AMAZONAS", Newspaper January 25 – Saquiribal <saqribal@racsa.co.cr> Mon., 26 Jan. 2004, Brasil and Costa Rica.

Shiva, Vandana (1989). "Development, Ecology and Women", in *Healing the Wounds. The Promise of Ecofeminism, Between the Lines*, Toronto.

— (1993). "The Politics of the Green Revolution", *Third World Resurgence*, No. 33, pp. 4-8.

— (1996). "Economic Globalization, Ecological Feminism and Sustainable Development", Paper presented at the Sixth International Interdisciplinary Congress on Women, Australia.

Smith, Robert and Claude Simard (2001). "A Proposed Approach to Environment and Sustainable Development Indicators Based on Capital", Paper presented at the Natural Capital, Poverty and Development Conference, 5-8 September, Toronto, Canada.

Tremblay, Claude and Daniel Malenfant (1996). "Estrategias Locales para Favorecer la Sostenibilidad de Acciones de Desarrollo El Caso del Proyecto de Conservacion y Desarrollo Arenal Costa Rica", Paper presented at the Congreso Mundial de Conservacion (Global Conservation Conference), held in Montreal, Canada, 17-21 October.

"The Madrid Declaration" (1994). *Third World Resurgence*, 51: and/or http://www.nativenet.uthsc-sa.edu/archive/nl/9410/0140.html

UNESCO (1995). (United Nations Educational, Scientific and Cultural Organization) General Conference. Twenty-eighth Session "Effects of Structural Adjustment Programmes on Education and Training." August 25, Paris.

— (1999). "Economic, Social and Cultural Rights. Effects of structural adjustment policies on the full enjoyment of human rights", Commission on Human Rights, Fifty-fifth session, Report by Mr. Fantu Cheru.

Vilas, Carlos, (1999). "The Decline of the Steady Job in Latin America", *Nacla, Report on the Americas*, 22 (4), (January/February), pp. 15-20.

Wood, Ellen M. (2002). *The Origin of Capitalism a longer view*, Verso.

World Bank (2003). http://www.worldbank.org/research/povmonitor/index.htm.

GIFT-GIVING, MOTHER-SENSE AND
SUBJECTIVITY IN VICTORIA WELBY.
A STUDY IN SEMIOETHICS

1. *Welby, Victoria Alexandrina, Lady Welby (1837-1912), who is she?*

Victoria Welby, philosopher of language and ideator of significs, now widely considered as the "founding mother" of semiotics, was born on 27 April 1837, the third of three children of his Grace the Duke of Rutland, Hon. Charles James Stuart-Wortley (1802-1844), second of three sons of the first Lord Wharncliffe, and his wife Lady Emmeline Charlotte Elizabeth (1806-1855), writer, poetess and traveller, second daughter of John Henry Manners, fifth Duke of Rutland, and Lady Elizabeth Howard, daughter of Frederick Howard, fifth Earle of Carlisle.

Victoria Welby was christened as Victoria Alexandrina Maria Louisa Stuart-Wortley by the Bishop of Salisbury in St. James' Church on 17 June 1837 with their Royal Highnesses Princess Alexandrina Victoria and the Duchess of Kent (the Queen Mother) acting as her godmothers and John Irving, Esq. as god-father. She was named after her first godmother. This event took on even greater significance when five days later Princess Victoria became first Queen Alexandrina Victoria and then, changing her signature, simply Queen Victoria.

Victoria Welby was appointed Maid of Honour to Queen Victoria in 1861 spending almost two years (1861-1863) at the royal court before her marriage at Belvoir, on 4 July 1863, to Sir William Earle Welby (1829-1898), military official, MP and High Sheriff, who with his father's death in 1875 became fourth Baronet assuming the additional surname Gregory. Consequently Victoria Welby's surname became Welby-Gregory.

Alternatively to a series of pseudonyms, she published under her full name until the end of the 1880s, under the name of Hon. Lady Welby from 1890 to 1893 and as Victoria Welby from 1893 onwards, although she continued signing all official and business documents with her full name.

After her husband's death and with the marriage of her son, Sir Charles Glynne Earle Welby (1865-1938), Assistant Undersecretary of State at War Office and MP, in 1887, to Maria Louisa Helena Hervey (d. 1920), her correct name was Victoria Lady Welby or simply Lady Welby since her daughter-in-law had acquired the right to place the title "Lady" before her Christian name. On marrying, her son also acquired the right to live at Denton Manor. Welby shifted to Duneaves her home at Harrow.

Her other two children were Victor Albert William (1864-1876) and her only daughter Emmeline Mary Elizabeth ("Nina") (1867-1955), painter, sculptress, writer. She also wrote her mother's biography and edited her correspondence in two volumes. Some years after her marriage, and following the Royal School of Art Needlework founded in 1873, Lady Victoria Welby-Gregory also set up and financed the Decorative Needlework Society. She was not at all attracted to life at court and soon after her marriage retreated to Denton Manor where she began her research with her husband's full support.

She contributed significantly to modern theory of signs, meaning and interpretation, introducing the term "significs", in 1894, to underline her own special focus on the interrelationship between signs, sense – in all its signifying implications – values and behavior. The term "significs" indicates her special approach to the study of meaning and interpretation, which she developed with reference to her meaning triad, therefore to the distinction between "sense", "meaning" and "significance". Welby's research is characterized by implications of an axiological order which she evidenced with the distinction between "meaning" and "significance". With the term 'significs' she differentiated her own perspective from others designated as "semantics", "semiotics", "sematology", and "semasiology". Welby strongly influenced such personalities as Charles K. Ogden[1] who co-authored with Ivor A. Richards a renowned volume of 1923 entitled *The Meaning of Meaning*. In this volume Ogden mentions Welby and her significs as well as her correspondence with Charles S. Peirce[2].

Besides numerous articles in newspapers, magazines and scientific journals (notably *The Spectator*, *The Expositor*, *The Fortnightly Review*, *The Open Court*, *Nature*, *Mind*, *The Monist*, *The Hibbert Journal*, *Journal of Philosophy*, *Psychology and Scientific Methods*) and a long list of privately printed essays, parables, aphorisms and pamphlets on a large range of subjects in numerous spheres – science, mathematics, anthropology, philosophy, education, social issues –, Welby's publications include six books. Apart from a travel diary (1852), written and published as a child, a book of critical reflections on theological and religious questions consisting mainly of extracts from her correspondence, *Links and Clues* (1881, 1883[2]), and a book of prayers (1892), Welby authored a collection of parables, critical reflections and aphorisms, *Grains of Sense* (1897), and two theoretical monographs specifically relating to significs, *What is Meaning?* (1903, 1983[2]), and *Significs and Language* (1911, 1985[2]). Other valuable sources include a biography by her daughter, *Wanderers* (Cust 1928), and on a theoretical level two volumes of correspondence between Welby and various interlocutors covering the years 1879-1891 and 1898-1911, respectively, *Echoes of Larger Life* (Welby 1929) and *Other Dimensions* (Welby 1931). Another major editorial event is represented by the publication of Welby's correspondence with Peirce *Semiotic and Significs* (Hardwick 1977).

From 1863 until her death in 1912 Welby was a friend and source of inspiration to leading personalites from the world of science and literature. She wrote regularly to over 450 correspondents from diverse countries including Great Britain, United States of America, France, Italy, Germany, the Netherlands, which testifies to her determining presence in the cultural ambiences of her day. She characteristically used her correspondence as a place for theorization in dialogue with others. Welby began writing to politicians, representatives of the Church, aristocrats and intellectuals as early as 1870 creating an epistolary network which expanded rapidly from 1880 onwards, both locally and internationally. She used this network for her own enlightenment, as a sounding board for her own ideas, as a means of circulating ideas – her own ideas and those of others. In addition to such personalities as

Peirce in the USA and Giovanni Vailati in Italy, her correspondents include such significant names as Bertrand Russell, Charles K. Ogden, James M. Baldwin, Henry Spencer, Thomas A. Huxley, Max Müller, Ferdinand C. S. Schiller, Benjamin Jowett, Frederick Pollock, George F. Stout, Herbert G. Wells, Mary E. Boole, Julia Wedgwood, Henry and William James, Henri L. Bergson, Michel Bréal, André Lalande, J.-H. Poincaré, Ferdinand Tönnies, Rudolph Carnap, Otto Neurath, Harald Höffding, Frederick van Eeden, and many others. Ogden was a young university student when he discovered Welby and her significs. He was committed to promoting significs and corresponded with Welby regularly between 1910 and 1911. His paper *The Progress of Significs* was published in 1994 in one of the four volumes collecting his complete works.

Thanks also to her social position and Court appointment as Maid of Honour to Queen Victoria, she counted friends and acquaintances among the aristocracy and Government officials. Because of her interest in religious and theological questions she corresponded with leading Churchmen of her day and subsequently with eminent scientists, philosophers, educationists whom she welcomed into her home where they met to discuss their ideas.

Nonetheless, in spite of general awareness of the importance and originality of Welby's work, she did not receive the recognition she hoped for, at least not publicl for many long years. In the attempt to avoid flattery, she either published anonymously or signed her work with pseudonyms, various combinations of initials, or simply as "Victoria Welby". The only honour she valued was "that of being treated by workers as a serious worker" (Hardwick 1977: 13). Though she had no institutional affiliations, she was a member of the Aristotelian and Anthropological Societies and one of the original promoters of the Sociological Society between 1903-1904.

Welby was an open-minded female intellectual in the Victorian era despite her complete lack of a formal education which led her to search for the conditions which made her theoretical work possible. She highlighted the importance of her extensive travels as a child with her mother, which often took place in dramatic circumstances and ended with her mother's tragic death in the Sirian desert leaving Victoria all alone until help came from Beirut. In a letter of December 22 1903 to Peirce who fully recognized her genius as testified by their correspondence, Welby made the following considerations:

> [...] I may perhaps mention that I never had any education whatever in the conventional sense of the term. Instead of that I travelled with my mother over a great part of the world under circumstances of difficulty and even hardship. The present facilities did not then exist! This I think accounts in some degree for my seeing things in a somewhat independent way. But the absence of any systematic mental training must be allowed for of course in any estimate of work done. [...] I only allude to the unusual conditions of my childhood in order partly to account for my way of looking at and putting things: and my very point is that any value in it is impersonal. It suggests an ignored heritage, an unexplored mine. This I have tried to indicate in "What is Meaning?" (Hardwick 1977: 13-14).

As her research progressed Welby increasingly promoted the study of significs, channelling the great breadth and variety of her interests into a "significal" perspective. Shortly after the publication of two fundamental essays, *Meaning and Metaphor*, in 1893 and

Sense, Meaning and Interpretation, in 1896, the Welby Prize for the best essay on significs was announced in the journal *Mind* in 1896 and awarded to Ferdinand Tönnies in 1898 for his essay on *Philosophical Terminology* (1899-1900). Important moments of a long attended official recognition for significs are represented by the publication of the entries *Translation* (Welby 1902), *Significs* (co-authored with J. M. Baldwin and G. F. Stout) (1902), and *Sensal* (with G. F. Stout) (1902) in the *Dictionary of Philosophy and Psychology* (Baldwin 1901-1905). However, the official recognition Welby had so tenaciously hoped for only came after approximately thirty years of "hard labour", with the publication of the entry *Significs* in the *Encyclopaedia Britannica* in 1911. The Signific Movement in the Netherlands, which developed in two phases from 1917 to 1926 and from 1937 to 1956, originated from Welby's significs through the mediation of the Dutch psychiatrist, poet and social reformer Frederik van Eeden (1860-1932).

Welby's scientific remains are now mainly deposited in two different archives: the Welby Collection in the York University Archives (Downsview, Ontario, Canada) and the Lady Welby Library in the University of London Library. The latter includes approximately 1.000 volumes from Victoria Welby's personal library and 25 pamphlet boxes containing pamphlets, reprints and newspaper cuttings, religious tracts, sermons and published lectures by various authors. Four boxes without numbers contain duplicates of most of Welby's own publications. The main part of her scientific and literary production is to be found at the York Archives, divided into 42 boxes. Boxes 1-21, that is, half of the collection, consist of Welby's yet mostly unpublished correspondence covering the years 1861-1912; boxes 22-42 are subject files (titles established by Welby) containing notes, extracts, commentaries on a variety of subjects – Biology, Education, Ethics, Eugenics, Imagery, Language and Significance, Logic and Significance, Matter and Motion, Numbers Theory, Philosophy and Significance, Significs (9 files), Time – speeches, lessons, sermons by other authors, numerous unpublished essays and a collection of poems by Welby, diagrams and photographs, translations, proofs, copies of some of her publications, newspaper cuttings, etc.

Suffering from partial aphasia and paralysis of the right hand due to bad blood circulation caused by flu caught at the end of January 1912, Welby died at the age of 75 at Denton Manor and was buried in Grantham (Lincolnshire), on 29 March 1912.

2. *The concept of mother-sense as gift-giving*

The generation of sense, value and significance in their most human expressions, that is, at high degrees of creativity, playfulness, openness to the other, excess, dialogism, intercorporeity and capacity for critique, occurs in sign processes of the abductive, iconic and agapastic type. In addition to Peirce and his research, this paradigm for semiosis in the human world also emerges from the theory of sign and meaning elaborated by Welby, her significs. Significs could also be described as a theory of the transcendent given that it conceptualizes signifying continuity throughout the sign universe, "synechism" in Peirce's terminology, therefore the tendency to surpass boundaries and limits – as imposed, in the last analysis, by the logic of identity – across sign systems which, however specific and differentiated, are always interrelated and interdependent, according to the logic of what we may call "dialogic otherness", in the terminology of Mikhail Bakhtin[3].

In a series of unpublished manuscripts collected under the title *Mother-sense* written at the beginning of the twentieth century (cf. References), Welby proposed the original concept of "mother-sense", subsequently replaced with the term "primal sense" and its variant "primary sense" (Box 28, Subject File 24). This concept plays a central role in her analysis of the production/interpretation of signifying processes in human signifying spheres and therefore in the construction/interpretation of worlds and worldviews.

Welby distinguished between "sense", therefore "mother-sense", on the one hand, and "intellect", therefore "father-reason", on the other. With this distinction it was her intention to indicate the general difference between two main modes – that in fact cut across sexual differences – in the generation/interpretation of sense which may be isolated for the sake of analysis but which are strictly interrelated in the reality of human behaviour, therefore in sense producing practices. Mother-sense may be understood in the double sense of the Latin verb *sapére* which means at once to know and to taste of (*scio* and *sapio*), and indicates a peculiar capacity for knowing, understood also as the capacity for transcending the very limits of knowledge itself when oriented by the logic of identity. What the intellect must exert itself to know mother-sense already knows in the double sense of *sapére*, and it is important to underline that such knowledge is related to the body.

Mother-sense also called "racial motherhood" is the generating source of sense and the capacity for criticism, says Welby; it is oriented by the logic of otherness and as such corresponds to the capacity for knowing in a broad and creative sense through sentiment, perception, intuition and cognitive leaps. With reference to Peirce we could say that it is the idea intuited before it is possessed or before it possesses us. As the capacity for knowledge, which we may also intend in the Peircean sense of *agapic or sympathetic comprehension and recognition*, or in the Bakhtinian sense of *answering comprehension*, mother-sense belongs to the human race in its totality, "an inheritance common to humanity", says Welby, without limitation to a given sexual gender, the female, even though in socio-historical terms the woman emerges as its main guardian and disseminator. Mother-sense, primal sense, racial sense or racial motherhood[4] is also that which is commonly indicated with a series of stereotyped terms including "intuition", "judgement", "wisdom". In any case it is common to both men and women, even though it is particularly alive in women owing to the daily practices they are called to carry out in their roles as mother or wife, which are mostly gift-giving practices oriented by the logic of otherness, of self-donation, giving and responsibility for the other, care for the other. Furthermore, Welby underlines the woman's influence and responsibility, as the main repository of mother-sense, in the development of verbal and nonverbal language and therefore in the construction of the symbolic order.

On the other hand, intellect, as understood by Welby, alludes to knowledge and inferential processes oriented by the logic of identity. As rational knowledge the intellect is connected with the processes of asserting, generalizing and reasoning about data as they are observed and experimented in science and logic. The limit of the intellect lies in the tendency to allow for the tyranny of data which we wish to possess but which, on the contrary, end up possessing us. The reign of knowledge covered by the intellect is entrusted fundamentally to the jurisdiction of the male, says Welby, mainly for socio-cultural reasons and certainly not because of some special natural propensity for rational reasoning exclusive to the male. However, the intellect derives from mother-sense and must remain connected to it if we are to avoid the intellect's homologation and levelling onto the logic of identity, emptied of the relation to the other, of the capacity for sense and significance. Consequently, for the full development of its cognitive and expressive potential, intellectual knowledge and science must be grounded in mother-sense and must not ignore it. Furthermore, mother-sense includes "father-sense" (even if latently), while the contrary is not true. Therefore mother-sense and the intellect must be recovered in their original condition of dialectic and dialogic interrelation on both a phylogenetic and ontogenetic level.

With the term "intellect", as understood by Welby, we are on the side of inferential processes of the inductive and deductive type, where the logic of identity dominates over the logic of alterity. In terms of Peirce's best known sign triad, induction and deduction may be associated respectively to symbolicity and indexicality. Instead, with mother-sense we are on the side of signifying processes oriented by the logic of alterity and by the iconic dimension of signs; mother-sense, or "racial sense", as Welby also calls it, alludes to the creative and generative forces of sense resulting from and in the capacity to associate things which would seem distant from each other while in fact they are mutually attracted to each other. In terms of argumentation mother-sense is associated with logical procedures of the abductive type which are regulated by the logic of otherness, creativity, dialogism, freedom, love and desire.

In this context important to signal is Welby's correspondence with her friend Mary Everest Boole, writer, political activist and wife of the famous logician and mathematician studied by Peirce, George Boole. Among her many merits Mary Boole authored a series of books and articles generally unknown to reading public: these include such titles as *Logic Taught by Love* and *The Forging of Passion into Power*. And, indeed, in their fascinating correspondence Welby and Mary Boole discuss the laws that rule over thought in terms of the intimate interconnection between logic and love, passion and power (cf. Welby 1929: 86-92).

Logic as understood by Welby is logic where the broader and generative dimension of sense, the original level, the primal level, mother-sense, racial sense, the "matrix" interweaves with rational, intellectual life in a relationship of dialectic interdependency and reciprocal enrichment. According to Welby, logic to classify as such must always be associated with primal sense. And, indeed, one of the major goals of significs is to recover the relation of "answering comprehension", in Bakhtin's terminology, or of "agapic or sympathetic comprehension", in Peirce's, and therefore the relation of reciprocal empowering between primal sense and rational life. This relation is necessary for the full development of our capacity for critique and, therefore, of our awareness of the value, meaning and purport of experience in its totality. Significs sets itself the task of recovering the relationship of reciprocal interpretation between the constant *données* of mother-sense, on the one hand, and the constructs of the intellect, on the other. Mother-sense, says Welby, is the material of "immediate, unconscious and interpretive intuition"; from an evolutionary point of view it constitutes the "subsequent phase, on the level of value, to animal instinct". Therefore, mother-sense is together "primordial and universal" and as such it is present at all stages in the development of humanity, even if to varying degrees (Welby 1985a: ccxxxviii); as such, recalling Emmanuel Levinas (1906-1995), it tells of significance before and after signification (cf. Levinas 1974c). Mother-sense concerns the real insofar as it is part of human practices and the ideal insofar as it is the condition by virtue of which humanity may aspire to continuity and perfection in the generation of actual and possible words and of signifying processes at large.

Furthermore, Welby's concept of logic may be associated with Peirce's when he describes the great principle of logic in terms of "self-surrender". And, as he also clarifies, this does not mean that self is to lay low for the sake of ultimate triumph, which must not be the governing purpose of our behaviour (cf. Peirce, *CP* 5.402, note 2).

Mother-sense is both analytic and synthetic, it determines a disposition for knowledge with a capacity for growth in both quantitative and qualitative terms, which implies the capacity for changing orientation and perspective, for proceeding by cognitive leaps and entering different cognitive paradigms. "Calculation gives useful results", says Welby in her unpublished manuscripts, "but without the sense and judgement of quality it can give no more than a description of fact".

Furthermore, mother-sense is defined by Welby as knowledge that is "instinctively religious", where "religious" is understood etymologically (*religare* = to unite, to relate, to link) as "feeling consciousness of the solar relationship"; a universal sense of *dependency* particularly developed in women upon something greater than the human (therefore, says Welby, a woman must not submit to her own creation, man); a universal tendency towards religion where by "religion" is understood a world that is other, vaster, more elevated, a world made of other origins and other relationships beyond the merely planetary, a world at the highest degrees of otherness and creativity. In Welby's description mother-sense is a transcendent sense, in other words it determines our capacity to transcend the limits of sense itself, and as such is the true sense and value of the properly human. As she further specifies, mother-sense does not imply "anthropomorphism", but far more broadly "organomorphism", on the one hand, and "cosmomorphism", on the other.

According to Welby, the history of the human race is also the history of the continual deviations operated by humanity in the social and signifying network, therefore, it is also the history of the loss of the sense of discernment and criticism, being the most serious of deviations. Such loss causes us to be satisfied with existence as it is, when, on the contrary, says Welby, what is needed is a condition of eternal dissatisfaction to the end of increasing our expressive capacity and of developing and improving the human race: "We all tend now, men and women, to be satisfied [...] with things as they are. But we have all entered the world precisely to be dissatisfied with it". Therefore, with her concept of mother-sense Welby signals the need to recover the critical instance of the intellectual capacity, the gift for unprejudiced thinking based on abductive logic, otherness, and dialogism, for the production of sense, for prevision and anticipation, for translation in the broadest sense possible across the different systems of signs and values.

Mother-sense underlines the need to develop a social consciousness that is radically critical, capable of transcending the limits of convention in the effort to improve what we might call a concrete abstraction, that is, future generations. Similarly to Peirce (ideator of the concept of creative love, agapasm) when he maintains that the evolutionary results engendered by the logic of love derive from love oriented towards something concrete, Welby too, though independently from Peirce, orients the logic of mother-sense towards one's concrete neighbour, that is, one's neighbour in terms of affinity or similarity, even though s/he may be distant in space and time, while criticizing the threat of "vague and void abstractions", as might be represented, for example, by the bad use of the concept itself of "future". On the level of inference the practices of creative love are abductive practices oriented by the logic of otherness, structured by the relationship with the other, the other in close "proximity" (Levinas), a "concrete abstraction" (Marx), therefore in its concrete "sign materiality" (Rossi-Landi) which also alludes to the subject's relation with a physical body, which is not a reductive relation of identification, as a condition for subsisting as a sign.

By rediscovering and reasserting the connection between mother-sense and the intellect, between mother-sense and behavior, we may recover the sense of symbolic pertinence present in the child. Critical work is inevitably mediated by language understood as a modeling device specific to the human species (cf. Sebeok 1986, 1994, 2001; Petrilli and Ponzio 2001 and 2002) and as verbal language, spoken and written. And, in fact, another fundamental aim of significs is the "critique of language" (cf. Petrilli 1998b), which presupposes the interrelation between language, consciousness, thought, and the subject, all of which are rooted in and engendered by mother-sense. Welby underlines the importance of developing a "critical linguistic consciousness" and, therefore, critical linguistic practices which when plagued instead by prejudice, ignorance and the lack of critical sense obstacle the exquisitely human propensity for answering comprehension, dialogicality, playfulness and creativity.

Mother-sense opens to the ethical dimension of signs and semiosis beyond the strictly cognitive. According to the project proposed by Welby with significs, logic must fully recover its connection with primal sense, the matrix of sense, in a relationship of reciprocal interdependency and enrichment. Therefore logic must also recover the connection with values and with common sense in all its signifying valencies, from instinctive-biological sense to the sense of significance. The aim is to work for the improvement of human behaviour and therefore for the health and happiness of humanity over the entire planet in a "significal", or, reinterpreting Welby and her significs in the light of recent trends in semio-philosophical studies, what we now propose to call a "semioethical" perspective (cf. Petrilli and Ponzio 2003).

3. *Subjectivity and gift-giving in the interrelationship between Ident and Self*

Welby's unpublished manuscripts include a file entitled *Subjectivity* with texts written between 1903 and 1910 which analyse the problem of subjectivity in terms of the complex and articulated relationship between the "I" and the "self". The subject's identity is modelled in the dialogic interrelationship among its parts emerging as multiplex, plurifaceted and plurivocal identity. The "I", or what Welby calls "Ident" introducing a neologism, develops relatedly to "self" or the multiple "selves" that form the various faces or masks of the "Ident". It is clear that in Welby's description otherness is a necessary condition for the constitution of subjectivity.

Dinstinguishing between I and self Welby establishes that "self is included in 'I', *but not conversely*. [...] The race like the individual *has* a Self because it *is* an I" ("The I and the Self", undated manuscript). The self is a representation of the I, a part of it, what we have and therefore cannot be; the I is what we are and therefore alludes to what we cannot possess. My "I" belongs to others just as "mine" belongs to (but does not coincide with) me. In her attempt to convey the idea of the distancing and shift between the various parts constituting subjectivity, Welby evokes the ancient use of the word "person" to refer to the masks of the actor. The I or Ident may be associated with "mother-sense", the matrix, while the self, or *person,* or mask may be considered as one of its possible expressions or realizations or, as Welby says, "representations".

In accordance with a dynamic and generative conception of existence as theorized by scientific research at the time of her writing, Welby maintains that the Ident is energy, a prime mover which manifests itself in the self and energizes the self, or better our multiple and ephemeral selves. Similarly to the body, the *self*, for which Welby also proposes the term *ephemeron*, is mortal, ephemeral. The I, instead, tends towards immortality beyond the mortality of the body and of self. The I coincides with the activity of giving, beyond the logic of exchange, beyond possession ("I and self", 9th January 1910). As understood by Welby, the Ident refers to that part of human identity which resists and is other – the subject's otherness with respect to itself, its sign materiality – in the continuous flow of change whose rhythm is beaten out in the succession, superimposition, multiplication and cohabitation of our multiple *selves*. Formed in this way, identity is not a unit but something more, an excess endowed with logical value understood in terms of the creative logic of abduction. In a manuscript of 23rd November 1907, Welby makes the following statements:

> The "I" *effectively IS*; since it belongs to the creative element of the universe, the energy of conception which includes the begetter and is both reproducer and evolvant (or evolutant?). Thus the I is one with the active and with the "actor" who can and does impersonate and play an inexhaustible variety of persons and parts, while remaining inviolably identical and illimitably representative (*I and self*, 23rd November 1907).

In Welby's thought system self does not coincide with the I but is one of its many representations, one of its openings, a means, an instrument, or modality, but never an end in itself (cf. also 7th July 1907). Therefore, contrary to the tendency to exalt the self, to establish between self and I a relationship of substitution, usurpation, identification, identity derives from the relationship of dialogical otherness between the multiple selves constituting the Ident, between self, rather one's multiple selves, and Ident. Human identity is the ongoing, generative and dynamic outcome ensuing from the intercorporeal relation of dialogical distancing and differentiation of self with respect to I. Welby's generative conception of human consciousness recalls Peirce's when in his discussion of thought and subjectivity he maintains that just as we say that a body is in motion and not that motion is in a body, we ought to say that we are in thought and not that thoughts are in us (cf. *CP* 5.289, n. 1).

Similarly to Peirce when he says that "self-love is no love" (*CP* 6.288), the ultimate "sin", says Welby (in "Who ARE we and what HAVE we", 9th April 1910), "consists in OUR giving our selves leave to demand and secure gratification, pleasure, ease, for their own sake: to be greedy of welfare at some human expense", in other words, it consists in allowing the *self* to trasform *selfness* into *selfishness*. Though the action of the centripetal forces of *self* may be necessary to "self-preservation *here*", to "survival *now*", the condition of being oriented univocally towards self generally defeats evolutionary development to the extent that it generates "self-regarding selfishness". Indeed, as says Welby, "Egotism, however, properly speaking, is impossible: I cannot love or centre upon I, for I am essentially That which radiates: that which IS the knowing, living, activity: it is only selfism that we mean; not egoism" (*The I and the Self*, cit.).

In Welby's view, hedonist ethics – the dominant ideology of the time – implied a reduction of the vastness of the cosmos to the status of mere annex of the planetary egoist, consequently it implied a reduction of the differences in the relationship between I and self to the advantage of a single self thereby reducing identity to the condition of what *à la* Bakhtin we might describe as monologic identity. On the contrary, the "supreme function of the Ident's *self*", as says Welby, is to put itself at the service of the Ident and to collaborate in engendering, knowing, serving, mastering and transfiguring our actual and possible worlds; the mission of our selves being "to master the worlds for Identity in difference [...]. The Ident is one in all, but also All in each. The Ident's name is first multiplex – We, Us, then complex, I, Me. That Ident has, possesses, works through – a self, or even many selves" (*I and Self*, 19th January 1910).

The Ident is a centre engendering multiple *selves* and at once a multiplicity inhabiting each one of our selves. The ontogenetic Ident corresponds to phylogenetic mothersense, the originating, generative source of all forms of responsivity and mental power, whether analytical or constructive, which calls the human being not only to react but also to create. *Self* is an expression of the I, the utterer, it is the means or instrument through which the multiple Ident works, through which it operates. While we do not distinguish between I and I, I and self do not converge. To be implies to become a nucleus of originating – though not original – power, to become aware of one's signifying potential and of one's worth both in phylogenetic and ontogenetic terms. The personal pronouns of the series I/we/you/they, as says Welby, tells of our "sense of universal order, our sense of mentally creative potency, our sense of worth as well as of reality, before all and above all our sense of sign and its signification, its natural significance and its intentional significance – its Meaning" (*The I and the Self*).

In tune with scientific progress of her time Welby calls attention to the dynamic and generative nature of subjectivity: "I suppose the greatest misfortune that can happen to a man is to be identified (except reflexively, that is as whole and part) with his self [...]. As *We* are never *It* we are never Self. We only *have* what is both". Indeed, Welby does not hesitate to describe her view of the I and the self as "essentially scientific": "selves are the product of Identic, somatic activity, its structure the product of its function" (*The I and the Self*, cit.). The relationship between the I and the self as theorized by Welby, between the I and its interpretants, is not of static equality, reduction of the differences, but rather of non correspondence, deferral, shift, difference and reciprocal otherness. Subjectivity is created in the dialogic interrelationship among its parts according to the logic of otherness, and in the interrelationship with the other external to personal identity. The role or function of I/we is determined structurally in the relation of distancing and deferral with respect to self. The I with its multiple selves belongs to the order of "motion" and "function" and, therefore, cannot be self-regarding; the self belongs to "matter" and "structure" and, therefore, is just there (cf. *I and Self*, 26th November 1906). Identity is becoming, acting, doing, giving.

The generative and dynamical character of the *Ident* is also determined by its triadic structure according to the model of father-mother-child, impulse-development-outcome, question-answer-act, which describes, as says Welby, "the process as the condition of true culmination, of attainment of an ascending ideal of which Nature is the parable as she is the exemplar". In Welby's conception, conscious identity represents a high degree in the development of evolutionary processes to the extent that it rises to interpretation of all things, of significance in the universe (cf. 21st January 1910, no title, undated manuscript).

Identity understood as a community of dialogically interrelating selves is engendered by the logic of otherness. The Ident as the resulting unit of signifying processes is dialectical and open with respect to the sum total of its parts, its multiple selves, with respect to which indeed it represents an overflow, excess value, a gift, as says Welby:

> In order to Be – and really to Be is to be Given – what is impotent for fertile being IS not; there *must* be overflow, there must be in some sense gift. True that in the arithmetical sense the bare unit may be added to and may multiply. But that is just because it has no content and no identity, as it has no fertility. Full identity is generative, is a Giver of its very self (11th December 1906).

In Welby's description, the I is centrifugal energy, while self is centripetal. The Ident is oriented towards the negation of self, towards being understood in terms of becoming, acting, giving, doing rather than of receiving, keeping, being *selfish*. The connection with Bakhtin is immediate when he describes the subject and language in terms of the dynamics between "centripetal forces" and "centrifugal forces", the processes of "centralization" and "decentralization", of "unification" and "disunification". Both the (partial) recognizability of the sign and its elusiveness, plurivocality, uniqueness are determined in the ephemerous space of an equilibrium that is always uncertain, unstable, attained among forces continuously struggling with each other (cf. Bakhtin 1975, It. trans.: 80).

The conventionalization and monologization of human consciousness constrain and reduce the potential for responsivity towards the other, for dialogism and critique. Instead, in Welby's view the properly human is the condition of maximum opening and responsivity towards the other. To exemplify this condition she cites the discourse of love and passion, of altruistic love, creativity of the genius, and literature, all considered as places in which our secret, unknowable, elusive and interrelational being is revealed in a play of veiling and unveiling forces. The other discussed by Welby is both the other self constitutive of my own identity as well as the other external to my own identity and which all the same concerns me and relates to me such that it is in this very relation that the other subsists for me as other. As Welby says, "the language of passion is a case of this or that other self, and what we find most interesting is the other, always ours (cf. *The I and the Self*).

Welby evidences the otherness of subjectivity which to be an Ident must always be other in the relation with self, indeed conscious identity develops in the play of deferral to its multiple selves and is always oriented towards surpassing the centripetal forces polarized in the self. Subjectivity emerges in the open space of the relationship with the other – the inner other and the outer other – in which identity of the subject is delineated in the deferral among its multiple parts without ever identifying with any one of them. In the last analysis, as the knower the I or Ident is unknowable, as s/he who possesses s/he is elusive, as s/he who utters s/he is the unutterable. The Ident is an orientation towards the other, towards the self insofar as it is other; a continuous transcending and transferral of the limits, displacement of the real as it is, of the *hic et nunc*. While the self represents that which to an extent can be identified, measured, calculated, the Ident cannot be definitively captured or possessed, but simply approached by approximation, tentatively and hypothetically, and only by working through the means at our disposal, that is, our selves.

In Welby's description and similarly to Peirce, the human being is a community of parts that are distinct but not separate. Far from excluding each other, these parts, or selves, are interconnected by a relation of reciprocal dependence. They are founded in the logic of otherness understood as the logic of unindifference among differences, which excludes the condition of undifferentiated confusion among the parts or of levelling the other onto self. As says Welby, to confound is to sacrifice distinction:

> But in *my* logic (if you will allow me any!) I see no great gulf, but only a useful distinction between methods proper to practical and theoretical questions. So then "Never confound, and never divide" is in these matters my motto. And I had gathered, I hope not quite mistakenly, that you also saw the disastrous result of digging gulfs to *separate* when it was really a question of *distinction*, – as sharp and clear as you like (letter of Welby to Peirce of 29th June 1904, in Hardwick 1977: 21).

To the extent that it represents an excess with respect to the sum of its parts, the I or Ident, says Welby, is not the "individual" but the "unique" (*I and self*, June 1907). Here we may interpret what Welby understands by "unique" – which has nothing to do with the monadic separatism of Stirner's conception of the unique, of singularity – with the concept of "non relative otherness" as understood by Levinas, or with his concept of "significance".The latter is also theorized by Welby in the context of her theory of meaning and the triad that distinguishes between "sense", "meaning" and "significance":

> [...] for we may represent the Unique. That is the word which might well supersede the intolerably untrue "individual". It is in fact just our individuality which constitutes the richness of

our gifts. We can, but must not be, divided; we must include the divisible in the greatest of Wholes, the organic Whole, which as risen to the level of the human, may crown each one of us as unique (*I and Self*, June 1907).

In Welby's philosophical system, similarly to Peirce's, love is directed to the concrete and not to abstractions, to persons, one's neighbour not necessarily in a spatial sense, locally, but in the sense of affinity, a person – to say it with Peirce, "we live near [...] in life and feeling". Love is a driving force where iconicity, abduction and creativity are clearly operative. Citing St. John's Gospel, whose evolutionary philosophy teaches us that growth comes from love, Peirce clarifies that love is not intended in the sense of self-*sacrifice*, that is, sacrifice of the other including one's own other to self. Nor is it understood as gratifying the egoistic impluses of others. Rather, to love is to sacrifice one's own perfection to the perfectionment of one's neighbour, "the ardent impulse to fulfill another's highest impulse". Applying the lesson learnt from St. John, with Peirce we may infer that the mind and the cosmos develop through the power of love understood as orientation towards the other, as care for the other. And recalling his essay of 1892, *The Law of Mind*, Peirce reminds his readers that the type of evolution foreseen by synechism, the principle of continuity, is evolution through the agency of love whose prime characteristic is that it enables us to recognize the germs of loveliness in the hateful and make it lovely (cf. *CP* 6.287-289).

Peirce polemically contrasts the "gospel of Christ" according to which progress is achieved by virtue of a relationship of sympathy established among neighbours, with the "Gospel of greed" which he describes as the dominant tendency of the time, consisting in the assertion of the individual, therefore, of one's own individuality or egoistic identity over the other (cf. *CP* 6.294). A parallel may be drawn between Peirce's critique of the supremacy of the individual and Welby's which, as we have seen, she develops in terms of her analysis of the dynamics between I and self, and of her critique of the self's tendency to transform selfness into selfishness or selfism. The principles of natural selection, the survival of the fittest, the struggle for existence as elaborated by Charles Darwin in his *Origin of Species* (1859) are translations of the concept of individual from nineteenth century political economy to the life sciences, from the sphere of economics to the spheres of biology and more specifically anthropology. On his part, Peirce privileged the agapastic theory of evolution and in fact considered his own strong attraction for this doctrine as possible proof of its truth (cf. *CP* 6.295).

Peirce distinguishes between self-love, love directed to another insofar as s/he is exactly like self, self-love which is no love, and creative love directed to what is completely different, even "hostile and negative" with respect to self, love directed to the other insofar as s/he is other (cf. *CP* 6.287). On this basis we could propose a typology of love passing from a high degree of identity to a high degree of alterity. But truly creative love, as both Welby and Peirce teach us, is love ruled by the logic of otherness, love for the other, directed to the other insofar as s/he is other. We could claim that the logic of otherness, altruistic and unindifferent otherness, is logic that is agapastic, dia-logic, abductive and creative.

4. *A dialogic exchange with Gen*

The following is an extract from an email message to me of 25th November 2002 from Genevieve Vaughan commenting a paper I sent her entitled *Subject, Body and Agape*, of 1997. The article I have presented for this current issue of *Athanor*, edited by Gen and dedicated to the presentation of her ideas about the gift economy, develops some aspects of that paper, in particular the concepts of "mother-sense" and subjectivity analyzed by Welby in terms of the relation between "I" or "Ident" and "Self", which are the object of Gen's considerations below:

I just read your paper *Subject, Body and Agape* and found it very exciting. I have not read anything of yours before. One thing I particularly liked was the way mother-sense or significs puts together logic and love. People have been saying to me that I should not use the word "logic" for the inter-action of gift giving so it is great to see that Welby did not separate logic from *other* orientation. The continuity between the "other oriented logic" and the "ego oriented logic" is the thread by which we can pull the mother back into philosophy. A challenge I admit but so necessary now with war pending. I think that there is a sort of ethical or even revolutionary basis – social agapism? – for interpreting semiotization in terms of other orientation and of what I think of as gift giving, in that only if you recognize the big picture need for social change can you see needs as the basis of production, including sign production. Needs have been blotted out of our discourse by the market which sees them only in terms of effective demand, instrumentalizing them to make a profit and so colored with selfishness (or less judgementally, and more systemically, ego-orientation). It is great to see how Peirce and Welby and Levinas have this approach towards the other. I am such a naive and uneducated "semiotician" I don't even know who my allies are.
A thought I had about Welby's self, I and Ident, has to do with the legal "I" as owner in mutual exclusion with other owners, a being which or who has things including perhaps a kind of relation of having with a self. Well that might not fit very well with what she says but I think it is an interesting consideration in that it abstracts the individual and the community, and now even corporations are considered on the same level as individual entities.
I am looking forward to reading other things you have written. Thank you for giving them to me.

Welby's thought system may indeed contribute to a semio-philosophical founding of gift theory for a better understanding of today's world and of the subject who inhabits it and, ultimately, for radical social revolution according to the logic of "social agapism" – to use the happy expression proposed by Gen. The bond between logic and love was theorized by Peirce, and quite separately from him by Welby who also did her research quite independently from academic institutions, just like Gen! Despite completely different historical and ideological contexts, to my mind many analogies may be established between Vaughan and Welby, the scholars and the women, their theory and their practice: both women turn to the community beyond self as a sounding board for their ideas, both women elect the community beyond self as the object of their gift-giving practices, their "disinterested generosity", the urge to "care for the other". Indeed, not only is the gift theorized, explicitly by Gen, but also by Welby with her concepts of mother-sense and Ident, both women dedicate their ideas and their practical resources to gift-giving with the same passion and enthusiasm deriving from a common fundamental conviction, that what they are proposing is a new model for radical social change.

Today's world is a world lacerated by war, hatred and the desire for vengeance, where bodies are exploded and torn to pieces, as dictated by the logic of power and dominion for the sake of identity logic and its interests. From their theoretical work and total dedication to care for the people and for life generally, women like Vaughan and Welby before her teach us that a new worldview is possible through radical social revolution oriented by the logic of love and otherness, that is, disinterested and uncalculating otherness, altruistic otherness.

Notes

[1] Charles Kay Ogden (1889-1957) was unquestionably a polymath, known above all for his book *The Meaning of Meaning* (1923) co-authored with Ivor A. Richards. As a student at Cambridge University, Ogden was one of the founders of the Heretic Society for the discussion of problems relating to philosophy, art, and science, as well as religion. He served as editor of the *Cambridge Magazine* and later of *Psyche* (1923-52), a journal of general and linguistic psychology. Among his various undertakings Ogden founded the Orthological Institute and invented Basic English, an international language comprising 850 words for people with no knowledge of English.

His research was strongly influenced by his relationships with Welby and with Richards. The unpublished correspondence between Ogden and Welby (which lasted roughly two years, from 1910 to 1911) is noteworthy from the perspective of the links between Welby's Significs and the conception of meaning proposed in *The Meaning of Meaning* (cf. Gordon 1990; Petrilli 1995, 1998b; Caputo *et alii* 1998). As a young university student, Ogden strongly promoted Significs, and in 1911 he gave a paper for the Heretic Society on "The Progress of Significs" (cf. Ogden 1994b).

In the *Meaning of Meaning*, Ogden and Richards propose a triadic schema of the sign. They describe interpretation and meaning in terms of relational processes, ensuing from the dynamic interaction among sign, interpretant and object, or in the authors' terminology, among *symbol*, *reference* and *referent*. In this book Peirce's importance for semiotics is acknowledged with the insertion of a section devoted to him in the appendix. As a result of this, Peirce's ideas were introduced and circulated in England for the first time alongside those of other important figures. Welby is also mentioned, but the significance of her research is underestimated.

[2] Charles Sanders Peirce (Cambridge, Massachusetts 1839-Milford 1914), an American scientist, historian of science, logician, mathematician and philosopher of international fame. He founded contemporary semiotics, a general theory of sign which he equated with logic and the theory of inference, especially abduction, and later with pragmatism, or as he preferred, pragmaticism. Peirce graduated from Harvard College in 1859 and then received an M.Sc. from Harvard University's newly founded Lawrence Scientific School in 1863. His thirty-one year employment as a research scientist in the U.S. Coast and Geodetic Survey ended in 1891. Apart from short term lectureships in logic and philosophy of science at the Johns Hopkins University in Baltimore (1879-1884), at the Lowell Institute in Boston (1866), and at Harvard (1865, 1869-1870, 1903, 1907), as well as at private homes in Cambridge (1898 and in other years), Peirce worked in isolation, outside the academic community.

He had difficulty publishing during his lifetime. A selection of published and unpublished writings were eventually prepared in the *Collected Papers*, the first of which appeared in 1931. But an anthology of his writings edited by M. R. Cohen and entitled *Chance, Love and Logic* had already been published in 1923. His works are now being organized chronologically into a thirty volume critical edition under the general title *Writings of Charles S. Peirce: A Chronological Edition* (Indianapolis, Indiana: Peirce Edition Project), the first volume having appeared in 1982.

In a letter to Welby of 23rd December , 1908, Peirce, who was nearly seventy, conveys a sense of the inclusive scope of his semiotic perspective when he says: "[...] it has never been in my power to study anything, – mathematics, ethics, metaphysics, gravitation, thermodynamics, optics, chemistry, comparative anatomy, astronomy, psychology, phonetics, economic, the history of science, whist, men and women, wine, metrology, except as a study of semeiotic" (in Hardwick 1977: 85-86).

As anticipated in a paper of 1905, "Issues of Pragmaticism", in Peirce's conception the entire universe, the universe of existents and the universe of our conceptual constructions about them, that wider universe we are accustomed to refer to as *truth* of which the universe of existents is only a part, "all this universe is perfused with signs, if it is not composed exclusively of signs" (*CP* 5.448, n. 1).

While developing a general model of sign, Peirce was particularly interested in a theory of method. His research focused specifically on the sciences and therefore on the search for a scientific method. However, in the perspective of Peircean pragmatism, knowledge understood in terms of innovation and inventiveness is not conceived as a purely epistemic process. Knowledge presupposes ethical knowledge, responsiveness to the other, which the self listens to both as the other from self and as the other self: for there to be an interpreted sign, an object of interpretation, there must be an interpretant, even when we are dealing with cognitive signs in a strict sense. The sign as a sign is other; in other words it may be characterized as a sign because of its structural opening to the other and therefore as dialogue with the other. This implies that the sign's identity is grounded in the logic of alterity. Consequently, learning, knowledge, wisdom, understanding and sagacity in their various forms are situated in a sign situation which, in the last analysis, is given over to the other, is listening to the other. Cognitive identity is subject to the other and as such is continually put into crisis by the restlessness of signs that the appeal of the other inexorably provokes. Therefore, insofar as it is part of the sign network by virtue of which alone it earns its status as sign, the cognitive sign is placed and modelled in a context that is irreducibly ethical.

[3] Mikhail Mikhailovich Bakhtin (Orel 1895-Moscow 1975), a Russian philosopher. He met Pavel N. Medvedev (1891-1938) and Valentin N. Voloshinov (1884/5-1936) in Vitebsk in 1920 and established relations of friendship and collaboration with them. Together they formed the "Bakhtin Circle" with the participation of the pianist and activist Maria Judina, the musicologist I. I. Sollertinskij, the biologist I. I. Kanaev, the writers K. K. Vaginov and D. I. Kharms, the Indologist M. I. Tubianskij, and the poet N. A. Kljuev. Even if only on an ideal level, Bakhtin's brother Nikolaj (1894-1950) may also be considered as a member of the "Circle". Having left Russia in 1918 N. Bakhtin eventually settled in Birmingham, England, where at the University he founded the Department of Linguistics, in 1946. He died there four years later.

During the 1920s Bakhtin's work interconnected so closely with that of his collaborators that it is difficult to distinguish between them. This would seem to confirm his thesis of the "semi-other" character of "one's own word", in spite of the critics who insist on establishing ownership and authorship. Bakhtin played a significant role in writing Voloshinov's two books, *Freudianism: A Critical Sketch* (1927) and *Marxism and the Philosophy of Language* (1929) as well as *The Formal Method in Literary Scholarship* (1928), signed by P. N. Medvedev. He also contributed to various articles published by the same "authors" between 1925 and 1930, as well as to Kanaev's article "Contemporary Vitalism" (1926). And even when the "Circle" broke down under Stalinist oppression, with Medvedev's assassination and Voloshinov's death, the "voices" of its various members were still heard in uninterrupted dialogue with Bakhtin who persevered in his research until his death in 1975.

Problems of Dostoevsky's Art was published in 1929, followed by a long silence broken only in 1963 when at last a much expanded edition appeared under the title *Problems of Dostoevsky's Poetics*. With Stalinism at its worst, in fact, Bakhtin had been banished from official culture and exiled to Kustanaj. In 1965 he published his monograph *Rabelais and His World*. A collection of his writings in Russian originally appeared in 1975 and another in 1979, followed by editions of his unpublished writings or re-editions of published works by himself and his circle (cf. in English, Bakhtin 1981, 1986, 1990, 1993).

Evaluated as "critique", in a literary as well as philosophical sense after Kant and Marx, Bakhtin's fundamental contribution to "philosophy of language" or "metalinguistics" consists in his *critique of dialogic reason*. He privileged the term "metalinguistics" for his particular approach to the study of sign, utterance, text, discourse genre and relations between literary writing and nonverbal expressions in popular culture, as in the signs of carnival. Bakhtin's critique of dialogic reason focuses on the concept of *responsibility without alibis*, a non conventional responsibility, which concerns existential "architectonics" in its relation with the I, with the world and with others and which as such cannot be transferred. Dialogue is for Bakhtin an embodied, intercorporeal, expression of the involvement of one's body, which is only illusorily individual, separate and autonomous, with the body of others. The adequate image of the body is that of the "grotesque body" (see Bakhtin 1965) which finds expression in popular culture, in the vulgar language of the public place and above all in the masks of carnival. This is the body *in its vital and indissoluble relation with the world and with the body of others*. With the shift in focus from identity (whether individual, as in the case of consciousness or self, or collective, as in a community, historical language, or cultural system at large) to alterity – a sort of *Copernican revolution* – Bakhtinian critique of dialogic reason not only questions the general orientation of Western philosophy, but also the tendencies dominating over the culture that engenders it.

Bakhtin and Welby never met in real life nor ever knew of each other, although they are easily related on an ideal level (cf. Petrilli 1990a, b, c).

[4] With the term "racial" Welby's reference is to the human race in general, to the genus *Homo* and not to a single race.

References

Bakhtin, Mikhail M. (1929). *Problemy tvorchestva Dostoevskogo* (Problems of Dostoevsky' work), Leningrad, Priboj; It. trans. and Intro. M. De Michiel, *Problemi dell'opera di Dostoevskij*, Intro. A. Ponzio, Edizioni dal Sud, Bari, 1997.
— (1963). *Problemy poetiki Dostoevskogo*, Moscow, Sovetskij pisatel'; Engl. trans. and ed. C. Emerson, *Problems of Dostoevsky's Poetics*, University of Minnesota Press, Minneapolis, 1984.
— (1965). *Tvorchestvo Fransua Rable*, Moscow, Khudozhestvennia literatura; Engl. trans. H. Iswolsky, ed. K. Pomorska, *Rabelais and His World*, Cambridge, The Massachusetts Institute of Technology, 1968.
— (1975). *Voprosy literatury i estetiki* (Problems of Literature and of Aesthetics), Moscow, Khudozestvennia literatura; It. trans. *Estetica e romanzo*, Einaudi, Turin, 1979.
— (1979). *Estetika slovesnogo tvorchestva* (Aesthetics of verbal art), Moscow, Iskusstvo; It. trans. *L'autore e l'eroe. Teoria letteraria e scienze umana*, Einaudi, Turin, 1988.
— (1981). *The Dialogic Imagination: Four Essays*, eds. C. Emerson and M. Holquist, University of Texas Press, Austin.
— (1986). *Speech Genres & Other Late Essay*, eds. C. Emerson and M. Holquist, University of Texas Press, Austin.
— (1990). *Art and Answerability*, eds. M. Holquist and V. Liapunov, Austin, University of Texas Press.
— (1993 [1920-24]). *Toward a Philosophy of the Act*, Engl. trans. V. Liapunov, ed. M. Holquist, University of Texas Press, Austin.
Baldwin, James Mark (ed.) (1901-1905). *Dictionary of Philosophy and Psychology in Three Volumes*, Macmillan, New York-London.
Boole, Mary Everest (1931a). *Collected Works*, ed. E. M. Cobham, Pref. E. S. Dummer, 4 Vols., The C. W. Daniel Company, London.
— (1931b [1905]). *Logic Taught by Love: Rhythm in Nature and in Education (1890)*, in M. E. Boole 1931a, vol. II, pp. 399-515.
— (1931c [1909]). *Symbolic Methods of Study (1884)*, in M. E. Boole 1931a, vol. I, pp. 239-333.
— (1931d [1910]). *The Forging of Passion into Power*, in M. E. Boole 1931a, vol. IV, pp. 1337-1413.
Caputo, Cosimo; Petrilli Susan; Ponzio Augusto (eds.) (1998). *Basi. Significare, inventare, dialogare*, Piero Manni, Lecce.
Cust, Mrs. Henry (Nina) (ed.) (1928). *Wanderers: Episodes From the Travels of Lady Emmeline Stuart-Wortley and Her Daughter Victoria, 1849-1955*, pref. Sir R. Storrs, Johnathan Cape, London.
Darwin, Charles (1998 [1859]). *Origin of Species*, ed., intro. and notes G. Beer, Oxford University Press, Oxford.
Gordon, Terrence W. (1990). "Significs and C. K. Ogden: The influence of Lady Welby", in H. W. Schmitz, (ed.), pp. 179-196.
Hardwick, Charles S. (ed.) (in collab. with J. Cook) (1977). *Semiotic and Significs. The Correspondence Between Charles S. Peirce and Victoria Lady Welby*, Intro., pp. IX-XXXIV, Indiana University Press, Bloomington-London.
Lévinas, Emmanuel (1961). *Totalité et Infini*, Nijhoff, The Hague; Engl. trans. A. Lingis, *Totality and Infinity*, Intro. J. Wild, Kluwer Academic Publishers, Dordrecht-Boston-London, 1991.
— (1974a [1949, 1967]). *En découvrant l'existence avec Husserl et Heidegger*, Vrin, Paris; Engl. trans. R. A. Cohen and M. B. Smith, *Discovering Existence with Husserl*, Northwesten University Press, Evanston, 1998.
— (1974b [1967]). "Langage et proximité", in E. Lévinas 1974a, pp. 217-236; Engl. trans. "Language and Proximity", in E. Lévinas 1987b, pp. 109-127.

— (1974c). *Autrement qu'être ou au-dela de l'essence*, Nijhoff, The Hague; Engl. trans. A. Lingis, *Otherwise than Being or Beyond Essence*, Duquesne University Press, Pittsburgh, 2000.

— (1987). *Collected Philosophical Papers*, Engl. trans. and ed. A. Lingis, Martinus Nijhoff Publishers, Dordrecht.

Marx, Karl (1857-8). *Grundisse*, vol. 28 of *The Collected Works of Marx and Engels*, Lawrence and Wishart, London (1975).

Medvedev, Pavel N. (1978 [1928]). *The Formal Method in Literary Scholarship: A Critical Introduction to Sociological Poetics*; Engl. trans. A. J. Wehrle, The Johns Hopkins University Press, Baltimore, 1978.

Ogden, Charles K. (1994a). *C K. Ogden and Linguistics*, 5 vols., ed. T. W. Gordon, Routledge-Thoemmes Press, London.

— (1994b). "The Progress of Linguistics", in Ogden 1994a, vol. 1, pp. 1-47.

Peirce, Charles Sanders (1892). "The Law of Mind", *The Monist*, vol. 2, pp. 533-559, in *CP* 6.102-6.163.

— (1923). *Chance, Love and Logic*, ed. Morris R. Cohen, Harcourt, New York.

— (1931-1966). *Collected Papers of Charles Sanders Peirce* [*CP*], eds. C. Hartshorne, P. Weiss and A. W. Burks, 8 vols., Harvard University Press, The Belknap Press, Cambridge (Mass.), (References are to *CP*, followed by volume and paragraph numbers).

— (1984a). *Writings of Charles S. Peirce. A Chronological Edition*, vol. 2, 1867-1871, Peirce Edition Project, Indiana University Press, Bloomington.

— (1992). *The Essential Peirce: Selected Philosophical Writings*, vol. 1, eds. N. Houser and C. J. W. Kloesel, Indiana University Press, Bloomington.

— (1998). *The Essential Peirce*, vol. 2, ed. by Peirce Edition Project, Indiana University Press, Bloomington.

Petrilli, Susan (1990a). "Sign and Meaning in Victoria Lady Welby and Mikhail Bakhtin: A Confrontation", in H. Walter Schmitz (ed. and Intro.), *Essays on Significs*, John Benjamins, Amsterdam/Philadelphia, 1990, pp. 197-215.

— (1990b). "Dialogue and Chronotopic Otherness: Bakhtin and Welby", *Discours social/ Social Discourse* 3, 1&2, pp. 339-350.

— (1990c). "The Problem of Signifying in Welby, Peirce, Vailati, Bakhtin", in A. Ponzio, *Man As a Sign: Essays on the Philosophy of Language*, Intro., trans. and ed. S. Petrilli, Mouton De Gruyter, Berlin, pp. 313-363.

— (1995). "Between Semiotics and Significs. C. K. Ogden and V. Welby", *Semiotica* 105-3/4, pp. 277-309.

— (1997). "Subject, Body and Agape. Toward Teleosemiotics with Peirce and Welby", *Working Papers and pre-publications*, Centro Internazionale di Semiotica e di Linguistica, Università di Urbino, 261-262, Febr.-March 1997, serie A, pp. 1-39.

— (1998a). *Teoria dei segni e del linguaggio*, Graphis, Bari, 2001^2.

— (1998b). *Su Victoria Welby. Significs e filosofia del linguaggio*, Edizioni Scientifiche Italiane, Napoli.

— (2004). *Percorsi della semiotica*, Graphis, Bari.

Petrilli, Susan; Ponzio, Augusto (2000). *Il sentire nella comunicazione globale*, Meltemi, Rome.

— (2001). *Sebeok and the Signs of Life*, Icon Books, London.

— (2002). *I segni e la vita. La semiotica globale di Thomas A. Sebeok*, Spirali, Milan.

— (2003). *Semioetica*, Meltemi, Rome.

— (2004). *Semiotics Unbounded*, Toronto University Press, Toronto.

Petrilli, Susan; Thomas A., Sebeok; Augusto, Ponzio (2001). *Semiotica dell'io*, Meltemi, Rome.

Rossi-Landi, Ferruccio (1973). *Ideologies of Linguistic Relativity*, Mouton, The Hague.
— (1982 [1978]). *Ideologia*, Mondadori, Milan; Engl. trans. R. Griffin, *Marxism and Ideology*, Clarendon, Oxford, 1990.
— (1985). *Metodica filosofica e scienza dei segni*, Bompiani, Milan.
— (1992a). *Between Signs and Non-signs*, ed. and Intro. S. Petrilli, John Benjamins, Amsterdam.
— (1992b [1968]). *Il linguaggio come lavoro e come mercato*, ed. A. Ponzio, Bompiani, Milan; Engl. trans. M. Adams et al., *Language as Work and Trade*, Bergin and Garvey, South Hadley (Mass.), 1983.
Schmitz, Walter H., ed. and Intro., I-IX (1990). *Essays on Significs. Papers Presented on the Occasion of the 150th Anniversary of the Birth of Victoria Lady Welby*, John Benjamins, Amsterdam-Philadelphia.
Sebeok, Thomas A. (1986). *I Think I Am a Verb*, Plenum Press, New York and London; It. trans. and Intro. S. Petrilli, *Penso di essere un verbo*, Sellerio, Palermo, 1990.
— (1994). *Signs. An Introduction to Semiotics.* Toronto University Press, Toronto, New ed. 2001; It. trans. and Intro. S. Petrilli, *Segni. Introduzione alla semiotica*, Carocci, Rome.
— (2001). *Global Semiotics*, Indiana University Press, Bloomington.
Tönnies, Ferdinand (1899-1900). "Philosophical Terminology" (I-III), (Welby Prize Essay, Engl. trans. Mrs. B. Bosanquet), *Mind* 8 (31-32), pp. 286-332, pp. 467-491; 9 (33), pp. 46-61.
Vaughan, Genevieve (1978). "Saussure and Vygotsky via Marx", *Ars Semiotica*, 2, pp. 57-83.
— (1980). "Communication and Exchange", *Semiotica*, 29, 1/2, pp. 113-143.
— (1997). *For-Giving. A Feminist Criticism of Exchange*, Foreword by Robin Morigan, Plain View Press, Austin, Texas.
Voloshinov, Valentin N. (1927). *Frejdizm*, Moscow-Leningrad; Engl. trans. I. R. Titunik, *Freudianism: A Critical Sketch*, ed. I. R. Titunik with N. H. Bruss, Indiana University Press, Bloomington, 1987.
— (1929). *Marksizm i filosofija jazyca*, Leningrad; Engl. trans. L. Matejka and I. R. Titunik, *Marxism and the Philosophy of Language*, Harvard University Press, Cambridge (Mass.), 1973.
Welby, Victoria (1881). *Links and Clues*, Macmillan, London, 1883².
— (1892). *A Week's Morning and Evening Prayers For Families and Institutions*, Menzies & Co., London (Vita).
— (1893). "Meaning and Metaphor", *The Monist*, 3 (4), pp. 510-525; now in V. Welby 1985a.
— (1896). "Sense, Meaning and Interpretation", *Mind*, 5 (17), pp. 24-37; 5 (18), pp. 186-202; now in V. Welby 1985a.
— (1897). *Grains of Sense*, J. M. Dent, London.
— (1902). "Translation", in J. M. Baldwin, 1901-1905, vol. 2, p. 712.
— (1903). *What is Meaning? Studies in the Development of Significance*, Macmillan, London; new ed., see V. Welby, 1983.
— (1929). *Echoes of Larger Life: A Selection from the Early Correspondence of Victoria Lady Welby*, ed. and Intro. Mrs. H. Cust, Jonathan Cape, London.
— (1931). *Other Dimensions: A Selection from the Later Correspondence of Victoria Lady Welby*, ed. Mrs. H. Cust, Intro. L. P. Jacks, Jonathan Cape, London.
— (1983 [1903]). *What is Meaning? (Studies in the Development of Significance)*, ed. and pref. A. Eschbach, IX-XXXII, Intro. G. Mannoury, pp. XXXIV-XIII, in *Foundations of Semiotics*, vol. 2, John Benjamins, Amsterdam-Philadelphia.
— (1985a [1911]). *Significs and Language*, ed. and Intro. H. W. Schmitz, pp. IX-CCXXXVII, in *Foundations of Semiotics*, vol. 5, John Benjamins, Amsterdam-Philadelphia.
— (1985b). *Significato, metafora, interpretazione*; It. trans., ed. and Intro., S. Petrilli, Adriatica, Bari, pp. 7-50.

— Unpublished Manuscripts. Welby Collection, York University Archives, York University, Downsview, Toronto, Ontario, Canada.

Welby, Victoria; Baldwin, John Mark; Stout George Frederick (1902). "Significs", in J. M. Baldwin, 1901-1905, vol. 2, p. 529.

Welby, Victoria; Stout, George Frederick (1902). "Sensal", in J. M. Baldwin, 1901-1905, vol. 2, p. 515.

Patriarchal Capitalism

Food is a Gift

You can give fire without losing it

The gift of language

PAOLA MELCHIORI

INSIGHTS ON THE GIFT
AND THE INSIGHT OF THE GIFT

The theory of the gift is a complex system of analysis at different levels, that runs transversally across different disciplinary fields, from economy to semiotics, to politics. When the idea of this article for *Athanor* came up one year ago, I was thinking of a more theoretical approach. Now, one year after, having, in one way or another, discussed, criticized, experimented "the gift" as a theory and as a practice, I realize that there is another level, beyond or beneath the theory, at which "the gift" works, catches and can be perhaps more easily shared. It has started to strike me how it is somehow extraordinary that despite the discussions, the reservations that one can have towards a particular aspect of Gen Vaughan's theory of the gift, so many women, almost by instinct, are taken by it, recognize in it the power of an insight, important because it changes a whole conceptual framework. It is this level, which lies behind and beyond the theory, that has started to interest me. I saw it at work with very different people and I have the impression that this is one important condition of its diffusion. It is that particular level that I want to focus here, leaving the clarification of the manifold aspects of the theory to its author. I would therefore "treat" "the gift", as we call it in our network, as a whole, without discussing its internal aspects, as an extraordinary insight, an orientation system, a tool for research.

1. *A certain functioning of a paradigm*

"The gift" marks, in the first place, a shift of paradigm. As happened in the emergence of feminism some invisible evidence comes to the forefront, to light, and this changes what we see and the framework through which we think. The emergence of feminism was the revelation of some of these invisible evidences. It made other voices be heard and other realities become active and visible. As in the famous gestalt drawings, you start seeing different pictures in the frame. That is true, also, for the gift. Its "evidence" corresponds to the reality of its diffusion, of its "being at work", all the time, everywhere, as women are in the world. Its invisibility corresponds to the strategic need that the diffusion, the importance, the dimension of this work of women (which is generally and commonly identified as motherhood but which is more than that), remain as usable and as invisible to the system as it is to the same subjects who do it. Our intention to dig it out from invisibility is a first step to recognize it, value it and… find other ways of functioning and recognition.

203

2. The "hidden life of the social fabric"

"The gift" reveals a hidden life in the structure of societies, making visible the real mechanism of its economies, and even more important, reveals the paradox of a simultaneous importance to the social fabric that is as intense as the need of its permanent invisibilization.

Somebody could argue that reclaiming the hidden role of women in economics is not so new. The "discovery" of the "hidden economic and emotional work of women", with its different forms in different societies dates back several years. That discovery was the beginning of feminism. It is today the calculated basis of structural adjustment programs. The discovery of women's work was more dramatic where the so called "domestic work" was in fact the economic work able to keep alive thousands of people. Even more dramatic was the fact that this evidence was and is invisible not only to politicians or academics but also to the very women who are the authors and the victims of it. This invisibility to the same eyes of the people who practice it is a condition that the gift shares with the invisibility of the work of women. But the gift is more than that.

Even if it is easy to reduce it to its economic aspect, the gift implies more than the revelation of a hidden work, of the hidden economy of gratuity, systematically plundered and used by the economic system. It restates the right priorities between economy and humanity, or politics. The gift re-affirms the absolute priority of the human relationships over its own creations, the economic and the social system. It is, in my opinion, the clarity of this message, as naïve as it might be considered, that is the reason why women "respond" or react to it so strongly. Today, because of the need for an economy of survival, in its most dense meaning, an economy of life which is opposed to an economy of self-destruction is more urgent than ever. It helps also in understanding why, when the discovery of the hidden work of women ended in an economic proposal for its recognition, many women did not like it. The gift goes to the root, to the relational meaning still embedded in any work, and gives an implicit explanation of the reason why the idea of paying domestic work had and has little appeal to women. The idea of "gift giving" as the basis of a society based on the idea of relationships goes to the foundation of economics, where the connection between human need and the system of economics is still visible. Perhaps this is the political meaning of its semiotic aspect: the gift aspect embedded in language is the real paradigm for and of a human relationship that can found the social fabric.

3. Losing all

To accept this statement of priority we need to imagine that "losing something", in this case our standard and pattern of life, "progress", privilege and "civilization" is not a loss, but the beginning of some new possibility. Unfortunately history has shown that human beings do not respond to laws of self preservation or self protection, or common sense. It seems that only "the day after", only the presence of a catastrophe, is able to teach something to human beings. A certain number of recent catastrophes have shown us that the gift is what essentially is left at work in times of "sinking ships", it works economically and psychologically: it keeps the social fabric going.

Some experiences in countries hit by economic and political catastrophes have shown us that what is a catastrophe from a certain point of view has also the capacity to make visible and arouse unforeseen possibilities. That is the case of Nigeria some years ago, when the economy had stopped and the central state disappeared in general strikes for a month. At the time of that crisis, a Nigerian friend on the phone was telling me how it was terrible… but fantastic too. "We are relying on ourselves and things start working better". It was an economy of barter but through barter some other relationships among people were made possible. The same happened more recently in Argentina. How many others we don't know of? When I met my friends suffering from hunger and loss of jobs wondering what I could do to help, I still remember my surprise when they arrived smiling in the lobby of the hotel, saying how much better they felt anyhow compared to before, how less depressed people were, struggling with real needs. The collapse of the economy, the loss of the value of money had re-awakened people's strengths, inventions, resources. Again the absence of money launched an economy of barter, yes, but the barter is a manifestation of the work of a relationship of trust which is the real gold, the basic currency, a gift.

So the exchange hidden in barter was hiding the joy of the possibility of discovery of the value of other relationships among people, who had to trust each other and to "give gifts" to each other. It was because there was no choice, yes, but this was allowing other possibilities to come out. During these months in Argentina something else was at work and this something else was relieving people's moods and spirits so that the terrible situation in which they lived was anyhow better than the terrible depression of seeing neo liberal laws winning everywhere. Many have observed that improvement even if very few have seen the gendered aspect of this economy.

The same thing was told to me by friends in Saint Petersburg, when in one night, the ruble fell and people found themselves poor. They said they had found something else precious and liberating. Other values. This is not a question of willing not to see the personal and political tragedy of these situations. The people themselves who lived them were the ones who highlighted this aspect. It is important to be clear that I don't bless these crises, created by a system devoted to the systematic destruction of lives, social bonds, nature and hopes. I only highlight that the crises are showing us these characteristics as well as some ways out, and these ways out sometimes include daring to make a mental leap, to imagine that some different ways can work.

In all these societies it was the gift at work: other economies were being created, all based on the absence of the symbol of greed: money. And in all these situations women were protagonists. Let us ask ourselves what this means.

4. *Which abundance?*

The gift is based on the idea that we are not in a world of scarcity but of abundance and that scarcity is being artificially created to keep power and control over people. Without being naive about this and recognizing the tragedies due to scarcity, the gift shows other priorities in human lives on which to build alternatives. It is based on the importance of human presence and on the priority of relationships and of the strengths that arise from the presence and sharing. Thinking of this frame as an abundance paradigm is a radical choice. It means accepting other values where "abundance" is made up of the possibilities of human beings, the inventions, the strengths of social relationships. In Northern countries also, the success of ethical commerce and banking, while still hidden inside the system of exchange, and trying to survive within the system of competition, clearly underlines that there is something important for people beyond interest and money. Saying, as in the Italian slogan of the ethical bank, that the "best interest is the interest of all" means to state the priority of social bonds over economics. The system is now trying to take advantage of the fact that despite all the criticism, many people believe in this statement. What is perhaps becoming clear is that even economically, ethical investments mean also better investments because transparent and made in more honest and solid businesses. The rapid appearance of ethical investments in many banks show at the same time the success and the ambiguity of this message and it opens the space for something in human beings which is perhaps not easy to prey upon and swallow: that people do not live, survive and desire only on the basis of private interest.

Although here the gift is obliged to work in the context of the market and through the market, nevertheless the strength of its growing in both successes and sustainability lies in something else. It has to do with satisfaction of the need for human relationships, community building, presence to the others. Before this can be recognized however, it has to reach a critical mass and to be validated by a strong community. And this works and reinforces itself like a spiral. At the moment these proposals are systematically made invisible or naïve and at the same time are systematically plundered by what asserts itself as the only real economy. A further effort should be made to sustain the ultimate meaning hidden also in these new economies. However the many catastrophes of the strong arrogant economic system are today helping the emergence of the not-only-utopian value of these proposals. They point out their growing realism.

5. Anticipation

Another characteristic of the gift is its possibility of anticipation of a possible future. Deciding to work with the gift initiates a series of theoretical and practical behaviours that allow us to look at things differently and to practice things differently. As Gen Vaughan might know better than anyone, to practice the gift, you need to live "already" in another world, to bear the weight of being considered out of the world, naïve, used up or worse, by "realistic" people, who think of themselves as the only ones with their "feet on the ground". Practicing a giving attitude in one's personal life also arouses interesting reactions. The most interesting one is a kind of slipping"disorientation".

It makes you see how people have lost even the possibility of thinking that it is possible to relate to others as human beings who share a common destiny. I have started to like this moment of dizziness, of looseness... I see there the (fortunate) loss of the normal paradigm which, like the floor where one walks, has become so strong as to be confused with a natural condition. Through this little hole of meaning something else, a small doubt, can open unforeseen paths: the still vague foggy notion that something else can work, exists, among people.

6. *Past and future*

The gift is a possibility launched towards the future but strongly rooted in the past. Everybody who has worked in Africa or in other communities where a survival culture and a community culture are still alive, knows that this is not an esoteric or a naïve message, but the result of the old wisdom of peoples who have learnt and refined a knowledge for survival through the centuries. And this survival is based on the possibility of overcoming the priority of economics. When goods and objects have abandoned us, the preservation of social relationships is the only "wealth of nations". It tells us what many real African friends consider richness and wealth: to have peaceful neighborhoods and keep good relationships in a community; and what they consider the basis of power: the ability to manage and solve the conflicts in a society. The basis of human relationship is the capacity of giving, without thinking of a return. A gift. Not in the obliged sense of Marcel Mauss, but in a sense which could free the receiver from the material and moral obligation to give back. To awaken this capability in the other is the open possibility of the gift which opens up for a return. This logic is the opposite of exchange, in its deepest meaning, not necessarily in its practice. It is in this sense that the gift is a challenge that fascinates. "The gift economy" is in general mentioned as an economy only when talking about "primitive" societies. Today it evokes naïvete, utopian dreams or primitive communities. I think, how strange: the more patriarchy has to rely on pure arrogance, the more the alternative proposals seem naïve, against common sense and impossible to practice. Instead there is not a single drop of nostalgia for the primitive societies here. The gift launches you into the future and at the same time is rooted in the wisdoms of the past, with the conviction that the only future we have lies in the ability to recreate the knowledge, technology and wisdoms that come from the deeply rooted laws that can help us to survive: the logic of relationship, which is the logic of the only "real economy" in the best sense of this word.

This is the shift of paradigm. And to live already "as if". Practice different "rules of the game", be it at a personal or a political level. Show how this paradigm works, in fact.

7. *Implications*

This is a choice full of implications. As a consequence, other aspects of theory are illuminated. I want only to make an example of one of these consequences. The most interesting to me is how the whole notion of rights and justice based on a notion of equality changes. Justice in the framework of the gift leaves aside any pretension of generalization and of returning the right amount, leaves aside the idea of punishment, of the compulsory reciprocity of giving back. Women's experiences are full of useful stories showing how what is apparently "equal and just" is not what is, deeply and profoundly, "giving justice". Perceived as "just", paying back is not healing the pain inflicted, the injustice done.

It helps to see that justice is not paying back, but doing something, which is sometimes the opposite of paying back, it is the healing cause by a small symbolic gesture. All the history of trying to find a way to redress the injustice of sexual violence shows the incommensurability of the notion of justice. Such justice cannot be general, but individualized, at the same time absolutely individual and precarious. It is not by chance that trying to apply justice, the normal paradigm, does not work with women. Not with their stories, not with the kind of crimes they are submitted to. The symbolic gesture that heals is generally a small, light sign, that breaks the pre-established mental setting which doesn't have the inner space, the mental possibility of seeing, of identifying something different. It breaks in like a wind from another mental dimension… and one discovers that "justice" can be a small, unforeseen gesture from which a person drinks a different water, a gift, the re-establishing of a relationship of recognition, of seeing the other.

When payments in money are proposed to redress injustice, women many times feel even worse, lawyers tell us. Why? Is it only because women are not "at ease" with money? They should become smarter? More developed? We could try to read this "inability" differently. Perhaps money back is not what is deeply wanted, or what is necessary.

But this "jumping out", this "practising a politics like frogs", means also the courage to get out from the notion embedded in "a politics of rights" which is the notion of the "Rightness of Equality". If we look at it with some mental freedom "equality" is not necessarily "justice". The appeal to equality does not even protect women, in the end. On the contrary, even if it uncovers the injustice, it creates conditions for other new injustices, at the same time, throwing women into a framework where they are not protected but are even more exposed to the laws of a world whose rules of functioning are not created by them and for them. Equality throws women into the Army. And this is not only the reality but also symbolic. This search for a different notion reminds me of the idea of justice and beauty by the woman philosopher Simone Weil. She worked much on the notion of justice, seeing it as re-establishing a feeling of balance, equilibrium, like the balance that a seaman finds trying to drive a boat in the sea, never established, always precarious and to be reinvented again and again.

8. *Opening paths: A conclusion*

These inadequacies show the need for other conceptual frameworks, in all fields of knowledge and practices, able to struggle against one logic by using a completely different one. What is required is a logic that does not work by mirroring the other, but finds other oblique, unforeseen, unlinear paths, jumping out from the system, which is also a mental framework. Again, the gratuity of the gift is one of those concepts, which alludes to this new paradigm, opens the space and the vacuum needed to invent it.

The Uruguayan writer Eduardo Galeano expresses the spirit of the gift well in this poem which could be our closure, helping to open the spaces and the courage in our minds to see and think out of our cages, differently.

The Soul in the Air

According to some old traditions, the Tree of Life grows upside down.
The trunk and branches downward and the roots upward.
The tree top reaches down in the Earth, while the roots look towards the sky.
It does not offer its fruits but its origins.
It does not hide under the earth what it has as dearest, as most vulnerable,
It throws it to the storms: it offers its roots, living flesh, to the winds of the world.

This is Life, says the Tree of Life.

Significantly, one of the songs written by Gen Vaughan has the title the *Tree of Life*.

SUSAN LEE SOLAR AND SUSAN BRIGHT

Violent crimes rip the souls and devastate the lives of everyone they touch. The question is – do we strike out in retribution, creating endless cycles of retaliation; or do we reach out to everyone the violence has eviscerated and heal the wounds? Just as surely as the victims' family members weep into the small hours of the morning, so too do family members on the offender side of the crime. Do we work to heal imbalances in our society from which crime manifests; or do we become perpetrators of more hate and violence?

In Texas, groups like "Justice for All", a support group for family members of crime victims, typify the exchange approach to solving human problems. "Justice for All" maintains that families achieve closure and peace only after the criminal has been executed. Afraid for the safety of other family members and wrapped in the fury of grief and revenge, a fury codified and sanctioned by the state, they demand that killers be killed – an eye for an eye. Governor, and later president, George W. Bush used the pain and outrage these victims endure to justify his stand for capital punishment in the same way he used the grief of September 11 families to justify his invasions of Afghanistan and Iraq. It was good politics to be tough on crime, good politics to go after terrorists.

It is impossible to have too much empathy for the surviving family members of murder victims. Lives are shattered, grief stained hours and dreams extend into drastic, frightening and empty futures for families who have their loved ones ripped away by violent crime. The same is true of the family members of murderers. It is difficult to even imagine the horror families of death row inmates who are innocent endure. For mothers and fathers and sisters and brothers whose loved ones have been unjustly executed, there is debilitating outrage plus the added trauma of public humiliation and stigma that lasts generations.

Worse perhaps, is what happens when this eye-for-an-eye logic degenerates to absurdity, when the victims strike out, not at actual perpetrators, but randomly, as happens usually in war and as much as half the time when the state executes human beings at the end of the profoundly flawed system that has evolved in the United States. Even if one could assume the right person would be executed for every murder, another death often lightens no one's burden of grief. Many family members discover retaliatory problem-solving does not bring peace or healing. Instead it paralyzes them in knots of anxiety and despair, the pain of which becomes impossible to bear. When that happens, some reach for another solution, one that is based on reconciliation. They go into prisons, meet offenders and work to alleviate social and economic problems that breed violent crimes.

Prison ministries such as Dove Prison Ministries, founded by Edwin Smith to serve death row inmates at the Terrell Unit in Livingston Texas, help inmates cope with unbearable conditions. They help prepare inmates for the spiritual journey to death. They also find pen pals and help prisoners communicate with international anti-death penalty activists and organizations who help raise needed funds for the dozens of court procedures on which inmates' lives depend.

The Restorative Justice movement is actually the original human solution to the disruption created by human conflict. A parent, finding one child has smashed the other across the face, will take measures to reconcile the children, not execute the offender. Violence needs healing, it does not require more violence. That is according to the first logic, the logic of the gift.

The leap of mind which assumes one human being will be healed by killing another comes from a deep disassociation between heart and action. The theory of the Gift Economy maintains this rift occurred when the boy child became disassociated from the nurturing mother so that he existed not as part of her, but in opposition to her. Suddenly the nurturing logic, is "wrong" and the opposite is "right". Capital punishment, like war, in a patriarchal society, is the logical outcome of this rift. Seen from the perspective of the first human logic, the logic of the gift, it makes no sense at all.

After 9/11 the Bush war campaign against Afghanistan and then Iraq ballooned on a tide of grief, fury and fear. The United Stated, led by a president who was not elected and in spite of the largest world-wide anti-war movement in history, destroyed homes, killed many thousands of innocent people and mobilized the enemy, who he said were "terrorists". Again it is impossible to overstate the immense grief victim's families of 9/11 have endured. And yet, many of these people, tears streaming from endless pools of grief, have been leaders in the anti-war movement. They have not wanted their grief to be used to further the political and economic goals of a neo-conservative administration or to justify the killing of any more innocent people.

At an anti-war rally in San Francisco on February 16, 2003, Matthew Lasar spoke out against Shock and Awe, the Pentagon plan to drop a bomb on Baghdad every four minutes for two days. "There is a word that describes the practice of bombing a city full of civilians in order to shock them into submission. That word is terrorism".

He went on to say:

We of "September 11th Families for Peaceful Tomorrows" know what terrorism means. We know what it means to wake up one morning and discover that a brother, or sister, or spouse or parent or child or uncle has been destroyed because someone wanted to fill us with "shock and awe". We oppose such practices, whether directed by Osama bin Ladin or George W. Bush. We of September 11th Families love this country. But our hearts break that it has come to this. Our hearts break as they did on September 11th, 2001, and they did when we visited the people of Afghanistan… We ask America, as citizens and as human beings – when will the cycle of violence end and the struggle for understanding and resolution begin? Let it begin with this enormous popular movement. Let it begin with us.

From the perspective of gift logic it is useful to link the reconciliation movement and peace work because they are existing alternatives to war and its civil equivalent, retaliatory justice. There is another way. It is not the way of blind forgetting. Good people are working endlessly to find ways to reach across the violent divides inevitably caused by patriarchal capitalism, which wastes to create scarcity to add value; when real value lies in the gift, an action which follows needs and perpetuates to enhance, not destroy life. Serious peacework involves addressing the conditions that create endless cycles of retaliation. There is a radically different way of seeing and acting in the world. People engaged in the restorative justice movement are doing that. They don't often see themselves as activists in the Gift Paradigm; but they are doing the work. Often it occurs that understanding the theory of the Gift Economy is first a matter of recognizing how it is woven through the threads of our lives. The gift, which has been morphed invisible by patriarchal structures for centuries, flourishes in the difficult and courageous work of reconciliation.

Delving into case histories of individuals on death row, one inevitably feels a deep empathy for victims' relatives: parents, children, grandchildren, siblings, spouses, lovers, friends. In the multitude of stories about Texas executions, relatives of the victims are most often quoted. Their stories range from cold fury to wrenching grief and loss that no act of justice can heal, to statements of astounding forgiveness, even love for the perpetrator. It is easy to understand the fury and desolation; what's harder for most of us is to imagine how one could arrive at a place of peace with the perpetrator of the most unforgivable damage imaginable. But some in our midst have done that, and their stories merit telling.

Thomas Ann Hines: Victim Offender Mediation Services (VOMS)

Thomas Ann Hines was the product of an abusive home, then an abusive husband. She left the marriage with her only child, a son who was the delight of her heart. A good kid, a good student, he went away to college. His freshman year, he took a study break in a video arcade between classes at Austin Community College. A young man asked him for a ride, then blasted him from the side with a handgun. They found him slumped over the wheel of his automobile. The seventeen-year-old killer fled, but was apprehended not long afterwards, and eventually sentenced to life, meaning 40 years before the possibility of parole.

Hines was consumed with grief and bitterness. She spoke constantly of hatred, pain and the senselessness of her son's murder. Friends tired of it. She now believes she was stuck in the anger stage of grief because she didn't know how to move forward. She never thought in positive terms about the future, only about the irredeemable past. She began volunteering in prisons in 1994, thinking it might lessen her pain. Over the next four years, she spoke to men behind bars about how they could change their lives, make different choices, no matter what they had done.

During a talk at the maximum security prison in Huntsville in which she had intended to give offenders a piece of her mind, she realized she was looking at a "sea of broken humanity". She was overwhelmed. "I looked at them, and all of a sudden, I became a mother again". After the presentation an inmate asked her why she had come. She told him: "If my son was sitting in this room, I'd want someone to reach out a hand and lift him up" (Evers 1998).

In 1998, thirteen years after the crime, she was led through the Victim Offender Mediation Services (VOMS), part of the Texas Department of Victims' Services, to the idea of meeting Charles, her son's killer. She agreed to have the meeting video taped.

She prepared for the meeting for three years, thinking at first she just wanted information about the last moments of her son's life. The killer was equally anxious about the meeting, afraid she would scream at him. When she got to the room where they would meet and saw the small table, she almost bolted, saying he would be too close; she didn't want to touch him. It was too late to change the table; the video cameras and mikes were all in place, so she toughed it out, telling the staff of VOMS that she'd already done the hardest thing a mother could do, bury her child and walk away.

The result is an astonishing videotaped encounter between a bereaved, tiny, middle-aged, white mother and a much larger, younger, black man who'd killed her beloved son. The turning point came when she asked him what books were read to him as a child. When he said "none", her heart began to open. At the point where he put his head down on the table and began to sob, she could no longer maintain the gap between them, and reached out to him. The meeting changed them both in ways no one could have foreseen, and brought her peace she had not imagined possible. Charles, for his part, no longer accumulates mountains of disciplinary write-ups for fighting and starting riots. These days, along with Thomas Ann, he speaks to groups about his transformation, though still serving the equivalent of a life sentence.

Gracie Jett: Victim's Mother becomes Death Row Mentor

Gracie Jett doesn't fit the profile of the typical ally for a man on death row. She is not European, to start with, or a minister, or enamored of a death row inmate, or a member of a human rights organization, or an activist of any kind. In fact, Mrs. Jett is the mother of a murder victim, whose accused killer is spending what may be the last days of his youth on Texas death row staring at an imminent execution. His appeals are well into the federal cycle, a journey from which few return alive.

It is a story of youthful neglect and abuse, addiction, gang culture on the street and in prison, drugs, thugs and deception. Cronyism, old boy networks and political ambition run through the story as well. The mother of the victim is convinced the person on death row for killing her son didn't do it.

Mrs. Jett didn't set out to challenge one of Fort Worth's leading prosecutors, a man named Mike Parrish, who has worked for the Tarrant County District Attorney since he left Texas Tech Law School two decades ago. She was minding her own business when she got a call from her ex-husband in the middle of the night, the kind of call every parent dreads. "Mike's been murdered", (Solar, taped interviews with Gracie Jett, 2/2001), her ex-husband told her. Their only natural son had just been killed near his childhood home in North Texas.

214

Jett is a native Texan who raised her family in a neighborhood on the north side of Fort Worth, which was safe and wholesome at the time. But Sansom Park was riddled with crime and drugs by September 1, 1994. That was when her son Michael Wayne Sanders was shot in the back. He died on the floorboard of his new Chevy truck in the parking lot of the Toro Car Wash on Long Street at 31st, just before midnight.

Gracie Jett says she used to believe in the death penalty and when her son was killed, she wanted the killer on death row: "People don't realize what losing a child is like". But now she is mentor for two young men on death row, and she feels like she should be included among families of the condemned inmates. "I just kind of dedicated my life to tryin' to help these two young men" (Solar, taped interviews with Gracie Jett, 2/2001).

Jett and her son's father investigated the crime extensively at their own expense because they were horrified that prosecutors had convicted the wrong person, probably, she later theorized, to get a gang kid off the streets. She wrote to then Governor, George W. Bush, TDCJ Director, Wayne Scott, the Texas Attorney General, and the Texas Board of Pardons and Paroles asking them not to execute Pablo Melendez, the young man falsely convicted of killing her son. "Here I am a victim's mother, begging the state not to kill the man that stands convicted of killing my only son, but he is not the killer... Pablo Melendez has made plenty of mistakes but one of them isn't killing my son"(*ibidem*).

"They don't need to be killing a boy that didn't do it", Jett says, adding that neither her son nor Pablo were angels, but "six feet under is not the answer […]. It's going to drive me crazy – another young man dead for nothing, a wasted life. And the real killer out there to put somebody's else's mother through what I've been through" (*ibidem*).

Ten years after the death of her son, Jett continues working with attorneys for Pablo Melendez to obtain his release from prison.

*Carol Byars: Murder Victims' Families for Reconciliation-Texas and Journey of Hope...
From Violence to Healing*

Carol Byars, the president of the first state chapter of "Murder Victims Families for Reconciliation" (MVFR), signed in June 2000 the first statement by a victims' group calling for a moratorium on executions. The first state branch of the national group was, fittingly, the Texas chapter, based in Houston, the capital of death row sentences in a state that leads the union and most of the world in state-sponsored killings.

Byars was the headliner in the press conference that formally announced the formation of MVFR -Texas, whose mission statement says they are committed to promoting healing through reconciliation rather than continuing the cycle of violence through retribution and vengeance.

Reporters issued a barrage of leading questions based on the opinion that the high rate of executions and capital sentences here reflects the public will, and that the MVFR position and a moratorium on executions would extend pain for victims' families and thwart the public will. Byars said she felt sympathy for the parents of murder victims and all their relatives, and that their pain was understandable, but from her own experience she believed the position of "Justice For All" encouraged the continuance of destructive pain.

"In my case I had children I wanted to raise in a positive atmosphere and show them there was a better way than revenge and retribution – that was Jimmy's legacy. My husband was worth more than teaching his children to hate. I'm doing what I'm doing to honor him". Later Byars added, "We are a healing organization; we don't promise revenge or retaliation. We believe you can't heal while you hold on to revenge and hatred. You can't do anything positive with all that negativity".

Byars has undergone a 22-year journey of pain and has emerged into healing and activism. She returned to her trailer home later that afternoon on the far northeastern outskirts of Houston to find her youngest daughter, born soon after the fatal attack on Carol's husband, exclaiming with friends over the TV coverage they'd witnessed of the event. But Byars had no time to discuss it. She was expected at work at the café next door, where she worked as a waitress, hoping to eventually earn enough to replace or repair her dysfunctional vehicle.

The formation of the Houston MVFR group was an effort inspired by Byars' participation in the "Journey of Hope" in Texas and Louisiana in 1998 where she met Ron Carlson, another Houstonian. Carlson's elder sister, Deborah Ray Thornton was killed with a pick-ax by Karla Faye Tucker and her boyfriend Danny Garrett. Carlson came to not only forgive Tucker, but to become a close friend and advocate for commutation of her sentence, and was present on her side of the witness divide at the Walls Unit in Huntsville at her execution in February of 1998.

Byars was 21 and nine months pregnant with her second daughter when the husband she refers to as the love of her life was shot in the stomach by a neighbor. A few years ago, she lost most of her material possessions when a friend who was her employer slowly slid into financial disaster and her wages were first paid by half, then half of that, then nothing. About that time, a Florida-based organizer against the death penalty who was setting up the "Journey of Hope" tour called and asked what her schedule was for the next few months. Byars told him she was free, and spent two months in what she describes as an incredible experience. She met Sunny Jacobs, who spent seventeen years in prison including five years on Florida's death row for a murder she never committed. Her common-law husband Jesse Tafero was executed for the same murder two years before an old childhood friend, film-maker Mickie Dickoff, uncovered and presented publicly the evidence of innocence that set her free.

New voices for compassion and reconciliation are speaking out in the most merciless state in the United States.

The James Byrd Jr. Foundation for Racial Healing

The family of James Byrd, Jr., arguably the most famous Texas murder victim since John F. Kennedy, Jr. found another path to heal raw pain caused by the senseless murder of their family member, a black man dragged to death behind a truck driven by white racists. The Byrd family created a foundation for racial healing in the name of their murdered loved one. In the small town of Jasper, they have reached out to the families of the perpetrators with compassion and a spirit of reconciliation, understanding with wisdom that can only come

216

from the deepest essence of our humanity. Their efforts for healing and reform have gained wide support.

Within three years of Byrd's murder, the State of Texas passed and Governor Perry signed into law the James Byrd Jr. Hate Crimes Act, which "strengthens penalties for crimes motivated by the victim's race, religion, color, sex, disability, sexual preference, age or national origin. It replaces previous hate crimes law that did not list specific categories of people who would be protected. In previous years, then-Gov. George W. Bush refused to support such legislation" (Interfaith Alliance Press Release, 5/2001).

Ross Byrd has become an outspoken opponent of Capital Punishment, joining abolitionists in vigil to protest the execution of his father's murderer. While he initially favored the death penalty for the men who killed his father, he experienced a change of heart. "When I heard King had exhausted his appeals, I began thinking, 'How can this help me or solve my pain?' and I realized that it couldn't" (Houston Chronicle, 7/3/02).

The Restorative Justice Movement

The Restorative Justice Movement searches for alternatives to the punitive and retribution models that are the basis of prison life and capital punishment. The community that gathers together in this movement includes not only victims' families, but abolition activists, defenders, the families of perpetrators and death row inmates themselves.

Jim Marcus, director of the Texas Defender Service, said that losing the case of Kenneth Ransom was devastating for him, although he said attorneys who take on capital defense cases have to be able to withstand such losses, given the odds against them. The families and friends of Odell Barnes, Jr., Pablo Melendez, Jr., Anthony Graves, David Stoker, Gary Graham, Kenneth Foster, Randall Dale Adams and Kerry Max Cook are also victims of a system that has declared their loved one dispensable, despite serious reason for doubt about their guilt. That has to affect one's self-esteem, one's worldview, one's sense of trust and hope in a benevolent universe. David Stoker's mother had a heart attack and died shortly after she learned her son's execution date had been set.

The families of those who admitted their guilt, like Larry Robison and Karla Fay Tucker, were traumatized for years by the fate hanging over their loved one. Is it disrespectful to the families of their victims to feel empathy for the families of murderers?

One of the daughters of James Byrd, Jr. demonstrated her answer to that question when (after John "Bill" King was condemned by a jury)she reached out to comfort the aged and grieving father of the man who tortured and dragged her father, in the most hideous way, to death. It was a powerful gesture of mercy.

International Models for Reconciliation

In March of 2001, Carol Byars left for Norway as part of a delegation focused on the death penalty in the United States. Byars wrote on her return that what she found in Norway was:

[…] a country that takes care of its own […] the police do not carry guns. It was hard for a Texan, like myself, to conceive of this way of life. Yet, their violent crime is very low. Their mentally ill are treated and general healthcare is provided […] they have few homeless by comparison. This was a world that was totally alien to me. I love my country, but the problems affecting the U.S. (seem) overwhelming. While I have been in the Human Rights struggle for some time, I had no real comparison to base my understanding of what a peaceful society is like. Coming home, I wanted to weep for America, and especially for Texas. I wanted to weep for what we could and should be (Solar, taped interview with Carol Byars, 6/00).

Byars contrasted Norway with Texas, where "the exorbitant amount of money spent on executions takes away from victims' funds, crime prevention, help for the mentally impaired, and education".

A Scandinavian psychiatrist named Sissel Egeland who works with violent offenders in rehabilitation offered to take a Texas death row inmate named Michael Moore who she believed to be borderline psychotic and who was scheduled for destruction in March of 2001. She offered to give him the treatment he would have received in her country had he committed his crime there: on-on-one care with a therapist in a nurturing, peaceful environment until he calmed down enough to begin to consider his future and to work together with specialists on constructing an individually tailored education and psychological treatment program that would mold him into a constructive member of society. It was a concept that is difficult to grasp as a reality, when one comes from Texas and has a knowledge of what the reality is here for violent offenders, even for nonviolent offenders.

"Journey of Hope" keeps a webpage devoted to stories of reconciliation. Carol Byars writes:

It is past time for being silent about the death penalty. In Texas, we're executing record numbers each year. Things have gotten so bad because people have all been silent and let things get bad. We are told many times that we are not supposed to forgive – that when people do horrible things to us we should do something just as bad in retribution. Those of us who know better – those of us who know the power of forgiveness – need to speak up. Every chance we get we need to challenge the mentality that compassion is a weakness. Compassion is the toughest thing of all, but it's the only thing that works to restore peace in our lives.

On August 8, 2003, in an address to Japanese delegates of the "Peace Boat", which included Nagasaki atomic bomb survivors, Beverly Eckert of "September 11th Families for Peaceful Tomorrows" said:

We're here today because we are the ones who hear the voices of the dead calling for an end to violence and hatred – voices that are telling us to rise above our fear in order to have a coherent and compassionate dialogue about the root causes of murderous strife; telling us that we need to shed our doubts about what a mere handful of believers can do; telling us that amid the ashes that covered this city two years ago and Hiroshima and Nagasaki 58 years ago, and amid the blood-soaked killing fields in countless nations overseas, we will find the wisdom, grace, unity and strength we need so that on some future September 11th, when we look around us, we will see a better world (2003).

These voices for reconciliation come from people who have been ravaged by terrorism, violence and war. They speak the logic of the first wisdom, the nurturing logic of the gift. The action of value, or gift, that violence requires us to complete is not retaliation but reconciliation.

References

Periodicals
"Byrd Son Fights for Life of Father's Murderer", *Houston Chronicle* (7/4/02).
Evers, Tag (1998). "Restorative Justice", *Yes!,* fall 1998, Positive Futures Network, Bainbridge Island, WA.

Internet
Byars, Carol, "Journey of Hope" website, Carol Byar's page. http://www.journeyofhope.org/people/carol_byars.htm
Eckert, Beverly. August 8, 2003, New York, Speech delivered to Japanese Delegates of the Peace Boat. September Eleventh Families For Peaceful Tomorrows website: http://www.peacefultomorrows.org/.

Unpublished Materials
Center for American History, University of Texas at Austin, Susan Lee Campbell Solar Texas Death Penalty papers, letter from Gracie Jett to Governor, George W. Bush; TDCJ Director, Wayne Scott; the Texas Attorney General; and the Texas Board of Pardons and Paroles.
Center for American History, University of Texas at Austin, Susan Lee Campbell Solar Death Penalty Papers, Interfaith Group Applauds Texas Governor for Courageously Signing "Hate Crimes Act", Interfaith Alliance Press Release, Washington DC, 5/15/01.
Center for American History, University of Texas at Austin, Susan Lee Campbell Solar Death Penalty Papers, taped interview of Gracie Jett, 2/8/01.
Center for American History, University of Texas at Austin, Susan Lee Campbell Solar Death Penalty Papers, taped interview of Gracie Jett, 2/24/01.
Center for American History, University of Texas at Austin, Susan Lee Campbell Solar Death Penalty Papers, letter from Gracie Jett to Governor, George W. Bush; TDCJ Director, Wayne Scott; the Texas Attorney General; and the Texas Board of Pardons and Paroles.
Center for American History, University of Texas at Austin, Susan Lee Campbell Solar Death Penalty Papers, taped interview of Carol Byers, MVFR, Houston, 6/14/00.

1. *Feminism in Bangladesh*

Feminism is a consciousness of everything that prevents a woman from realizing her full human potential and is a commitment to challenge and change these conditions, in solidarity with other women. It is necessary to know its different evolving strategies in relation to colonialism and global issues. Women, whether as feminist activists or as mothers, daughters, wives, have a passion towards human values. Their nurturing and caring efforts work towards improvement of social, economic, political and human rights.

History and background

Women in Bangladesh are constantly deprived of their rights. Feminist theory highlights that such deprivation is discrimination against the female gender as a whole. However, many Bangladeshi women blame themselves and do not recognize the true source of their troubles. Men control women's productivity both inside the household and outside in paid work. Women provide all kinds of free services to their children, husbands and other members of the family throughout their lives. Men control women's labor outside the home, both by imposing work on them and by preventing them from working. They also exclude women from better-paid jobs. Women are used as a cheap labor force in Bangladesh. They are also voiceless regarding their reproductive power. They have no right to decide when and how many children they want. It is astonishing that patriarchy is controlling women's reproduction even through so-called "family planning programs".

In the long history of women, almost the only thing to be found is their exploitation and deprivation due to caste, class and gender disparity. Historically they appear as prostitutes, call girls, temple dancers, pious and good housewives, which is not comparable with men's history. Those stereotypes have ignored women's knowledge in agriculture, their technological skill and artistic creativity. In fact, the social evolution and patriarchal hegemony of colonialism prevents women's empowerment. Patriarchy is continuously controlling women's existence in public and in private space.

Therefore the main purpose of feminism can be seen as spreading information and building consciousness among the people about the patriarchal structures of society that create the obstacles in women's life. Only when women see their common problems can initiatives be taken toward improvement of women's situation in a sustainable way. The lack of women in high income positions is not due to their lack of ability to keep such jobs but to the socialization and education of all the people into the patriarchal system.

However, feminism is not a new phenomenon for Bangladesh. The book *Sultana's dream* by Rokeya Shakhawat Hossain (1924) showed that a wonderful, equal, women-directed Utopian feminist world, free from exploitation, is possible. Sultana's struggle for existence and her work for women's emancipation is an example of feminism. The political message of gender is very clear in her other acclaimed book *Padma Raag.*

The "empowerment" approach to women is applied much more by Third World grass roots organizations than it is in First World countries. So it is a fact that feminism is not a recent Western or middle class idea, nor imposed by the United Nations upon women, but it has its own history in Third World countries like Bangladesh.

Since the beginning of the nineteenth century, Third World countries have been giving importance to the changing role of women but this has taken place while these countries were in the trap of colonialism and in a world economy that is exploitative. So Bangladeshi women have to be united against the present situation and search for an alternative economy. The current predominant economic model is that of the Exchange Economy, where goods and services are exchanged for equivalent valuables.

How are the problems of the individual women linked to the Exchange Economy?

a. Family

The parents normally arrange the marriage in Bangladesh. After the wedding the woman is expected to leave her own family and move into her in-laws' house. This practice affects the way that children are looked upon. Boy children mean support of the parents in old age while girl children are only temporarily staying in their parents' house and will add nothing to the prosperity of the family. Girls are given less food and also in times of crisis mothers are expected to be the first to cope with less for the sake of the rest of the family. Maternal morbidity and mortality is common. The head of the family is always the oldest man. Discrimination is rooted in the family in terms of food, education, health, freedom of choice and expression, and even interpersonal relationships. The same discrimination exists in access to and control over money, as well as in decision-making processes. A study showed that in relation to access to the economy, the participation of all classes of women is low except for the cheap labor done by poor and landless women. Women came to international attention because of their cheap and bonded labor. Traditional patriarchal household practices helped women to go readily into the garment factory. Women transformed their previous roles to become income earners in the family. This was the first time women got the chance to gain control over money and scope of mobility.

b. Community

The community has great controlling power over all members. Communities in Bangladesh tend to be very rigid and do not accept deviance from social customs and practices enforced by men. A double standard in the judgment of the morality of the behavior of women and men exists. Most crimes committed against women are considered women's fault. Therefore being divorced, raped, beaten and/or mistreated creates a negative image of the woman. This leads to greater ill-treatment of the victims. Even the respect women receive in the society depends on position of their husbands and fathers.

c. Wider social structures

There is very little possibility for women to get socially accepted jobs, not to speak of higher positions. Therefore judges, professors, politicians, doctors and policemen are almost all males. This often results in obstacles to women who need to use the institutions where those men are employed.

d. Traditions and culture

The traditional role model of men and women is of crucial difference. The glorified ideal of female virtues makes it almost impossible for women to be emancipated and respected at the same time. Good women are supposed to be shy and selfless. Women questioning or even trying to improve their situation inevitably will get into conflicts and often be outcast because of the social pressure of not fitting into the accepted ideal.

c. Religions

The family law in Bangladesh varies according to the religion of the family concerned. This creates problems since for example the Hindu religion proscribes no marriage registration so the possibility that a case of divorce might occur is also not foreseen. The religious family law is a way of ignoring human rights, even if they are granted in the constitution. This is a reason for unjust practices. Examples of bad practice in Muslim family law are many: men getting custody of the women, or men easily able to divorce and abandon their wives, taking second and third wives, the lack of mobility of women, etc.

e. Environmental problems

Women are the caretakers of the household, where a main part of the work is the caring and bringing up of children, washing, cleaning, fetching water, food processing and participating in 80% of the agriculture work. Women are the keepers of all the traditional knowledge of conservation and preservation of bio-diversity. Bangladesh is a country with a high variety of rice, fruits, vegetables and herbal plants, which are the responsibility of women. But globalization, a new kind of patriarchy, gives patents on their skills and knowledge. Also their bondage to the household makes it hard for them to move when there is an environmental disaster. The new structure of mechanized irrigation systems lowers the normal water level and if a water crisis occurs it is often up to the women to go long ways to fetch water. The environmental degradation is a threat and makes women even more vulnerable.

2. Economy in Bangladesh

The economy is patriarchal, led and run by men. Evidence of the patriarchal power structures in the economy can be found when looking at the ruling class, the rich and economically successful people who are predominantly male. The global economy is very hierarchical. It can be said that the hierarchy of political power is slowly transforming into an order where economic success determines position. An example of this is that of the hundred leading economies in the world, only about half are states, while the other half are private companies. This is leading to the point where private companies have greater power in decision-making than governments that are elected to power by the people. Decisions regarding payment rates, environmental law etc. are taken in favour of the big companies and not of the people, because the states can not afford to impose laws and lose the support of these powerful enterprises. Often government representatives are also part of the elites, who conspire to retain their positions and power through such decision-making, at a cost to the masses.

3. *The recent changes in the economy have important effects on individuals and the community*

In the global economy, Bangladesh stands in the position of the margins. However, the small economic elite of the country has widely adopted the capitalistic world-view, which originates in the West. Furthermore this elite carries parts of the patriarchal cultural heritage of past rulers in the area. Because of its weak economic power, Bangladesh is deeply dependant on foreign investments.

The garment industry, which forms the most crucial part of the country's GDP and its exports, is closely tied to the industrial world's markets. The garment industry also faced depression when the U.S. industry sloped downward after the September 11th incidents. Unemployment increased.

Recent studies by the organisation "Rights" declared that every day 100 women and 50 children are illegally trafficked for a range of bonded labour activities. About one million women and children are trafficked in India, Pakistan and the Middle East. In Pakistan there is a market for selling women and a big trading net work earning 10-20 billion dollars per year and connected directly to a sub-economy.

On the other hand, there is a strong demand for imported products (e.g. pharmaceuticals, foreign textiles, foodstuffs) in Bangladesh. There is an increasing addiction to imported products because when they first appeared on the market they were seen as superior, and therefore caused the disappearance of the local equivalent products. With the disappearance of traditional knowledge an alternative to imported goods disappeared.

For an agricultural country like Bangladesh some concrete results of these actions are the introduction of hybrid seeds, pesticides and chemical fertilizers, which slowly replace the local varieties and techniques. Farmers, who gradually lose their ancient knowledge, cannot reproduce it anymore by themselves. This process creates further dependency on the multinational companies.

Another factor that strengthens the need for imported products is the declaration of patent rights given to foreign companies. This deprives Bangladesh of the possibility of fulfilling its own demands by producing local products.

The development programs aimed at building infrastructure do not take into account the needs of the majority. Western structures are copied hastily and without sustainability. For example, supplying TV cables in a country where most people do not even own a radio is missing the point.

The dependent nature of Bangladesh, which makes it hard for the government to implement economic protection policies, in combination with the increasingly embedded poverty, has a big impact on individuals.

4. *What does a gift-economy mean?*

The system of the market is in theory based on the exchange of goods for equivalent valuables. Where there is profit coming from the exchange there has obviously been an unequal exchange. This we call forced gift giving. But next to the economic market another system exists. A lot of valuables are given away without the expectation of getting anything in return. Women traditionally give these valuables that do not fall within the traditionally recognised economic market. These include housework, raising of children, giving birth, knowledge passed on to friends and family members. More and more this system of payment-free receiving is taken over by the economic market through a new form of patriarchy: globalization. This applies also to land, water and bio-diversity, which used to be seen clearly as common goods, not private property for sale.

A gift economy is not conditional like exchange for money. It is not incorporated with the exchange economy. Traditional long-practiced gift giving can be a vital force in supporting an alternative economy.

5. *How can the gift economy be used in the local context? How could it be used to improve the empowerment of women at the grass root level? How can it be integrated with a global vision?*

The gift economy can be found in different forms. Traditional knowledge, skills and plants which are freely passed on from one generation to the next is one of them. Patent rights slowly destroy this existing gift economy. The following gifts can act in the local economy to empower women and create a feminist option to integrate with global vision:

A) Biodiversity and the different natural species now under the threat of globalization are the best gift resources for an alternative economy. Women from the SUS (Sabalamby Unnayan Samity) self-reliance organization in rural villages expressed their opinion regarding these resources:

– Traditional knowledge of food preservation.
– Conservation and preservation of different local seeds.
– Traditional organic agriculture to save nature.
– Traditional system of seed preservation and innovative new appropriate low cost technology.

– Exchange skill and knowledge within the community according to its value and nature.

– Save traditional knowledge about irrigation and adapt new appropriate technology for overcoming future water crises.

– Use collective traditional coping mechanisms for facing disasters and floods according to the geographical area.

– Collect and save different traditional knowledge including knowledge of herbal plants; protect and prevent those from patenting and pharmaceutical companies.

– Encourage mobilization and documentation of all kinds of natural resources under the local community.

– Initiate biodiversity fair to reclaim diverse wealth.

B) Cultural, religious and traditional gifts. Those are very important to create an alternative economy. The rural women from SUS northeast part of the area offer their opinion:

– Traditional ceremonies like donation as religious duty, gift giving as traditional culture for all. These ceremonial gifts can transform into new innovative alternative.

– Sharing wealth as a part of religious duties can accumulate wealth in the local economy, for example, Zakat, Fitrah in Islamic religion.

– Disseminate collective traditional folk culture and analyze its internal spirit to transform it into innovative knowledge.

– Small handicrafts works like pottery, knitting, carpentry, home gardening, small fish and poultry farming culture which was long tradition can act as localized economy.

C) Women as the root of Mother Earth are the best gifts to our society. The rights and empowerment of women are the important strength for a gift economy. The SUS women from the rural and urban areas offer their opinion regarding women's values:

– The work of women's reproductive, social and cultural roles is being transferred to the free market as cheap labour, instead of transforming their knowledge as gift economy. It is a most important task to recognise them and ensure their basic and fundamental rights.

– It is necessary to recognise women's long traditional, spiritual and political knowledge and its integrity.

– Discourage use of women's body for amusement and commercial propaganda for transnational corporations.

– Discourage the use of family planning methods or devices only on women, as it takes away their good health and peace of mind. Indigenous methods are preferred by them. Maybe look at safer alternatives; reproductive rights are fundamental to the freedom of women. How to encourage a man to wear a condom in Bangladeshi society is a challenge. What are the indigenous methods? Are there clear examples? are they safe? And don't forget multiple births kill women every hour.

– Discourage drinking Coca Cola, Sprite, Seven-up, Fanta, etc. Replace by local green plain drinking water, coconut water, lemon water and processed local fruit juice.

– Encourage a debate or campaign on local fruits, local seed conservation and preservation, use of surface water as irrigation instead of deep water pump.

In this way the gift economy can play a role in mainstreaming localization to complete and integrate with a global vision.

I've been a community radio practitioner for more than thirty years, and during that time have observed several kinds of controversy erupting within the field. In this paper, I will examine radio and especially community radio in terms of gift economy concepts, and explore the hypothesis that much of the conflict that emerges within community radio can be seen as a conflict between a nurturing gift model and a hierarchical or patriarchal-exchange model.

> In order to reject patriarchal thinking, we must be able to distinguish between it and something else, an alternative. – Genevieve Vaughan in *For-Giving: A Feminist Criticism of Exchange* (1997: 18)

First, how is community radio different from other kinds of radio broadcasting? In actual practice, the definition of community radio is somewhat inconsistently applied, and can overlap with other categories such as public radio, state radio, and association radio[1], and even commercial radio. However, in December 2003, the Civil Society initiative of the World Summit on the Information Society divided mass media into three sectors that it said need to be recognized: commercial media, public service media, and community media[2]. Each of these sectors can be described in terms of a gift analysis.

Commercial radio is a radio station (or network) set up as a business. Its owners sell advertising to raise revenue, and a money bottom line is usually the prime driver. It's often said of these stations that in business terms the product is the audience, which is sold to the advertiser for a profit, and that the content of the station is simply a means to attract the audience so that the audience's attention can be sold. Station rankings are determined by surveying selected people from the potential audience to find out what percentage of "market share" each station has captured, in terms of gender-and-age and economic groupings. For example, males 18-34 living in families making more than $100,000 a year would be a pretty desirable demographic, because it's relatively easy to get them to spend money on advertised goods. It's also fairly certain that you can attract a sizeable amount of them with the right bait. The preference for a male demographic tends to skew broadcasting content towards lowest common denominator fodder for males, such as sports, smart-ass commentary (and on television, sex and violence).

In the United States, the Federal Communications Commission (FCC) formerly interpreted the Communications Act of 1937 to mitigate the commercial nature of broadcast media and require that it give something of value to the public.

The FCC took the view, in 1949, that station licensees were "public trustees", and as such had an obligation to afford reasonable opportunity for discussion of contrasting points of view on controversial issues of public importance. The Commission later held that stations were also obligated to actively seek out issues of importance to their community and air programming that addressed those issues. With the deregulation sweep of the Reagan Administration during the 1980s, the Commission dissolved the fairness doctrine[3].

Congress passed a law in 1987 to try to restore the Fairness Doctrine by writing into law what had formerly been only administrative regulations of the FCC. However, President Reagan vetoed the bill, and other attempts have failed. Other obligations of commercial broadcasters that have been dissolved since the 1980s in the U.S. include obligations to air news and public service programming, to give a right of reply against attack[4], and "to offer 'equal opportunity' to all legally qualified political candidates for any office if they had allowed any person running in that office to use the station"[5]. This final requirement was suspended for 60 days by the FCC, shortly before the 2000 election, and resulted in, for example, some Belo Corporation TV stations reportedly refusing to air Democratic Presidential Candidate Al Gore's ads.[6] The suspension of the equal time rule was supposedly in anticipation of a court ruling striking down the rule on grounds that it violated broadcasters' right of free speech; however, as of the present writing the courts have not definitively ruled on this matter[7].

The rhetoric of the broadcast regulation that emerged in the U.S. from the 1937 Broadcasting Act turned upon the issue of scarcity. Because broadcasting spectrum was a scarce resource and was interpreted as belonging to the public, this supposedly justified putting requirements on broadcasters to meet community needs. In 1980, broadcasters were required to make an annual survey of 19 categories of potential community needs and show how they responded to this with programming; by 2000, they were only required to keep a public file of any community issues and programs on them. Within this time frame, the Telecommunications Act of 1996 changed the rules to permit the same owners to have almost unlimited numbers of radio stations. "Family owned" radio stations that might have some human ties to the local community have virtually disappeared, swallowed up and chased out by a very limited number of fiercely competitive conglomerates[8].

The commonly stated rationale for permitting these ownership changes is that with the availability of more kinds of media outlets (for example, cable TV and radio, satellite radio and netcasting), there is no longer a scarcity of media outlets. However,

Since 1994, the Federal Communications Commission (FCC) has conducted auctions of licenses for electromagnetic spectrum. These auctions are open to any eligible company or individual that submits an application and upfront payment, and is found to be a qualified bidder by the Commission[9].

In effect, by permitting a few of the largest cash- and credit-rich companies free reign in enclosing the commons, government is colluding in an artificially enhanced scarcity of broadcasting spectrum. In the words of former Clinton-appointed FCC Chairman Bill Kennard:

> Of course, spectrum has always been in short supply. But never in history have we seen more intense demands on the spectrum resource. We are in danger of suffering a "spectrum drought" in our country[10].

In the words of Bebe Facundus, who was forced by economics to sell the commercial women's radio station she had created in Louisiana, "Only 3 entities own everything [i.e., all the commercial radio stations] in the city of Baton Rouge, and that's happening throughout the country"[11]. These conglomerate owners could buy up the most powerful stations with the best reception and greatest audience reach; they could undersell her in advertising, using economies of scale, until they drove her out of business, and they (and the casinos) could hog and drive up the price of billboards used for radio promotion. Facundus tried to make her station both attractive and useful to women in her community – an example of how a commercial station that is locally owned can cross over category and be oriented towards meeting needs. Facundus put a large amount of her own money into the station; but she was unable or unwilling to absorb a big financial loss as the conditions in the community changed. She also says about her experience that she had a problem with male investors, whom she had to buy out because "if men come in with any money they think they own everything"[12].

The loss of local ownership and local accountability is now recognized by the public in the US, and has generated such a backlash against the FCC that in October 2003 the federal regulatory body created a "Localism Task Force":

> I created the Localism Task Force to evaluate how broadcasters are serving their local communities. Broadcasters must serve the public interest, and the Commission has consistently interpreted this to require broadcast licensees to air programming that is responsive to the interests and needs of their communities. – Chairman Michael K. Powell[13].

A North Carolina TV station's web site contained this reporting about the hearing in Charlotte, which was attended by Chairman Powell and other commissioners:

> Powell, one of three Republicans on the commission who backed the new rules, has said he believes the issue of how broadcasters serve their local community should be addressed separately from the ownership rules.

> But he could not stop speakers from bringing up the ownership dispute at the Charlotte hearing. "To try to talk about localism without discussing media ownership is avoiding the issue", said Tift Merritt, a singer-songwriter from Raleigh who told the FCC members she was unable to get her songs on her local radio station. Her comment drew applause from the packed hearing[14].

In contrast to 1960, when "Payola" (companies paying to get their records played on radio stations) was a crime, today in the US: "Listeners may not realize it, but radio today is largely bought by the record companies. Most rock and Top 40 stations get paid to play the songs they spin by the companies that manufacture the records"[15]. This affects not only local artists and the local audiences who would like to hear songs on the radio that reflect local culture, but they also shut out smaller and independent record-labels. (If you travel, you may have noticed that the music on airlines is sometimes all from a single recording company, too, e.g., Sony Music).

Several extreme failures by conglomerate radio stations to meet local need were widely publicized and became one of the main reasons for the FCC localism hearings. For example:

> In January 2002, a train carrying 10,000 gallons of anhydrous ammonia derailed in the town of Minot, causing a spill and a toxic cloud. Authorities attempted to warn the residents of Minot to stay indoors and to avoid the spill. But when the authorities called six of the seven radio stations in Minot to issue the warning, no one answered the phones. As it turned out, Clear Channel owned all six of the stations and none of the station's personnel were available at the time[16].

And then there was the report, also from the North Carolina, that the Bob & Madison Morning Show on WDCG-FM had included a lot of hate talk directed at cyclists, including discussion of how much fun it was to run cyclists off the road. Cycling organizations' protests got the station to promise to run road safety announcements, but these public service announcements were reportedly also parodied and derided by the morning show hosts[17].

So-called shock radio with hate elements, including sexism, has become standard fare for many commercial radio stations across the U.S., especially in the most widely listened-to time slots. Howard Stern, a shock jock syndicated by a CBS subsidiary, got away with advocating rape, among other things[18]. According to FAIR (the New York-based NGO Fairness and Accuracy in Reporting), hate radio is political[19]. This assessment would seem to be borne out by the fact that Stern's show was cancelled from all the stations of the vast Clear Channel network in February 2004. While CNN reported that this was because Stern violated the FCC's new decency standards[20], Stern himself was widely quoted as saying that it was because "I dared to speak out against the Bush administration and say that the religious agenda of *George W. Bush* concerning stem cell research and gay marriage is wrong"[21].

Hate radio for political purposes is far more widespread than just in the U.S., of course. According to Radio Netherlands, "Hate radio killed more than 800,000 people in the last decade". They maintain regularly updated listing of examples of both Hate Radio and Peace Radio stations[22]. Among the examples of hate radio they list:

> Radio Télévision Libre des Mille Collines (RTLM) is the most recent and widely reported symbol of "hate radio" throughout the world. Its broadcasts, disseminating hate propaganda and inciting to murder Tutsis and opponents to the regime, began on 8 July 1993, and greatly contributed to the 1994 genocide of hundreds of thousands.

The hate radio station in Rwanda was succeeded in 1994 by two peace radio stations, *Radio Agatashya* (*"The swallow that brings hope" in Kinyarwanda*) and *Radio Amahoro* (*"Ra-*

dio Peace"). Apparently both these stations were short-lived. Radio Netherlands describes the funding crisis of Radio Agatashya thus:

> It was originally set up by UNESCO and Reporters Sans Frontières in August 1994, but was taken over by the Swiss-based Fondation Hirondelle (Swallow Foundation) from August 1995. In June 1994 it was pledged a US$20,000 grant by UNESCO, which it never received, and turned down a French government gift of 250,000 French francs owing to the French military involvement in Rwanda. It was funded by the UNHCR, European Union and the Swiss government. (…). The radio has been off the air since 27 October 1996, mainly d[u]e to a funding shortage.

In 2000, I attended the United Nations Commission on the Status of Women and met a UN delegate from Rwanda, who told me that she was interested in getting a women's radio station started in Rwanda because that would be a good way to promote peace. In 1997 an organization called Health Unlimited organized a team of Rwandans to produce a women's radio soap opera and a 15-minute women's radio magazine program that were aired twice a week on Radio Rwanda, starting in 1999 and apparently continuing to the present time[23]. Another radio station for peace is Radio UNAMSIL, established in Sierra Leone by Sheila Dallas, to promote the UN's peacekeeping mission. The story of this successful effort is told by Dallas in radio program #28-03 "Peace Radio in Sierra Leone" from the Women's International News Gathering Service[24].

The association between women's radio and peace has a flip side in that shock radio, also described as "aggressive reality" radio, finds more of its listenership among males[25]. Not surprisingly, it is also understood to be a tool of a religio-Republican hierarchical ideology that has been struggling hard against feminism and environmentalism in the US. Patrick Burkart analyzed this phenomenon in an essay in the collectively-published magazine *Bad Subjects: Education for Everyday Life*[26]:

> Using Clinton's election in 1992 as a basis for a backlash, talk show programs directed momentum-building campaigns of mass fax-and-phone call petitions to national politicians, especially in response to changing federal policies towards abortion restrictions, discrimination against gays and lesbians, and strengthening national educational standards.

Burkart makes reference to earlier studies of Nazi radio, as well as to the methodology of contemporary right-wing talk radio, which is absolutist and builds a false sense of consensus:

> On the market, talk radio is inherently conservative because disagreement and dissent are programmed out of talk radio shows de facto, by reaching only those audiences with lifestyles that support consumption of this entertainment technology.

Groups ranging from Fairness and Accuracy in Reporting in New York[27], to the Coalition Against Hate Radio in Portland, Oregon[28], among others, recommend liberals to mount campaigns that include calling in to hate radio programs. However, Burkart explains in his article that the shock radio programs today use technologies such as pre-screening callers and using a delay to allow editing calls even on live radio, in order to build up a picture of monolithic public opinion supporting the hosts' fascistic pronouncements.

As Genevieve Vaughan writes in *For-Giving*:

> An environment is created in which some ideas fit together and thrive because they are validated as permissible and respectable, while their alternatives are discredited. The so-called "free market" of ideas, like the economic free market, often promotes the benefit of a (genetically superior?) few while appearing to be good for everyone. [...] Systems of ideas which have been taught us as the truth back up the political and economic systems of which they are a part (1997: 19).

Burkart's analysis of right-wing radio is corroborative of that insight:

> Shock radio is a technocratic forum, portraying its ideological perspective... delivering daily, oracular, absolutist insights. Rush Limbaugh reminds his audience regularly that he is the only voice of the truth in "he media".

Commercialism also has a role in less "mainstream" hate radio, whose purveyors simply buy time from commercial operators that exercise no control over the content. This, for example, appears on the web site of famous Nazi sympathizer Ernst Zundel:

> With only a limited budget, anyone can buy airtime on hundreds of AM or shortwave stations throughout America. Almost everyone listens to the radio! Ernst Zundel urges his listeners to join the "Freedom Evolution" towards Truth and Justice, by participating in this bold new venture in mass communication[29].

Zundel is presently fighting deportation from Canada to Germany, where he would face criminal charges of "inciting hate"[30].

Public Service Radio is a second category of media that the 2003 Civil Society initiative of the World Summit on the Information Society says must be recognized. Public service radio could mean many things[31], but you can get an idea of the generally accepted range by looking at the membership of the European Broadcasting Union. Its members are "radio and television companies, most of which are government-owned public service broadcasters or privately owned stations with public missions". Support and control relationships between public service broadcasters and governments vary. Stations and networks may be owned by the government like Radio Mozambique[32]. They may be owned by a foundation partly controlled by the government, like Swedish national radio[33]. They may be owned by a state-initiated private company, funded by a dedicated tax and with nominal government control, like the BBC. In the case of National Public Radio in the US, you have a non-profit corporation indirectly funded by a line in the government budget, with the money laundered first through the Corporation for Public Broadcasting (a bipartisan politically directed body) and then through a network of member stations that are also listener-, donor-, and business-funded. Looking at these structures, you can infer that public service radio is intended to be for the public benefit, but not "by the people". In many cases, the government makes show of an arms-length relationship, but I think it is fair to say that these entities are expected to promote stability in the present system and cannot afford to be radical. It is a fact, however, that in the current climate of capitalist globalization even maintaining the status quo can become radical by default.

Remember that radio itself is only about 100 years old. In 1894, Marconi "made a bell ring using radio waves". In 1902 there was a "public demonstration of radio". Not til 1906 were the first radio set advertised and the first music broadcast on radio. Radio transmitters interfering with each other soon became an obvious problem. The first U.S. law to regulate broadcasters was passed in 1912[34]. This was, incidentally, the year the Titanic sank, a ship that had a radio but couldn't reach anyone with it. The nearest ship did not have a 24-hour radio operator. It was also the period of the First World War, and governments could certainly see the building power of radio for war, not only at home but also in their colonies.

New Zealand passed the first law to require government licensing of radio, in 1903[35], while it was still a British colony[36]. Private broadcasting was introduced there in 1923, but in 1936 the 22 private broadcasters were nationalized to create a state broadcasting monopoly. In 1947, New Zealand became one of many colonies that gained full independence from Britain. Like other former British colonies (and most of the rest of the world) it retained monopoly broadcasting and looked to the BBC for ideas. However, the BBC's programming was supported by government-levied licensing fees for radio receivers, and New Zealand was too small a country to make much money that way; hence, they took advertising, with its attendant pressure to make programs attractive to wealthy businesses. They also bought the majority of their programs from BBC [In 1983, a UNESCO study showed that Britain had 85% local programming on TV and New Zealand had only 25%].

In the mid-1980s, a New Zealand Royal Commission "advocated a strong public service system with limits on advertising levels and a local programme quota". But instead, national broadcasting was made into a state-owned enterprise that was supposed to return a profit to the government. Bids for programs the government wanted produced were let out for bidding to private companies. One big project the government funded was the medical soap opera *Shortland Street*, "NZOA's major prime-time vehicle for representing a changing national culture". *Shortland Street* is a wonderful example of how government funded programs can be politically shifted. Watched by 700,000 Kiwis every weeknight, the show has been top-ranked drama in the country ever since its debut. But as its web site describes, it has changed:

When Shortland Street began in 1992, "privatisation" and "business practice" were the buzzwords of a health system reinventing itself. The direction of healthcare seemed to lie in the private accident and emergency clinics springing up around the country. The forward-looking clinic Shortland Street A&E Medical was the way of the future.
Ten years later, faced with a decline in the demand for specialist private clinic services, Shortland Street has become a public hospital, funded by a district health board, and managed by a DHB-appointed CEO. Reflecting the health services most in demand in the fictional suburb of Ferndale, it provides a 24-hour accident and emergency service, community services (including GPs and preventative health care programmes), and elective surgery facilities[37].

The program had been initiated by the right-wing National Party during the Labour Party interregnum of 1990-99, with the obvious political aim of normalizing privatized healthcare. Perhaps unfortunately for the Labour Party when it returned, it wasn't as simple to turn around broadcasting policy as it was to change content. In 1991, New Zealand under the National Party had dropped all restrictions on transnational ownership of broadcasting, and the results had been disappointing to some:

> Although the introduction of competition has significantly increased the number of television services available within New Zealand, there is heated debate as to whether it has extended the range of programming on offer.
> Critics of the reforms point to the cultural costs of the minimal restrictions on commercial operators, the intensified competition for ratings points, [...] the absence of any quota to protect local programming, to NZOA's inability to compel stations to show the programmes it has funded in favourable slots; and to the marked increase in advertising time which gives more space to commercial speech and less to other voices[38].

The National Party had not only deregulated New Zealand's broadcasting sector, it had made a gift of it to the corporations and corporate-controlled states through GATS (the General Agreement on Trade and Services), an internationally negotiated trade pact.

> New Zealand deregulated its broadcasting sector and listed it as a covered service under the GATS. It is thus constrained from reintroducing content quotas, despite a change in government and a clear public will to re-regulate the sector[39].

Most other countries have similar points of struggle to New Zealand's. There are governments that still maintain broadcasting monopolies, but far fewer now, even in Africa and Asia. Zimbabwe remains one of the few governments that maintain total monopoly over broadcasting. Recently a high-ranking minister there cancelled the popular national anti-AIDS TV soap opera *Mopane Junction*, because funding had come from the Centers for Disease Control in the United States[40].

Canada is a country that still has a major government-funded public service broadcaster. Through a combination of budget cuts and exponential growth of its competition, the CBC has lost ground in the ratings, but is still the major opinion-testing ground of the nation, and clearly courts more diversity of opinions than the U.S. commercial talk radio referenced in the beginning of this article. Canada also has stiff requirements for Canadian Content (CanCon) in the music played on its radio outlets; and the province of Quebec has additional quotas for playing songs that include at least some French. (This can be contrasted with the Canadian film industry. The government still puts substantial, if shrinking, amounts of money into subsidizing Canadian filmmaking through the Film Board of Canada; however, as movie theatre ownership is overtaken by American-based chains drawing on American-based major distributors, Canadians often bemoan the fact that it's very hard to find places to view Canadian films outside of festivals).

With so much shared border and so much shared language between Canada and the economically and culturally aggressive US, the results of dropping Canadian cultural quotas and subsidies would be instantly noticeable and highly unpopular. Canada was one of the countries that brought the 2003 Free Trade Area of the Americas (FTAA) to a halt in the fall of 2003, largely over the issue of protection of cultural diversity. In July of 2001, Canada proposed this phrase to be part of the preamble of the FTAA:

> [...] countries must maintain the ability to preserve, develop and implement their cultural policies for the purpose of strengthening cultural diversity, given the essential role that cultural goods and services play in the identity and diversity of society and the lives of individuals [...] (FTAA.tci/w/04)[41].

Other countries share Canada's concerns. The UNESCO Executive Committee recommended in 2003 that a Convention on Cultural Diversity be developed as a legally-binding international instrument, citing:

> – There is a growing awareness that aspects of globalization are leading to cultural homogenization and increasing the difficulties for local and diverse cultural production.
> – Bilateral and multilateral trade agreements make the situation worse by limiting the ability of nations to support their own artists, cultural producers and institutions. Trade in "products and services" of the "entertainment industry" is big business, accounting for an increasing share of the trade balance of several countries.
> – "Exempting" culture from trade rules has been ineffective in preserving cultural sovereignty. WTO rules have been applied to cultural activities by trade panels. Cultural policies are increasingly made to conform to trade commitments. Developing nations cannot promote their own indigenous artists and cultural producers even when they have the capacity to implement appropriate policies.

Sweden provides a tidy example of public service radio at the service of national policy[42]. The current guidelines for Sweden's public service broadcasting were vetted by a committee appointed by the government that included members of all the parties in the Riksdag (Parliament). What they accepted includes this definition:

> In general terms the task of *public service radio* and TV can be described as giving everyone access to a balanced and independent selection of high quality programmes with no commercial advertising. Among other things this means that the broadcasts shall reach people throughout the country and that the broadcasts shall be so composed that it ranges from programmes of general interest to the more specialised, at the same time as the citizens are given new and unexpected choices of programmes and genres. The broadcasts shall be characterised by the fundamental democratic principles by which the state is governed and shall meet the requirements of impartiality, objectivity and independence of both state and private interests, and of political, economic and other spheres of authority. All programmes shall be of high quality. Another important aspect is that the broadcasts shall reflect the country as a whole and that programmes therefore shall be produced in different parts of Sweden.

One may note within the description above a number of phrases that are typically used for keeping station and programming decision-making within establishment boundaries, such as "of high quality", and "objectivity"[43]. "Diversity", explicitly mentioned elsewhere in the guidelines, is largely described in terms of geography and alternative languages. But we also see, later in the same document, indicators that Sweden intends public service broadcasting should be something of a counterweight to private media consolidation:

> Public service radio and television enjoy high status and will become increasingly important when there is greater competition. The Government proposes that the fundamental principles for public service broadcasting shall continue to apply and considers that there is broad agreement on having well-established *public service radio* and television companies in Sweden in the future. Vigorous *public service radio* and television can provide a strong balancing force in a media landscape that otherwise risks being dominated by a few actors.

In early 2004, there's been conflict in the UK around the independence of the BBC from government control. I had imagined when I began researching this that BBC was a government entity that had been granted independence by sufferance, but when I looked into its history, I found that it was actually a private-public partnership from its inception in 1922:

> Though it was the Post Office that had initiated the meeting, it was the six main manufacturers of radio equipment (the Marconi Company, Metropolitan-Vickers, the Western Electric Company, the Radio Communication Company, the General Electric Company, and the British Thompson-Houstan Company) who were asked to form a committee to prepare the plan for broadcasting in Britain.

The formation of the BBC involved companies making a capital investment for setting up transmitting stations that would reach all of Britain, thus creating a demand for radio receivers. The "new BBC was to undertake to sell only British-made sets, to pay to the Company 10 per cent of the net wholesale selling price of all broadcast receiving apparatus". BBC was also forbidden to accept money for carrying any message or music, except with written permission from the Postmaster. In 1927, Parliament joined the troika with the Postmaster-General and the corporate governors, and was nominally given "ultimate control" of the BBC; but basically "broadcasting had become a monopoly, financed by licensing fees on radio receivers, and administered by an independent public corporation"[44].

One of the stumbling blocks BBC had to get around when it began was opposition by the British newspaper industry. Initially the industry won a rule saying that the BBC would have to buy and pay for its news from existing print news services. Before long, of course, it outstripped these other sources – it still pays rather well, but has its own relationship with correspondents. Recently the conflict between BBC and newspapers has heated up again, though, and the crux of the matter is related to gift-giving.

In August 2003, a headline appeared reading "Dyke to Open Up BBC Archive". Greg Dyke, Director General of the BBC, had announced that

> […] everyone would in future be able to download BBC radio and TV programmes from the internet. The service, the BBC Creative Archive, would be free and available to everyone, as long as they were not intending to use the material for commercial purposes […].

"The BBC probably has the best television library in the world", said Mr Dyke, who was speaking at the Edinburgh TV Festival. [...] "I believe that we are about to move into a second phase of the digital revolution, a phase which will be more about public than private value; about free, not pay services; about inclusivity, not exclusion. [...] it will be about how public money can be combined with new digital technologies to transform everyone's lives"[45].

Dyke's announcement of free content fell in the middle of a spate of decisions by other UK news agencies that they were going to start charging for content on the internet. An analysis appeared on the University of Southern California's *Online Journalism Review*:

The BBC has the most popular British news Web site by far, with 16 to 20 million unique users per month. But it has pockets £ 2 billion ($ 3.32 billion) deep, filled with taxpayers' money. While it does not run advertising, most commercial newspapers believe that the BBC makes it harder to compete and survive because it poaches potential readers and subscribers.

The BBC response is to claim the public service defense. "We believe that the news we provide is a valuable service for the UK's license fee payers", said Pete Clifton, the newly appointed editor for BBC News Online. "It delivers to them, on an increasingly important platform, a rich source of BBC News content which they may have missed elsewhere. This content, paid for by them, covers news from local to international, and we feel it is right to make this available on the Web".

Newspapers are eagerly awaiting the British government's online review, which will report on the market impact of BBC's Web business next year. Many in the industry want curbs placed on the BBC Online; they hope the online review will make recommendations to that effect.
All of the United Kingdom's bigger online news operations are focused now on growing profits – and doing that is naturally more difficult in a marketplace where one of your competitors is deeply subsidized and giving away top product for free[46].

This controversy reflects a very deep conflict in societies around the world between models of socially provided goods and services that are collectively supported for all, and individual payment on the barrelhead for everything (even essentials of life like water). In the case of public service radio in the UK, "free" access to information and entertainment was made possible by over-the-air broadcasting to all who have the receivers, and those who bought the receivers paid for this information through dedicated taxes. Now public access to what is essentially collective wealth is being vastly extended by the BBC's opening its archives to all who have sufficient internet tool access, and this is considered an attack by those who need a condition of scarcity to help them make money on selling information.

It is important that the resemblance between the issue of information access and water access is not merely coincidental. Both are the subject of extremely heated trade negotiations, legislative activity, regulatory interpretations, and court fights all over the world, brought by a corporate sector that seeks to privatize valuable resources in both the material and the information commons. New laws formed in these arenas are extending copyrights, so that the products of creativity are not coming out into the public domain. They are newly criminalizing the copying of "intellectual property" even for individual use, research, or critical analysis. They are giving broadcasters and distributors new ownership rights over material that they did not create. And they are extending enforcement jurisdiction not only to those who actually copy or share protected intellectual property, but to those whose services or equipment designs are used in these newly illegal activities. That means internet service providers and engineers being held liable for what might be done by others. ISPs in some places are being subpoenaed to provide the names of their users who might potentially be sharing music files, for example, and coerced to provide this information under penalty of law[47]. As pointed out by attorney Robin Gross of the organization IP Justice, these new laws and trade regimes contravene an international human right, Article 19 of the Universal Declaration of Human Rights:

> *Article 19. The Right to Communicate.* Everyone has the right to freedom of opinion and expression; this right includes freedom to hold opinions without interference and to seek, receive and impart information and ideas through any media and regardless of frontiers.

This brings us then to the final section of this article, and a discussion of *community radio*. Community radio is the form most clearly concerned not only with people's ability to seek and receive information through media, but also with our ability to "impart information and ideas" to one another. As Genevieve Vaughan has pointed out in *For-Giving*: "'Comuni-cation' is giving gifts (from the Latin *munus* – gift) together. It is how we form 'comuni-ty'" (1997: 25-26).

Even more than for commercial or public service radio, the parameters of community radio can be hard to define.

> Some stations are owned by not-for-profit groups or by cooperatives whose members are the listeners themselves. Others are owned by students, universities, municipalities, churches or trade unions. There are stations financed by donations from listeners, by international development agencies, by advertising and by governments. – *"Waves for Freedom". Report on the Sixth World Conference of Community Radio Broadcasters. Dakar, Senegal, January 23-39, 1995*[48].

The World Association of Community Radio Broadcasters (AMARC [Association Mondiale des Radiodiffuseurs Communautaires]), based in Montreal, promotes mutual support among community radios around the world. They organized the Dakar conference of community broadcasters referenced above, as well as seven others since 1983. AMARC has members that are licensed and members that broadcast illegally; members that are free-standing stations, members that do community radio in the permitted niches of state broadcasters, and members that share frequencies with stations that may have incompatible aims to their own. If you go to the AMARC web site < www.amarc.org > and click on "What is Community Radio?" you'll find instead of one definition a series of quotes submitted by members in different regions. For example, from Latin America, where community radio stations are numerous and are often strongly linked to anti-oligarchical struggles:

> Radio stations that bear this name do not fit the logic of money or advertising. Their purpose is different, their best efforts are put at the disposal of civil society. Of course this service is highly political: it is a question of influencing public opinion, denying conformity, creating consensus,

238

broadening democracy. The purpose – whence the name – is to *build community life*. *"Manual urgente para Radialistas Apasionados"*. José Ignacio López Vigil. 1997

In Latin America, there are approximately one thousand radio stations that can be considered community, educational, grassroots or civic radio stations. *They are characterized by their political objectives of social change*, their search for a fair system that takes into account human rights, and makes power accessible to the masses and open to their participation. *"Gestión de la radio comunitaria y ciudadana"*. Claudia Villamayor y Ernesto Lamas. AMARC y Friedrich Ebert Stiftung. 1998

From Canada, where community radio is obligated by government to promote diversity and Canadian culture:

The tone of each community radio station is well modulated in the image of its listeners. The important thing is to seek out differences. Community radio is an element of closeness, a bridge, a step toward the other, not to make the other like us, but to have him become what he is. It is not a question of having more, but of being, that is the real mission of community radio stations in Canada. Isn't the most meaningful definition of culture the act of making people aware of the greatness they possess? *Alliance des radios communautaires du Canada, ARC. Canada.*

From France:

Free, independent, lay radio stations that are linked to human rights and concerned about the environment. They are many and pluralistic. refuse mercantile communication. They scrupulously respect the code of ethics of journalists and work to disseminate culture by giving artists broader expression within their listening audiences. They have association status, democratic operation and financing consistent with the fact that they are non-profit organizations. They are solidary toward each other and constitute work communities that make it possible for each member to fulfill its mission to the utmost.
Charte de la Confédération Nationale des Radios Libres, CNRL. France.

From the Philippines, where radio was very powerful in mobilizing People Power that overthrew the Marcos dictatorship:

Stations collectively operated by the community people. Stations dedicated to development, education and people empowerment. Stations which adhere to the principles of democracy and participation.
TAMBULI – Communication Project. Philippines

From India, where virtually all broadcasting has long been controlled by All-India Radio, which is both the national broadcaster and the regulator, and has occasionally doled out bits of airtime to community broadcasters under a tight rein:

Community radio programming is designed by the community, to improve social conditions and the quality of its cultural life. The community itself decides what its priorities and needs are in terms of information provision. VOICES. India.

239

From Africa:

The historical philosophy of community radio is to use this medium as the voice of the voiceless, the mouthpiece of oppressed people (be it on racial, gender, or class grounds) and generally as a tool for development. *"What is Community Radio? A resource guide"*. AMARC Africa and Panos Southern Africa. 1998.

A far-reaching example of community radio organizing originated in Africa was started by women, during the period when government-controlled radio was the rule across the continent. In 1988, the Zimbabwe chapter of the Federation of African Media Women (FAMW) resolved to get more rural women's participation into broadcasting, and came up with the idea for radio listening clubs[49]. These professional women communicators contacted women in rural villages, asked them to listen to the radio as a group, and then recorded the rural women's comments and questions. Next the journalists took the rural women's questions to public officials and asked them to respond[50]. Programs combining these elements were aired on Zimbabwe Radio 4; the rural women listened to the programs, again responded, and the series went on in this vein. Eventually, having observed how little it took to make the recordings, the rural women asked to be given their own recording equipment, and told the professional journalists they were no longer needed during the discussions[51].

Radio listening clubs spread first to other countries in the Southern Africa Development Community (SADC) region, and then to other parts of the world. It became a model for other feminist and community media projects in film, video, and still photography. And it's been copied by governmental and non-governmental development agencies seeking to accelerate social change. In the PhD dissertation "Media and the Empowerment of Communities for Social Change", Chido Matewa writes of radio listening clubs: *grassroots participation is what sets this project design apart and distinguishes it from other rural radio which is in line with the agenda setting theory of McCombs and Shaw, i.e. that the media agenda (MA) leads to the people's agenda (PA): MA»»PA*. [italics in original][52]. [I can't resist commenting that the "MA leads to PA" formula might be phrased in a more feminist manner: "MA leads PA"].

According to Matewa, radio listening club membership declines when radio sets become more available in villages, so expansion has been in ever more remote areas. Another problem may be that the association of radio listening clubs with state radio, and the adaptation of the radio listening club model to the aims of development agencies change the experience from participatory to didactic, and reduces its value as a gift. One gets a hint of local contempt for such coercion in a speech delivered by Kate Azuka Omunegha at the World Forum on Communication Rights:

One thing that seems to be glaring in Nigerian media is the near absence of women as newsmakers. One possible reason for this is the new news value, which privileges prominence, who is involved. Closely related to this again is the idea that Nigerian media seem to work with what we call the ideology of developmental communication. The media are seen as the mouthpiece of the government[53].

As more governments have opened up space for independent broadcasters, though, some community radio stations have been created that incorporate values from radio listening clubs and also consciously draw on the values taught by Brazilian popular educationist Paolo Freire, values such as starting with people's own lived experience, *concientizacion* (a word that is very popular in Latin America, but whose closest common North American equivalent is "consciousness raising"), and emphasis on dialogue that involves respect and working together[54].

There are community radios in Africa consciously promoting those values. The one I visited, Radio Ada, was first set up to serve the coastal fishing community of Ada; but because they could uniquely fill a need for local, participatory radio programming in the Dangme language, they ended up serving the entire region of about 500,000 Dangme-speaking people, half of whom are not literate. The station's mission as reported on the web site of their funder, UNESCO, is "to support the development aspirations and objectives of the Dangme people, give a voice to the voiceless, sustain the growth of Dangme culture, and encourage, promote and contribute to informed dialogue and reflective action"[55].

I visited Radio Ada in 2003, in the company of the coordinator of the Ghana Community Radio Network, and was fascinated by a description of how they work on reflective action in the public sphere. First, I was told, they ask the people what their problems are, then whose responsibility it is to deal with the problems. Then they go to those responsible, often public officials, and ask what they have done to meet their commitments around the problem. Then they give everybody time to think and work on the problem. This groundwork is done before beginning any recording, so no one is shamed on air before they've had a chance to improve their practice. I was told that this was normal procedure for all four stations in the Ghana Community Radio Network[56].

A traditional underpinning for this kind of relationship to authorities was stated by Ntombi, a Zimbabwean woman active in rural community publishing:

What is democracy? What is governance? [...]. You get the meaning of governance from the old people in the village, and they will tell you "governance in our times was a servant of the people, to do what the people want you to do, and once they don't approve of what you are [...]. When you govern people you are not their master, you have to be their servant and respect [...] being a governor in our time was being the people's slave, and it could go like the dew[57].

Another African station that grew directly out of the radio listening club movement was Radio Mama, the women's station in Kampala, Uganda, regrettably shut down by the Ugandan government on January 8, 2004 (reportedly for not having paid its license fees)[58]. According to an interview I conducted in 2002, Radio Mama had been assigned a broadcasting frequency that could not be picked up on car radios, a staggering handicap for developing an audience.

The issue of who is the audience, in other words, who is the recipient of the gift of radio, is a crucial one for community stations. To be community stations in the sense of "giving gifts together", the audience and the operators of the station should be interrelated categories.

Radio Ada co-founder and Deputy Director Wilna Quarmyne clearly subscribes to this view. She is originally from the Philippines, where she was also involved in the community radio and popular education movements. She writes that the approach to training in the station's activities was

> originally developed in 1997 for and at Radio Ada, the first full-fledged community radio station in Ghana. The approach is continually being enriched and has succeeded in enabling a group of volunteers with no previous training or experience in broadcasting to operate a full-scale, 17-hour-a-day service entirely on their own. Some of the volunteers have grown into trainers. The approach has also been extended with positive outcomes to other member stations of the Ghana Community Radio Network, as well as to a prospective community radio station in Ethiopia[59].

In some stations, the radio audience may be virtually coterminous with the presenters. The legendary Margaretta D'Arcy is an AMARC member who runs Radio Pirate Women in Galway, Ireland – a pirate (unlicensed) station that operates during periodic Women's Radio Festivals, using a transmitter small enough to fit in a purse. When a reporter asked D'Arcy how many listeners the station had, she stated that listeners were completely unimportant – that what is important is that the women talk on the radio, they listen to each other, get all fired up, and then they go out in the street and they demonstrate!

Larger and more permanent community stations usually have doors open for volunteers but also have some kind of long term paid staff for facilities management, and may also have staff setting programming policies. To maximize the gift-giving potential of community radio, leadership should ideally be nurturing and give-way[60] to the needs of the organization, promote horizontal giving, and promote "abundance through the cessation of waste"[61]. However, most stations also exist in a context of patriarchal hierarchicalism that can be insidious. In the United States, for instance, the Corporation for Public Broadcasting gives money to noncommercial radio stations that meet certain criteria, which in recent years have included having not less than five full-time paid staff members. This can provide an opening for stratification, and be in conflict with the kinds of values that often emerge from collective activity, where paid positions are often part-time or rotating jobs that help subsidize people of small financial means who are also volunteers. Professional aspirations of staff to earn higher salaries without moving on can lead to cutting in other areas[62]; and staff desires to minimize conflicts and hassles and streamline decision-making for themselves can lead to imposition of rules and loss of flexibility. Allowing breaking of rules so as to be flexible for some people and not others is then a likely source of cronyism and dissatisfaction.

Another entrée for hierarchicalism is provided by the "ownership structures" of many noncommercial stations. In order to qualify for noncommercial frequencies, receive public funds, and offer tax-deductible status to donors, stations generally have to have boards of directors. In the US, only one state, Wisconsin, even permits nonprofit organizations to have a cooperative structure, and even those have to have boards of directors[63]. Directors have the legal liability for the station, the rights to change its bylaws and approve its budget, and are in effect treated by the law as the owners of the station. (And as volunteers have sometimes found when they tried to go to court against boards of directors, "ownership is nine-tenths of the law"). A famous recent struggle within the five-station Pacifica network turned in part on directors' decisions to change the board from elected to self-selected, and a suggestion that they would change the bylaws to allow board members to make a profit from activities performed for the station. In both staff and board hierarchies, you can see a potential for imposition of one-many structures, where the one or ones who are staff or board substitute and take over from the many who are volunteers or listeners (or both). This pattern can be found not only in community radio, but in many kinds of nonprofit organizations. A corollary of such a development is that volunteer contributions are devalued and raising and spending money takes over as the dominant activity of the organization. In the case of U.S. community radio, the Corporation for Public Broadcasting promoted such substitution by changing the way it awarded public funds. Where formerly stations' "match" for public funds they received could include volunteer hours assigned value in monetary terms, this was changed so that stations had to raise actual dollars to match the federal dollars they might be given[64]. This discounting of volunteers' gifts of their labour and denial of economic means to support that work seems related to the following statement in *For-Giving*:

> Free giftgiving to needs – what in mothering we would call nurturing or caring work – is often not counted and may remain invisible in our society or seem uninformative because it is qualitatively rather than quantitatively based (1997: 24).

Many community stations run on very little funding, but even they have financial needs, for equipment, for electricity, for materials, and usually for at least some paid staff that can spend the concentrated time to coordinate volunteers and keep things running smoothly. Whether the funds come from NGOs, foundations, the government, or business advertiser/underwriters, they often come with some kind of mandate, pressure or temptation to modify or abandon a social change agenda. Even listener donations can tempt community radios to play to the richer elements of society. One of the most frequently heard debates within listener-supported radio is whether the value of the program should be measured by how much money is donated to the station when that program is on the air, and whether shows that don't raise enough money should be dropped, even if they serve a disadvantaged audience.

A related conflict is whether the value of a station can be measured by the number of its listeners. Commercial radio stations use commercial measuring services to come up with audience "ratings". The sample of people asked to give data on their listening habits is supposedly randomly selected from fixed demographic categories (e.g., males 18-34). Standings in the Arbitron ratings are used to rank stations in terms of "market share" both geographically and demographically, and these figures in turn are used by stations to set advertising rates. That is the process by which the invisible product of human attention to radio is made visible and sold[65]. Similar methods of audience measurement have been adopted by National Public Radio in the US. Their audience surveys include asking whether their listeners use or buy long lists of products, but have little (usually nothing) about the listeners' social change activities. Starting in the 1980s, a well-publicized goal of their audience research department was to "double the NPR audience", and the announced plan for doubling the audience was to have stations program so that the same people would keep listening longer. This led to a conscious effort to program more for the well-off white male, the same demographic that commercial radio found most desirable. While some editions of *The NPR Audience* noted that older women are actually more generous and consistent listener-donors, they were considered a shrinking part of the audience, and of course they were less attractive to underwriters. (Underwriting is a form of quasi-advertising that NPR, PBS, and most U.S. public radio and television stations now pursue heavily).

Within U.S. community radio, two divergent streams of thought emerged around the question of audience. One faction believed and promoted the concept that pursuing similar strategies to NPR's would be good for community radio and give it more listeners, more money, and greater stability. Their approach was to change stations so that there would be more paid programmers and hosts, a more consistent sound, and more mainstream kinds of music and information. This was similar to the usual public radio formula, and often included airing offerings from the major public radio syndicators, NPR and Public Radio International. Programs most likely to be cut included women's programs and other kinds of programs run by collectives or groups, the reason given usually being that shared responsibilities and changing hosts led to inconsistent air-sound. The other community radio faction, however, developed a very different self-identity, rejecting some of the advice that was being promoted to them through the collaborative efforts of the National Federation of Community Broadcasters and the Corporation for Public Broadcasters. In 1996, breakaway stations from NFCB created a new annual conference, the Grassroots Radio Conference, "as a reaction against the homogenization of commercialization of public radio"[66]. The founders of the GRC, Marty Durlin of KGNU in Boulder, Colorado, and Cathy Melio of WERU in Maine, wrote an article explaining their movement. I excerpt here from a version found on the web:

What is grassroots radio?
You can recognize a grassroots community station anywhere in the country. There is a freshness you'll not hear elsewhere due largely to the variety of voices and connections the station has with its community. Local programming is the backbone of community radio, [but] another element that connects grassroots stations are the independently-produced national programs many of us broadcast, including Alternative Radio, WINGS (Women's International News Gathering Service), National Native News, and Making Contact.
These national programs connect the grassroots stations, while our local programs ground us in our own communities. [...] Sometimes the performances of inexperienced programmers are rough [...] [but] those new voices become competent and creative broadcasters before our very ears [...]. It is insulting the intelligence of people to think that they can not accept or appreciate variety of programming [...]. We believe in expanding the audience for the variety, not reducing the variety to expand the audience. [...] Important principles to maintaining a community involved grassroots station are: participatory governance, with active committees involved in decision-making, community and volunteer involvement in all major decisions, openness on the air (no gag orders!), elected volunteer representatives serving on the board of directors, open access to the airwaves, active recruitment and ongoing training of volunteers, commitment to diversity, consideration of those under-served by other broadcast media, and diverse programming[67].

The GRC has done much to strengthen the self-identity and resolve of community radio in the US, and its model has had a strong impact. Throughout the eight years of GRC conferences, it has also provided a national venue for the struggles of volunteers and listeners to reclaim the five-station Pacifica network from its runaway board. Many of the GRC stations were affiliates of the syndicated programming distributed by the Pacifica network, and organized among themselves to support striking Pacifica news reporters and withhold affiliation fees in support of the struggle. After the volunteer-listener victory and re-organization of Pacifica, GRC co-founder Marty Durlin was overwhelmingly elected to chair the reclaimed board of the Pacifica Foundation, in March 2004.

In 2002, at the World Social Forum in Porto Alegre, Brazil, Brazilian popular education activist Moema Viezzer took me to visit a special community radio station. It had been set up with city government support for the use of the youth at the conference. They were broadcasting primarily via loudspeaker to the youth camping area, and to a landless-persons' camping area nearby. The studio was a large log building with a packed earth floor, and inside were rows of computers, and a complete broadcasting studio. Over the microphone was a sign, which Moema Viezzer translated for me: "A microphone is not a piss pot".

What did this mean?, I wondered. Finally, this occurred to me: radio is gift-giving, and gift-giving is transitive[68]. When you speak into a microphone, you don't do it to relieve yourself. You do it to reach people with something that will meet their needs.

Notes

[1] Notably, Meridien FM in Tema, Ghana.

[2] http://www.worldsummit2003.de/en/web/229.htm accessed January 25, 2004.

[3] http://www.museum.tv/archives/etv/F/htmlF/fairnessdoct/fairnessdoct.htm accessed March 5, 2004.

[4] Corollaries to the fairness doctrine – the "personal attack" and "political editorializing" rules – were thrown out in October 2000 by the U.S. Circuit Court of Appeals for the District of Columbia. http://www.firstamendmentcenter.org/Press/topic.aspx?topic=press_broadcasting, accessed March 5, 2004.

[5] http://www.museum.tv/archives/etv/F/htmlF/fairnessdoct/fairnessdoct.htm accessed March 5, 2004.

[6] WINGS #4-01 Revenge on Big Media: Dallas's cat-killers. Radio program produced by Mary O' Grady for Women's International News Gathering Service and released in 2001.

[7] "Section 315 of the Communications Act – the section that imposes an equal time requirement for all broadcasts featuring candidates – may itself be unconstitutional". Michael C. Dorf, on web site http://www.cnn.com/2003/LAW/08/22/findlaw.analysis.dorf.arnold/, accessed March 5, 2004.

[8] http://www.listenerchoice.com/essays/BroadcastingShift.html accessed March 5, 2004.

[9] http://wireless.fcc.gov/auctions/ accessed March 5, 2004.

[10] http://www.ncs.gov/N5_HP/Customer_Service/XAffairs/SpeechService/SS00-056.htm accessed March 5, 2004. I am using the U.S. as my primary example because I am most familiar with the process there, and because the process of enclosing the commons there is very stark. However, as will be discussed in the section on government radio, there is more than one way to ensure control through scarcity.

[11] Interview notes by Frieda Werden, on web site http://www.womensradiofund.org/femradio.htm accessed March 5, 2004.

[12] Werden, Frieda, "A Woman's Local Commercial FM Station", on web site http://www.womensradiofund.org/batrogue.htm accessed March 5, 2004.

[13] http://www.fcc.gov/localism/ accessed March 5, 2004. Chairman Michael Powell is the son of the U.S. Secretary of State Colin Powell. To see what is the "community" of media owners in the U.S. (and transnationally) today, see the

web page "Who Controls the Media?" maintained by the National Organization for Women, as part of their campaign against lifting media ownership restrictions: http://www.nowfoundation.org/issues/communications/tv/mediacontrol.html

[14] "FCC Localism Hearing Draws Large, Vocal Crowd" on web site http://www.wral.com/news/2574901/detail.html POSTED: 9:52 p.m. EDT October 22, 2003, UPDATED: 10:18 p.m. EDT October 22, 2003.

[15] Eric Boehlert in "Pay for Play", http://dir.salon.com/ent/feature/2001/03/14/payola/index.html

[16] "#17 Clear Channel Monopoly Draws Criticism", on web site http://www.projectcensored.org/publications/2004/17.html – summarizes coverage by Jeff Perlstein from September 2002.

[17] http://www.mediageek.org/archives/002169.html, posting dated October 23, 2003.

[18] Jennifer Pozner, "I'd Take Them Out with Sex: Journalists trivialize Howard Stern's advocacy of rape as 'Insensitivity'" in *Extra*, July/August 1999. Found on web site: http://www.fair.org/extra/9907/stern.html

[19] See collection of back articles from FAIR on http://www.fair.org/media-outlets/talk-radio.html

[20] http://www.cnn.com/2004/SHOWBIZ/News/02/25/stern.suspension/, dated Feb. 26 2004. NB: These new "decency standards" are also quite political, a reversal of the entire trend toward deregulation of media content pleasing to the fundamentalist sector of the U.S. political right.

[21] "Stern Feels Bush-Whacked, End is Near", dated March 3, 2004, on web site http://www.fmqb.com/Article.asp?id=20252 [I can't resist mentioning here that in my research for discussion of the rationale for shock radio's popularity, I found web sites selling term papers on this topic for $9.95 a page!].

[22] http://www.rnw.nl/realradio/dossiers/html/hateintro.html, viewed March 6, 2004; page last updated February 10, 2004.

[23] http://www.comminit.com/pdsradiodrama/sld-9388.html, Case Study 9: Rwanda – *Urunana* (Hand in Hand).

[24] http://www.wings.org/2003.html

[25] Heidi Dietrich, "Polite market: Area not known for shock radio", in Puget Sound Business Journal, October 17, 2003. Print Edition, archived on the web at http://seattle.bizjournals.com/seattle/stories/2003/10/20/story3.html accessed March 6, 2004.

[26] Patrick Burkart, "Radio Shock: Talk Radio Propaganda", in *Bad Subjects*, Issue # 23, December 1995, archived on the web at http://www.eserver.org/bs/23/burkart.html accessed March 6, 2004.

[27] "Challenging Hate Radio: A Guide for Activists" on the web page http://www.fair.org/activism/hate-radio.html: "Call in to the show. Call the on-air line during the show and try to challenge the racism, sexism or homophobia calmly and directly. It often doesn't take much to demonstrate the absurdity of bigoted arguments. If several people call in, it can change the entire show".

[28] "Groups Demand End to 'Hate Radio'" by John C. posted Wednesday, Apr. 24, 2002 at 7:23 PM *on the web page* http://www.indybay.org/news/2002/04/124735_comment.php

[29] http://www.zundelsite.org/english/catalog/audio_catalog.html accessed March 10, 2004.

[30] Greg Bonnell, "Holocaust denier Ernst Zundel to remain in jail pending immigration hearing", Tuesday April 1, 2003, in *CNews Law and Order*, archived on web page http://cnews.canoe.ca/CNEWS/Law/2003/03/31/55093-cp.html accessed March 10, 2004.

[31] In the US, the term "public service radio" is sometimes applied to emergency radio communications used by police and fire departments, and "public radio" is used for the noncommercial broadcast stations.

[32] http://www.tvradioworld.com/region3/moz/ accessed March 12, 2004.

[33] Christina Ruhnbro, private e-mail, March 15, 2004.

[34] "Radio Broadcasting History" timeline, archived on web page http://senior.billings.k12.mt.us/otrannex/history/radio.htm accessed March 6 2004.

[35] "A Brief History of Regulation of Radiocommunications in New Zealand 1903-2003" on the web page http://www.med.govt.nz/rsm/publications/pibs/radiohistory/footnotes.html#fn09 accessed March 6, 2004.

[36] "Timeline: New Zealand" at http://news.bbc.co.uk/1/hi/world/asia-pacific/country_profiles/1138430.stm accessed March 6, 2004.

[37] From the Shortland Street web site, FAQ http://shortlandstreet.nzoom.com/faq/ accessed March 11, 2004.

[38] http://www.museum.tv/archives/etv/N/htmlN/newzealand/newzealand.htm accessed March 6, 2004.

[39] "Advancing Cultural Diversity Globally: The Role of Civil Society Movements", on web page http://www.incd.net/Conf2003/INCD_papers2003_Convention.htm, accessed March 10, 2004.

[40] Musi Khumalo, private communication February 2004.

[41] FTAA Trade Negotiations Committee Canada, "Paper on Cultural Diversity in the FTAA Negotiations", September 23, 2003, on http://www.ftaa-alca.org/TNC/tnw195_e.asp, accessed March 10, 2004.

[42] Ministry of Culture, Sweden, "Public Service Radio and Television 2005" on the web page http://www.google.

ca/search?q=cache:mWfBSHFt2QgJ:kultur.regeringen.se/inenglish/pressinfo/pdf/Public_service_%2520eng.pdf+%22public+service+radio%22&hl=en&ie=UTF-8 accessed March 11, 2004.

[43] See, for an example of such discussion, Noam Chomsky's book *Objectivity and Liberal Scholarship*, which discusses objectivity as an ideological mask for championing mainstream self-interest against mass movements for change.

[44] "The Unofficial Guide to the BBC" on web site http://www.vaxxine.com/master-control/BBC/ chapters/Bbc_form.html accessed March 11, 2004.

[45] http://news.bbc.co.uk/1/hi/entertainment/tv_and_radio/3177479.stm accessed March 12, 2004.

[46] Daithí Ó hAnluain, "Free Content Becoming Thing of the Past for UK's Online Newspaper Sites", in Online Journal Review, posted Feb. 13, 2004. Web site http://www.ojr.org/ojr/business/1067472919.php accessed March 12, 2004.

[47] Robin Gross, speech at the Community Media panel on Intellectual Property Rights, World Summit on the Information Society, 11 December 2003. Recorded by Frieda Werden, and forthcoming as an audio program in WINGS: Women's International News Gathering Service.

[48] "What is COMMUNITY RADIO?" on www.amarc.org/amarc/ang accessed March 16, 2004.

[49] Chido E. F. Matewa, *Media and the Empowerment of Communities for Social Change* (PhD dissertation 2002), "Chapter Five: Participatory and development communication in Zimbabwe" archived on the web at http://www.comminit.com/idmatewa/sld-6133.html accessed March 15, 2004.

[50] Note that CEDAW – the United Nations Convention on the Elimination of All Forms of Discrimination Against Women, requires that all signatory states provide mechanisms for the participation of rural women in public decision-making. Zimbabwe finally ratified CEDAW in 1991.

[51] Elizabeth Karonga in radio program "WINGS #44-00 Media for Women's Development" produced by Frieda Werden.

[52] Matewa, op. cit.

[53] Omunegha, "Women, Poverty and the Media", speech at the World Forum on Communication Rights, Geneva Switzerland, December 11, 2003, recorded by Frieda Werden and aired in Voix San Frontieres, AMARC audio feed, March 21, 2004.

[54] http://www.infed.org/thinkers/et-freir.htm accessed March 22, 2004.

[55] "Ghana: Radio Ada Goes on the Air", on web page http://www.fao.org/docrep/003/x6721e/x6721e30.htm accessed March 14, 2004.

[56] N.B.: "We are not using the violent methods of the system but are looking for other ways to change it from within". – Genevieve Vaughan, *For-Giving*, p. 23.

[57] Interview by Elizabeth Robinson, recorded at the African Village exhibit at the World Summit on the Information Society, December 10-12, 2003; aired in AMARC, *Voix sans frontiers*, March 21, 2004.

[58] "MAMA FM Closes, on web site http://radio.oneworld.net/article/view/73528/1/ accessed March 15, 2004.

[59] Wilna Quarmyne, "A 'Kente' Approach to Community Radio Training: Weaving Training into the Community Empowerment Process", February 2001, on web page http://www.comminit.com/africa/st2004/sld-1467.html accessed March 22, 2004.

[60] *For-Giving*, p. 96.

[61] *For-Giving*, p. 98.

[62] Lyn Gerry, "KPFK Programmers Ordered to Mainstream Content; Advocacy Journalism is 'Out'", dated May 26, 1998, on the web page http://www.radio4all.org/fp/mainstream.htm accessed March 16, 2004.

[63] Norm Stockwell, General Manager, WORT-FM, Madison, Wisconsin, small group discussion, July 22, 2000.

[64] Anonymous, [Pacifica] PROGRAM DIRECTOR MEETING (PART II) ALBUQUERQUE, NEW MEXICO FEBRUARY 28, 1995 on web site http://www.radio4all.org/fp/pdmeet1.html

[65] I should mention here that community broadcasters, including both FIRE (Feminist International Radio Endeavour/Radio Internacional Feminista, based in Costa Rica) and the great community station Bush Radio in Cape Town, South Africa, are coming up with new and appropriate ways of not only measuring but valuing their audiences.

[66] http://www.kgnu.org/grassroots6/ accessed March 22, 2004.

[67] Marty Durlin and Cathy Melio, "The Grassroots Radio Movement in the US", found on the web page http://www.morelater.com/kaos/forum/messages/43.html accessed March 16, 2004.

[68] Vaughan in *For-Giving*, p. 36. See also, p. 24: "[G]iving to needs creates bonds between givers and receivers. Recognizing someone's need and acting to satisfy it, convinces the giver of the existence of the other, while receiving something from someone else that satisfies a need proves the existence of the other to the receiver".

References

Vaughan, Genevieve (1997). *For-Giving: A Feminist Criticism of Exchange*, Plain View Press, Austin, Texas.

Introduction

It was sometime in the very beginning of the 60's. They came together in a university lab to do an experiment. No one paid them to do it and they did not have to pay anyone either. They were not calculating, they just wanted to make one computer be able to communicate with another, thus passing and sharing information back and forth. Free and open distribution of information.

At the time computer technology was hardly accessible to people in general, because computers were not very compatible then, and also because personalized computers had not emerged the way they have today.

They did have access to computers because they were university students and scientists, struggling to share information faster, and what they wanted to share was nowhere to be found in print. They were trying to share new developments and discoveries they were producing in physics.

But beyond the pragmatism behind their motivations, lay a philosophical and political conviction: the free exchange of information would have to be embedded in the internet culture that would emerge, otherwise it made no sense! They developed it quietly because they knew what they were up to. Such communications systems were secretly being used by the military alone.

They were determined to make it work, for the sake of free sharing of information by civilians. And they did. No one remembers what the first words were, but when they appeared in the second computer, connected to the first via phone line, the joy was out of this world.

The day was November 21, 1961. They did it at the UCLA science department computer which communicated with the computer at the Stanford Research Institute near Palo Alto, also in California. They developed it into what was known as ARPANET, a network that joined four university sites, which became twelve and then grew to sixty two and to 200 by 1981. ARPANET was discontinued in 1990. The World Wide Web was created in 1991 by Tim Berners Lee in Switzerand, also for research sharing by scientists and students, and soon became open to others (Kaku 1997: 49).

Along another line of purpose and use, the Pentagon had created its own parallel internet communications for military purposes, keeping it in secrecy for their warfare purposes.

Once the Cold War was over, they opened it up, and the corporations came in to make it a profit-oriented business. But the spirit, objectives and strategies of that first experiment not only survive, but thrive in the hands of peoples and social movements across the world today.

Gift giving is one of the names under which the development of "open" (for some) or "free" (for others) software for the use of the internet and World Wide Web has emerged and developed alongside the commodified corporate way and the warfare actions of the military.

Gift giving has been defined by many, but the definitions that FIRE will use here come from feminist activist Genevieve Vaughan and from the Transaction Network, in terms of internet gift giving.

Vaughan's definition is as follows:

[…] the direct satisfaction of the needs of one person by another is perhaps the basic human interaction. This interaction constitutes the fundamental logical pattern of mothering and of many other aspects of life in which it has not been recognized. Human interactions of unilateral gift giving create relations of communication and community, as giver and receiver relate themselves to each other, to the items given and the needs satisfied […] gift giving is the basis of communication, and […] signs and especially the signs of language can be understood as gift constructions at different levels of abstraction. The market, which denies and cancels gift giving through exchange, is thus a mechanism of distorted and contradictory communication, which models and provides a niche for adversarial patriarchal relations. By seeing language and communication as gift giving we can revise the self image of our species so that we can consider our humanity as based on nurturing not on domination, and act accordingly. We can alter our collective self-fulfilling prophecy (2003).

The Transaction Network defines it like this in "Countless Exchanges in the Gift Economy: Toward a New Understanding of Transactions" in their web page (TN 2003).

Over the last two decades, the resurgence in non-competitive money systems have demonstrated that money need not store value (in the form of accrued interest), and in fact works better when its sole function is to facilitate exchanges. This definition of money – as Bernard Lietaer puts it, "an agreement within a community to use something as a medium of exchange" – allows us to envision a new type of "gift economy" in which money need never be hoarded and members of a community are therefore free to exchange all their gifts and services. The "gift economy" model might be extended if each individual exchange or transaction were likewise redefined. As it stands now, even in interest-free money systems, each exchange must be quantified in hours, Green Dollars, or some other form of unit. But if we understood "transactions" to include unilateral goodwill gifts from an individual to an entire community, we might encourage community members to focus not on counting hours or Green Dollars or other units, but instead on weaving together a network of reciprocal gift-giving.

These definitions differ in that the feminist definition does not consider that everything has to include exchange. What they have in common is that both recognize that exchange is not the only way to interact!

The Internet and its free and open software are examples of gift giving, so strong, that in the evolution of the internet and the WWW, movements have rejected time after time every intent to control and fully commercialize it or impose overall copyrights. The way in which the flow of information in the web happens remains pretty much the same as that first civil society experiment: computer to computer communication, so that information can flow freely and openly since the cost of copies and of distribution is open and oftentimes free.

That is the structure, despite governmental and corporate efforts to control, commercialize and copyright it. As Tim Berners-Lee points out: "Concepts of intellectual property, central to our culture, are not expressed in a way which maps onto the abstract information space. In an information space, we can consider the authorship of materials, and their perception; but [...] there is a need for the underlying infrastructure to be able to make copies simply for reasons of [technical] efficiency and reliability. The concept of 'copyright' as expressed in terms of copies made makes little sense" (Burners-Lee 1996: 11).

Much water has run under the bridge of cyberspace in the time between 1961 and 2004. In 1998, there were 95.4 million households worldwide with personal computers, about half of which (45.2 million) were online. At the time, the prediction was that by 2000, there would be 113.6 million PC households, of which 66.6 million would be online. In 2003, Google reported 2 million searches per day (1/3 from the US, the remainder in 88 other languages). VeriSign, a company that operates much of the Internet infrastructure worldwide, reported in 2000 that they had processed 600 million requests per day (to go to websites of .com, .net, etc.). By 2003, there were 9 billion requests daily (Thompson & FIRE 2004: 7).

New compatible technologies have emerged that make old time computers seem like the equivalent of a dinosaur, seen by a lizard. Alongside the hardware came software for all kinds of activities and possibilities. Most of it as we know it has been commercialized (...) but not all.

Despite the commercialisation of a lot of activites and software in cyberspace, the users ensure that the gift economy that exists and flows through the internet continues to flourish. Tim Berners-Lee, in "Realising the Full Potential of the Web" says that the structure of the WWW has been developed to encourage open cooperation among its participants, as the users are the ones who are constructing the system together when they send e-mails, participate in listserves, post their information in web sites and newsgroups, participate in electronic conferences and produce web sites (Bernes Lee 1997: 5).

The vast wealth that software corporations amassed in the eighties and nineties was largely due to an interesting phenomenon linked directly to the very nature of software. It is possible to create a software application and then reproduce it any number of times with very little additional cost. This aspect of software has allowed corporations like Microsoft to achieve revenues surpassing the gross national product of most countries while employing hardly more than 15,000 employees world-wide. Open software is not only a lot more cost-effective but it distributes technical power democratically. While many leaders of the open source community reside in the US, the power is very well distributed internationally. In fact the most famous open source programmer of all, Linus Torvalds, is from Finland.

People in the South who have been utilizing open source software benefit in many ways. Firstly, the actual cost of open source software is usually zero. Hundreds of billions of dollars can be saved yearly by using open source software. Secondly, the implementation of open source projects requires in-depth knowledge. Technicians in the developing world are no longer reduced to following instructions handed down to them, they can work shoulder to shoulder with their peers in the open source community. Thirdly, the majority of money that is spent on implementing software projects stays in the community and is not concentrated in the hands of a few. Fourthly, local technologists implementing the solutions are far more in-tune to their own local needs than foreign corporations are. They no longer have to adapt their organizations to fit software designed for others; they can create solutions appropriate for themselves, which greatly increases the effectiveness of the technology (FIRE & Nomadic Solutions 2003: 10). Due to the fact that knowledge and brainpower is the true mover of open source there is a great opportunity for women who have basic Internet access to learn and to adjust programs to their own needs and strategies.

New movements and new technologies have emerged in this context. They struggle to keep the structure and flow open, despite corporate effort to revert this gift giving trend. The open source movement and the free software movement are part of the social movements that have been able to become global, precisely because of they use open and free access to the internet.

Open-source software (OSS) is software for which the source code is freely and publicly available, though the specific licensing agreements vary as to what one is allowed to do with that code. Free Software is a movement that stems out of an ethical and political stance to mean freedom from corporate control in order to give information as a gift.

The concept of Open Source Software (OSS) has become a true technological – and political – revolution. The basic idea is very simple: Computer programmers create the software programs and share them at no cost with others, who in turn are able to add or change the characteristics and codes of the programs according to their own needs, and share them further with the user community (who are also free to change them) of OSS users around the world. Thus, the open source programs are constantly evolving through an open and shared development process. Open source technology is considered to be more stable, secure and creative than its commercial counterparts from Microsoft.

One example is the issue of instant messaging, one of the most popular services on the Internet. Unfortunately, there are several issues facing Instant Messaging in its current form.

1. Proprietary, standalone systems. Popular systems such as Microsoft's MS Messenger, AOL Instant Messenger, and Yahoo Messenger are separate, incompatible systems. No intercommunication is permitted between any of these different networks.

2. Instant Messaging is insecure. There are many security concerns regarding the current Instant Messaging systems. Firstly, it should be known that all the chat traffic has to go first to a main Instant Messaging server before getting transmitted to its final destination. All conversations in any of these corporate-run Instant Messaging systems can be monitored at will. Perhaps of greater concern is the fact that the majority of these systems still send the chat traffic in plain text over the Internet. Not only is it feasible for an entity to monitor chat traffic, it is easy. In many countries the number of Internet connections to the world is minimal and usually concentrated in one place. A government that wants to monitor Internet traffic can easily do it. This is not science fiction, it is done daily in the U.S. in a widely-known FBI project known as Carnivore – the Internet's equivalent of a phone tap. People working on social justice issues in unfriendly environments may be at risk if certain parties are able to eavesdrop on their conversations.

3. The most popular Instant Messenger services are owned by large corporations. For now, most Instant Messaging systems do not charge although several companies are starting

to look for ways to take advantage of their captive clients. In the near future this phenomenon of "free" messaging may all but disappear. It is important for Instant Messaging services to be taken back from corporate control.

Jabber is an open source project that offers a standard, interoperable, extensible, and secure protocol for creating an Instant Messaging system. There are many free versions of the client software that run on Microsoft Windows, Apple Macintosh, and Linux based computers. Setting up a server that supports several tens of thousands of users is feasible with very little resources. The Jabber protocol also supports decentralization and interoperability between various Jabber networks. While the project may start out with all women using the main server in Costa Rica to access the system (see graphic) it is possible to have several servers around that world that maintain local traffic local and pass messages as needed to their final destinations. The Jabber system also supports secure encrypted traffic which maybe desirable under many circumstances (FIRE & Nomadic Solutions 2003: 10).

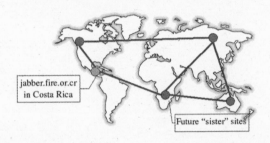

The APACHE server, which today is the most popular worldwide, was originally created and is currently used by many people in the open source community. Its operating system of open source is called GNU/Linux and is used not only for Internet computers but also for creating special effects in Hollywood, as well as for administrative systems in hospitals. It is very popular among activists, including those struggling against monopolistic corporate power, because it represents a concrete alternative example both technically and socio-economically.

As such, open source technology redistributes the power of technology, enabling users to copy the programs at no cost, and adapt them to their needs. Thus any of the users who have even some knowledge of computer programming can produce and create open source programs, and so they are not merely acting as commercial servants to the mass technology monopolies. Thus, gift giving in the Net is about democratizing and it is about a paradigm shift in economics.

The case of FIRE: Open source technology in the hands of women

One example among thousands worldwide is the case of FIRE – Feminist International
Radio Endeavour and its use of free or open source technology.

Last November in Costa Rica, FIRE held a workshop that shared such gift giving. An Internet server called APACHE, using LINUX, an Open Source operating system, was created during their workshop entitled "Internet Technologies for Our Political Action". The server had two functions: to share a non-corporate Internet operating system with the 32 workshop participants from throughout the Latin American and Caribbean region, and to offer these same participants a local server to use for practice during the workshop.

For the experimental server used in the FIRE workshop, each participant had her own website, access to e-mail, and a link to the internal server network for the workshop, all in a free form that was created and designed for the event itself and the participants. The participants were able to use a free version of FTP to create and modify their websites.

By adding her own presence to the internet, every user contributed to the collective knowledge accessible to those already on-line, another dimension of gift giving. As a result of the training workshop, "New Technologies for Political Activism", female activists from 15 grassroots organizations designed and published web pages for their organizations. The "first time" for each of them opened a Pandora's box: a new window to the world that taught them that the Internet is a tool, not only for gathering information, but for making their own voices heard worldwide.

An activist for Honduran Afro-descendent black women's rights, Nedelka Lacayo of the Enlace de Mujeres Negras (Honduran Black Women's Network), along with a Mayan Guatemalan indigenous women's rights activist, Marta Misa of "Kaqla" (Mayan word for rainbow), had used e-mail before attending the workshop and had surfed the Web for information. Likewise, a maquila women's rights activist and Salvadoran activist, Dina Salas of Centro de Orientación Radial para Mujeres (Center for Training of Women in Radio) had experience with e-mail, as had a Nicaraguan rural community organizer, Maria of the Asociación de Mujeres de Jalapa (Association of Women of Jalapa) "OYANKA" (Indigenous word for new road), among others.

Surrounded by a closed circle of 24 computers in the conference room of the Hotel Comfort Inn in Santa Ana, Honduran Nedelka Lacayo clutched the computer keyboard as her new "key" to the world wide web. "I even learned how to put my own voice in the page. Come and see... oops... come and hear, as you open the page, I welcome people to the site of my organization. It's almost like magic!" exclaimed Nedelka.

Some women's organizations already had web pages when they came to the workshop. Guatemalan Laura Asturias, producer of a regional feminist electronic bulletin, La Tertulia, and co-producer of the monthly women's newspaper, *La Cuerda*, shared her extensive internet experience and skills at the worskhop. She trained other participants in making feminist electronic bulletins, as did Margarita Salas of Fundación Acceso (Access Foundation) in Costa Rica, who conducted a worskhop on the design of forums and discussion lists. Katerina Anfossi of FIRE and Jackie Siles of the International World Conservation Union (UICN) trained others in the use of chat rooms for activism. As the participants opened their first "AMLAT Women" chat session, the first online message someone typed said, "Is this a private meeting or can others come in?". Of course all were welcome.

"Cibersives" was the name adopted by one of the working groups who shared with others their experiences in the use of the internet for political activism in the region. Guatemalan radio producer Ana Silvia Monsón of the radio program "Voces de Mujer" (Women's Voices) explained that through e-mail her organization was able to generate international solidarity and pressure when the administration of the radio station wanted to cut airtime for her program. The women radio producers were able to stop the threat. Ana Silvia noted, "They (the administration) learned that we were not alone, that we are part of a global movement of women doing radio and that this movement was not going to allow this to happen. We learned that we have stronger negotiating capacity when we have the support of others".

One after the other, all participants in the group shared similar experiences that speak to the fact that access to the internet allows for their voices to be heard in the midst of big media control. "Cibersives" declared that there is a relationship between claiming a media of our own and the right to self determination and bodily integrity. "We are our bodies" was the topic selected by the group for the production of a collective web page. Upon opening this unique web page, what appears is a carefully designed collage of different parts of the bodies of participants. At the center is AWID's (Association of Women in Development) T-shirt which calls for globalizing women's rights, saying "globalizalos".

The issue of Internet policy was also discussed in the workshop, resulting in a final resolution which was developed and approved by the 25 participants. The ownership structure and flow of global information and communications technologies was addressed by Katerina Anfossi of FIRE in a panel presentation at the workshop. "Today, the power of the media is concentrated in the hands of 10 companies who define who and what are socially and politically relevant, rendering invisible many sectors of the population, especially women", Katerina continued,

The human right of all people to communicate for themselves is a cornerstone of a democratic media. But the road to democratic communications faces many challenges: the concentration of media ownership in ever fewer national and international monopolies; the unidirectional flow of information from North to South; and the pre-established ideological content of media that are overwhelmingly sexist, violent and that alienate many. The rapid development of new communication technologies with access to the Internet, challenges us to ensure that these trends will not duplicate the fate of traditional broadcast and print media. Will these new technologies deprive us of the voices of the majority of the world's inhabitants or will they instead benefit those who in the past were excluded?

FIRE among others, is addressing the digital divide, both because it is an international channel of communications based in the Global South, but also because it is in the hands of women. Recent research has made it evident that although the world is ever more globalized, the development and use of new technologies have not been made accessible to all, and instead have deepened the divide between the "haves" and "have-nots" in terms of access to information, or a voice in media, and to other kinds of connections. FIRE is working to ensure that women are given access to new technologies and that their voices are heard in the world's media. Only by creating international communications venues, appropriating new media venues for diverse voices and connecting multiple voices, strategies and technologies, will a truly democratic media become a reality.

FIRE's experimental open source server during the workshop served to showcase that women's ownership of servers is possible and furthermore, that it can make the use of the internet a lot cheaper and more accessible to more women. Spanish feminist activist, Monserat Boix of Mujeres en Red in Internet (Women's Internet Network) in her country said

It is good to know that there is a confluence of feminist proposals about democratization of media and the creation of internet tools such as open source. It would be great if we could organize an international meeting where we can discuss all of those issues and coordinate strategies so that we can do much more together.

Interactivity: A necessary component for gift giving in the internet

Although interactivity is assumed to be a "natural" component of new communication technologies, FIRE feels it is urgent to develop a feminist conceptualization of this term, as part of the ongoing rapid development of computers, programs and resources. Otherwise women run the risk of being only users of information, and marginalized as creators of information and the power that brings, as built and articulated through the Internet.

Most often in virtual ideology, interactivity of the Internet is defined more as a technical term, rather than one with political or social meaning. As such, it generally refers to the two-way interface of communication and information flows in the Internet. However, the Internet is a system of communication and information flow based on the capacity of computers to enable users to "speak" to each other as with a telephone system, radio waves, etc. Web resources that allow such interactivity include chat rooms, electronic forums, bulletin boards and other interactive mechanisms built into web pages.

But this marvelous technical process which never ceases to amaze particularly those of older generations who had in the past relied only on one-way flows of media, information and communication, also has a socio-political dimension. As Internet users are able to interact technically, those who are communicating or producing the information are also developing relationships with each other. And this is rarely acknowledged much less analyzed in depth.

Women can interact in the Internet by channeling information flows, and communicate with others by transmitting their productions, art, writing, actions, identity, programs and operating systems, etc. Women who are often employed in a technical capacity as workers in the information industry play a critical role as facilitators of these processes, but all too often remain invisible, and even transparent!

Based on this perspective, the RIF/FIRE workshop was comprised of a series of activities involving training in technical capacities, including how to download and upload 256 information from the Internet, using technical resources and programs for creating web pages, and maximizing the use of search engines. Women participants also learned to use chat rooms, electronic forums, listserves and bulletin boards in Internet, considered by many the key elements in gift giving in the Internet.

But beyond the technical training, a socio-political dynamic sustained the workshop from beginning to end. Women participants collaborated in groups to design political and social action campaigns on issues of their choice, and had the option to upload that information to the Internet, along with biographical information and photos of themselves as Web authors. They also produced live webcasts in which they launched these campaigns, and also were able to design specific political actions from the results of the workshop based on their experiences and in order to promote their own rights and needs.

Conclusions

Gift giving in the Internet happens because people's movements keep using it for the same purposes and within the same framework that the originators of civil society cyberspace created: a way to freely and openly share information.

Its evolution as gift giving has meant both creating the necessary alternative software and technology, but also the political activism to expose and counteract corporate Internet trends.

Both will probably continue to exist, but civil society's best bet is to contribute to its free and open flow. For that to happen, people, especially women, have to empower themselves collectively and personally to develop such an alternative paradigm.

FIRE has been a pioneer in providing written and audio content on the Internet for several years. Only a small percentage of the population has access to Internet Radio directly, however it has been shown that FIRE's content is being downloaded and re-transmitted in many forms around the globe. Therefore the people that need the content have the resources to access it. In the future Internet Radio will be a medium for the masses and FIRE will be ready when the technology advances.

The case of FIRE is but one example of the way in which women and people do this on a day to day basis. Millions more experiences exist, that make up the world wide movement to democratize and socialize the voices, hopes, dreams and struggles for a better world, free of corporate greed and full of people's sharing and gift giving. Another world is possible. It is happening in the Internet and elsewhere.

References

FIRE & Nomadic Solutions (2003). *FIRE's Feasibility Study for a Feminist Open Source Server*, unpublished document.

Kaku, Michio (1997). *Visions: How Science will Revolutionize the 21st Century*, Anchor Books, New York.

Thompson, Margaret and FIRE (2004). *FIRE's Interactive strategy in the Internet*, ISIS Manila, Philippines.
Vaughan, Genevieve (2003). "Semiotics for Social Change, the Mother or the Market?", in *Logica, dialogica, ideologica*, Susan Petrilli, ed., Mimesis, Milano.

Internet
Transaction Network (2003). at www.transaction.net/biz/models/opensource/
Berners-Lee, Tim (1996). The World Wide Web: Past, Present and Future at http://www.w3.org/People/Berners-Lee/1996/ppf.html)
— (1997). Realising the Full Potential of the Web at http://www.w3.org/1998/02/Potential.html

1.

Let me take a few stars from the sky
and light a fire for us
listening to the women gathering around it:
weavers, gardeners, dancers, drummers,
storytellers,
telling stories from the dailiness of their lives
stories of denigration, of dispossession
yet also, of *survival*
also telling stories of *resistance*
of refusing to turn against dreams
dreams written on the insides of trees
dreams written on the insides of their skins *hidden*:
subversive knowings; subjugated knowledges
that come from generations of unconditional love
that challenge the dominant ways of knowing
that begin to draw the contours of another world view
painting with the colours of *another logic*
a logic that must disrupt, disturb
master narratives, master houses, houses of reason
one that speaks to an *ethic of care* and *concern*
of connectedness and community
an ethic of celebration,
offering another logic, a logic of the gift.

A weaver tells the story of the Trinjan:

It is said that there was once a village, where, as is customary in most villages in the Punjab, the men met together at the *chopal* at nightfall to relax and discuss the day's work. The women too had their *chopal*, the *trinjan* where they brought their unspun yarn to work and talk and spin the night away.

We are told that gradually, and over a period of time, the sharing of knowledge and resources that took place at the *trinjan* wrought a wonderful and visible change in these women. They became more sure of themselves, more self-reliant, more confident.

It would have seemed that it was now a time for rejoicing. But strangely enough, or perhaps it is not so strange, it was at this time that the tranquility of the village was disrupted. Rumours began. It was whispered that these women were dangerous – that they had gained secret knowledge; that they were familiar with the black arts and were a danger to society.

The whispering soon became news and then news became fact. From every corner of the market place fearful voices clamoured that Religion was in danger! Society was in danger! Civilization was in danger!

Then the village council met and the men agreed that the source of danger lay in the *trinjan* and in the women who possessed this knowledge. With this belief came the recognition that these women whom they feared, were no strangers. They were the mothers and the wives, the daughters and the sisters on whose love and service depended the security and comfort, not only of the present gathering but that of the future generations as well. And then the decision to act was taken.

That night, when the *trinjan* met and the merriment was at its height, shadowy figures crept out of the surrounding darkness and set the thatched pindal on fire. The pindal and its inmates were razed to the ground, and its ashes dispersed with the wind.

Simorgh Women's Collective, Pakistan, 1993.

the wind writes the story of the *trinjan* on the barks of trees
mothers tells the story to their daughters for generations
a mystical even magical fabric of timeless care.

Women are weavers in all cultures:

In Polynesia women own at least one but often many *tifaifai*,
which when translated we are told loses the meaning, memory and magic of the word.

tifaifai belong to the women and are women's personal wealth:
tifaifai are often given as gifts to express emotion – love, honour, loss:
tifaifai is about compassion and connectedness.

Starquilt, AWHRC, 1995.

Quilts of the slave women are pieces of their painful history recorded in their weavings; the comfort women of Asia (former sexual slaves of the Japanese Imperial Army of World War II) wove their stories of rape and violence into their quilts; offerings of their *memories against forgetting*: precious gifts indeed!

Many women sitting around the fire have held or are preparing to hold what we call the *Courts of Women* which someone described as daring and audacious. A Court, yes but a

Court of Women! In these Courts, women offer their stories of pain, of resistance, of hope: there are thousands of stories, each story a gift.

We will listen to a few voices:

My name is Mauria, Mauria from Havana.

I belong to a pedagogical movement in Cuba and when I was younger remember how thousands of us, though children ourselves, *helped to teach smaller children.*
We have been blockaded for many, many years. Too many.
But during these difficult years we turned our country into a seedbed of primary and secondary schools: we gave working mothers the wonderful right to have kindergartens for their children, we gave birth to politechnical institutes and special schools for disabled children and we opened the doors of the universities for post graduate studies for professionals. Thus, economically surrounded *ad absurdum*, we made true the dreams of people about having opportunities through a huge campaign that *combined tenderness and science for all, with all.* All through the years of the blockade we have continued to plant schools, *plant hope.*

When the world socialist system collapsed, the siege grew more intense:
the U.S. blockade has tried to asphyxiate us, starve us, defeat us.
but we have continued to live. […]
I could tell you a thousand stories of women who stitched old uniforms of children so that other children could have one; of people who bring old chairs to our schools so that children could study with a little comfort; school books that are carefully repaired and distributed to the next set of children; women looking for firewood to cook food for the children, food sharing, *a thousand acts of giving.* No one can stop the giving.
No laws: no economic blockade: not even the USA!
By depriving us, the possibilities for giving and receiving become abundant.

(Mauria Herrera Lobato, telling about the dailiness of survival at the International Court of Women Against the Economic Blockade, Havana, Cuba, March 2002 – Original testimony in Spanish).

This is a true story:

I am a mother who, together with her sick husband Uzeir, survived all horrors of this war. My name is Dautovic Mejra, called *the Mother.* My son Edwin was born in 1965 and my daughter Edna was born in 1969 in Brcko.

The party SDS won in April of 1992, a year later SDS took over in the most brutal way, and created concentration camps for non-Serb population. When Bosnia was literally in flames (April 1993), in Prijedor we had an oasis of peace. We never thought for a second that *our neighbors and friends would kill us.* On May 22, first Hambarine, a part of the city was destroyed, killing and exiling people. After they shelled Hambarine, the *chetniks* went for cleansing other areas and we thought they were searching the houses, but they were killing everything alive that happened to be before them. The *chetniks* attacked Kozarac, a town on the other side of Prijedor where they were ruining and murdering the non-Serb population. Seven to eight thousand people were killed

261

and taken into *camps of death*. Thousands of Kozarac residents found themselves in these camps, and many of them were killed or executed. On June 14 the police entered and brought a list that was handwritten which had twenty five names on it of persons to be taken away to the concentration camp. Among those names was the name Edna Dautovic, my daughter. They called her to report to the police station since she had participated in actions defending the city of Prijedor. Edna stood up, dressed as if she was going on her last journey from home. After an hour, my husband went to the police station, but she had already been taken away to the concentration camp Omarska because she did not want to give a statement. At that moment I fainted and for thirteen days I ate or drank nothing.

Edna became a pile of bones with a bullet hole through her head.

We started to search for Edna. We went to Omarska camp a few times. We asked all our Serb friends to help us find Edna, but they remained uninvolved. We learnt after two months when the camp Omarska was closed, from women who were with Edna and survived all horrors of this camp that they did all the worst things to her and her brother Edwin had to watch all of it. He was himself captured in June and taken to Omarska. Edna also had to watch how her brother was tortured, both of them had to survive and live through many humiliations.

When people started to come out of the camp, they said that Edwin was in the concentration camp, in the white house of death. I could not believe that Edwin also ended up in the camp. No one could convince me of that. *After eight years I learned the truth.*

I have been all over Bosnia and the Republika Srpska searching for my children. My path through hell continued because *I was helping thousands of persons even as I looked for my children.*

The book *Mother Mejra*, which I wrote and which is published, offers and seeks to find the truth. The book holds all my suffering and pain in my search for my children. One year after the book came out, I learned the truth about my children. I went to all *the mass graves/graveyards* to see if I could identify or recognize my children *in all the remains* found. So God wanted that I find my Edwin in Lusca Palanka nearby Sanki Most, in a hall where he was one of the 146 other after-death remains from the Kemljani mass grave; all were murdered in Omarska. I recognized him by his teeth and his bones. When I gave my statement to the judge from Edwin's birth to his death, his height, weight, the doctor brought me teeth of two bodies. I took one of them, and the other one I put down. When I took the first one, I said *this is my son's*. Never has a body remains pulled me so much as at that time when I took his teeth. For three months, I went there every week to learn something new from the remains.

I learned about a mass grave of Lisac where with my own eyes I saw the digging of the death remains – among which was my Edna's. I recognized Edna by her tooth, because it got chipped the day before she was taken to the concentration camp.

I found my children after eight years of searching during which the whole of me
was dedicated to searching for the missing, the disappeared.

[Mejra Dautovic, Bosnia. – Testimony of a Mother in Exile on Mass Graves. World Court of Women against War for Peace, Cape Town, South Africa, March 2001. Original testimony in Bosnian].

We have begun to believe that we are fragments; *that our stories are disconnected from each other*; the enemies are safely ensconced within our minds and hearts, and none of us escapes.
This World Court is a moment of connection to remind us that we are in the movement: and *that we do have power.*
We must forge new definitions of manhood for all our fathers, for all our sons; so, collectively we can restore the power of love and courage...
Perhaps the time has come to light up those parts of ourselves we have kept hidden in fear, in shame, in ambiguity; *to hear our voices come from deep within.*

(Pregs Govender, Expert Witness on Militarization, Patriarchy and Racism, World Court against Racism, Durban, South Africa, August 2001).

Listening to the many voices speaking; listening to the many more unspoken
The *Courts of Women* are about breaking new ground, crossing lines, our dreams of trespass. In a very modest way, the Courts challenge the dominant ways of knowing, the dominant global system, the universals: reminding us that in the dominant world view of the universal, there is no place for the gift.

We need new stories for our times:
even new storytellers.

2.

We live in violent times:
times in which our community and collective memories are dying;
times in which the many dreams are turning into never-ending nightmares,
and the future increasingly fragmenting;
times that are collapsing the many life visions into a single cosmology that has
created its own universal truths – equality, development, peace;
truths that are inherently discriminatory, even violent;
times that have created a development model that dispossesses the majority, desacralizes
nature, destroys cultures and civilizations, denigrates the women;
times in which the dominant political thinking, institutions and instruments of
justice are hardly able to redress the violence that is escalating, and intensifying,
times in which progress presupposes the genocide of the many;
times in which human rights have come to mean the rights of the privileged, the
rights of the powerful
times in which the political spaces for the other is diminishing, even closing;
the world, it would seem, is at the end of its imagination.

Perhaps, we must no longer be afraid to ask the non-questions, to analyze what is considered the non-data, the non-rational, the non-scientific. Perhaps we must begin to search outside the dominant discourse, beneath the required level of scientificity and beyond the established parameters of knowledge, discovering the disqualified knowledges of civilizations and cultures that are non-western, the social knowledges of those who are on the edges, tribals, indigenous peoples, dalits, women and to discern in their mythologies, in their metaphor, in their motif, in their *logic*, other world views. We must move away from traditions of the dominant discourse and find ourselves in that terrain which has been denigrated by the discourse – the eastern, the black, the indigenous, the woman. To discover the hidden knowledges of the *South in the South*; of the *South in the North*. To listen to the wisdoms of these vernacular, local knowledges against all that is dominant and hegemonistic. Perhaps, we may then move to creating new political visions that are holistic, more holographic, responding to the complexities of reality, more critically, *creating a world in which many worlds can be embraced.*

The Universal Mode

The *South* has for too long accepted a world view that has hegemonised its cultures, decided its development model, defined its aesthetic categories, outlined its military face, determined its science and technology, its nuclear options, and moulded its modes of governance through the modern nation state. For the modern idiom of politics is the eurocentric world of nation states; centralized, bureaucratized, militarized, some even nuclearised. The nation state in its homogenization of the polity has subsumed all cultural diversity, all civilisational differences, into one uniform political entity, which now belongs to the *new world order.*

A cosmology constructed of what has come to be known as *universal values*; a cosmology whose philosophical, ideological, and political roots were embedded in the specific historical context of the culture of the west. What qualified it then to be termed *universal*? The vision of the world in which the centre of the world was Europe and later North America (West) encapsulated all civilizations into its own western frames: it reduced their cultural diversities into a schema called *civilization*; it made universal the specific historical experiences of the West. It announced that what was relevant to the West had to be a model for the rest of the world: what was good for the centre had to be meaningful for the periphery. *All that was western simply became universal.* Every other civilization, every system of knowledge came to be defined and compared vis-à-vis this paradigm submitting to *its insights as imposition, its blindness as values, its tastes as canons, in a word to its euro-centricities*[1].

The *Other* in this cosmology was the civilizations of Asia, the Pacific, Africa, Latin America, the Arab world. *Scarcely twenty years were enough to make two billion people define themselves as under-developed*, vis-à-vis the post war growth model, the market economy and the international economic order conceived of at Bretton Woods. It minisculed all social totalities into one single model, all systems of science to one mega science, all indigenous medicine to one imperial medicine, all knowledge to one established regime of thought, all development to gross national product, to patterns of consumption, to industrialization, to *the western self image of homo-economicus with all needs commodity-defined*, and *homo economicus has never been gender neutral*[2].

This cosmos of values has determined the thought patterns of the world, as also the world's ecological patterns: indicating its scientific signs, giving it the development symbols,   264 generating the military psyche, defining knowledge, truth: *universal truths which have been blind, to cultures, race, class, gender.* Universal *patriarchal* truths, whatever the cultural ethos, whatever the civilisational idiom.

A universal world order that has subjugated the women in its androcentric matrix and which in its dominant motif has been *patriarchal*. A universal world view that has subsumed the civilizations of the world in its eurocentric mode; a universal mode that has been deeply *racist*.

> Western civilization has articulated its struggle for domination in terms of the holy battle of humanity against barbarism; reason against ignorance, science against magic, rationality against passion, what in fact has happened in the course of the civilizing process, is the redeployment of violence [...] violence has been taken out of sight, rather than forced out of existence[3].

And this *invisibilisation of violence* was perfected during the era of colonization in which were perpetrated unimaginable horrors against entire peoples and civilizations. A horror that has today been hidden in the mists of distorted histories. A people who lost their land, their lyric and their lore to the devastating logic of laws like the *terra nulliu*s. A violence that was sought to be hidden by hollow claims to *civilization* and *progress*; a violence that was sought to be sanitised by respectable scholarship in ethnography, anthropology, eugenics, developmental psychology and socio-biology; a violent history that was sought to be valorized in narratives of colonial conquest that were rewritten to read like benign narratives of discovery and scientific exploration.

The altered memories of the Native Americans and the Mayan Indians, the Maoris, the Aboriginals, the Pacific islanders, among others, bear mute witness to this *forgotten genocide*.

Testimony: around the fire

I am here to speak of slavery: slavery, which began around 1657 when the Dutch East India Company decided to settle and colonise this land. So we have a long history of slavery in our country. People were bought and sold: and even now if you walk in our small towns in the Northern Cape, people will show you and say there's a slave house down there that's where they sold my grandmother.

So, we've not had a long time to forget:

We have been silenced but we remember what has happened to us, as first peoples who were enslaved in our own lands. We have experienced slavery not only as a system of racism but as a system of sexist oppression: a system in which rape is normalized; so normalized that in South African society it was a rite of passage for the son of a slave master to rape a slave girl. That's how the Whites knew he was a man because he raped the slave women; the rape became institutionalized ensuring the White man's supremacy.

265

(Yvette Abrahams, excerpts from testimony on slavery/colonialism, World Court against Racism, Durban, South Africa, August 2001).

Testimony: around the fire

It all began with the invasion of Columbus:

When the boats came they said they could smell the sweetness of the land before they landed. It was so pure and so full of bounty with everything that we needed. Now, after his invasion the pilgrims came; they kept moving us further and further west; then they sent the missionaries with their bibles and sewing machines; they sent the army full of guns and *blankets full of smallpox.* That was in the 1700's. One of the *first germ wars* perpetrated on Native Americans.

(Pamela Kingfisher, excerpts from testimony on Indigenous Women in the USA and Colonialism, World Court of Women against Racism, Durban, South Africa, August 2001).

A similar extermination happened in the Congo.
Belgium's King Leopold II issued a decree in September 1891 which gave his representatives in the Congo, a monopoly on trade in rubber and ivory; by the same decree, natives were obliged to supply both rubber and labour which in practice means no trading was necessary.
Leopold's representatives simply requisitioned labour, rubber and ivory from the natives without payment. Those who refused had their villages burned down, their children murdered and *their hands cut off.*
Baskets of amputated hands were sent to the King as a proof of the *progress of civilizations* and the fate of anyone who resisted[4].
In recent times, the Revolutionary United Front in Sierra Leone chopped off the hands of anyone who resisted their rule and their politics. We are told that the practice is barbaric, *uncivilized.* Colonization sowed the seeds of bio terrorism only it was called another word then *Civilization.*
We need to replace *history* with *memory.*
For colonization was the archetypal racist project that not only inaugurated the era of *universalized violence* but also sought to establish and institutionalize the supremacy of the White, the European, the West. While the legacy of colonization has been multilayered, the master narrative remains that of the *Other* – a creature and creation of the modern dualistic mind. A mind that needs first to *externalize* and *exorcise* the monster within, through the creation of the *Other*, who then proceeds to *experiment* with and *exterminate* as an object that can be sacrificed at the altar of modern science and then ensure its total *erasure* through its co-option into the *New Global Order* either as a consumer, commodity or object of conservation. From the creation of the *Other* through the colonial project of the European Enlightenment and expansionism that saw the *non west as resource* to be exploited and appropriated and *non western people as barbarians* to be developed or destroyed; to the erasure of the *Other* in the neo-colonial project of globaliza-

tion that has institutionalized structural racism and perpetuated a pervasive pattern of discrimination and disadvantage for specific ethnic and racial groups – the *subordinated races* of the former colonial empires.

The circle is complete.

And in this master narrative the woman has been created and recreated as a permanent *gendered Other*; reduced to a biological object that has become the site of conflicts of many kinds. Whether it is as a victim of rape, as a form of ethnic cleansing or in caste conflicts; as a womb in which was born the stolen generation; in which was implanted the seeds of a nuclear future; whose femininity is a threat that has been permanently fettered by a fundamentalist paranoia; the migrant and the refugee woman who is trafficked and who most often than not is poor, dalit, minority, third world, south.

While the global project of colonization has created the *universal Other*, culturally specific power hierarchies too have created the *Other* within different contexts – be it the Dalits/Untouchables in India, the Buraku in Japan, the gypsies, the Rroma, the Sinti, the Amazeeg in the Maghreb, minorities, the women. The privileging and consolidation of these cultural hierarchies under the regime of colonization is one reality we live with, while the deepening of violence against them in the era of globalization is another. *Organized violence* by the dominant castes against the dalits in India, *pogroms* against ethnic minorities as in Bosnia, *systemic silencing* of the women by fundamentalist organizations like the Taliban, products also of the nation state, are disturbing evidence of the growing intolerance in highly aggressive, competitive, *masculinised, militarized and racist societies*. For finally it is the *colonization of the mind* that has proved to be the legacy that has been most enduring and devastating. Racism that continues to recreate itself in contemporary times, is a tragic testimony to this fact.

Testimony: around the fire

It is a great challenge for me to speak to you about resistance after apartheid: the resistance is a challenge to break the silence of making us accept; our government must listen to us.

We have the right to say we want a house; we want land: can you imagine that we, Black people live only on 13% of the land? The humiliation and the dehumanization of our people during the years of apartheid has scarred us; *we continue to carry these scars*.

We are told to forget and forgive, to reconcile.

We are told not to remember.

Mothers who do not know the graves of their children, must forget. So we go out and say we need the land, we are homeless, we want a roof over our heads. We want jobs: we want to redress the imbalance of apartheid.

We are told we are being unreasonable.

We say we want equality, equal opportunities.

We are condemned that we practice *racism in reverse*, so we do not want to be seen as racists, we want to be seen as those who forgive and forget: so with all the pain and anguish inside us, we put on our masks and sing and chant and dance – *it is a way to survive*: One of the greatest challenges of the post apartheid era is that the resources, skills, land are still with the White people: we must find new ways of resistance after apartheid: what we urgently need in South Africa is the *liberation of our minds, our imaginations.*

(Nise Malange, Expert Witness, Resistance after Apartheid, World Court of Women against Racism, Durban South Africa, August 2001).

Scientific rationality and militarization as the by products of colonialism, together produced the most genocidal form of extermination ever-*nuclearisation*. It is not by coincidence that the process of going nuclear was highly racist; it has been established beyond doubt that the nuclear bombing of Hiroshima and Nagasaki and the nuclear tests conducted on Bikini islands in the Pacific by the USA were deliberate scientific experiments conducted on a *population* that were by definition and choice, *non whit*e.

There exists therefore in this universal, racist mode a deep commitment to a cosmology that is scientific. Underlying its fundamental categories is a construction of knowledge that is rational, objective, neutral, linear and also *patriarchal*. Cosmologies that did not fit into the framework, whose basis was the certainty of scientific knowledge were dismissed and ridiculed: the cosmologies of *Other* peoples, of women, destroyed. There emerged only the *one, monolithic scientific paradigm in all its rationality* and objectivity that dominated all civilizations, *in all its patriarchality*, that denied all women.

As in the eurocentric knowledge construction, the West came to be the norm and the *universal*, excluding other civilizations, other cultures, in its androcentric dimension, the male became the norm, and in its masculine mind set excluded the feminine. This knowledge generated a patriarchal scholarship in which the lives and experiences of women were invisible. The codification of knowledge is a cumulative process with silence built on silence: *for generations women have been silenced in patriarchal discourse unable to have their meanings encoded and accepted in the social repositories of knowledges*[5]. Their meanings of power for instance: what is enshrined in the different disciplines and social order is a concept of power that the male uses – the power to control, the power to manipulate, the power of the winner. This concept of patriarchal power pervades all cultures. In cultures where concepts of women power, *Stree Shakti*, exist, it has been pushed to the periphery: woman's power remains on the margins of knowledge, of life.

Moving out of the patriarchal mind set would mean refusing the mono dimensional definition of power, seeking to re-define power, to re-locate power, to discover *alternate concepts of power*, to find new patterns of power: *power to name the world differently from world views that are non-modern*. Because the modern world view is dualistic, it divides: it separates ideas from feelings developing the capacity to take ideas to their objective, rational conclusion without being burdened by feelings. Real science requires the suppression of emotions. It must: for there are no categories that can contain personal experience, no mathematical formulae to measure emotions, no place in the traditional sciences obsessed with objectivity to explain the subjective.

The personal could never be political.

3.

A violence that is silent, sanitized: a violence of order and of universals: a violence of the new global economic order.

The new global economic order ushered in by the Bretton Woods financial and trade institutions like the World Bank, International Monetary Fund (IMF) and the General Agreement of Tariffs and Trade (GATT) became the post colonial instruments to impose the West's industrial and economic systems on the two-thirds world countries to maintain the latter's colonial status as suppliers of cheap raw material, exploitable labour and capital and market sinks for their finished products, without which they would be unable to maintain their non negotiable lifestyle[6].

Guided by *an irrational faith in Western Economic Science*, third world governments allow themselves to be trapped into a suicidal bond of debt and conditionalities imposed through Structural Adjustment Policies; blinded by the ephemera of progress and prosperity, to the extermination and extinction of their own people; racing towards the post industrial project of the construction of the virtual global village through powerful new information and communication technologies.

A global village in which traditional nation state borders are crumbling into irrelevance in the face of the invasion by Trans and Multinational Corporate Warriors; in which new modes of governance are being created to cope with the demands of a free floating global economy; in which cultures are being recrafted to suit the fickle taste of the new secularized citizen for the multi ethnic flavour of the day.

Local cultures are deemed to have *values* only when they have been fragmented and these fragments transformed into saleable goods for a world market. Only when food becomes *ethnic food*, music *ethnic music*, and traditional tales *folklore* and when skills are harnessed to the production of *ethnic objects* for the tourist industry, can the capital accumulation process benefit from these local cultures[7].

A global village in which technology has lost forever its human scale, size and scope. The violence of this technological expansion and explosion in the modern age is unmatched in speed and range compared to any other period in the history of technology. More forests have been destroyed and natural minerals mined and exploited over the past two centuries than in the past two millennia. Paradoxically this *age of reason* that is celebrated for the flowering of human knowledge has grown at the expense of culturally distinct human traditions and communities that have been systematically silenced.

For this global market seeks to destroy community wisdoms and knowledges by appropriating them as individuated intellectual property: laying claims to the invention of even life and life forms; Corporations are now claiming patents on *knowledges pirated from the third world*. For example, the *neem (Azarichta Indica)* for pesticide and fungicide was claimed by a multinational corporation, W. R. Grace, a clear example of biopiracy which leads to situations where the South will soon have to *pay for its own knowledges* which has evolved over generations.

Life in the great global market is for sale to the highest bidder. And so while biopiracy by Corporations from the North has become legitimate business, saving lives for self survival has become a criminalized activity. Across countries of the *global South*, hunger has grown to genocidal proportions as a result of structural adjustment and trade liberalization policies. It is however a crime for countries to ensure that their hungry are fed for this involves laws, policies and financial commitments, which are declared *protectionist* – the ultimate crime in the regime of globalization.

Globalization is genocidal greed: greed based on the monetisation of all aspects of life and living.

The gradual economization of all aspects of life and the total integration of traditional, premodern and subsistence societies into the world economy has created a more debilitating condition than that of *global poverty* that development is supposed to be a panacea for. The processes of development have legitimized a *standard of living* evolved by an exclusive minority that is displacing and destroying the *living standards* of a majority. By doing so it has not only destroyed a way of life and living that was sustainable for all, but also the people *incapable* of achieving this standard.

As Majid Rahnema says "the myth of global affluence based on economic productivity left no room for *moral poverty*, that is the old perception of modes of life based on the ideals of simplicity, frugality and respect for every other living person including nature"[8]. The universal mode therefore universalized notions of richness and poverty so that the modern rich can never redeem themselves by subscribing and having access to a *moral notion of poverty* while the modern poor displaced from homes and livelihoods are condemned to remain in permanent exile, migrant and refugee from an *over consumptive paradise*.

Poverty today has little to do with the poor.

For the poor in the new globalised economy have been rendered invisible, faceless and voiceless. Reduced to being *targets* their only identity is that of a percentage that survives under a mythical construct called the *poverty line*. Indicators of *growth* like the Gross National Product and Per Capita Income ensure that poverty by becoming economized can only be alleviated through loans and aid being routed through international agencies like the World Bank and the IMF which can only help to globalize, capitalize and centralize the economy into the hands of the (not so) Free Economy.

This economized notion of poverty has also made invisible deeper notions of *scarcity* that is silently perpetuated by eroding and rupturing collective life visions and life-worlds and homogenizing all forms of living systems whose development does not necessarily lie only in the pursuit of the great dollar dream.

This scarcity reflects most sharply in the lives of women. *Feminization of poverty* means more than the fact that women are the poorest of the poor; or that *poverty has a woman's face*. Dragged into the economized world of productive labour, woman's *wealth*, traditional skills and knowledges that she shared and nurtured along with her family and community have been made redundant and therefore devalued. She is therefore not only being denied the very means of survival and worth but the *gendered worlds in which these skills were nourished* are also being destroyed. With the erosion of subsistence economies,

270

women's integral contributions to the production process has also almost disappeared. In the profit economy too, on the other hand, due to greater mechanization and modernization, women (largely) in the *unskilled* sector are being retrenched and displaced. In the *informal* sector where women are primarily dealing with *nontradeable goods* their capacity for survival has been threatened with the definite emphasis on *tradeable* goods. Denying people their access to resources and sources of livelihood like land and forests, forces them to migrate both internally and outside their countries in *search of livelihoods*. As casual migrant labour in cities and countries, women become more vulnerable to exploitation and violence.

We do not need additional indicators or measurements of poverty: perhaps what is required is to construct an *index of violence* to understand the violence hidden in the new globalised economic order, that has created *poverty as scarcity*; to find an *ethic of care* that would enable us to see the new victims; to recognize the many generations and *communities* that need to be *sustained* and nurtured. Perhaps we need a *new notion of rights* to set right the many violent wrongs being perpetrated by the universal mode.

Perhaps we must begin to unearth the truth in all the *universals*, to look more closely at what has been accepted as the universal concept of human rights, set in a *common standard of human rights achievement* for *all peoples* and *all nations*. An understanding which has informed not only classical human rights thinking but also the contemporary political institutions and the human rights discourse in our times.

The discourse and legacy of human rights historically, had its philosophical and ideological foundations in the liberal creed of the Enlightenment period. This historical conjuncture ushered in the industrial mode of production, the rise of the market economy and the nation state system; bringing with it the materialist ethic. A cosmology that proclaimed a society in which everyone would be committed to the rational pursuit of self-interest. The liberal philosophers announced their political programme through private endeavour. Their political faith was anchored in the concept of *possessive individualism* which essentially meant that the individual was the proprietor of his own person or capacities, unrelated to society. They emphasised the importance of private interests, private profits; competition and utilitarianism were its cornerstones. A world view therefore, rooted in these concepts, generated an image of an individual who owed nothing to society. The individual was a product of the machinations of the market economy and human labour, like every other commodity, could be bought and sold, beaten and used. This point of view was encouraged and propagated by those sections in society who in their attempt to develop their *self-interest* converted human rights to mean the rights of the privileged, the rights of the powerful. Human rights then, over the centuries, came to mean that the claims of the strong and the powerful took precedence over those of the powerless: and that for some classes to have human rights, the masses had to surrender their right to be human. It was a dialogue within a civilization; and even so, it was *a partial dialogue within a civilization*. This vision of the world in which the centre of the world was the West encapsulated all civilizations and cultures into its western frames. It made universal the specific historical experiences of the west. It underlined that what was relevant to the West had to be the model for the rest of the world. What privileged the constructs of one particular culture to be endorsed with universal values? This understanding had its ideological and political moorings embedded in the specific historical context of the culture of the West: what qualified it to be termed *universal*?

> Any resistance then to the hegemonic dimensions of the existing universalisms of the human rights discourse is not seen as resistance to any historical power group but to the universal morality of human rights[9].

Every other civilization, every other system of knowledge, every other cosmology, came to be defined vis-à-vis this paradigm. It hegemonised all peoples, tribes, minorities, ethnic groups into the one polity of the *nation state*. It made all *citizens* of the state faceless citizens mediated and manipulated by the market. It portrayed the one civilization of *universal man*, flattening all diversities, ignoring all historical specificities, homogenizing all aspirations into universal norms of freedom, liberty and equality.

And all this was done with great violence.

It was in these exploitative aspects of liberal society that the concept of the sovereign state developed. The state was seen as the guarantor of individual freedoms; a strong state, could prevent the disintegrative forces of the market economy from breaking up society. It is this kind of liberal rhetoric that has provided the basis for the United Nations Declaration on Human Rights as it addresses itself to the sovereign nation states of the United Nations. The fiction of the social contract underlines the state-individual relation blurring the stratifications and communities in society. It developed a particular notion of the state, individual rights and personal freedoms. A notion of politics, therefore, in which individual rights and freedoms provided the essential tenets on which the edifice of human rights was built and developed. And for which, the nation-state was the guarantor. The United Nations Declaration on Human Rights, to which the nation states are signatories, clearly elucidates the *rights* that must be assured to the citizens of the state. The nation states then are given the responsibility of upholding these rights. However, in the name of human rights, the nation states who are signatories to the Declaration may then legitimise the most inhuman conditions of life, the most brutal repression of its own people which are then seen as the *internal* concern, the *law and order*, the *national security* of these sovereign nation states.

The state, we know, is often the greatest violator.

And the human rights discourse and praxis legitimises what is described as state violence and state terror. Human rights become the expression of politically legitimated power. It does this not only vis-à-vis the rights of the citizens who it pretends to protect against the state, but more important it also legitimates a particular concept of violence – the violence of poverty, of famine, of malnutrition, of multinationals, of militarization, of ecological destruction and technological terrorism; the violence of the war on terrorism and the terrorism of war. These are not recognised forms of violence which the state through its development models, its technological choices, its wars and its weapons culture perpetrates on peoples.

Perhaps what must not be forgotten is the fact that *terrorism* as this contemporary face of barbarism is not only a product of cold war politics between the two super power ideologies of capitalism and communism but also of state terrorism going global, patented by the USA, copyrighted by the CIA and franchised to all modern day nation states the world over. *Fundamentalist* or *terrorist* violence of any kind cannot be justified under any circumstances, particularly when the danger is that of hegemonic geopolitical interests perverting civilisational imperatives in the name of a *Crusade, Jehad* or a *Dharmayudh.*

And it is here that deeply dangerous theories like Huntington's *Clash of Civilizations*, need to be challenged. For only then can we begin to seek ways of recovering *lost faiths* and regenerating *compassionate politics* that will not need the *Other* to perpetuate its racist, intolerant self. The politics of fundamentalism is enveloping large areas in the world, striving to hegemonize other faiths, unleashing a *cycle of violence that must return to destroy.* Can we return the spiritual to the material? Can we find the feminine in the increasingly violent male, civilisational ethos?

Can we bring back the sacred to the earth?

4.

Let us return to the fire and listen to the wise woman Grace Black Elk:

In a different place, in a different time, Grace Black Elk heard the song of the wind
I saw myself on the central mountain of the world,
the highest place, and I had a vision because I was seeing in
the sacred manner of the world, she said
Remember she said, she was seeing in the sacred manner of
the world
And the sacred, central mountain was a mountain in her part of the world
"But", Grace Black Elk continued to say: "the central mountain is
everywhere".

The old categories, the old concepts imperialist as they are, have become insufficient; they are almost *unable to grasp the violence of the times.* While we need to extend the horizons and to deepen the existing human rights discourse, we need too, a *new generation of human rights.* We need to urge the passing of a paradigm that has understood human rights as the rights of the powerful: we need to listen to the voices of those who do not share that power. *To see these violations through the eyes of the victims* – victims of development, of progress, of technical fixes, of war; through the eyes of those who have been denied privileges and power in the system; *through the eyes of the powerless*; through the eyes of those whose cultures have been ransacked; whose peoples, ruined; through the eyes of those who have been on the margins, the fringes: through the eyes of *peoples on the edges*: through the eyes of the *South in the South*; of *the South in the North*; through the eyes of women.

Because they will tell us very different stories.

273   It is not difficult to see that we are at the end of an era, "when every old category be-

gins to have a hollow sound, and when we are groping in the dark to discover the new"[10]. Can we find new words, search new ways, create out of the material of the human spirit possibilities to transform the existing exploitative social order, to discern a greater human potential?

What we need in the world today are new universalisms; not universalisms that deny the many and affirm the one, not universalisms born of eurocentricities or patriarchalities; but universalisms that *recognize the universal in the specific civilisational idioms in the world*. Universalisms that will not deny the accumulated experiences and knowledges of past generations but that will not accept the imposition of any monolithic structures under which it is presumed all other peoples must be subsumed. New universalisms that will challenge the universal mode – the logic of development, science, technology, patriarchy, militarization, nuclearism, war. Universalisms that will respect the plurality of the different societies, of their philosophy, of their ideology, their traditions and cultures; one that will be rooted in the particular, in the vernacular, one that will find a resonance in the different civilizations, *birthing new cosmologies*.

This could be the wind from the South *rising in all its grandeur* bringing much to this cosmology. The South then, as the movements for change in the world, the South as the voices and movements of *people on the edges*, wherever these movements unfold; the South as the *visions of women*; the South as the development of *new frameworks*, seeking a new language to describe what it perceives, rupturing the existing theoretical categories, breaking the mind constructs, challenging the one, objective world view as the only world view; the South Wind as the *seeking of new knowledges*, refusing the one, mechanistic scientific knowledge as the only legitimate knowledge; the South as the *discovery of other knowledges* that have been silenced; submerged; the South as an *insurrection of these subjugated knowledges*; the South as the finding of new definitions of knowledge, of politics, creating *new paradigms of politics; new paradigms of knowledge*.

The South must reclaim the subjective and the objective modes of knowing, creating richer and deeper structures of knowledge in which the observer is not distanced from the observed, the researcher from the researched, poverty from the poor. This new cosmology will move away from the eurocentric and androcentric methodologies which only observe and describe; methodologies which quantify, percentify, classify, completely indifferent to phenomena which cannot be obtained or explained through its frames. We need to deconstruct the dominant mythology, *disallowing the invasion of the dominant discourse*; refusing the integration of the South into the agenda of globalization. The South invites us to create a new spectrum of methods which depart from the linear mode of thought and perception to one that is more *holistic, holographic*. It urges us to search more qualitative methodologies in oral history, experiential analysis, action-research, fluid categories, *listening for the nuances, searching for the shadow*, in poetry, in myth, in metaphor, in magic. It invites us to a way of knowing that refuses to control and exploit Nature, to use and abuse Nature, but one that finds our *connectedness to Nature*; to place together these fragments, to discern the essence, to move into another space, another time, recapturing hidden knowledges, regenerating forgotten spaces, refinding other cosmologies, reweaving the future. *It is here perhaps, that the notion of the gift is nurtured*, here *that the sacred survives*; it is here in the cosmologies and rootedness of cultures, here with peoples on the peripheries that we must seek the beginnings of *an alternate discourse*.

Our imaginaries must be different.

We need to imagine alternative visions for change: to craft visions that will evolve out of conversations across cultures and other traditions; one that will not be trapped either in the *universalisms* of the dominant discourse tied as it is to a market economy, a monoculturalism, a materialistic ethic and the politics and polity of the nation state; neither must it be caught in the discourse of the *culture specific* but one that will proffer universalisms that have been born out of a *dialogue of cultures and civilizations*. And this will mean another *ethic of dialogue*. We need to find new perspectives on the universality of human rights: *in dialogue with other cultural perspectives of reality*, other notions of development, democracy, even dissent, other concepts of power and governance; other notions of equality, other concepts of justice because *human kind proffers many horizons of discourse*, many horizons of life.

Take the *universal* discourse on *democracy*.

The dominant understanding on democracy is tied to the notion of individual rights, private property, the market economy; *we are all equal we are told*. But the market works as the guarantor of inequality, of unequal distribution, of how only a few will be rich and how the many must live below the poverty line. What shall we do with the rhetoric of political equality on which this democracy is built, while the majority live below poverty lines? We must seek new concepts of democracy that will include a concept of freedom that is different from that which is enshrined in the Enlightenment and its Market. There is an urgent need to reinvent the political; *to infuse the political with the ethical*.

An ethic of care

In 1996, Madeleine Albright the then US Secretary of State was asked what she felt about the 500,000 Iraqi children who had died as a result of U.S. economic sanctions (in the name of the UN Security Council), in the context of the continuing war. Was it a high price to pay? She replied that it was a very hard choice but *yes, all things considered, we think that the price is worth it*.

Lives of children lost in wars are considered *collateral damage*;

And the Project for The New American Century has also brought with it new words – regime change, pre-emptive strike, enemy combatants, confiscations, embedded journalism, military tribunals;

New words: *words soaked in blood*.

We live in a world being uprooted.

We need to find new imaginaries to develop another social imagination for *sustainability* as a basis for living and for the enhancement of life, an imaginary where people of the margins of the universal, of the *global south* are subjects of their own history, writing their own cultural narratives, offering new universals, *constructing a new radical imaginary*.

In its *Declaracion de Managua*, the III Encuentro Continental de Resistencia Indigena, Negra y Popular, in 1992 reaffirming its campaign against the 500th anniversary (1492-1992) of colonialism, was incisive, passionate and compassionate.

An extract:

After five hundred years we stand:
Regrouping ourselves from our own roots, men, women, without distinctions of skin colour, language, cultures, territorial demarcation or frontier: recovering what is ours and constructing an alternative project to the one that threatens and attacks us; a project in which misery and suffering are excluded: in which our culture, languages and beliefs flourish with neither fears nor prohibitions; in which we take back the forms of self government that made us great in the past; in which our aptitudes for art and beauty are strengthened; in which we destroy the chains of oppression on women; and in which Mother Nature is reconciled with her human children in her lap: in which war remains a memory of bad times; in which we can look each other in the face without feeling the shame of hate or scorn; linked, then, in love, solidarity and life.

The new imaginary cannot have its moorings in the dominant discourse but must seek to locate itself in a *discourse of dissent* that comes from a deep critique of the different forms of domination and violence in our times. Any new imaginary cannot be tied to the dominant discourse and systems of violence and exclusion.

As the poet says, "we should now break the routine, do an extravagant action that would change the course of history, the logic of our development". What is essential is to go beyond the politics of violence and terror of the times and *to find new imaginations, to sing our root song, to refind and touch the dream.*

The fire still continues to burn with help from the stars, so there is time for another little story; a story from the women, located in this discourse of dissent; inspired by an imaginary offered by a *South Wind*. A little experience proffered as an expression of this new imaginary that we explore not as expert, but as witness; *a witness who is not a mere spectator: who looks but also listens; who remembers so that nothing is forgotten.*

It is a story of the *Courts of Women*:

It was a dream of many years ago. It began in Asia and through the Asian Women's Human Rights Council who with several other women's groups has held nine Courts in the Asia Pacific region; and encouraged several more in other regions of the world – Africa, Arab world, Central America, Latin America, Mediterranean.

The *Courts of Women* are an unfolding of a space, *an imaginary*: a horizon that invites us to think, to feel, to challenge, to connect, to dance, to dream. It is an attempt to define a new space for women, and to infuse this space with a new vision, *a new politics*. It is a gathering of voices and visions of women from the *global south*, locating itself in a discourse of dissent: in itself it is a dislocating practice, challenging the new world order of globalization: listening to the voices and movements in the margins.

The *Courts of Women* seek to weave together the *objective* reality (through analyses of the issues) with the *subjective* testimonies of the women; the personal with the political; the analytical with the intuitive; the *logical* with the *lyrical* (through video testimonies, artistic images and poetry) urging us to discern fresh insights, offering us other ways to know, inviting us to seek deeper layers of knowledge; towards creating a new knowledge paradigm.

The *Courts of Women* are public hearings: the *Court* is used in a symbolic way. In the Courts, the voices of the victims/survivors are listened to. Women bring their personal testimonies of violence to the Court: the *Courts* are *sacred* spaces where women, speaking in a language of suffering, name the crimes, seeking redress, even reparation.

While the *Courts of Women* listen to the voices of the victims/survivors, it also listens to the voices of women who resist, who rebel, who refuse to turn against their dreams. It hears the voices of women from the women's and human rights movements; it hears of survival in the *dailiness of life*; it hears of women and movements resisting violence in their myriad forms- war, ethnicity, fundamentalism; it hears of women struggling for work, wages, their rights to the land; it hears of how they survive – of their knowledges, their wisdoms that have been inaudible, *invisible*. It hears challenges to the dominant human rights discourse, whose frames have *excluded the knowledges of women*. The *Courts of Women* repeatedly hear of the need to extend the discourse to include the meanings and symbols and perspectives of women.

It speaks of a new generation of women's human rights.

The Courts of Women invite us to write another history; a *counter hegemonic history*, a history of the margins. The *Courts of Women* are a journey of the margins: a journey rather than an imagined destination. A journey in which the dailiness of our life proffers possibilities for our imaginary, survival and sustenance, for connectedness and community. For the idea of imaginary is inextricably linked to the personal, political and historical dimensions of community and identity. It is the dislocation expressed by particular social groups that makes possible the articulation of new imaginaries. These social groups, the margins, the global south, the south in the north, the anti-war movements, the women are beginning to articulate these *new imaginaries*.

The construction of these imaginaries occur when stable structures of meaning are breaking: the existence of antagonism and dislocation are necessary to the emergence of new imaginaries[11].

The peasants in Chiapas, Mexico, describing their *new imaginary*, explain their core vision in their struggle for their livelihoods and for retaining their life worlds. And in their profound and careful organisation, in their political imagining and vision do not offer clear, rigid, universal truths; knowing that the *journey is in itself precious*, sum up their vision in three little words: *asking, we walk.*

The asking in itself challenges master narratives, masters' houses, houses of reason, *universal truths*, of power, of politics.

The *Courts of Women* invite us to *dismantle the master's house*; and as the poet Audre Lorde says the master's tools will never dismantle the master's house. There is an urgent need to challenge the *centralizing logic* of the master narrative implicit in the dominant discourses – of class, of caste, of gender, of race. This dominant logic is a logic of violence and exclusion, a logic of civilized and uncivilised, a logic of superior and inferior.

This centralising logic must be decentered, must be interrupted, even disrupted.

The *Courts of Women* speak to this disruption, to this trespass.

The Courts of Women, to borrow the title of Fatima Merinissi's book, are our *Dreams of Trespass* offering new imaginaries that must be feminine;

Let us listen to two more voices around the fire:

The World Court of Women against Racism has dared to *storm the bastions of power* and to give a *hearing to the disempowered*. Thank you for defying the darkness of racism and hatred to shed light on the *invisible victims*: thank you for challenging the master narrative and providing a forum for the authentic narratives of the *silenced* to enable them to gain mastery over their lives. The *Courts of Women are a tribute to the human spirit*: in which testimonies can not only be heard but also legitimised. The Courts provide witnesses, victims, survivors and resistors not only validating their suffering but also validating the hopes and dreams that they have dared to harbour.

(Dr. Hanan Ashrawi was invited to deliver the Opening Address at the World Court against Racism at Durban, South Africa at the NGO forum, World Conference against Racism, Xenophobia and Related Intolerance on August 30, 2001).

Another voice of an indigenous woman from Hawaii:

Through resilient testimonies received by the Court, we see that women's human rights cannot be privatized, individualized or domesticated either under national or international law. Current trends in the economic and political arenas maintain the old masculine paradigm, which favors consumption, exclusivity and militarism. This is our greatest challenge. To replace the old paradigm not with a new paradigm but with the first paradigm – the *paradigm of the feminine*. Women from traditional matrilineal cultures have kept the knowledge needed to *return balance to the world* in which we live. The indigenous women's worldview stands in stark contrast to the patterns of globalization. Our traditional grandmothers recalled the original instructions of the Creator – to live as a guardian of the sacred earth, honoring all life forms. We must return to the path of our grandmothers, *walking in the vision of our cultures*.

(Mililani B. Trask, Hawaai; Member of the Jury: Nga Wahine Pacifika, Pacific Court of Women, Aotearoa, September 1999 and World Court of Women against War for Peace, Cape Town, South Africa, 2001).

we need new stories for our times.
even new story tellers.
we need new myths, magic and mystery.
we need to find *new spaces for our imaginaries*.

and then to end with a last gift from the very beautiful words of the poet Chrystos[12]

you have come gathering
you have made a circle with me
of the places where I have wandered…
I want to give you the first flower opening from the earth I have sown

I give you seeds for a new way
I give you the moon shining on a fire of singing women
I give you the sounds of our thoughts flying
I give you the sounds of our feet dancing
I give you the sounds of peace

Notes

[1] Taylor, Clyde (1986). *Eurocentric vs New Thought at Edinburgh*, Mimeograph, October.

[2] Illich, Ivan (1981). *Shadow Work, Vernacular Values Examined*, Marion Boyars Inc. London.

[3] Bauman, Fredrique Apffel-Marglin (1989). *Rationality, the Body, and the World: From Production to Regeneration*.

[4] Lindqvist, Sven (1996). *Exterminate all the Brutes*, The New Press, New York.

[5] Spender, Dale (1980). *Man Made Language*, Routledge and Kegan Paul.

[6] Periera, Winin, Seabrook, Jeremy (1994). *Global Parasite, 500 years of Western Culture*, Earthcare Books.

[7] Mies, Maria and Shiva, Vandana (1993). *Ecofeminism*, Halifax, Farmwood.

[8] Rahnema, Majid (1999). *Banyan Tree, Essays on the Violence of Globalization*, El Taller International.

[9] Asaria, Iqbal (1994). *The Culture of Individualism in the West and Its Impact on Human Rights*, International Seminar on Rethinking Human Rights, Just World Trust, Malaysia.

[10] Thompson, E. P. (1982). *Exterminism and The Cold War*, Verso Books, London.

[11] Ruiz, Lester Edwin (1994). *Towards a Radical Imaginary Constructing Transformative Cultural Practices, Alternatives*, Volume 19, Number 2, Spring.

[12] Chrystos, Starquilt (1995). Asian Women's Human Rights Council.

In the world today there are more than 600 million poor children, the children of the Third World. But poor children can be found in the rich people's world too.

The children of the Third World are easily exploited and treated badly. In fact, often they are forced to work, to go to war, to leave their mothers. In some cases the mothers are even forced to sell their children, to get money and maybe give food to their other children.

Such a disaster occurs because of the poverty and exploitation of the people in countries such as Africa, South America and Asia.

The UN organization was born in 1945 with the aim of ensuring peace, freedom, justice and respect for human rights. In 1959 the UN approved a Declaration of the rights of children. Obligatory rules were written that were meant to be followed by the parents of the child and by all other adults. For example: the child has a right to nourishment, housing, entertainment and adequate health care; if he is in a situation of physical, mental or social inferiority, the child has the right to receive psychological treatment, loving care and education and the special care he needs. All children need to be loved, protected and welcomed into the world with joy.

Even in developed countries like Italy, there are poor people and children who work already by the age of 10 and earlier. Italy is the country in Europe with the highest number of children who leave school to go to work.

There are some poor children who don't get affection, attention and understanding from their parents, either because they don't have parents or because they were sold, like the protagonist of a story that really happened.

There was a 12 year old boy by the name of Iqbal who lived in India as a slave in a factory of carpets with many other children. He started working at 4 years old and stopped at 10. Iqbal met a union worker who was dedicated to the problem of the exploitation of minors, of children in slavery. A great friendship was born between Iqbal and the union worker. Iqbal reported the system of exploitation of minors to the whole world. But because of this our dear fried Iqbal did not live long, on the contrary he died early, too early…

With his reports, Iqbal threatened the interests of the industrials who were losing profits because of him. The boy was shot from a car while he was playing on a bike with his friends. It was Easter day 1995. And that was the end of Iqbal's life, the end of a martyr.

In today's world, which is the world of globalization, urgency increases and children are getting worse, poverty and exploitation of minors are growing. Even in Italy, and precisely in Bari, where I live, I see various children in my neighbourhood who instead of going to school, spend their day on the streets, some of them work and some just hang around. Isn't there a rule, at least in Italy, that says that children have to learn to read and write? Aren't there laws that protect children from those criminals who also spend their time on the streets? Where is there space to play with other children that is not on the streets?

If all of us would give a chance to the children or their parents, we wouldn't have people begging. You and I, have we ever asked ourselves why when we are in the car, children come up wanting to wash our windshields? And we are talking about Italy, of the rich and developed world, as adults say! Have you ever asked yourself why these children are forced into "jobs" of that kind or why they beg? I can answer all this because there is only one explanation: because some people have a bunch of money and they spend it egotistically only for themselves, for their clothes, which they probably have lots of already, for cars like limousines or Ferraris or for other costly cars on the market. And why do you think they are there? I can answer this question too: to be bought! and because people think they have value: but, on the contrary, these things aren't worth anything at all, they have no value beyond market exchange value!

In facing all this we have to ask ourselves "what can we do?". The most important thing to do is to be aware of the problem, realize what poverty many children are living in and therefore the exploitation, the dangers and the violence to which they are exposed. Many poor children live like little slaves and nobody loves them, they don't have food, they don't have a mother, not even a place to sleep. We have to talk about all this with our school mates, in the family, in our city, with all the children of the rich countries and report these injustices. Internet and the email serves this objective too! And when we finally recognize the problem it means that we can make plans and do something to help our little friends, nearby or far away, but always close to our hearts.

We need to know that there is enough food for everyone on the earth, and instead, children die of famine, have you ever asked yourselves why? I know! Because there are a lot of egotistic people who don't think of the children, who don't care if they are well or not, whether they have food, whether they go to school, whether they have the care they need to grow up healthy and happy, whether they can play instead of gathering garbage or instead of living in the sewers! Many people think of money, of making money grow, only for themselves. Many people are thirsty for power and think only of accumulating richness and material things, and I am sure they are not even very happy!

Each one of us children can help our little friends on the planet Earth, for example avoiding to buy products on the market which we know are made exploiting children's labour. And unfortunately these products are very many. I am thinking of the brands that us children in the rich world buy or demand from our parents, like things of the brands Nike, Puma, Adidas or foods like Nesquik, Cornflakes, etc.

Instead, there exist very rare people who know how to spend their money, who care for others and help people in need, including poor children, like a very special friend I know who has dedicated all her life to showing the way to a better world.

Bari, 31/5/2004
Translation from Italian by Amelia Rossi-Landi   282

Introduction

As a woman sociologist[1], I knew I had come to a different cultural space when I arrived in Nova Scotia. It was over thirty years ago that I moved from Columbia University's graduate school in New York City to Nova Scotia's capital city of Halifax, the major Canadian city east of Montreal[2]. My early research in Halifax (PhD dissertation on newcomers in Halifax and studies of citizen participation) indicated that it took longer in Halifax than in other places in North America, based on what the scholarly literature was reporting, for a newcomer to be considered to be part of the community. "Newcomers", "birds of passage" (a term coined by an elected member of the governing city council), or "come from aways" (a common Newfoundland phrase) were not welcome by local inhabitants. Newcomers in the early 1970s were frequently asked at public meetings on planning and development issues: "How long have you been here? And where are you from?" Being able to claim birth in Halifax definitely added credibility to what was being said.

I noted that social relations in this region were also different then. Family status had a structural importance in community life not unlike class or caste in other societies around the world. Henry Hicks, the former President of Dalhousie University and politician, is reputed to be able to greet incoming students to the university and be able to place them in a genealogical picture based on their last name and their geographic location. Most Haligonians would ask about a stranger's family (and the stranger's genealogical location within it) as a mechanism for socially locating a stranger in the same way that people now would be more likely to locate a stranger by occupation (with a questions such as "what do you do?"). When I said at a dinner party in 1968 that I did not know the maiden names of my four great grandmothers, the Lieutenant Governor's wife called across the room to her husband at another table, telling him of this startling phenomenon. I had clearly broken the social expectation that everyone is embedded in a genealogical picture of prime social significance both for themselves and for others in the community.

It was thirty years later and only after being introduced to Genevieve Vaughan's concepts of the "gift economy" that I recognised the gift's place in this regional culture. The first part of this paper draws illustrations of gifting relationships in this region from my personal memories and research in the city of Halifax, in the Maritime region (which includes the provinces of Nova Scotia, Prince Edward Island and New Brunswick) and in Atlantic Canada, the larger region which encompasses both the Maritimes and also the province of Newfoundland and Labrador. I then address what first appeared to be a surprising and apparently contradictory idea about the gift which I recently encountered from a woman in a small Nova Scotian fishing community and use sociological analysis of the gift to recognise its very different meanings and its appropriation and transformation by capitalist societies and cultures. No wonder the gift is viewed with suspicion by some people. The paper concludes with a discussion of the feminist significance of the gift as a hopeful alternative paradigm and pathway toward life-affirming social relationships and the non-patriarchal societies of the future.

Illustrations of the gift in Nova Scotia

My most vivid recollection of the gift economy is from the early 1970s after we had moved to a nearby fishing community. One morning we were awakened by a banging on our door. There stood a neighbour, with a piece of freshly caught halibut for us. There was no special "occasion" for this gift. He said very little but that he had more fish than he needed and thought we might like some of it. What an understatement. The fact that he was thinking of us helped us to feel part of the community. The delicious taste of fresh fish still lingers among the multi-layered memories of such neighbourly gifts and gift-giving in that community. As a sociologist who had lived previously only in suburban and urban places, I remember how different it was to live in a place such as this where diverse relational and communal norms rather than individualistic norms prevailed.

Another recent example illustrates that the Nova Scotia gifting tradition continues although, sadly, not as dominantly in the community where we now live. In September 2003 my husband and I were driving home after a long trip. We were on the main highway in a rural area of Nova Scotia after dark when our left front tire went flat and we pulled off to the side of the road. It was a dark moonless night; trucks and cars whizzed by and both of us were still trying to find the jack, the instructions and the flash light when two men came up to us from a side road. A father and an adult son said they had noticed us and thought we might need help. They changed the tire and refused to accept the monetary gift my husband tried to offer "in return".

The hospitality that still marks Atlantic Canadian culture is often noted by strangers to the area who are unaccustomed to generosity, especially from those whom they consider to be "less well off" than they are. Newspapers in Nova Scotia and Newfoundland often contain letters of thanks to the community, including from the grieving relatives of those who died in the Swiss Air disaster off Nova Scotia's coast in 1998 and from the plane passengers who were guests for days in Newfoundland and Nova Scotian homes and communities when many planes returning from Europe were suddenly grounded in this region on September 11, 2001 after two planes attacked the towers of the World Trade Center in New York City. Moreover, stories abound in the region of travellers taken in by those living along a highway until a storm subsides and of community cooperation following natural disasters.

Research in 1999 in Nova Scotia's coastal communities also provides evidence of less visible but daily acts of generosity, gifts which are often so taken-for-granted that they are unrecognised and unseen by both the giver and the receiver. These taken-for-granted acts of neighbourliness include drives given to friends and neighbours who are without transportation, food delivered to elderly or shared with those living in poverty and offers of care in times of emergency. In interviews with women whose communities were being devastated by the fishing moratorium, we found that gifts of personal services were not considered as "volunteer work" by those who carry it out. We also found that women in these communities were grieving not only for their own family's misfortune but for what they could no longer do for their neighbours; without money for gas or insurance for their cars, their elderly neighbours and the local children no longer had a way of getting to the doctor, to the store or to local events.

Women's community work in Labrador

In some parts of Atlantic Canada the model of gift giving by the mother is extended to women's caring for the community itself. Like mother's work of giving gifts, however, the contributions are often invisible and unrecognised to outsiders and insiders alike. It becomes taken-for-granted and unspoken, unarticulated and not calculated by social, economic and policy planners. My research in some coastal communities in the mid to late 1970s found that it took a long time to recognise the strength and presence of local women and their extensive community work for the following two reasons.

1. I arrived having internalised the popularist version of women's movement teachings of the day, which drew a deep dichotomous distinction between (backward) "traditional" and "modern" women (among whom I prided myself). This dichotomous interpretation originally led me to consider the women there as "backward" based on what I saw. When I went to a public meeting, for example, I saw women sitting on one side of the room and not saying very much and men on the other side, the centre of the visiting (male) governmental attention; other women were at the back of the room, serving coffee, and the all-male panel of government officials and dignitaries were at the front. It was only after considerable research and analysis that I began to recognise that this "traditional/modern" dichotomy assuming "progress" was a false one. It had led me to jump to unwarranted interpretations about the stereotypical "traditional women" I first witnessed in Labrador at this meeting, as will become clear below.

2. Community relationships were clouded by a strong patriarchal veneer. Government visitors and academics alike (see Matthews, 1976) described the culture as male dominated, despite evidence to the contrary, which I gradually began to notice.

In fact, I was first introduced to the Matthews book entitled *There's No Better Place Than Here* by an irate woman leader in Labrador. She dragged me away from a dinnertable when she heard I was a sociologist; she wanted to show me what she considered to be an outrageous, biased and discriminatory book which was totally wrong about people like her. The book's methodology rationalises the exclusion of women from the study's sample by some methodologically problematic arguments and the claim that women are not leaders in Newfoundland and Labrador; it then goes on to conclude, later on, that one of the three com-

285

munities studied would not have survived without the actions of a particular woman, a description which seemed to indicate women's leadership. In addition to the outrage of this Labradorian woman leader at what she considered blatant sexist discrimination, indications of women's presence included the fact that the executive director of the community organisation was female and the Women's Institute had a position on the community development association's Board. Indeed, at the time, women had more public presence than they did in similar situations in the supposedly more "progressive" Halifax and other urban areas where there were higher levels of misogyny (hatred against women) among women themselves.

When I went back to the site of my research with a specific focus on women, I was told time and time again by women that "without women, there would be no community". Women pointed out how "government or religious men from away" did not understand that women were the ones who made things happen in the community (see Christiansen-Ruffman, 1980, 1995). When I told men about my return to their community for research on women, generally they at first expressed surprise and consternation at the topic (since I was obviously violating the patriarchal veneer), but then, after growing silent for a few moments, they would describe how important their mother was to their family and to the community. They tended not to mention their wives, although it was adult women of all ages whom I saw running the households, including the household business and its accounts, raising money for community work, meeting to discuss community issues and dealing with community crises.

Unlike the highly privatised household in which I grew up, specific parts of the home in these northern communities were considered public. Women's kitchens effectively served as public community spaces, open to all who came through the unlocked door to sit for a while, perhaps to get warm or chat or rest or hear the news or have a cup of tea from the pot which always seemed to be cooking on the stove. I was never completely comfortable with the non-proprietary cultural practice of not even knocking on the door or otherwise announcing my entrance. Having experienced the biting cold northern wind, I could understand this cultural practice as a community gift, one that encouraged sociability, or, perhaps more accurately, supported social relationships by taking community relationships for granted. Women were the providers and managers of these public spaces.

"Business As Usual?" An alternative meaning of the gift and its implications in Nova Scotia

In 2003, I was sitting around a table with seven women in a small coastal community in rural Nova Scotia, discussing current issues and problems. One woman asked how she could feed her husband the food he now needs for health reasons. Earlier in the week his doctor had given her a list of healthy food, but none of it is available at the local food bank. Amidst discussions of life's problems in the community – inadequate money for food, lack of housing for single women, problems of employment and the recent death of a parent whom one of the women had cared for "non-stop" for fifteen years, one woman, whom I shall call Mary, made a surprising statement. She passionately introduced the idea of the gift into the conversation as one of her major problems of the times. I was astounded. I had been thinking about how so many items discussed in the conversation were accomplished by gifting relationships – women caring, creating support and training opportunities for others, caring for parents, providing the infrastructure for the food bank, the transportation to look for a place to live… But Mary was the only one to use the word "gift" – and she hated it. She said it was ruining her life. She spoke with such vehemence in describing how her sister in law would spend $300 to $500 per child on gifts for the children at Christmas. Gifts like that were impossible for her, totally out of her reach. The gift was destroying her relationships with her family, making them impossible.

This discussion shows several features of the gift in contemporary Nova Scotian society. Sociologically, it indicates how many community relationships are based on "free gifts" or "giving gifts" which were invisible and often even are unrecognised as gifts by people in the community – both those giving gifts and receiving gifts. Indeed, gift-giving and generosity toward one another might well be a large part of what it means to be "a community". Gift-giving relationships and community relationships seem to be inextricably associated. Perhaps because of their taken-for-granted nature in some settings, people seem to be more likely to describe them in the abstract or once these relationships have been lost rather than describing them in their daily lives.

Secondly, the vehemence and intensity of Mary's concern with the "problem" of the "gift" is associated with a societal and cultural shift in its social meaning. The gift is increasingly becoming commoditized and appropriated to signify some of the worst features of capitalist relationships. Increasingly the gift feeds into and reinforces a market-oriented materialist society. The gift as material commodity is reinforced by advertising, stores and an increasingly consumer-oriented culture. The dominance of this commoditized gift in Mary's mind is not surprising given the dominance of the gift as commodity motif in advertising and in stores throughout Atlantic Canada; in December 2003, before the Christmas sales were complete, local chains of "drug stores" were full of gifts for Valentine's Day, 2004.

Thirdly, the explicit use of the word gift is associated in the public mind with the idea of "exchanging gifts" or gift exchange, with the very explicit notion that the exchange should reflect social relationships. The translation of gifts to monetary value along with the idea of equality begins a process of reciprocal inflation among friends and relatives. Gifts become symbolic signifiers of social relationships, with a tendency among friends and siblings toward equal exchange. This idea of equality of exchange may either reinforce equality in social relationships or shatter the relationships themselves when reciprocation is impossible; when one party is not able to participate in "equal exchange", a "charity model" is seen to become operative. This whole process establishes and reinforces ideas of hierarchy and social class when gift relationships are seen to fail.

The unexpected diatribe from Mary is an indicator of what we might call "false manifest equivalence". The word "gift" is the same but takes on two very different meanings because of appropriation of the gift by capitalist and patriarchal cultures. New characteristics are ascribed to public meanings of the term, often fueled by the market and advertising, and by dichotomous "readings" and evaluations by the public of what is being said. In the case of Mary, for example, the "value" of the gift is no longer measured by its thoughtfulness or the time involved in creating it; the only way of measuring a gift has become its monetary value on the market, which trivialises and "makes fun of" quaint or "cheap" or non-monetary gifts. Even more importantly, the notion of "gift exchange" has come to mean the equivalency of market value. This cultural appropriation of the concept of what constitutes a gift illuminates a common way in which the powerful are able to shift the social agenda in significant and subtle ways which are difficult to counteract, even when this social process is recognised.

Research in coastal Nova Scotian communities found that women's sense of themselves, of their communities and of their social relations were being shattered by a set of processes related to the fishing moratorium initiated by what was called an "environmental crisis of overfishing". Government restructuring, the corporatization of fisheries, a shift away from rural-friendly and people-friendly policies, what was reported as a deliberate divide and conquer governmental strategies and a shift of all policies and culture toward individualism and economic fundamentalism were the set of neo-liberal policies which responded to this crisis. Government of Canada officials brag about the "success" of the fisheries, now more lucrative than ever before in terms of the value now being extracted from previously underutilised species. These neo-liberal solutions and the policy of switching the fisheries to "underutilised species" will in all likelihood exacerbate the environmental crisis in the long run – as well as undermine the social infrastructure which has sustained these maritime communities and their gift-giving traditions over the centuries.

The erosion of this social infrastructure is both a direct result of economically-oriented government policies aimed at restructuring, corporatising and professionalising the fisheries and invisible to government because it is not captured on the standard economic measures used by policy makers and policy planners. It shows up, instead, down the road in cycles of poverty, despair and growing dysfunctionality of both individuals and communities and the shift to the individualistic, greed-based economic where everything of value can be measured in monetary terms and even social transactions are reduced to calculations of self-promotion.

This individual and local level dynamics is related to what has been happening at the global level in the last few decades. The neo-liberal agenda and its individualistic market-oriented ideology along with restructuring of Nova Scotia's rural infrastructure has been undermining the cultural, economic and community basis of the gift economy. The ideology of support to those in need characteristic of the welfare state with its social safety net has given rise to an ideology of individualism and greed. Rural communities are under threat as hierarchies are introduced. Globally both within and between societies, we see the reintroduction of a commoditized gift economy which parallels the growing gap between the rich and the poor both within and between societies and communities around the world.

Conclusion

As in all non-dichotomous interpretations, both discouraging and promising elements are apparent from this analysis. Mary's negative attitudes toward the gift is a sign of the dubious impact of globalisation on human lives and communities. The vast research on the negative impact of structural adjustment programs on women in the economic south tells a similar story. The current cultural values of economic fundamentalism harm features of life that cannot be reduced to monetary value or the exchange mentality. Mary's attitude toward the gift is one of many signs that Atlantic Canadian life and culture is being adversely affected by neo-liberal policies. The increasing presence of individualism, greed and a commodification of culture and history makes it harder and harder to practice a gift economy in this region – or even to describe it.

Underlying this neo-liberalist agenda are patriarchy, capitalism and colonialism. As values of patriarchy and colonialism (with their dichotomous, hierarchical and dominating assumptions over life – by violence and other means) continue to combine with capitalism (with its exploitative and monetarist assumptions), we can see how easy it is to produce instrumental individualism with its machiavellian assumption that the end justifies the means. If we look around us, we can see the emergence of a logical result – the buying of people and body parts; new forms of slavery emerge in a variety of hierarchical forms – from sports figures to trafficked women. The end, the value, in this case, is money and wealth. Women, children, men, the environment are only there to be exploited in this neo-liberal equation. It – and the life it shapes – are based on false economic assumptions.

The good news is that almost everyone still knows that the above view of life is partial and exclusionary while it pretends to be complete and open to all. Almost everyone can still imagine another possible world based on life-giving, gifting values and practices – a world which they still experience but which is shaped by different assumptions. The fact that it has been existing and that we do not have to start from scratch, from nothingness, is also appealing. Its traces are there in mothering behaviours and community practices, especially in what are now considered marginalised parts of the world. In articulating cooperative, communities, in valuing multi-centredness and diverse equalities, global feminisms also contain such hope and vision.

We can all start by asking these question: "What do I value most in this world?" and "What does it 'cost'?". And then ask ourselves: "What in the world costs the most?" and "What value would I put on this most costly item?". When we share the answers to these questions with each other, we will begin to understand different forms of wealth and of giftgiving relationships which recognise our common humanity and begin moving toward another possible world.

Notes

[1] This paper is based, in part, on my previous sociological research and in part on memories, experiences and reflections of living in two very different social, cultural and geographic spaces – each in North America and each diverse in its own, unique way – both then and now. My in-depth grounding over time in these two spaces provides an ideal condition for reflective qualitative comparative analysis and for autonomous feminist theorising, which is similar to inductive research and grounded theory but with a feminist perspective which recognises women's specificity (see Miles 1996). Autonomous feminist theorising is necessary because knowledge is based on patricentric assumptions (see Christiansen-Ruffman 1989). In writing this paper I recalled, again, how inadequate I had found sociology's dichotomous concepts (e.g., rural versus urban, traditional versus modern, Gemeinschaft versus Gesellschaft) in trying to understand Nova Scotian society.

Developing new concepts is not the purpose of "normal" hypothesis-testing science, and feminist scholars found it necessary to develop qualitative methodologies which were more in tune with this exploratory conceptual objective and which were able to build on understandings embedded in society (see Maguire 1987; Christiansen-Ruffman 1998). This paper uses a feminist methodology which recognises as significant: the reflective personal, political and intellectual experiences of a researcher/ theorist; the social, political, economic, cultural and historical importance of contexts;

and qualitative comparative methodologies of sociological research, including removal designs. In this case, the move between two places which are apparently the same but culturally and socially very different helps to remove the taken-for-grantedness of culture to reveal governing norms and thereby help in creating new understandings.

Nevertheless, autonomous feminist theorising is still very difficult because our knowledge is so full of patricentric assumptions which are so taken-for-granted that they are very hard to see, and even once they are recognised, we must still communicate in patricentric language and with many of the patriarchal assumptions which we have been trained to use.

[2] I also began living and doing research in its rural surroundings and had also been a research assistant in Africa and had done research in Appalachia, one of the most rural and poorest parts of the United States at the time. These different positional perspectives allowed me to appreciate the diversity of cultures and to avoid dichotomous thinking.

References

Christiansen-Ruffman, Linda (1976). *Newcomer Careers: An Exploratory Study of Migrants in Halifax*, Ph.D. Dissertation, Columbia University.

— (1980). "Women as Persons in Atlantic Canadian Communities", *Resources for Feminist Research*, Special Publication No 8, pp. 55-57.

— (1987). "Wealth Re-examined: Toward a Feminist Analysis of Women's Development Projects in Canada and in the Third World", Working Paper #140, *International Development Publication Series*, East Lansing: Michigan.

— (1989). "Inherited Biases Within Feminism: The 'Patricentric Syndrome' and the 'Either-Or Syndrome' in Sociology", in Angela Miles and Geraldine Finn (eds.), *Feminism: From Pressure to Politics*, Black Rose Books, Montreal, pp. 123-145.

— (1995). "Researching Women's Organization in the Labrador Straits: Retrospective Reflections", in Carmelita McGrath, Barbara Neis and Marilyn Porter (eds.), *Their Lives and Their Times: Women in Newfoundland and Labrador, A Collage*, Killick Press, St. John's, pp. 249-263.

— (1998). "Developing Feminist Sociological Knowledge: Processes of Discovery", in Linda Christiansen-Ruffman (ed.), *Global Feminist Enlightenment: Women and Social Knowledge*, International Sociological Association, Montreal and Madrid, pp. 13-26.

Lord, Stella, Ariella Pahlke and Linda Christiansen-Ruffman (2000). *Social and Economic Stress and Women's Health in Fishing Communities*, Research Report, Canadian Research Institute for the Advancement of Women in association with Nova Scotia Women's FishNet, Halifax; also (2002), published in *Good Policy, Good Health*, a community tool authored and organised by Janis Wood Catano, Halifax, Nova Scotia Women's FishNet.

Maguire, Patricia (1987). *Doing Participatory Research: A Feminist Approach*, The Center for International Education, Amherst, Massachusetts.

Matthews, Ralph (1976). *There's No Better Place Than Here: Social Change in Three Newfoundland Communities*, P. Martin Associates, Toronto.

Miles, Angela (1996). *Integrative Feminisms: Building Global Visions, 1960's-1990's*, Routledge, New York.

Activism is a gift to the community.

Sunlight is a gift.

Water is not a commodity; it is a gift.

Plants give us oxygen, we give them carbon-dioxide.

Starlight is a gift if there are eyes to receive it.

The dandelion gives the gift of its seeds. The artist
gives you the gift of the drawing of the dandelion.

STONEHAVEN RANCH:
A PROJECT OF THE FOUNDATION FOR
A COMPASSIONATE SOCIETY

Stonehaven Ranch is a 200 acre Conference and Retreat Center, which is owned by women, and operated by women. The purpose of the ranch is to accommodate and serve progressive groups who are working for social change and peace. Stonehaven is also a center of networking and resources. Stonehaven ranch is provided free of charge or at a very low cost. The meals, the cook and staff are provided. Stonehaven Ranch is one of many projects created and in accordance with the theory proposed by author/owner Genevieve Vaughan in her book *For-giving. A Feminist Criticism of Exchange* (1997).

The Gift Economy theory is a sociological/economic blueprint for creating a modern matriarchal society. Giving to areas of need, however we can, until something sustains on its own, are things all mothers do (and men who have been given this kind of love), and it is life supporting.

It is evident and clear to the majority of the people in the world that the patriarchal systems (male dominated profit motivated world economy) have not worked and are not working. Within this context, we are facing terrible human rights injustices, great human suffering, global environmental destruction, war, greed, multi-national control of the world, and people ruled by armies. The United States as a society must start to think in a different way. We must change the "powers that be" to nurturing instead of dominating, to giving instead of taking. We, as the people, must do what we can and all we can to make this change for our children and the next 7 generations. Anything you can do, helps. It is a natural way of existing.

In the original teachings of all religions and cultures, "giving" was/is a core value, and it existed without exchange, as instead patriarchy demands. In societies before the "Inquisition", this was the way of life. In the language of all Indigenous cultures this is within the language that is still spoken today. Giving creates a consciousness. We must renew and restore these values, and matriarchal systems, to the modern times we live in. These things are the foundations for the Gift Economy theory, which is a blueprint for change.

Restore the mother image as the human image and giftgiving as the human way. In our personal lives empower ourselves with gift values, gratitude, community, turning towards the earth, spirituality. We must pay attention to needs. Validate empathy. Learn to give with dignity and sensitivity. It is our sweet and sacred responsibility (Vaughan 2002).

Stonehaven Ranch is an example of the Gift Economy. Stonehaven is given as a "common ground"/home, for all. And the ways of gift giving are in effect, by all. It is everyone's home, and a gift to the next generation.

Stonehaven holds us all safe, like a big mother's love. We are safe from the world we have come from, the world we are trying to change. You give us clear thoughts, good hearts, and successful meetings. Stonehaven, you hold the prayers, the good intentions, the fortitude, the courage and the joy of all the people that have come before, and us. Those things live in the stones of your lodge walls, and upon the earth of you. You renew life in us. And, in the darkness of the night and the hanging stars, you give us good dreams. A guest.

Stonehaven Ranch is in the ancient homelands of the Indigenous peoples, the Choctaw and Natchez nations, and the medicines of the south, where the earth is covered with a vast array of plant life, medicines, yucca, stone, oak trees, caves, and water. Stonehaven is also wild animal and bird sanctuary, where many endangered species still live. Stonehaven is in the beautiful hill country of Tejas, 32 miles from the "progressive" city of Austin, Texas.

Stonehaven Ranch sits on a hill boldly facing all directions. All of the buildings are made of stone from the area. There is a Main Lodge, the Mother house, that will sleep 20 people in 7 bedrooms. There are also two other houses for guests, the Madre and the Carriage that will accommodate another 12 people, 32 total. There are vast dining and living rooms in the main lodge. The floors are oak and tile. There are 2 big stone fireplaces in the living room. All interior walls are tall and made of stone. The ceilings and overhead beams are cedar. There are vast stone patios that surround the main lodge. There is a pool and hot tub year round.

Stonehaven can accommodate 300 campers for conferences and gatherings. There are an outdoor kitchen, outdoor showers and a large fire pit. There is a "tennis court" turned "pavilion", with a stage, for speakers and entertainment. There are several meditation and sitting areas. And there is a prayer tower. It's the old windmill/well tower. The life size sculpture of the Goddess Sekhmet, by Marsha Gomez, is there.

Stonehaven is approx. 200 acres with no development bordering her in any direction. 15 acres are as "common grounds" which are mowed and maintained and patrolled by Faye, the Stonehaven dog. The rest of the ranch land is wild, with walking trails.

There are vast aquifers under the earth in the hill country here. Rivers come out of the ground in this area and run all the way to the Gulf of Mexico. So, there are many birds here. The majority residents are the bright red cardinals. They zoom thru the air chirping at each other all day. If you find one of their feathers, legend has it you will have luck in love! There are parrots from Chiapas, Mexico that migrate to this area in the summer. When you hear them for the first time, you will think you are on the TV set, of "wild queendom". Large herds of deer come thru and sometimes sleep on the grounds. At night, all the animals on the hill come feast at the new compost pile in the garden, gifts from the guests. It is a "golden buffet" for the raccoons, foxes, armadillos, birds, squirrels, skunk and deer. And at night in the winter you can hear the coyotes (but sometimes it's the guests, in the hot tub laughing and telling stories).

The staff lives on site. We are like contemporary "Grass Dancers" (those who prepared the meeting grounds for the tribes, in the old days). A modern day F-Troop. Ms Stonehaven demands to be looking nice and everything fixed, and a big dinner cooking in the kitchen, for the guests who she knows, are coming. She can be quite demanding, so the staff is not in need of "going to a gym"! The groups coming are some of the best people that there are, so Friday arrivals are exciting.

And, as "staff", we are fortunate to be examples of the economic blueprint within the Gift Economy. We have a "job in the market in a non-polluting and non-exploitive business. We give money, time and creative imagination to social change activities while validating the gift paradigm and our own gift giving both socially, intellectually, spiritually, and in our individual relations". We are encouraged to do this by Gen Vaughan. Thus we are able to be our natural selves, live a full life, and participate in gift giving, that helps others.

"Stonehaven, all of us that have come and gone from you, are strengthened. You have healed hearts, minds and spirits. You have given us all a home. You have given clarity to the meetings, and blessings to the intentions and endeavors of all. You have given us a place to touch the earth, be close to the stars, to pray, to dream, to laugh, and to dance. You have held descendants and ancestors, and us. You will always be in our hearts and part of us will always be here too". The staff.

Stonehaven Guests 2003: 39 groups/ approx 1,050 guests
American Friends Service / San Antonio American Indian Center / Spiral Door workshops / National Organizer Alliance-Immigration Caucus / Artist Workshop / Sisters of the Moon Artist Workshop / Tibetan Buddhist Conference / Permaculture Workshops (2) / Tejas Web / The Joy Workshop (2) / Women of Color Writers Workshop / AFSC Women and War Conference / ALLGO / Youthful Creations-Bilingual Theatre Group / The Goddess Salon / Jump Start Activist Theatre Group / Full Circle Drumming Workshop / Fellowship Of Reconciliation: Activist Youth Training / Unity Church of Austin / Texas Civil Rights Commission / Diana's Grove Mystery School / Sisters of the Red Moon / Memorial-Anna Lee LaBar / Unity Church of San Marcos / Quakers Board Meeting / Secada Recovery (2) / The 11th Annual Goddess Festival / Indigenous Two Spirited Conference / National Organizers Alliance / MANA Midwives Conference / Unconventional Mothers of Austin / Brujas Workshop / La Pena Cultural Gathering / Roxanne's House for Youth / The Hildegirls Workshop / Memorial-Erin First / Peace Group of San Marcos

Stonehaven Ranch Guest List 2002: 44 groups / approx. 1,000 guests
United for a Fair Economy / Unity Church of San Marcos (2) / AFSC: Women & War Conference / U.S.-Cuba Women's Peace Summit / Texas Comm. on Family Violence / Texas Civil Rights Project / Elder Women's Workshop / La Pena Cultural Arts Commission (2) / Divine Redeemers of San Antonio / Feminist Perspectives / Gift Economy Int'l conferences (2) / Wounded Healers Workshop / Spiral Door Workshops (5) / Unitarian Church of Austin / Esperanza Peace and Justice Center (2) / Full Circle Drum-dance workshop / Women of Color Writers Workshops (2) / UT Multicultural union: Poet honoring / Diana's Grove Mystery School / The 10th Annual Goddess Festival / Statewide

Latina women's meeting on El Paso murders / The Goddess Salon / Women Rising: HIV advocacy / Ywca girls group / Katherine Ann Porter School / Domestic Violence Counselors Retreat / Triple Goddess Retreat / Sisters in Action-Youth Training / ALLGO / Secada Recovery Project / Tibetan Buddhist Retreat / Tibetan Buddhist Workshop / Quakers National Board Meeting & Retreat / Marsha Gomez Memorial Accommodations / AFSC National Women's Board Mtg.

Stonehaven has been in operation since 1984 with approximately 1000 guests per year.

"Gratefulness is the angel standing at the edge of the abyss".

This saying has followed me around for many years now and seen from the viewpoint of the exchange paradigm it could be a powerfully poisonous mantra sending us into the endless orbit of obligating co-dependency. Seen from the vantage point of the *gift*-paradigm it is the expression of the consciousness of the *giftedness* of life itself. Seeing how I am *gifted* in my life, how life flows to and through me has made me free of fear. As serendipity has it, I am entering into a greater consciousness of this reality now and during the past few months than ever before.

The first time I came across the term *gift*-economy was sometime early last year. I received one of those e-mail circulars which usually wander un-read into the e-bin. But this time, I read the text and the word *gift economy* struck a cord in me somewhere. So I replied to the sender, a woman from Finland who I did not know at all, and asked what this gift-economy was all about. She told me of the author, Genevieve Vaughan who had written the book *For-Giving*. I should write to her and she would send me the book *as a gift*. Thinking I could do nothing wrong by following these instructions, the book promptly arrived and I was struck dumb when I started reading.

Here I found somebody who described my life and how I always had lived it. Somebody validated my experience, which has always been ridiculed and belittled by members of my family.

I had always loved to work and give of myself to others. I always longed for a family where I could do *"legitimised giving"* but being 47 and single now without children and never married, it was not to be. So I always felt like the odd one out, being single and not being interested in climbing the career ladder. All I wanted was to live in a community where I could use my various skills and be with other people in support of one another. But I was always told that I was being totally unrealistic and I should "wake up to the real world". I am glad I did indeed wake up to the real world, the feminine way and it is indeed the world of *giving*.

And interestingly, when I first started reading Gen's book, I skipped over the bits which were too academic for me, on language theory, I did not connect with the academia at all, and still find it difficult now. But it is actually through language, and being bilingual, that this experience of rich giftedness has been granted to me.

301

I am a German national, and was dyslexic as a child. I can still remember the day when I went to the new school, 5th grade. Nearly everybody was going to English classes, except a few very "weak" kids. The teacher had known my brother who was such a gifted kid he rarely needed to do any homework and still made good grades. Making the assumption that I would be similarly gifted (and indeed I am) this teacher tried to push me into the English lessons and I held onto the door frame for dear life, crying.

I could not see how I could start to learn another language when I had not mastered my own. With my 10 years I was able to stand up to her, and was sent into a special course for dyslexic children instead.

We had here in Germany a three tiered school system, and I was at the bottom rung. I had accepted that I was somewhat "stupid", as dyslexia was not even recognised as a disorder at that time. Then during 8th grade I had the *gift* of a wonderful teacher who saw my potential under the frightened shell. One day, as we were talking about the future and possible professions, she made a very unconventional suggestion. At this time, in the early seventies, there were not many options for a girl not inclined to academia: shop assistant, hair dresser, secretary, nurse. None of those really appealed to me. She suggested I go back to 7th grade into what was called "Middle School" and if I did not like it I could just come back. This was a very unusual thing to do, and I followed her suggestion and never looked back.

I had to start English from scratch, when all the other kids had already studied it for 3 years, so my parents found a private teacher with whom I could study in the afternoons trying to catch up with the others. The *gift* of this extra time with an adult was very special for me. Because I was quite a "live wire" at school, any lack in written work was made up for by my enthusiastic and lively participation in class.

The next step was going to grammar school to study for the baccalaureate, the entry examination for university, which is called "Abitur" in Germany. A group of girls from the same class went to a special school which took children from the Middle Schools to train them for this examination. This school was in a small town with an American Army Installation and some of us started going out with the young GI's. Soon after that I was fluent in spoken English. I repeated one of the grades for non-attendance because I was so busy seeing my boyfriend, but in the end I managed to achieve a good average mark.

During this time I had fallen in love with a black American soldier and there has always been something about black people which pulled me strongly, something of this zest for life which I was feeling inside, but found no expression in most of my surroundings. He left me for another woman. I was as deeply depressed as I can remember and felt bereft and desolate. One day hitching home from Frankfurt, a black American woman picked me up. I poured out my heart to her and consequently we became friends. She was very interesting: a gospel and jazz singer and psychologist and a member of a local American Pentecostal Church.

To make a long story short I had a very powerful conversion experience and because I had no frame of reference for this experience I swallowed everything the church (mainly men) told me "hook, line and sinker", and became involved in a very fundamentalist approach to Christianity for many years. And here the teaching of *gift giving* was stressed very much. And I can remember regularly tithing (giving 10% of my income to the church) and during that time I did not have financial problems, there is something like a letting go that sets in when one is willing to give a part away. There was always enough money to meet my needs. And the basic teaching of Jesus to my mind still confirms the gift-giving paradigm for me, which existed of course long before him. When I give from a free and loving heart, somehow this giving will be returned to me. It is like a spiritual law: what is given freely will come back. Of course there are numerous Christian and Esoteric books on the market both teaching this law. But the problem is you can not just try to follow the law, always looking toward the outcome, really being driven by one's fear of not having enough. And there are some really disastrous outgrowths of a spiritual reality which people try to "fit into the exchange-paradigm" such as the Health and Wealth Gospel movement and various esoteric cult teachings as well.

I never did chose the path of academia, for fear I could not master it, but on the outside I "despised" the often very arrogant "upper class" kids, because they despised me, working class kid and felt I could not keep up with them. I was always afraid of the harsh competition, be it in sports or in class, and I expected the university to be even worse.

Having always admired working with my hands and wanting to prove myself I applied to train as a carpenter, but the atmosphere was so sexist and belittling that I changed my mind. At this time, early 80's, there were not many woman in the field of carpentry. I trained in horticulture instead which was more women friendly. This gave me a love of nature, and a true appreciation of the *giftedness* of life. And this is really where I understand the whole idea of the gift paradigm takes its origin from, in the abundance and richness of life which nature provides.

I trained in a conventional ornamental house plant production company, but quickly turned to organic systems which were just taking off in Germany. During this time there was a real movement towards living in community and living off the land. Many folks bought land and set up farms to live a self-sufficient frugal lifestyle which would work in co-operation with nature instead of trying to dominate it with agro-technology and agro-chemicals. Many Germans went all over the world to start up organic farms to get away from the rat-race.

After I finished my apprenticeship in horticulture I worked for an organic grower for a while, but at that time I was really looking for a Christian organic farmer or better still a farming Christian community. So off I went in my search to the "promised land" the U.S. I ended up in what I call now my "fundamentalist Boot camp", a missionary group run by two ex-army members. Women were to be "under the cover" of a man, so not being married I was supposed to submit to the male leadership. Of course they were infallible, almost like the Pope who was of course criticised for his stance. But disobeying the authority over me was like disobeying God himself, as the scriptures say, God has installed those who are governing us. Despite this, looking back now, it gave me a real experience of "living by faith" or trusting that if I do what my heart desires, all my needs will be met. I had a group of friends who sponsored me financially and I was never in need of anything. There was only one other single woman there who was very kind to me and supported me in many ways, which kept me sane in an insane situation.

After two years in the US I retuned to live in Germany to look after my dad who had become very ill with cancer. Emotionally I felt very unstable, I was unemployed in Germany and eventually found a job in London, England with a Christian Company who were whole-saling wholefoods.

We used to have a prayer meeting at the company I worked for every morning and learning to take responsibility for this meeting taught me a lot about self-expression and speaking publicly. It was a very intense time and I made friendships with people which remain today especially with some of the women.

During all this time I loved celebrating and organising celebrations and bringing people together. My search went on trying to find the life where I could give of myself and not worry about my daily needs. After working for Community Foods I lived in a convent for a year, observing the religious community with the view to joining the noviciate, while I ran their small organic vegetable garden. But it was quickly clear that this was not for me.

During my time in London I also trained as a therapist for two years sensing that I had gifts in this area. I discontinued the training because for one I fell out with the director, and also during the mid 80's to the mid 90's I saw a therapy "industry" growing up around me which made me wonder about the motivation of many of its proponents.

During my first contacts with therapy and reading very many books about the subject I kept thinking "This work ought to be done by 'the body of Christ' for love, not for money". There were some free services of different Church groups, but as the field got more and more "professionalised" it got more and more expensive.

There were two main reasons why I personally went for therapy: one was my seeming inability to stay in any relationship longer then a year or two, and an eating disorder which was growing more and more ferocious. The connection between compulsive overeating and sexuality was one I only understood much later. I started to attend 12-step groups for compulsive eating. This was really my first conscious experience of *gift-giving* with a real powerful effect. Here was a group of addicts who were simply listening to each other and "sponsoring" each other. The concept of the sponsor is very important in the 12-step groups, as it is the very act of "giving away" your sobriety which keeps you sober (meaning sharing it with others and giving of your time and attention and financial support as well).

The main benefit of my experience in these groups has been the practice of "encountering" a benevolent higher power, not a punishing God who I feared from my fundamentalist Christian time. The experience that one could chose any higher power one wished, or none at all, the support could also be the group itself. As I watched people getting better I understood how this "faith" worked. It was the constant reinforcement of a positive approach to life which slowly changed my inner world. This experience did more for me than any of the smart books I had read, as it convinced me that life is good, if I let it be good to me. At the same time a very helpful tool in the groups were the little sayings or proverbs, which would pop up at the appropriate time and help me to resist the compulsive acting out. This again demonstrates the relationship between language and giving. These are some of my favourite examples:

One day at a time.
This too shall pass.
We can't think ourselves out of our addiction; but we can only act ourselves into serenity.

Let go and let God.
God says today, the devil says tomorrow.
If the devil can't get you with poverty, he will surely get you with success.
Coincidences are God's way of staying anonymous.
Whether the cup is half full or half empty depends completely on your viewpoint.
When the pupil is ready the teacher appears.

These sayings were like little beams of light which would shine into my often unmanageable everyday life. I valued the support of those who sponsored me, who would take time to sit with me and listen to my feelings and fears, who would not judge me but could identify with my experiences. In return I had the sense of really having something to contribute when I sponsored others. Attending these groups was a very healing experience for me. My continued interest in communities led me to become involved in a large group experience called Community Building. I was involved in this for many years in London. The most exciting thing I learned there was, the truth of my life and my past, my very own experience, with all its joys and pains and paradoxes will be the well-spring of my future. So the act of acceptance is what enables me to build on the building blocks of the past, this is where gratefulness for the gifts one has received comes in again. And the other very important two points, to speak when I feel moved to speak and let the words just flow without being afraid of not knowing what to say next. The experience of the passing of emotions, the hard to handle anger and aggression and fear, all will pass, liberated me to trust more in the life that was given to me. Life is in constant flux, we can not control it, not only that, the very act of trying to control life mostly makes it unbearable. It's like stemming up flowing water, the pressure will eventually destroy the vessel used for its arresting, or the water will find a way around the blockage.

Then I moved on from London to live in Ireland, still looking for a community. I ended up living in West-Waterford, a small village called Dunmore East, living on a farm which was run by an Amish-Mennonite family, growing vegetables for a box-scheme and a small farm shop. The farmer was a lecturer at the local technical college and only ran the farm part time. I really enjoyed my work there, but the church was way too narrow for me. Again principally the same dogmas, no equality for women, and a very strict dress code as well.

The farmer eventually decided to give up the commercial farming, since he made more money as a lecturer and the children were not really into working so hard and the rest of the church was also more into trading rather than growing food. So I was a bit shocked that after having given up everything in England to come over to Ireland I was told after one season growing that it was not to be continued. I applied to attend a small college course on organic horticulture and went to work at a Camphill community while I was waiting for the course to start.

The Camphill communities are a good example of how the *gift-giving* can function. People work in these communities without fixed pay. All their needs are taken care of: housing, clothing, food, recreation, and they get a small allowance and if they need extra money they apply for it and it will be paid from a special fund. I stayed there for 8 months and really enjoyed it, even though it was hard work. I worked in one house cooking in the mornings and gardening in the afternoons. Camphill communities are based on the Philosophy of Rudolph Steiner. Then I joined the college and lived in a shared house with 4 other students, mostly younger people from many different nations. We always had big celebrations in the house we lived in and everybody brought food to share and we made music and danced a lot. There was a great sense of giving to each other all the time. What comes to mind here is the aspect of relationship which is stressed by Gen, that giving establishes relationship.

We were 5 students and we lived in the biggest house on the square in this quaint little Irish village in West-Limerick called Dromcollogher. Our landlord was a self-made man and very wealthy, he owned a lot of property and several factories. Because of his success he was not well liked by many villagers, and I heard how difficult he was. I quite took to him when I first met him, and gave him the benefit of the doubt. So I established a relationship with him just by being friendly to him and not begrudging his wealth. Our house was a very lively and unusual place and he obviously liked coming for visits, always getting "strange, foreign" food from us. I was friendly to him and he was friendly to us. As a consequence, when I asked him to do certain jobs in the house that needed doing he would always do it quite promptly, because I had established a relationship with him. He also owned a small house next to ours which was also rented to students and they always complained to me about him, as they saw him as the rich landlord. I just saw him as the man who owns the house we lived in, and a funny man on top of that. So I saw and experienced how this giving works.

I would like to raise another issue which I think is very important. When I first started to read Gen's book the issue of co-dependency came up for me very strongly. I know that my giving has often been very manipulative, I wanted to "buy friends" at a certain time of my life, so what looks to the outside as very generous, is really an act of manoeuvring. In this sense the act of giving can be a weighing up of my input to see whether or not I get an equivalent back, just as it is in the exchange paradigm. I think this is one of the reasons for inventing money, to avoid having to deal with emotional issues and having to relate. One does not have to be a decent person to have one's needs met when there is money, one can buy everything, even sexual gratification. But if one lives in a society which is based on relational process one has to adapt to the "rules" of this society. Our ego-centric narcissistic society has come about through the way we related, we use each other. Ann Willson-Schaef talks about an addictive society, everything in our society is based on addiction, and addiction is a way to escape from intimacy.

In the year 2000 I returned to live in Germany because my mother had become very ill with cancer. She was bedridden for many months, and living with my sister who was a few weeks away from the delivery of her third child. My sister called me up in Ireland and asked me to come back home to help with our mother. At that time I had just finished the college course anyway and was in the process of wondering what to do next. The timing was perfect so in September 2000 I moved back home after 16 years abroad.

My idea was to live with my family, but this was not to be, strained relationships made it hard to find common ground between my sister and me and my brother and me. So I now finally live in a house-community with one other woman and one man, and it is really working well. There is a sense of being welcome and appreciated for who I am and therefore my gifts can really flourish and I bring out in others the giftedness in them.

306

Gift-giving and the civil society movement

One of the things I got involved in when I returned to live in Germany is to be a volunteer for an anti-globalisation NGO called attac, which has a group of people doing online translations of texts and also interpreting at various events.

To have been involved in this did two things for me, it helps me hone my skills greatly and it gives me a sense of being involved in something I considered worthwhile. So as I am *giving* of my skills and time to the various tasks, they get more and more refined and I am meeting the most interesting people. The fact I am writing this article now has come through the contacts I made at the first ESF (European Social Forum) in Florence in 2002. I am not a trained translator or interpreter, but I have the skills to do it and I am able to do it in a context I am happy about.

There are thousands of young people involved in this group called "Babels", the volunteer translators and interpreters of attac and it helps them to feel involved, with something they can contribute. There are more and more individuals who are involved in bartering circles all over Germany with some of them having their own regional currency.

There is a groundswell of interest in real alternatives to the current system and gift-giving is the basis of all of those systems. And as Gen rightly says the first priority now has to be to recognize where gift-giving is still in existence and validate and protect it, both in the so-called developing world (developing from gift-giving into the exchange mode!!!) and in our society as well. It is incredible once my eyes were opened to see it, I started to see it everywhere.

I feel I have been blessed with some very important teachings from the dying themselves. I feel preparation for dying needs to become more of an accepted practice. With someone who is slowly dying, and is bedridden, you may still be the only person on the spot who needs to know what is needed. Depending on what that person has chosen regarding her/his death, and if you are a friend or relative, you will need to find out just what is going on and how you can be of service, without your own agenda. So, primarily, one needs to learn to simply show up and be in the moment with what is. You cannot know "what is" until you are in that moment.

This requires a simplicity of being, not of doing. This skill requires you to know how to be present – not by what you say, but by who you are. If you are ambitious about being the wonderful care-giver and "s/he who knows", you will only get in the way. I feel that a person's actions can have a strong psychic affect on the dying – even if they are not able to say so. I feel that dying people are exceptionally sensitive, and an inappropriate behavior can cause anger and fear in them. Once when a hospice assistant came to bathe my mother the day before she died, the woman washed my mother's face and my mother quietly spoke from a deep place of wisdom "she has hurt someone". I noticed the woman had a roughness about her, and reported her to hospice. My mother, in having her face washed by this energy, could feel the harm in it.

The image of a loving mother who gently tends and nurtures her child is a most powerful image to hold in working with the dying. Loving mothers just know what to do, how to be and what to give to the needs in the moment. There is no thinking or intellectualizing – there is only giving and caring. Loving mothers do not have selfish agendas nor are they judgmental. They are present with their love as an offering – as a gift. I see loving mothers as free – they are not controlled by a fear-based male religion telling them how to behave. They are grounded in the spirituality of the Great Mother, the Goddess, who informs their true nature. Where are these mothers?

I think these mothers are remembering ourselves and our ways. The mother culture is a far different culture than this patriarchal one in which we are all trying to survive. The mother culture is free from violence, domination and control. It is rooted in the earth, and is governed by the magical rhythms of the moon-mind. To remember these ways is to

bring back the wisdom of our foremothers who did, indeed, midwife the dying and tended their journeys as they left this world and passed into the next. These ancestral mothers understood the secrets of life, death and rebirth and their rituals were woven with this sacred knowledge.

Midwifing someone in motherly love in their death means just that – loving them from a pure heart. You cannot go wrong with this kind of attention. Kind and loving words, soothing silent presence, gentle singing, tender touch, creation of beauty in the environment, acceptance of the process, the offering of non-invasive support, protecting their dignity, affirming their precious worthiness, giving permission to them to let go, using compassionate prayer, whatever can be given in the spirit of love and kindness are all the offerings of motherly love. While motherly love fights fiercely for life, it also knows when to let go. Motherly love trusts the entire process of life on its journey and helps it to pass gently and peacefully. In this manner, this kind of love assists the dying person to meet death with a sense of surrender instead of paralyzing fear.

Perhaps in this, death then, can be a kind of celebration/initiation that can only be experienced at the time – a passage through a portal into the next world. It seems to me that if we can die without fear, we are creating for ourselves an opportunity to be open and conscious to what is as we leave this life and enter a new one. It makes sense to me that how we die – that is, what our intention is at the time of our death – affects the coming experience. We celebrate birth and new life when a baby is born. Would it be so different to celebrate the death of a person as they are born into another world? The moment of my mother's death was filled with light, awe and wonder. Though she suffered from cancer, and I believe her cancer was connected to the anger she carried all of her life, all traces of suffering seemed to disappear as she surrendered. On this side of the veil, it is hard to know, though it seems our ancestors had a strong sense of the other side as the regenerative transformative domain of the Goddess.

I believe midwifing the dying in simplicity of being and motherly love is based on giving. It is not based on exchange. When you sit with someone in their dying, you are not looking for payment or something for yourself. You are simply giving your presence. The gift of giving is its own reward, as it fills the hearts of the giver and the receiver with a warm love, communication and compassion. This gift-giving is the foundation of motherly love. Our whole society and economy are based on exchange, so how do we know what giving really is, especially in a time of need? If we don't understand the nature of giving, then we also don't understand the nature of receiving. Exchange is not about either one of these. Exchange is linear and patriarchal, based on an expectation of "getting".

Gift-giving is cyclical and circular, ushered forth from the very Earth Mother who gifts all of us. Gift-giving creates true community and communication – "muni" is Latin for "gifts". If we have lived a life in giving, then we can die in the same experience. If we have lived a life dependent on exchange, we have limited ourselves to always seeking "what's in it for me" and feeling we don't have time to give unless we get something in return. It is no wonder that we live in a death-denying society. The patriarchal mind sees death as a "there's nothing in it for me" situation. There is no sense of a giving back to the Mother in this denial. A mother gives unconditionally because she simply loves. She is capable of loving and giving. And yet, this giving does not just happen effortlessly. Any mother will tell you that nurturing requires mindfulness, great effort at times and the ability to put another's needs before one's own. This is not a blind giving away of self, as has become the condition women find ourselves in patriarchy, but rather a sharing of the self.

Another way of viewing this capacity to give is learning to exchange self for other – putting yourself in the shoes of another, or seeing them as yourself. Mothers do this naturally, all the time. Why do we have male authority figures in our religious traditions telling us how to love like a mother? Who knows best how to do this? Why when men speak of this, are they listened to, and when women do it, are we ignored? Author of *For-Giving, a Feminist Criticism of Exchange* (1997), Genevieve Vaughan writes: "By not recognizing gift-giving as an important independent human way of behaving with its own logic, the continuity between mothering and other types of activity are lost. We must become wise enough to shift paradigms towards the mothering way" (1999).

It is self-evident that this continuity is all but lost in the current ruling paradigm. There is nothing more important to do than restoring this continuity in our lives.

I see many people who are not able to freely love and give. And the odd thing is that all of us want to be loved and to be gifted, as well as to give love and to give our gifts. So we are desperate for the very thing our fear pushes away: fear of allowing someone to love us because they might take advantage of or hurt us, like someone may have done when we were little, fear of being visible and seen for who we really are, fear of not knowing, fear of being wrong, fear of being right, fear of fear. How can people learn to shed this fear in the face of death? How can people learn to shed this fear in life and not wait until death has arrived? Genevieve states that when we are ready to truly create a gift-based society then we will be able to create a community with the spirits of the dead forming a "practical heaven on earth" (1999).

I do want to speak to violent death, as it is difficult to think of death as a celebration in the face of such grievous pain. I know that many people, many women and children die horrific and violent deaths in patriarchy. I do not want to say that these deaths are celebrations. I know these deaths are very difficult for the living to accept, and to have any sense of deity when a child dies a violent death must be unspeakably difficult. And yet, while we are on this side looking at the violence that has stolen our loved one, what is happening on the other side to the one whose life was taken?

I remember when four women were murdered in Yosemite in 1999. They were: Carole, a mother, her fifteen-year-old daughter, Julie, Julie's sixteen-year-old friend, Silvina, and twenty-six year-old Joie. The crimes were particularly heinous, committed by a woman-hating man who was completely consumed by demons, though apparently appearing to many people to be "gentle". He was so manipulative that he fooled the FBI after having been questioned several times. The FBI even engaged his help in collecting possible evidence at the scene of the crime of the murders of Carole and Silvina, where he worked. What is important to note is that a female journalist went to the crime scene, spending a night at the lodge where these women were murdered.

In the evening, she got in the hot tub that was occupied by one other person – the murderer. She of course did not know this, but after talking with him for a short time, she felt extremely uneasy and left to go back to her room. There, she pushed up chairs and a table against the door – something she had never done before. What was it this woman felt? Why didn't any of the FBI men feel anything like this? She knew he had been questioned; nevertheless, she intuitively felt his energy, and as it turned out, she was correct. I went to Joie's grave, the last of his victims whom he decapitated in the pristine wilderness near her rustic cabin, leaving her headless body in the creek beside her home. When I sat at her graveside, I wept in bewilderment and rage. How could this loving, sweet Goddess-child, naturalist and wonderful teacher about Yosemite's environment to many children, have been taken in such a manner? I still have no answer for that question, but as I sat there, I was overcome with a sense of peace. I had told her in prayer I was going to Yosemite with a group of women to do a healing ritual to cleanse the energy where the murders had taken place and asked her if there was anything she wanted me to do.

I then had a vision of a beautiful butterfly, but instead of an insect body, it was a woman's body, wings outstretched glistening in radiant color. I knew it was Joie. She said to me "make the world safe for the children". She was not in pain, nor was she suffering. She was beautiful and at peace. As I got up to leave, a butterfly appeared and landed on the flowers marking her grave. I felt completely blessed. While her death was grotesque, I knew she was in a place of celebration. When my friend, Monica, and I talked about the death of her youngest child, who was killed by a car in 1985, she said that the look of peace on young Leif's face at the very scene of the accident gave her a sense that he was in a good place, that he had been "met" by loved ones. Her agony at his loss cannot be described, but he came to her later in a dream and said "love is all that matters". Are his words an honoring of a kind of celebration of spirit?

Though I would never ask a mother who has lost a child to regard that death as a celebration, because of her own loss and grief, I do have to wonder what is taking place on the other side for the one who has died. While I know that the Mother is not always serene and nurturing, that she is sometimes wild and fierce, mysterious and untamable, I trust She knows what is going on.

While I do not understand why certain things happen the way they do, I have felt She is there on the other side, guiding and loving. When Monica shared with me what Leif had communicated to her, I replied that he was the child of the Mother, speaking Her wisdom. We both agreed this was true. And her pain is still her pain, as is true for Joie's mother, Silvina's mother, and the family of Carole and Julie. Sometimes I think a deep piercing of the heart opens us up to things we would not otherwise know. A mother's love for her child knows no bounds. This is a fierce kind of love that is feared in patriarchy. We need this love more than ever now as we face tremendous odds for our survival in this new millennium.

References

Vaughan, Genevieve (1997). *For-Giving, a Feminist Criticism of Exchange*, PlainView Press, Austin, Texas.
— (1999). "Gift-Giving and the Goddess, a Philosophy for Social Change", *Avalon Magazine*.

Introduction

The following interview gives an example of women who see a problem and solve it for others as well as themselves. This problem solving can be understood as the satisfaction of a social need, addressed with creativity and determination, individually and in community with others. Although the problem arose here in a market-based context, and its solution involves the return of property to its rightful owners, the actual solving of the problem is a unilateral gift given by the women who have dedicated themselves to doing it in spite of great difficulties. It is a gift to society as a whole, not just to the individuals who have had their land restored. I would say that it is even a gift to the powers that be, because it has kept them from perpetrating yet another evil upon the people. Social activism can be thought of in this way, as gift giving to society. That is, the gift of social change is the most necessary gift in our times. It can have huge multiplier effects, by changing the system that is causing the needs, and by spreading the example and the hope that this can happen. The gift of the Movimiento de Mujeres is particularly important because it shows a non violent method of problem solving, satisfying also the need for ways to social change that are not based on killing and counter killing – ie. exchange. The videographer who wrote the story and videoed the protests is also giving a gift by contributing to the multiplier effect of the women's protests. That is she is satisfying the needs of all to know about this gift. The threads of gift giving combine to weave the tapestry of the international women's movement, which contains the picture of a better world.

Genevieve Vaughan

Auction in Chivilcoy, September 13, 2003

I have been making a documentary on the Movement of Agrarian Women in Struggle for some months now, with the difficulties and discontinuities that go with independent production, difficult also because, as everyone knows, one must continue with work and the usual obligations. This lets me see the women only every once in a while, traveling to their locations. The known fragments of their story, regarding the paradigms of Argentina in the 90's had really captured my attention.

Small agrarian producers throughout the country used to believe in the then President Menem's "productive revolution" and in the eternal equality of the peso with the dollar, but most of all they believed that because of technological changes and international competition, they had to "modernize". They asked for loans of ten, fifteen, or twenty thousand pesos/dollars to buy machinery, improve infrastructure, increase crops. A few years later, between lion sized interest rates and devaluation, those loans had transformed into hundreds of thousands of dollars, of course un-payable. The mortgages and guarantees had used the fields as collateral, as the banks wanted. Then auctions began, that were making hundreds of small agricultural producers disappear at the hands of the usual speculators re introducing an old national tendency from the beginning of the last century: the concentration of the best lands in the country in a few national and foreign hands.

The assumption is that everyone knows what land means to a man of the fields, which is why when they knew they were losing it, the men got depressed to the point of isolation or suicide. There was nothing left for the women to do but – as they always say – "take off their aprons" and go out to fight. Directly from the kitchen to the streets. Lucy de Cornelis got started in a small village in La Pampa, but soon there were hundreds of women from all over the country. And, unaccustomed to the traditional militant ways, they began in the way that occurred to them: they got together to stop the auctions – not theirs, but anyone's, anywhere – and to call upon women to join, and men also, if they would leave their negativity behind.

There they would sit in the front row and, as soon as the auctioneer began with the bidding, they would sing the national anthem and begin praying out loud to stop the auction. The curious thing is that the movement, apart from expanding rapidly throughout the different provinces within the country, was joined more and more by women who had no land and no debts, but were there out of pure solidarity.

The establishment was stupefied: what to do with these crazy women (so similar to the mothers of the Plaza de Mayo) who confronted economists, auctioneers, auction houses, municipalities, police and other forces of order with only their bodies and their voices? Also, they were women rooted in the home: women who were experts in the kitchen, washing and ironing, raising children and giving their husbands attention when they came back from the fields. The fact is that the state of confusion generated by the using the national anthem as the original instrument of struggle, and more than anything, the tenacity of the solidarity of these women, caused the majority of the auctions to be stopped as the auctioneer would grow tired of listening to them sing for an hour non-stop and the presiding judge would say over the phone that, well, for that day it would be suspended and that they would see about it later. This postponement allowed them to get new deadlines, mortgages, even finally refinancing the debt for twenty years with the Banco Nacion (Nation Bank). The last two years before I got involved had added greater flexibility because of the national crisis, and the auctions had been practically stopped.

That is, until a peasant from Chivilcoy was not able to pay the bank. His lands (42 hectares, so you can get an idea) were called to be auctioned on September 12 at 11:30 in the Centro Comercial de Chivilcoy, in the province of Buenos Aires, at the auction house of Villarino.

The women called upon themselves, as always, and by 10:00, Lucy and Chiquita from La Pampa, Ana, Ana Maria, Ema and Sara from Santa Fe, and Olga and other partners from

Junin were already in the plaza. Remember: 8 women. Then the owner of the land that was being auctioned and his wife joined along with their family, friends and neighbors. They had called me to see if I wanted to film the auction for my movie, because I had not filmed one yet. I went with my cameraman and the assistant, with the excuse that we were sent by an agricultural program for cable television. Even though the women were in good, almost angelic, spirits, the red flag on the entrance door hit my stomach when I walked in and told me that things were going to end up badly. Particularly because of the vast quantities of men – and one woman – with that bullying look that one can easily detect.

I asked who they were and they spoke of the "leagues" of buyers, representatives of the bigwigs under the protection of auction houses, loaners and auctioneers, who show up like crows at the auctions to take, for a few pesos, lands that are later re-sold for large amounts. The auctioneer began the function, authoritatively strolling through the aisle, saying that he would not tolerate any disturbance from anyone who was there to upset the order. Then he got up on the stage and proceeded to read the "marvelous characteristics" of the land, whose base price was 42,000 pesos (some $15,000). He then asked for the offers to begin.

The women, then, in an old recovered ritual, stood up together and began to sing the national anthem loudly, accompanied by the peasants. Signs ("the land must not be sold, it must be defended"), prayers, and a national flag waving ceaselessly were added. The auctioneer made a sour face; the people from the "league" made uncomfortable gestures; the police looked at each other disconcerted. And after half an hour of so much singing and flag waving, the commissioner (called in a hurry by the auctioneer) said he was going to consult the judge on what should be done. The "buyers" went down to the street and the women – who did not allow themselves to be taken out of the hall – sat patiently waiting for the decision. After reminding me that the judge usually phoned in to cancel the auction until further notice, the women dedicated themselves to showing pictures of children and grandchildren, conversing about acquaintances and about a future agrarian reunion, and passing around "mate" and cookies, because it was already one o'clock. And no one was going to move from there even if they were hungry.

But the judge – who was assigned to the town of Mercedes, 70 km away from Chivilcoy – did not telephone this time to cancel. He finally arrived at 2:30 in the afternoon and came up surrounded by the auctioneer, the "buyers", and police. He communicated to the peasant and his wife that the auction was legal, that they could not keep it from happening, and that he was there to establish law and order. Then he publicly announced that he came to guarantee that the auction would take place just as it had been convoked and that at the first disturbance he would ask the police in attendance (and there were a lot of them) to "proceed". I had a premonition of what was to come and I asked the cameraman to go outside, behind the gathering, to preserve the camera and the cassette of what had been filmed. But I still could not believe they had the guts to do it.

And they did it. Lucy, sitting, made the sign of the cross. Then she stood up, holding the hands of the partners on each side, the rest followed, and they started singing the anthem again with all their strength. In front of them were lots of policemen, the judge, the supposed buyers and many more men with a bullying look.

They were only 8 older women singing the national anthem. The judge told the police to "proceed" and the women were taken away with forced kicks and shoves, in a very violent situation. It took a moment for me to regain my reflexes (at the same time as the cameraman) and we were able to film most of what happened and I am telling you about. Outside there were five patrol cars waiting (remember? there were only 8 women) and they put four of the women in one and left the others on the sidewalk.

When we went to see them in the commissioner's office, they told us that the women were incommunicado. The women on the outside began rounds of calls to functionaries, lawyers, the press, deputies, and the women were released on Saturday at midday, after pressures and threats. The peasant had also been arrested in an attack of desperation. And his 22 hectares, the wonders of which the auctioneer had been describing as "being the best land in the country", where the tax rate is $4,500/hectare, were auctioned at 155,000 pesos (some $50,000).

The women did not give up and on September 22 they were able to get a judicial recourse (in the last two hours before the legal deadline) asking for the annulment of the auction because of all the irregularities committed.

What we had captured on video was fundamental as evidence and for the time being, the operation is suspended. Now we can only hope that for once, justice will be served and that these poor peasants will not lose their land to the hands of the usual speculators.

INTERVIEW WITH LUCY (who began the struggle in the province of La Pampa and is president of the movement)

Lucy de Cornelis is lean, around 60 years old, with the figure of a traditional and austere woman. She would seem fragile, if one had not seen her transform during the auction into a fighting lioness protecting her pack. There is an air of oppression in her look, the product of an accumulated tiredness in these years of endless battles, and above all of a lot of solitude, when she comes home to the domestic environment where her family barely understands or supports her. However, she hurries to affirm that before leaving for every auction, picket or interview with functionaries, she leaves everything done at home: the food cooked, the clothes washed and ironed, some cake if there is time.

All the contradictions and problems of her gender seem to have incarnated in her – as well as the strength to confront them. We went to interview her in Winifreda, the small village where it all began that autumn night in 1995.

I am interested in your telling me the story of the movement, for the ones who come afterwards, for the memory of the struggle: How did it all begin?

On May 27, 1995 the auctioneer came to my house to see the condition it was in. I have four daughters but none of them were there, so I was alone and I knew that things were going badly even though my husband hid the problem, because he would work, work, and each day he would make more effort, and we did not know anything about it. When the auctioneer left, I began to pack my daughter's paintings, the lamps. I wanted to keep what belonged to the family, its history. When my husband came home I did not tell him about

316

it, and that night I was alone, alone, alone and I asked myself: "What shall I do? I do not have much life left". So I grabbed the bible, and I heard a voice telling me, "You can", and a fire came into me, a strength. We were middle class, in a village where it is difficult to go out and say what you think, because you know that many are glad when you fall. We had an accounting business and a field and, well, the next morning it came to me to go to the radio of my town and talk about what was happening to me. I took the bicycle and I told the boy at the radio that I wanted to make an appeal; and I made the appeal and afterwards women were waiting for me outside of the radio station. I was not alone.

What did the appeal say?

That we needed to do something about what was happening, because everyone knew we were working, that we were not delinquents, but that because we had wanted to buy a tractor in 1989, in no time we were in debt for ten tractors. My husband kept on getting into more debt, kept on signing; he would take me to the bank and they would tell me that I was crazy, that I should sign for my husband, and would you just sign the documents. Well, the thing with the radio was all spontaneous, no thinking or anything, and then I went to the radio in Castex to make another appeal. Other women were going to come with me but they got scared so I went alone and made the second appeal 40 km north of my little town, Winifreda. So I made the appeal and there, also, women were waiting outside for me. I decided to go to a rural program in Santa Rosa, the provincial capital, which was about 80 km more, and make another appeal. When I got home the phone started ringing because there were thousands and thousands like me, women who had never before been so animated. So we women decided to hold an assembly on June 3rd and I said – just spontaneously: "We have to wave the Argentine flag and sing the anthem". Well, that's when Chiquita and a whole bunch of other women joined in: 350 women from 21 localities. At four o'clock in the afternoon there was nobody, but from one moment to the next the hall was filled to overflowing until nine o'clock at night. Everyone was crying, they all broke down. I was at a big empty table, so I invited the women to accompany me. Since I had never organized an assembly or anything, it was all very spontaneous that there it was decided that a petition of eight points would be made to the governor of the province. The first and foremost point was to stop the auctions, the recalculation of the debts (we were asking for ten years at that time) and interests, plus two years of grace. And from that moment on we said we would not permit anything to be taken from anyone; we would stop all the auctions in the country, beginning with the ones in La Pampa. We went to the governor thinking that everything would be solved there because the provincial governor knows about the fields. But he had made a study on what we were asking and he said that what we were saying had been fabricated by a lawyer, by an accountant, and that this could not have come from us women. He kept us there for a few hours and asked us to wait a week for a reply. After the week passed, he did not answer us. Instead, the minister of production told us that our husbands were useless, that they did not know how to plant or how to work and, well, it's over. He had us from three o'clock in the afternoon until seven in the morning. The news began to spread, women from other provinces would call us and meanwhile we kept on stopping auctions, because they were happening very fast.

How was it that the first auction was stopped?

We all went to it; I do not remember anymore who was there. We all showed up and when the auctioneer began to read the edict we started to sing the national anthem and we stopped the auction, it was saved. But you know they do come back, so we started to go to all of them.

How many women were there?

Lots of women, and men too, because it was the families that accompanied us in La Pampa. Other provinces started hearing about us and when the auction information came they would call my house, so I tell the women that we should hold a national assembly, and it was done on September 21, 1995 with one thousand women from all the country. There were women from the south, Rio Negro, Santa Fe, Formosa, Cordoba, Buenos Aires; that's how the movement began to form. There people asked for more time, because ten years was not enough and we began to make petitions for twenty years to pay and recalculate the debt, which were principal points. Everyone was also totally committed to stopping the auctions at a national level.

Who did you give this petition to?

Well, to the President of the nation, ministers of the nation, deputies. We began to have a dialogue with deputies in La Pampa. We would meet and they would help us. Then came the exposition in La Rural and that year we women went to Buenos Aires, to La Rural, where they closed their doors to us. Afterwards, they let us pass in groups and someone had to guard each group. President Menem was there and they left me outside. So I had a chance to have all the press to speak to and that helped us grow. We went knocking on everyone's door in Buenos Aires, functionaries would cry because of what was happening to us, because we were going to lose everything, but they didn't solve anything and neither did the President of the nation. Meanwhile different assemblies were being held in different parts of the Argentine Republic, and the women were always telling me we should go to Buenos Aires in a big march, but I said no because that would cut off the dialogue. We were still channeling the appeal up the hierarchies to the directors of the National Bank and we were still speaking with all of them. When I saw that this was leading nowhere, we took on the big goal of March 8, International Women's Day in 1996: there were 2,500 of us women who went to Buenos Aires – with some men – on a big march with an old tractor. So when you get started, people who want to buy you and shut you up start coming to your house, isn't that true? We had the march, delivered the petition, but nothing happened. So they asked themselves how could we end this? They saw it growing with so many women, and said: "We have to auction their president". First they came to buy me, and I said no, that I had begun this struggle and that it was for everybody because if God gave me the strength it was for something, not just for myself, so even if I had to lose everything it didn't matter. The governor sent people over and told me to settle my accounts and how much was it that I wanted and that I should not act like the Virgin Mary because I was not going to solve anything fighting for everyone. But they could not silence our wills, which were the screams of silence because in the fields everyone is very alone and the farm worker is ashamed of not being able to pay, of telling his family he failed. I always say we are the screams of silence that come out to defend ourselves.

Why do you think women come out and not men?

Because I think that in our culture, our roots, the man was the one who managed everything, and even more so the man from the fields, so it was very hard on him. In my particular case, it was very hard on my husband to see me in the streets because I had always been by my daughter's and family's side, I had not been to Buenos Aires, and he always had had the final word. There are people who know me and ask: "how were you able to break through that?". And I think when you have worked a lifetime and see all the effort of the family go to nothing, that is what gives you the strength, even to face your own family, because my husband would shut the door and lock me out. People began to call saying we were not in Buenos Aires in this struggle but instead we were sleeping with men, that we had other partners, a big quantity of lies when I was not there. So he would close me up, one day he even broke all the windows of my kitchen. That was very embarrassing because women came from all the provinces and my husband would lock them out. So the people said that they had to shut me up, that they could not buy me but they could auction my land and that everything would end. When my auction was about to happen, about fifteen days before, my husband suffered a blood pressure attack and was left paraplegic. So on top of everything this was added to my struggle, I used to have a strong husband and now my companero is an incapacitated boy. It's hard but I think it also gives me energy to continue with the fight.

And what happened with the auction?

Well, the day of the auction came; it was September 24, 1996. The night before, people from all over the country started coming to the village, from the most remote areas. The press helped us and lots of media from Buenos Aires came, the most important ones, because this has begun to be a big thing. So the hour of the auction came and some people had raised money to buy me back the house, at least I would have the house to live in because if not I would be out on the street. A discussion began: some women said we should stop it and others said we should buy the house. Someone came and told me that my husband wanted to come and I said it was too much for him in his state of pain, but he insisted and they brought him in the state he was in. The women formed something like an assembly and asked me what I wanted. I said that I was not going to let them buy the house for me in any way: we were going to save it because that was the way we would all be saved. What is the use of having something if the same thing is going to happen in the rest of the country? I think this was when I fell apart – and the women understood. So the auction came, my husband had been an auctioneer in Banco Nacion but he had quit, and when the auctioneer appeared it was a kid that he had trained. The auctioneer began to read the edict and we began to sing the national anthem. Such an outcry was formed inside that we thought it would be suspended. But, in a week they began a second auction, so I say, "With the money that was raised lets make a hearing on the biggest creditors of 1996". So you get the idea, in my case, we had borrowed 15,000 pesos (equivalent then to dollars) from the bank of La Pampa, in 1994, and in 1996 we owed $ 240,000. The hearing begins in 2001 and the judge says I only owe the bank of La Pampa $ 47,000.

Why?

Because the judge determines that the rest is usury, and that was when I began to understand, because we used to not know anything about these things. Well, then the waves of auctions began all over the country. We began going out to stop these auctions with our only weapons being the national anthem and prayer, but the police also began to come in and beat and drag us and arrest us. It was a tremendous situation. However, since they saw they could not stop us, for example in little towns, many of the police came over to our side and we began to grow so much and get so strong that they could not stop us. All this helped to get an extension of twenty years to pay the debt in Banco Nacion, because they held the mortgage on the best 14 million hectares of land in the country. So we began to understand that they were not just trying to get our land but the sovereignty of Argentina. In my speeches I began to tell the women about sovereignty, that they were coming for our land and all the land. And we were the ones who kept the land from being taken away from 400,000 small producers. That is, the big landholders wanted to be what they were in the beginning: to go back to the big land holdings and the business of finance. And what the people lived on was going to disappear. We began to understand little by little. We learned from lawyers. We know what is due to us, it is just that expansion that leads you along, but we never hesitate. It is very hard because there have been many things. Once they put drugs in a car I was saved from in Buenos Aires because God told me: "Get out of that taxi because you are being set up". All the federal police that were following us were there; we were investigated by the Army, by five captains, and we asked for an explanation from the Air Force. We had spies within our movement through some of the women who would join. There are many things... I think it was our resistance and our great faith that saved us. When we got the twenty-year bonds, I had to set the example and at that time they were taking 400 cows for the bonds. I was the first in La Pampa and in the republic. If I had them today I would have over a million and a half in capital, I would have paid and I would have been saved, but I had to set the example. I was the first and then there were many more. We used to say that the exchange rate is what brought us to this as well as the corrupt financial system. Because our interests were high, what we produced was worth nothing. They took our crops at extremely low prices that were not even enough to pay for our expenses. It was a system that was foreign to us and I believe the people who work in the fields did not even think about it while it was happening. For a while people who did not have debts said we were crazy, but then they would also be taken away, because this is like AIDS, it goes knocking on people's doors and just takes them away. Later we started to get a lot of recognition, even from the traditional agricultural organizations that had not wanted us in the organizational discussions where they plan the projects for the fields, because we are women. We had to struggle a lot with the men in the organizations because they always work things out for their own farms, negotiate and regulate their own things and none of us particularly wanted to regulate anything. Last year because of the devaluation, we got the chance to sell absolutely everything but to save the land. Being president means a lot of pressure, many things happen to you. When we start- 320 ed investigating, the figureheads said they would kill us, that they knew where our children were and, well, I will not shut up and I will continue to fight until the last day of my life. I got the chance to be in Mexico at the International Meeting of Agricultural Debtors; there were a thousand of them. They were men and they could not believe that women were doing this. There I was diagnosed with diabetes that almost killed me – this also takes your health away – but it does not matter and I am probably going to end up saving my land. But until I save every little piece of land of every producer I will not give up this struggle. If it allows me to be more free, not thinking about the judge maybe calling and saying that they are going to take it away, that is tremendous. It sickens you. But I will not stay in my house and I will go to every producer that calls me. And, well, because of this we gained a great respect from the Banco Nacion, thank God. Yesterday we came from seeing the new president of the bank, who is not only a partner but a sister, because with every woman we are sisters, or more than sisters because sometimes between brothers and sisters things happen to separate them. And we came also because we want to save everyone. I want to fight for every Argentine, because fighting was how we gave lives to our children and we also have to give them a future. That is why when we speak of the land, it is individual but also an Argentine patrimony because it belongs to every Argentinian. When the land does well, factories work and everything works. Because the peasant never says he is going to keep it, no, it is for investment, for machinery, for wire, for seeds, he leaves his family without things so he can give to the land. This is what I want understood in every village, in every city, that this is not for us. With my 57 years I say: "All my life I worked to have a united family and make my children good people; if we don't leave them the answer that this struggle is for everyone, and if they do not understand, nothing will make sense". We are back and we care about money, material things, and everyone's well being. It cannot be that in Argentina children are starving when there is so much land, holy land that God gave us and they are dying; we are guilty; we are guilty if we do nothing.

Apart from the landholders there is the ghost of adopting foreign ways

Imagine how easy it is for foreigners to come and make contracts with the dollar being so cheap. I do not think there is any other country that allows foreigners to come and keep the land more than here. We said this and it happened, and the idea of privatizing the Banco Nacion is to hand over lands. I had information from the exterior that Japan was interested in our lands because they have overpopulation. Every one of us has the commitment to put this in our land and what is left over we will export. We have to industrialize our products; they are taken them away as raw materials. With what is kept back from what is taken away from the producers today, subsidies can be given to heads of families who have nothing to eat. But the day that the land is owned by foreigners there will not even be production; they will take it all away. This is very serious, and I say that we are still not conscious about what can happen.

Are you doing something about this?

Putting up Argentinea flags in every field bought by foreigners, denouncing them, and making a study. You become cold when you see that Spanish landholders bought 15,000 or

321

20,000 in this part or that part, the best hunting lands. We are born naked and we leave naked. I do not want to take anything, but I do want to leave a free and sovereign land to my grand-children so they can live in peace and give food where there is hunger in the world, because we have a lot of land to produce and feed the world. But the culture of work has to be taught because the small and medium-sized producer is the one that is opening the rut every day. Last Saturday, the son of a producer came and said that when his uncle received the notification of the auction from the bank he hung himself. Another one's mother died of a heart attack. When they call you and you know you cannot get there and the producer kills himself, you are left with anguish, you feel like you are useless, that you cannot help people. Then it becomes like a self-help family program, a large family.

That is very particular to women.

Yes, it is very much up to women to protect the family, so it is her they have wanted to destroy. But they will not succeed.

What happened with the men after the first reaction? Did they understand and join? With the children, what happened?

For the children, in my particular case, this took away their mom, their mom was out. I try to fulfill my obligations – sometimes I have nothing left to give – but I leave everything organized at home: from the food, the clothes, the cleaning, everything. And in the morning I wake up very early, organize the house and at 8:30 I always say that I put on my Argentine shirt and go out to fight. Children do not want you to be out in the street, but I know they are proud anyway. In my case, for example, my husband did not want this and that is why I tell Chiquita [her friend who accompanies her] that what I would have liked the most was for him to come with me. Sometimes I see it with her and her husband and I feel a solitude [she cries].

You think he still does not understand?

I think he understands because he looks at me a certain way when I go to the banks, to see if I saved some fields but sometimes he is afraid.

It is difficult for women to have to be everywhere, to fill all the roles, to do everything.

Yes, it is very difficult. The sickness of my husband made everything more serious. My girls, especially the oldest, are depressed because they see him like that and all this has led me to be absent in some important moments for the family, like for the birth of my grandchild, because I was out defending the people or I missed a birthday and my grandchildren still do not understand this.

They will understand. And the girls, what do they do?

The youngest graduated and I had to come to live in the city because my husband had an accident out in the fields and was left paraplegic. I wanted to be there because he would choke, and 322 since my daughter was studying agronomy we came until she graduated. I also baked and went out and sold whatever I could. Now she got work and she helps us, until we can recuperate our lands and leave them to her. I have asked that I want my life to end on those fields, on that land.

Which women do you remember who have interesting stories in different places within the country? You were speaking of one especially.

Yes, Joaquina, but she is in bed unable to move, speak, or write with a very cruel disease: multiple sclerosis. I think from going around everywhere she was worn down… She lives in the fields, she is a producer who had no children or debt and she joined our battle with everything. She is also from La Pampa. It kills me because I wanted her to see our battle realized.

With whom does she live? Alone?

She always lived alone, but now she has two women who take care of her. I was in the hospital with her until they gave me her diagnosis: she would look me in the eyes so she could know. We went through many things together. And she was very lucid. At the beginning she would write but not any more. We have women fighters in all the provinces. They have made pickets in the south and we have to go. They communicate and we go. Now it is very difficult to know how to go on because of the telephone bills. There is a bond in circulation to be able to pay for the expenses and the trips because we can no longer handle it. We were taking money away from our families to fight. I think we gave our lives and the few things we had for all the Argentines. They would call us crazy, those crazy women.

That's curious, no? The mothers of the Plaza de Mayo were called crazy. It seems that every time women go out to fight they are called crazy.

Because they think we are not there for our families but for searching for our freedom. And it is the contrary. I carry within me all of them. The day that my grandson was born, in the moment he was born on October 23rd, I was putting a flag in foreign-owned land.

That is the last grandchild?

The last grandson. I have: a child of 15 who decided now to live with me, a child of 14 whose birthday is tomorrow, a child of 13 who has a marvelous voice and sings to feed the poor. And that last one, Salvador, who I say came to save us because from that moment on we have been able to pay our debts. Another of my daughters is studying. She should have graduated already, but with all this she got a depression, and being far away, first from her father and her mother. They were studying in San Luis. I have a daughter who went to live in Bariloche and the second one is married to a manager from Banco Nacion who is marvelous and has given me food so that I never lack it. God has never left me. I would have nothing but then someone always would come and give me a little and I think that in a little over a year I will be able to live from the fields.

323

Go back to the fields?

Go back. I am going to plant aromatics so my grandchildren can love that land. The question they would ask me was this: "and with that fighting you will save the land?". I would say "Yes I will save it", even though I knew that behind it all were the bankruptcy and the auction. And now I say "I will save it", I think it is practically saved. But it is very difficult struggling with power; it is very, very hard and harsh.

Is there always a lot of loneliness?

Yes, there is loneliness, it is tremendous. But now I have to always be doing something for the people because if not I can no longer live.

One comes into this and can no longer go back.

No, you can't. The other day Chiquita was worried because I hardly sleep. I keep on going day and night and do not sleep. I am practically always awake. And she said I had to find someone to help me at home because I cannot handle everything. I try, for example, to knit for them like I used to. Stay in for the night to tell them: "Look at what I made". I try to make the same foods, cook for them and leave things done so that they feel they will always have their mother. If they all come I try and fix beds for everyone.

It worries me that our country, which used to be the grain capital of the world, is becoming a one-crop culture of genetically engineered soy. This is a serious problem, fed by the compliance of the agronomy schools that defend it because they receive funds from transnationals, and by the lack of information of the peasants who, for example, do not know that Europe does not want to accept genetically-engineered foods. The recent flooding in Santa Fe also has something to do with this.

Yes, it is a subject we have discussed a lot with the kids in the university and with my daughter, who is an agronomist. I think now people are beginning to see that this is organized by the North to destroy us and take our best lands. They want to buy it so that the land is productive for them and not for us.

And what about the Patagonia? What happens with the Mapuche communities?

I was with them, and you know their lands have been mortgaged to the World Bank. The governments have used the lands that were originally theirs, the piece that was given to them, as collateral, for corruption. But, well, I always say that Latin America is bathed in Indian blood because the land was originally theirs. We had a meeting with indigenous women fighters and I go to them when there is a problem. In the south there was a woman in the movement who was working for a transnational and the women rightly sent her away because she was investigating the Mapuche community. We are not sectarian, and we have organized ourselves so that every one of us, when she believes she is defending a just cause, is there.

Is there any important activity, and auction, march, or land-taking, in the near future?

The auctions now are suspended, and hopefully they will not come again. Marches are economically difficult now, but we went to Buenos Aires the other day with a tractor. In the foreign owned lands we will continue to put flags and now we are determined to negotiate the debt of those who are left. We also have to say that sometimes we are not many, because many of the ones who solved their problems stay home.

That happens in movements. I still think, however, that your battle is changing the ways of women and society.

Yes, yes. For society we are no longer the crazy ones, we are still the crazies for the functionaries. We ask to be heard. Until now a President has never received us, and we will see what happens with this new government that seems more open to problems. We are also thinking of what can be done with those who have lost their land, and if it is possible to give them some land so they can produce again.

It seems very interesting that within the movement there seems to be a politically concrete plurality.

Yes, everyone has a political position but the movement belongs to no one, and we are very strict about that because we know we can destroy ourselves from within. And because of this we keep on growing: in Chaco, Formosa, Cordoba, Rio Negro. We want to see how we can again travel throughout the country because there are places where things cannot move and we have to find the resources.

What is the situation now of your lands?

When they took my last cows to the fair it was so sad because they mooed to me in such a way it seemed like crying.

And you will not get more?

I do not know and I am unable to tell you. I still am not able to stop paying because they expect something from the president and if I fail it's like giving them a victory. That is why I will pay every last cent and I will be free.

How much is left?

325   Very little.

THE OTHER WOMEN (Fragments of the testimonies registered for the documentary)

Province of La Pampa

Chiquita: It is very important to highlight the courage that Lucy had in making the first appeal which initiated the movement, because maybe at that time she also felt alone and thought that she was the only one that faced that problem. And it turned out that thousands of Argentines, thousands of homes were facing the same thing. In that moment, the men managed practically everything and women were in the homes. And when Lucy's appeal was made it allowed us to open our minds and say, "No, we are seeing the disintegration of our family and the loss of the lands that belonged to our fathers and grandfathers". Because of this, women came out and defended what is ours. We saw that it could be done.

Province of Santa Fe

Ana (Vice-president of MML): The women of this movement have similar histories. We are the daughters and granddaughters of those immigrants who came to the port of Buenos Aires with their little suitcases, went to some village in the interior of the country, took a piece of the land, and were tenants until, after many years of tremendous sacrifices and struggles, like the *Grito de Alcorta* in 1912, they were able to become owners of that little piece of land during the Peron epoch (the decades of the 1940's and 1950's). That meant a mortgage of thirty years with the Bank and working very hard to pay it off; but one could live with dignity and my generation was able to have other commodities (like electricity) and could attend the secondary school of the village. All of a sudden in 1989 and 1990, neo-liberal policies were applied to the country. And there was even a minister of agriculture who, in the process of the implementation of the Menem-Cavallo model, said it very clearly: that 200,000 small and medium-sized producers did not fit into the model because of the amount of land they had and that they were condemned to disappear. So we lived really sad situations because the peasant indebted himself to modernize (like the model required) and when he could not pay he became depressed and lowered his head in shame because he could not administer the land that he inherited from his parents and grandparents, who had sacrificed so much. He would not speak about it to his children or his wife; it took many years to convince the peasant that it was not his fault that he was failing. Do you know how many suicides there were? How many paraplegics because of the strokes? So the women came out and fought tooth and nail, saying: "No, no we are not guilty. It is an economic model and a government who want to take away our lands". And, as Lucy always says, "Since we have been mothers, we will not allow that our fields be auctioned". And they began to stop the auctions singing the national anthem, praying, seeing functionaries, and fighting in the banks. In every family the submissive wife who would be cooking and waiting on her husband and kids would whip off her apron and say: "I will win this or win this". Because it has to be understood that for the man and woman of the fields, land is not just a way to make a living, it is a way of life, the only thing known. It is an identity. You should have seen my mother, in her 80's, when the justice official came to kidnap her tractor and tools and tell her they were going to auction her land… and they delegated it all to me, the only woman, because my brothers were destroyed. Thanks to the struggles of all these years we still have our fields, even though we still have debts. But, well, the struggle has been worth it because we have been able to save many producers and, above all, expose the perversity of that economic model that began with the dictatorship of 1976 and has deepened in Argentina within the last decades, that strives to achieve the large scale process of concentration of land to restore the practice of absentee ownership. And such was the silence about this, since the peasant would not speak, that no one believed us until the last agricultural census demonstrated that there are 145,000 less small producers than in 1988. And it was not just stopping the auctions, but also demanding the minimum price, the re-financing for 20 or more years, the recalculation of the debts, and in some cases (like in the impoverished northern states) the pardon of debts, because we believe we have already paid them off and then some throughout these years. Also, with the arrival of this new government that is more popular, we have been the first to embrace the Banco Nacion to avoid its privatization and to stop the foreign investors from keeping our mortgages. When I am asked: "Why the women?" I remember that with the kidnappings of the youth during the dictatorship, although these kids had fathers and mothers, it was the women who went out to fight and with this land it is the same; women have a strength that allows us to do this.

Ana Maria (lawyer of the Movement): I am from the 1970s, of the ones who wanted to change the world, when the fall of everything that was collective came during the dictatorship.

At the height of the neo-liberal epoch, the movement made its public debut on March 8th with a 2,000 women march in Buenos Aires that confronted the "end of ideologies" with a solidarity network to avoid the auctioning of the land of the people we did not know. And each auction caused a town of people to come together, joining the grandmothers (who prayed so that it would not happen), the classmates and teachers of the kids of the indebted peasants, the businessmen who knew the peasant and knew that he always paid his debts, the priest who would ring his bells, the firemen who would add their sirens, all confronting a wicked economic model. My grandfather, just arriving from Italy, defended the Indians whom the landowners were massacring, so I feel that the movement is the historical continuation of the struggles of the Indians, Creoles and immigrants who fought for the land they worked and that is why it is my place on this Earth. And we are establishing the agrarian model we want for the country: thousands and thousands of farms, no vast ownership of lands. The womens' movement is a whirlwind that has incorporated itself massively to the struggle in the past years, starting off small, gathering force to never be stopped.

Maria Luisa (80 years old, one of the early settlers): My parents were immigrants from Galicia and my mother came to Argentina to work in "family homes" as a domestic maid, as was the custom of the time, when in Europe it was believed that easy money could be made here and that one progressed quickly. When I was a girl, the fields were a marvel, full of peasants, work, and parties. Then it was depopulated because of the debts and the introduction of soy that threw people into the cities, but what would happen if we went back to the old time agriculture and cattle-raising? If I have to buy the milk and vegetables in town, I become ill. I joined the Movement when I was invited to the first meeting in Rosario, and I have accompanied them when I have been able to, even though my husband held me back because he was afraid. I do not have the courage to confront the military like they do, but I contribute with my grain of sand and I hope I do not die without seeing our dreams accomplished.

Maria (peasant): At the time I was invited to join the movement my husband had died and my daughter was due to be married in five months time, so I was very depressed and without desire to live. But in that first meeting I was hooked and I did not let go. I had no debts; I went to help the others. Sometimes things got messy, like when we all ended up in the commissioner's office in Canada Honda. I continue working my fields like before, but I started to live again with this struggle. We have been everywhere, I have learned a lot, and I feel rejuvenated since I began to fight. Sometimes it is not easy, but we forge ahead.

Norma (cattle-raiser): I was born and raised in the fields. When I got married I came to this house with my husband, who already had a small cattle-ranch, and I worked with him in addition to raising the four kids, who are already big and are studying. When the economic crisis began, neighbors who could not longer buy bottled milk asked us to deliver milk to them and we became old-fashioned milkmen: my husband and I would set out at dawn towards different directions to deliver milk. When the first meeting was held in Rosario for women of the field, we were few. After a year and a half it was decided that we would go to Buenos Aires on a large march. But we knew that to call attention there we needed to be thousands, and since we were not so many, the idea of going with a tractor emerged. They asked me if I would drive it and, since I will do anything to help out, that day I became the tractor-driver of the movement. Women have been the historical progressives, because in times of big decisions men are depressed by impotency, and women rebel. That is why, today, we are the protagonists of the large battles of these epochs, even though sometimes our families hold us back. Men negotiate in a more individual way while women, since they always had to defend themselves in conjunction with others, have more solidarity. A woman cannot ask for food for her children and pass by a starving child without giving.

Provinces of Rio Negro and Neuquen

Andrea (agronomist, initiator in the south): The situation in the Valley of Rio Negro and Neuquen is one of small fruit producers facing high costs and not enough protective State policies, who must compete in the international markets with subsidized products of other countries. In the 1990s they had to get credits, which is why now 3,000 producers and 800 farms are in the hands of the Banco Nacion. Later, they turned to private banks and lenders, who are much worse. There was an economic, political, and social crisis that extended beyond our country, and, along with the debt of the small producers, there was a concentration of riches within monopolistic exporters who, with foreign capital, are keeping the farms. They gave long-term bonds to the producer to lift their debts, and they held captive for many years the production of the farmer without even giving them a chance to ask how much they would get paid. Farmers are also held captive by the big laboratories that give them agro-chemicals and the pesticides that provoke resistancies and bring about a negative environmental impact. When I wanted to begin the movement in my area in 1998, my grandmother, a producer, 87 years old, helped me to find women peasants and it became explosive; we put out a call over the radio and first 60 women came and later 40 from all over the valley, which extends for 400 km. Then we tried to join with other sectors, above all agricultural producers, and we partic- 328 ipated in tractor rallies and pickets. By ourselves we had stopped 50 auctions, and with each one we would get as excited as with the first. We are women with differences of age, customs, and political ideas, but we are united by the fight to help every producer in need. Men would isolate themselves, because the producer is already individualistic due to his work and social environment; so the debt would not be spoken about. Women are different, you touch their nest and they jump, and the nest is the farm that belonged to their parents and grandparents and that is intended for their children. A woman is shameless, she jumps, she pushes through, to go out and search for equals: it was through the radio that women called out to other women. And the ones with and without debt came; many are not even farmers. We have teachers, social assistants, a hairdresser. Most of the time we do not even know the person whose farm we are going to save. We are growing in size because we have united with other sectors and because of bigger problems, like the introduction of foreigners in Patagonia. Indigenous communities are being moved from their land, and the landowners expel the Creoles and Mapuches to city slums. There is clear spoiling of the land and also a strong environmental impact because of gold mine and petroleum exploitation.

Susana (producer): Since my grandparents, we have been a family of fruit producers, and I joined the movement because of the appeal of two of my cattle-raising girlfriends who did not have debts. Later, a hailstorm ruined our pear crop and we had to get credit, but we were able to pay it off with a lot of sacrifice. I will continue as long as the auctions continue. Our news runs through word of mouth. An auction that we hear about is an auction we go out to stop. The anguish each time is greater, as if it were our own. Afterwards we are exhausted and we hug each other and it is a very nice feeling. And sometimes it is very sad: on two occasions we could not stop it. Coming into this was unintentional. We were housewives and most of us had no debts. It was a question of solidarity. Afterwards, the peasants asked for help; before, they had shame, and some have died of sadness. Now only 30% of the lands in the Valley are in the hands of the producers, 70% already belongs to the big businesses. But we will fight so that none of that 30% is touched. Like our motto says: "From our grandparents to our children". We do not want to lose anything else. We do not want anyone to lose anything else.

Olga (producer): I am in charge of the farm while my husband delivers fruit in the south. I take care of the animals and of everything until harvest time, which is when I classify and pack the fruit so he can commercialize it. My daughter spoke about the Movement, because it seems she had learned about it from a teacher, and got me into joining. I did not have debts, but I received a lot of love from the girls and I began to help – with a lot of nervousness in the first auctions. We do not know where we get our strength, but on those occasions we are transformed, we think of the person whose farm will be taken away, which is like cutting off their arms, and then we can. We also have other activities with different sectors of the areas, like the Central de Trabajadores Argentinos (CTA) [a worker's union] and other organizations with which we participate in rounds against the ALCA [free-trade agreement with USA]. For example, we were collaborating with the Mapuche community in Corcovado (100 km from Esquel) against gold mine exploitation in the area, and now we have been invited to participate in one of their religious rituals.

Abuela Molinaro (producer): I came from Italy when I was five with my parents, who already had five Italian children and would have five in Argentina. I am now 87 and I came to this place in 1939, when I got married. I later had three sons. In those times, the comforts of today were not available in the fields and we had to do everything with hard work: building a brick oven, planting fruit trees, taking care of the animals. At the beginning it was hard. Then the boys worked and we could do better. Today it is an immense pear and apple plantation. We had many auctions but we could stop them. The whole family participated in tractor rallies and pickets. I do not even remember anymore how many auctions I went to with the women. Now they don't let me go because I am sick, but I am always close to them. Of course I never had as much courage as Lita, who would pinch the military men with needles, or like Andrea, who was arrested. But they had to let her go.

Marta (producer): My grandparents arrived in Villa Regina in 1924 and I was born in 1948 on a farm, when times were best. Now we have returned to the old times, very difficult, when what is tilled one day is erased by the wind the next. Valle de Rio Negro became a paradise with the work that followed, a kind of big cooperation between farmers, like a happy family. Later, everything changed and we began opposing the first auctions, because you tend to have solidarity with people in need. Now there is a farmer with six hectares who they want to remove, and we are going to stay there with him so they cannot do it, because it is not fair that they make us pay for what they have given away to the large corporations. We have been asking for a provincial or national horticultural fruit law to protect the small producers for a long time, but we still have not succeeded.

Liliana (hairdresser): I do not own land, a farm or anything; I am a hairdresser. My work is solidarity, and when I have to stop an auction I charge my batteries as if I owned 20 farms. And the girls love me a lot. They always call me. I did not know what a bank debt or an auction was, but as we started acting I started learning and I feel like I am a part of this. Today they called me because of the auction in the morning. I was cutting hair 20 km from here. I took two buses, a taxi, and I got here when it was ending, but I got here.

Lita (retired social worker): I come from an agricultural family; however, I have no land or debt. I am a social worker and I got into this because I am against a perverse system, seeing how my friends in the area were sinking. I am a militant for human rights; I have a brother-in-law that is missing because of the dictatorship, my sister died from it, and I belong to a group against unpunished crimes. When I met Andrea in a women's meeting, she convinced me that we could fight not only for the dead but also for the living, and I helped her start the movement here. The calling had great effect, we began to fight together and now I take it personally. I have eight cases pending. We defend ourselves; we sing the anthem and pray. But if they push us, we carry sewing needles and we pinch the military men and they run back. And in other moments, we have looked for any possible weapons. Once, in an auction, I could not impede the only person bidding, a gypsy, to hold up his hand. So, the only thing I could think of in the desperation was to slap him and when the press and the rest of the people came to see what had happened, I said he had touched my ass. I am a big woman so this caused a big scandal. He got mad saying I was crazy, but he left and since he was the only bidder the auction was stopped. There is a story for each one… I know I will never give up, because this is my struggle.

330

Assetou Madeleine Auditore (Madou) was born in Yaou, Ivory Coast on 14th December 1993, of parents migrated from Burkina Faso. She now lives and studies in Bari, Italy, where she has just completed grade five primary school. She is also an Australian citizien. She studies music at the Conservatorium Nicolò Piccinni in Bari. She enjoys playing sports, dance and cooking.

Rokeya Begum is from the northeast part of Bangladesh. Born in 1948 in a lower middle class family, she married when she was only thirteen and a mother at the age of 16. Her husband and parents in-law became angry that she had a daughter and tortured her physically and mentally. Her beloved father, who had taken the wrong decision for her life earlier, came forward to help her get a divorce. She restarted her unfinished education, completed High School and took teachers training which helped her get a teaching job. Her bitter experience led her to start a women's group to work with those women who were victims of societal superstitions and different kinds of violence. She now leads SUS, an organization of 27,000 women in Bangladesh. She also works with different groups addressing globalization, education and women's and children's rights, as well as networking for alternative development through the gift economy.

Susan Bright is the author of nineteen books of poetry. She is the editor of Plain View Press which since 1975 has published one-hundred-and-fifty books. Her most recent book, *The Layers of Our Seeing*, is a collection of poetry, photographs and essays exploring peace and justice issues post 9/11. She was named Woman of the Year by the Austin (Texas) Women's Political Caucus in 1990. She now works as an activist and editor for the Center for the Study of the Gift Economy. She is editor of Susan Lee Campbell Solar's book on the death penalty, from which the essay on reconciliatory justice in this collection is derived.

Linda Christiansen-Ruffman is Professor of Sociology and Women's Studies at Saint Mary's University and co-founder of WWIFUN. She has been President of the Canadian Research Institute for the Advancement of Women (CRIAW), the Canadian Sociology and Anthropology Association and Chair of Research Committee 32 of the International Sociological Association on Women in Society and partecipates in local feminist organisations in Halifax, Nova Scotia.

Leslene Della Madre is a "shemama" – a practitioner, student and teacher of the feminist shamanic healing arts. Studying and practicing for over 35 years, she serves as spiritual midwife to the living and dying. She is founder of "Winged Women", a center for healing of body, mind and spirit in Sonoma County, California. She is the author of the forth-coming book *Midwifing Death: Returning to the Arms of the Ancient Mother* and serves as spiritual adjunct to the medical, psychological and psychiatric professions, assisting doctors and therapists in cutting edge healing work.

Eila Estola [Finland] is a senior in the Faculty of Education in the Department of Educational Sciences and Teacher Education, University of Oulu, Finland. Her main interests centre on narrative-biographical teacher research, especially the moral dimensions in teachers' stories.

Norma Fernandez is University professor of Anthropology, journalist with a degree in Cinematography, and makes video documentaries. She is a member of the Institute of Studies of the Central Organization of Argentinian Workers (CTA) and is an activist with the World Social Forum (Argentinian Committee). She is married and has three sons and many friends.

Heide Göttner-Abendroth is woman philosopher and researcher in culture and society, focused on matriarchal studies. She was born in Thuringia (Germany) in 1941 and is the mother of three children, two daughters and one son. In 1973 she took her Ph.D. in philosophy at the University of Munich on the subject of the "Logic of Interpretation". There she taught philosophy for ten years (from 1973-1983). She published various books on matriarchal society and culture and has become the founding mother of modern scientific matriarchal studies. In 1986 she founded the "International Academy HAGIA. Academy for Matriarchal Studies and Matriarchal Spirituality" and is its director. Her main work in several volumes is *Das Matriarchat* (1988, 1991, 2000 etc.) *Matriarchy* (soon to be translated). In the year 2003, she was organizer of the first "World Congress on Matriarchal Studies" in Luxemburg.

Mechthild U. Hart is Professor at DePaul University's School for New Learning. She moved from Germany to the United States in 1972, worked in a number of women's and community organizations, and has been teaching and mentoring at the School for New Learning since 1987. She has published several articles, book chapters, and two books on international and social divisions of labor, with special emphasis on poverty and motherwork.

Ana Isla is a member of Toronto Women for a Just and Healthey Planet. She is an assistant professor at the Faculty of Women's Studies and Sociology at Brock University. She was born in the Peruvian rain forest and is the mother of two children.

Kaarina Kailo is professor of Women's Studies and Multiculturalism at Oulu University, Finland. She is also co-founder of the Finnish Ecopsychology association, coordinator of the Finnish FemAttac and a member of many other peace and feminist organizations. She has published/edited or co-edited books on ecospirituality, ecofeminism, Indigenous women and postcolonialism, violence vs. women and many other feminist issues.

Corinne Kumar (India/Tunisia), with an abiding faith in women's knowledges and all vulnerable wisdoms, is a woman deeply committed to issues related to women's and human rights, peace and mi-
ism. Academically qualified with a Masters Degree in Sociology and a Masters Degree in Politi-
Sciences, she abandoned pure academia after two years of pursuing a Doctorate in search of a
relevant and enhancing political praxis. Through the Asian Women's Human Rights Council
HRC) and El Taller International she has envisioned and coordinated, along with several organs in different parts of the world, a series of innovative and challenging initiatives called the
of Women. She is sometimes poet and always pilgrim of life.

Rauna Kuokkanen (Finland/Canada) is currently completing her PhD titled "Toward the Hospitality of Academia: The (Im)Possible Gift of Indigenous Epistemes" at the University of British Columbia, Canada. She has been actively involved in Sami society for many years and is currently engaged in the protection of a sacred Sami site in her home community. She has edited an anthology on contemporary Sami literature (*Juoga mii geasuha*, 2001) and has published several articles on Sami and other indigenous literatures, decolonization and Sami research paradigms.

Lee Ann LaBar was born in Dallas, Texas, in 1958. From 1979 on, she has been working on environmental justice and human rights for Indigenous People land based research, documentation and public awareness. She also does radio documentaries and benefit concert tours. She has been working at Stonehaven Ranch, a project of the Foundation for a Compassionate Society near San Marcos, Texas, for 2 1/2 years.

Mari Lahtinen (Finland), is a MNSc and PhD student who works as a researcher at the Department of Nursing science in the University of Oulu. She is interested in ethical foundation of nursing and she teaches nursing ethic at the University of Oulu. She is preparing her doctoral dissertation on nursing ethics from an ecofeminist perspective.

Paola Melchiori is founder of the Free University of Women in Milan, Italy and of its International branch Crinali. Since the mid-1980s, she conducted field operations in North-South cooperation projects in the context of cross-cultural women exchanges. She is a consultant for the EU on issues related to poverty, gender and civil society. She has represented Italy in many UN and academic international conferences and committees.

Bhanumatu Natarajan (India/Norway) is an ethnobotanist and has done research on the use of medicinal plants by women in India. She is also active in issues related to property rights, the conservation of biodiversity and traditional knowledge.

Susan Petrilli (Australia/Italy) is Associate Professor of Semiotics at the University of Bari, and works at the Department of Linguistic Practices and Text Analysis, at the same University. Her principal research interests include sign theory, subject theory, theory of meaning and language, communication theory, problems of ideology, translation theory. She has edited three volumes of the series *Athanor* on theory and semiotics of translation. Her major publications include: *Su Victoria Welby. Significs e filosofia del linguaggio* (1998), *Teoria dei segni e del linguaggio* (1999); (with A. Ponzio): *Signs of Research on Signs* (1998), *Fuori campo. I segni del corpo tra rappresentazione ed eccedenza* (1999), *Philosophy of Language, Art and Answerability in Mikhail Bakhtin* (2000), *Il sentire della comunicazione globale* (2000), *Thomas Sebeok and the Signs of Lif*e (2001), *I segni e la vita. La semiotica globale di Thomas A. Sebeok* (2002), *Semioetica*, (2003); (with T. A. Sebeok and A. Ponzio): *L'io semiotico* (2001); recently she has edited *Translation Translation* (ed. 2003), *Linguaggi* (ed. 2003), *Ideology, Dialogue and Logic in Semioethic Perspective* (ed. 2003); her most recent monographs include *Percorsi della semiotica* (2004), *Semiotics Unbounded* (2005).

Jutta Ried (Germany), 47, single without children has lived for 16 years in 4 different English speaking countries (Canada, US, UK and Ireland) which has given her a deep insight into the functioning of different shades of the Western industrialised society.
Her original professional training is gardening, leading to a detailed knowledge and experience of nature and an appreciation of the inter-connectedness of all life. After returning to live in Germany in the year 2000 she has become involved in interpreting and translating (English/German/English) for attac and the HAGIA Institute on matriarchal research.

Susan Lee Campbell Solar (USA, 1941-2002) was an artist, activist, journalist and teacher. Under the trademark Ssymbols she created goddess jewelry. While working for the Foundation for a Compassionate Society, she created The Earth and Sky Women's Peace Caravan for a Nuclear Free Future. When she died unexpectedly in 2002 she had almost finished a book about the death penalty in Texas, from which the article in this volume about restorative justice is derived.
Her chapter was edited and modified for inclusion here by Susan Bright, who is the editor of Solar's book on the death penalty.

María Suárez Toro is a Puerto Rican and Costa Rican feminist, journalist, communicator, teacher and human rights activist in local, national, regional and international arenas through work as co-director of FIRE-Feminist International Radio Endeavour between 1991 and the present. She worked as a human rights activist and literacy teacher at the grassroots level in El Salvador, Costa Rica, Nicaragua and Honduras in the 1970s and 1980s.

Genevieve Vaughan is an independent researcher. In 1963 she moved to Italy from her native Texas. Her two early essays *"Communication and exchange"* (*Semiotica* 1980) and *"Saussure and Vigotsky via Marx"*, Ars semiotica, (1981) deal with language and economics. In 1978 Vaughan became a feminist, participating since then in the Italian, US and international feminist movements. In 1983, Vaughan returned to Austin, Texas where she created the Foundation for a Compassionate Society (1987-1998), an all-woman activist foundation, which initiated many innovative projects based on the politicization of "women's values". Her book *For-Giving, a feminist criticism of exchange* (1997) can also be found on the internet at www.for-giving.com. She is active in the anti-globalization and peace movements.

Hildur Ve (Norway) is Professor Emerita of Sociology, Department of Sociology, University of Bergen, Norway. She holds a PhD on Social Class Differences in Socialization and Reproduction of the Labour Force (1975). Her main works include *Society and the working class: Parson's view of the workers' situation in a Marxist theoretical perspective* (1977), *Class and gender: role model consideration and liberation in advanced capitalism* (1981), S*ociology and the understanding of Gende*r (1991), *Action Research and gender equality work in school* (1992), *Education for change: action research for increased gender equalit*y (1998), *Rationality and identity in Norwegian feminism.*

Frieda Werden (USA/Canada) has been a producer in public, commercial and community radio, and a journalist covering U.S. public broadcasting. Since 1986, she has produced and syndicated WINGS: Women's International News Gathering Service < www.wings.org >. She's a board member of the Association Mondiale des Radios Communautaires and the International Association of Women in Radio and TV. She lives in Vancouver, BC, Canada.

Liliana Wilson (Chile/USA) was born in Valparaíso, Chile. She studied at the Instituto de Bellas Artes de Viña del Mar and also obtained a degree in law at the Catholic University of Valparaíso. In 1977 she traveled to the United States and subsequently settled in Austin, Texas. She studied drama at Austin Community College and painting at Southwest Texas State University in San Marcos, s. She has exhibited throughout the United States as well as in Italy. She has also worked for 15 as a graphic designer helping promote the theory of the Gift Economy.